Data Hiding and Its Applications: Digital Watermarking and Steganography

Data Hiding and Its Applications: Digital Watermarking and Steganography

Editors

David Megías
Wojciech Mazurczyk
Minoru Kuribayashi

MDPI • Basel • Beijing • Wuhan • Barcelona • Belgrade • Manchester • Tokyo • Cluj • Tianjin

Editors
David Megías
Universitat Oberta de Catalunya
Spain

Wojciech Mazurczyk
Warsaw University of Technology
Poland

Minoru Kuribayashi
Okayama University
Japan

Editorial Office
MDPI
St. Alban-Anlage 66
4052 Basel, Switzerland

This is a reprint of articles from the Special Issue published online in the open access journal *Applied Sciences* (ISSN 2076-3417) (available at: https://www.mdpi.com/journal/applsci/special_issues/Digital_Watermarking_Steganography).

For citation purposes, cite each article independently as indicated on the article page online and as indicated below:

LastName, A.A.; LastName, B.B.; LastName, C.C. Article Title. *Journal Name* **Year**, *Volume Number*, Page Range.

ISBN 978-3-0365-2936-3 (Hbk)
ISBN 978-3-0365-2937-0 (PDF)

© 2022 by the authors. Articles in this book are Open Access and distributed under the Creative Commons Attribution (CC BY) license, which allows users to download, copy and build upon published articles, as long as the author and publisher are properly credited, which ensures maximum dissemination and a wider impact of our publications.

The book as a whole is distributed by MDPI under the terms and conditions of the Creative Commons license CC BY-NC-ND.

Contents

About the Editors vii

David Megías, Wojciech Mazurczyk and Minoru Kuribayashi
Data Hiding and Its Applications: Digital Watermarking and Steganography
Reprinted from: *Appl. Sci.* **2021**, *11*, 10928, doi:10.3390/app112210928 1

Amna Qureshi and David Megías
Blockchain-Based Multimedia Content Protection: Review and Open Challenges
Reprinted from: *Appl. Sci.* **2021**, *11*, 1, doi:10.3390/app11010001 7

Luca Caviglione
Trends and Challenges in Network Covert Channels Countermeasures
Reprinted from: *Appl. Sci.* **2021**, *11*, 1641, doi:10.3390/app11041641 31

Marco Botta, Davide Cavagnino, Marco Gribaudo and Pietro Piazzolla
Fragile Watermarking of 3D Models in a Transformed Domain
Reprinted from: *Appl. Sci.* **2020**, *10*, 3244, doi:10.3390/app10093244 47

Weitong Chen, Na Ren, Changqing Zhu, Qifei Zhou, Tapio Seppänen and Anja Keskinarkaus
Screen-Cam Robust Image Watermarking with Feature-Based Synchronization
Reprinted from: *Appl. Sci.* **2020**, *10*, 7494, doi:10.3390/app10217494 63

Franco Frattolillo
A Watermarking Protocol Based on Blockchain
Reprinted from: *Appl. Sci.* **2020**, *10*, 7746, doi:10.3390/app10217746 89

Najeeb Jebreel, Josep Domingo-Ferrer, David Sánchez and Alberto Blanco-Justicia
KeyNet: An Asymmetric Key-Style Framework for Watermarking Deep Learning Models
Reprinted from: *Appl. Sci.* **2021**, *11*, 999, doi:10.3390/app11030999 107

Han-Yan Wu, Ling-Hwei Chen and Yu-Tai Ching
Block-Based Steganography Method Using Optimal Selection to Reach High Efficiency and Capacity for Palette Images
Reprinted from: *Appl. Sci.* **2020**, *10*, 7820, doi:10.3390/app10217820 129

Benjamin Aziz, Jeyong Jung, Julak Lee and Yong-Tae Chun
A False Negative Study of the Steganalysis Tool Stegdetect
Reprinted from: *Appl. Sci.* **2020**, *10*, 8188, doi:10.3390/app10228188 145

Eric Järpe and Mattias Weckstén
Velody 2—Resilient High-Capacity MIDI Steganography for Organ and Harpsichord Music
Reprinted from: *Appl. Sci.* **2021**, *11*, 39, doi:10.3390/app11010039 163

Jörg Keller and Steffen Wendzel
Reversible and Plausibly Deniable Covert Channels in One-Time Passwords Based on Hash Chains
Reprinted from: *Appl. Sci.* **2021**, *11*, 731, doi:10.3390/app11020731 177

Yan-Hong Chen, Chin-Chen Chang, Chia-Chen Lin and Zhi-Ming Wang
An Adaptive Reversible Data Hiding Scheme Using AMBTC and Quantization Level Difference
Reprinted from: *Appl. Sci.* **2021**, *11*, 635, doi:10.3390/app11020635 189

Andrea Tundis, Gaurav Mukherjee and Max Mühlhäuser
An Algorithm for the Detection of Hidden Propaganda in Mixed-Code Text over the Internet
Reprinted from: *Appl. Sci.* **2021**, *11*, 2196, doi:10.3390/app11052196 . . . . **203**

About the Editors

David Megías, Professor at the Universitat Oberta de Catalunya (Barcelona, Spain). David Megías received his B.Eng., M.Eng., and Ph.D. degrees from the Universitat Autònoma de Barcelona (Barcelona, Spain) in 1994, 1996, and 2000, respectively. He is currently Full Professor at the Universitat Oberta de Catalunya (UOC), Barcelona, Spain, and Director of the Internet Interdisciplinary Institute (IN3) at UOC. He has authored more than 120 research papers in international conferences and journals. He has participated in different national research projects both as a contributor and as a principal investigator. He also has experience working in international projects, such as the European Network of Excellence of Cryptology of the 6th Framework Program of the European Commission. His research interests include security, privacy, data hiding, protection of multimedia contents, privacy in decentralized networks, and information security. He is a member of IEEE.

Wojciech Mazurczyk, Professor at the Warsaw University of Technology (WUT) (Warsaw, Poland). Wojciech Mazurczyk received his B.Sc., M.Sc., Ph.D. (Hons.), and D.Sc. (habilitation) degrees in telecommunications from the Warsaw University of Technology (WUT), Warsaw, Poland, in 2003, 2004, 2009, and 2014, respectively. He is currently a University Professor with the Institute of Computer Science at WUT and head of the Computer Systems Security Group. He also works as a Researcher at the Parallelism and VLSI Group at Faculty of Mathematics and Computer Science at FernUniversitaet, Germany. His research interests include bio-inspired cybersecurity and networking, information hiding, and network security. He has been involved in the technical program committee of many international conferences and also serves as a reviewer for major international magazines and journals. Since 2016, he has served as Editor-in-Chief of the open access *Journal of Cyber Security and Mobility*. Between 2018 and 2021, he served as an Associate Editor of the IEEE Transactions on Information Forensics and Security. He is also a Senior Member of IEEE.

Minoru Kuribayashi, Associate Professor at the University of Okayama (Okayama, Japan), Minoru Kuribayashi received his B.E., M.E., and D.E. degrees from Kobe University, Japan, in 1999, 2001, and 2004, respectively. Here, he served as a research associate from 2002 to 2007 and an assistant professor from 2007 to 2015. Since 2015, he has been an associate professor in the Graduate School of Natural Science and Technology, Okayama University. His research interests include multimedia security, digital watermarking, cryptography, and coding theory. He serves as an associate editor of JISA and IEICE and as a vice chair of the APSIPA Multimedia Security and Forensics Technical Committee. He is a member of the Information Forensics and Security Technical Committee of the IEEE Signal Processing Society. He received the Young Professionals Award from the IEEE Kansai Section in 2014 and the Best Paper Award at IWDW 2015 and 2019. He is a senior member of the IEEE and IEICE.

Editorial

Data Hiding and Its Applications: Digital Watermarking and Steganography

David Megías [1,*], Wojciech Mazurczyk [2] and Minoru Kuribayashi [3]

1. Internet Interdisciplinary Institute (IN3), Universitat Oberta de Catalunya (UOC), CYBERCAT-Center for Cybersecurity Research of Catalonia, Castelldefels, 08860 Barcelona, Spain
2. Institute of Computer Science, Warsaw University of Technology, Nowowiejska 15/19, 00-665 Warsaw, Poland; wojciech.mazurczyk@pw.edu.pl
3. Graduate School of Natural Science and Technology, Okayama University, Okayama 700-8530, Japan; kminoru@okayama-u.ac.jp
* Correspondence: dmegias@uoc.edu

Citation: Megías, D.; Mazurczyk, W.; Kuribayashi, M. Data Hiding and Its Applications: Digital Watermarking and Steganography. *Appl. Sci.* **2021**, *11*, 10928. https://doi.org/10.3390/app112210928

Received: 10 November 2021
Accepted: 17 November 2021
Published: 19 November 2021

Publisher's Note: MDPI stays neutral with regard to jurisdictional claims in published maps and institutional affiliations.

Copyright: © 2021 by the authors. Licensee MDPI, Basel, Switzerland. This article is an open access article distributed under the terms and conditions of the Creative Commons Attribution (CC BY) license (https://creativecommons.org/licenses/by/4.0/).

Data hiding techniques [1] have been widely used to provide copyright protection, data integrity, covert communication, non-repudiation, and authentication, among other applications. In the context of increased dissemination and distribution of multimedia content (text, audio, video, etc.) over the internet, data hiding methods, such as digital watermarking and steganography, are becoming more and more relevant in providing multimedia security. Due to the complementary nature of general requirements of these methods, i.e., imperceptibility, robustness, security, and capacity, many data hiding schemes attempt to obtain optimal performance.

There are many potential applications of data hiding techniques. Copyright protection via content proof of ownership, owner identification or transaction tracking (digital fingerprinting), broadcast monitoring, content authentication including tampering detection or localization, copy control, device control, and legacy enhancement stand out among the applications of digital watermarking. On the other hand, secret communications are the focus of steganography, either for military reasons, for dissidents, or for criminal organizations. The military and criminal applications of steganography have led to an increased interest of the academic community in steganalysis, i.e., the techniques used to detect steganographic communications.

Apart from the classical applications of data hiding, mentioned above, new application scenarios have emerged in the last few years [2]. These new applications of data hiding include privacy-preserving transaction tracking, digital watermarking for data provenance, digital watermarking for forensics, network flow watermarking, network steganography, VoIP steganography, steganography for criminals and terrorists, and steganography for malware injection, among others.

The goal of this special issue is to focus on the improvement of data hiding algorithms and their different applications (either the traditional or the emerging ones), bringing together researchers and practitioners from different research fields, including data hiding, signal processing, cryptography, or information theory, among others, to contribute with original research outcomes that address current challenges in data hiding methods. The list of topics/keywords covered by this special issue is the following:

- Steganography
- Steganalysis
- Digital watermarking
- Zero watermarking
- Digital fingerprinting
- Coverless data hiding
- Reversible data hiding and applications
- Forensic aspects of data hiding

- Embedding capacity/payload
- Emerging applications of data hiding in IoT and Big Data
- Applications of data hiding
- Ownership Proof/Copyright Protection
- Covert channels
- Traitor-tracing
- Extraction/detection
- Data integrity
- Distortion measurement
- Transform coding
- Information theory
- Information entropy
- Signal processing
- Data segmentation

In response to the call for papers, nineteen papers were submitted to this special issue among which twelve were accepted for publication. These twelve papers include two review papers/surveys and ten contributions that address several research challenges of data hiding schemes.

In one of the accepted papers, Qureshi and Megías [3] present a systematic review and future directions for blockchain-based multimedia content protection schemes using data hiding techniques. The survey provides a detailed analysis of multimedia content protection applications using blockchain and proposes a taxonomy to classify these applications based on the technical aspects of blockchain, content protection techniques, digital rights management, digital watermarking and fingerprinting, and performance criteria. The paper concludes that there is a relevant research gap regarding blockchain-based multimedia copyright protection systems. In addition, the paper discusses some technical challenges and outlines future research directions.

In another survey paper, Caviglione [4] presents a systematic literature review of the most recent approaches for counteracting network covert channels. Network covert channels are increasingly used to distribute malware (stegomalware) and the detection of these kinds of attacks is difficult since those channels typically carry very low data rates, and it is difficult to identify where the secret information is hidden. Apart from the literature review, the paper identifies the major research challenges and the most promising development trends and discusses the advancements needed for building a more robust and consistent framework to obtain protection against network covert channels and stegomalware.

Among the research papers, four of them focus on new watermarking applications, including watermarking for 3D models [5], a watermarking scheme robust against screen-cam attacks [6], a watermarking protocol based on blockchain [7], and a watermarking framework to protect Deep Learning (DL) models [8].

In Ref. [5], Botta et al. present an algorithm for integrity protection of 3D models represented as a set of vertices and polygons. The proposed approach uses fragile watermarking on the vertices of the 3D model introducing a very small watermarking noise. The watermark is embedded into a secret vector space defined by the Karhunen-Loève transform obtained from a key image. The proposed method outperforms the state-of-the-art techniques in terms of performance, especially distortion and security.

Chen et al. [6] present a screen-cam robust image watermarking scheme using feature-based synchronization. Taking pictures of a screen with mobile phones or cameras is one of the main methods to leak image information. The paper analyzes the distortions caused by the screen-cam process and classifies them into five categories, namely, linear distortion, gamma tweaking, geometric distortion, noise attack, and low-pass filtering attack. After that, a watermark synchronization method is proposed based on the construction of a local square feature region (LSFR), a Gaussian function, a modified Harris-Laplace detector, and a speeded-up robust feature (SURF) orientation descriptor. Then, the message is embedded in each selected LSFR with an embedding algorithm using a non-rotating embedding method and a preprocessing procedure to modulate the discrete Fourier transform (DFT) coefficients. This approach makes it possible to improve watermark detection from the captured information. The effectiveness of the method against screen-cam attacks is shown and the scheme outperforms the state-of-the-art techniques not only against screen-cam attacks, but also when they are combined with other desynchronization attacks.

In Ref. [7], Frattolillo presents a watermarking protocol based on blockchain. "Buyer friendly" and "mediated" watermarking protocols can ensure both correct content protection and the easy participation of buyers in the transactions to purchase multimedia content, offering an alternative to more traditional "buyer and seller" watermarking protocols. In this paper, a new watermarking protocol is proposed combining the "buyer friendly" and "mediated" approaches with blockchain technology. The resulting protocol supports limited and balanced participation of buyers and content providers in transactions of protected digital content and avoids the need for a trusted third party directly involved in transactions. This reduces the risk of protocol violations by the buyers or the sellers by colluding with other parties. The proposed approach achieves security properties that are comparable to those of the state-of-the-art schemes, which require trusted third parties. Although the performance is somewhat penalized by the consensus mechanism of the blockchain, the next generations of the blockchain will make it possible to implement better algorithms and improve performance.

Jebreel et al. [8] propose KeyNet, an asymmetric key-style framework for watermarking DL models. DL models are used to solve many complex engineering tasks, including computer vision, speech recognition, natural language processing, or stock market analysis. Building representative and highly accurate DL models is a very costly task that involves devoting significant computational resources to process large amounts of proprietary training data, which is also hard to collect. Hence, the owners of DL models seek compensation for the incurred costs from commercial exploitation of such models, but this makes DL models attractive for attackers who try to steal them and use them in an illegal manner. KeyNet is a novel watermarking framework that satisfies the main requirements for an effective and robust watermarking of DL models. In the proposed framework, any sample in a watermark carrier set can take more than one label based on where the owner signs it, where the signature is the hashed value of the owner's information, and her model. Then, multitask learning (MTL) is used to learn the original classification task and the watermarking task together. Furthermore, a private model is added to the original one to act as a private key. Both models are trained together to embed the watermark while preserving the accuracy of the original classification task. To extract a watermark from a model, the prediction of the marked model on a signed sample is passed to the private model which can provide the position of the signature. The proposed KeyNet framework is then tested on several data sets to show its effectiveness and performance. The obtained results illustrate that KeyNet preserves the utility of the DL model while embedding a robust watermark. The watermarking application is carried out in an innovative way that makes it possible to embed a large amount of information, to establish a strong link between the owner and her marked model, to prevent attackers from overwriting the watermark without losing accuracy in the original task, and to uniquely fingerprint several copies of a pre-trained DL model for a large number of users in the system.

Then, four other papers present different advances in steganography and steganalysis: a high-capacity block-based steganographic scheme for images [9], an evaluation of the false-negative rate of the Stegdetect tool [10], a steganographic scheme for the MIDI format [11], and a reversible and plausible deniable covert channel for one-time passwords (OTP) based on hash chains [12].

Wu et al. [9] propose an efficient and high-capacity block-based steganographic method using optimal selection for palette images. The main goal of steganography is to provide a large steganographic payload with statistically undetectable methods. A typical approach to reduce statistical detectability in steganography is to increase the embedding efficiency, defined as the number of bits that can be hidden per embedding change. Methods with higher embedding efficiency are less detectable since, under the same capacity, they change less pixel values compared to lower efficiency methods. Block-based steganography methods are designed in order to improve the embedding efficiency under a limited capacity, but they often skip the blocks with larger distortion and require a location map to record the blocks that carry embedded data. The method proposed in this paper applies block-based steganography for palette images and does not require a location map. The proposed scheme embeds several bits in a block with, at most, a pixel change, which minimizes the embedding noise. This makes it possible to embed data in all the blocks of the image, leading to a larger capacity compared with other schemes known from the literature. Experimental results comparing the proposed scheme with other works evidence an improvement in the trade-off between embedding efficiency and capacity.

In Ref. [10], Aziz et al. analyze the false negative rates of Stegdetect, a modern automated steganalysis tool. Steganalysis is a collection of techniques aiming at detecting whether some media carries secret information previously hidden using steganography. Detecting steganography is essential to fight against secret criminal communications or malware that is transmitted using covert steganographic channels. In the paper, an extensive analysis of Stegdetect is conducted by embedding random messages in 2000 JPEG images using JPHide steganography to establish the false-negative rate of the tool. The study concludes that the sensitivity parameter of Stegdetect is a key factor of the false-negative rates. The false-negative rates with Stegdetect are high for sensitivity values between 0.1 and 3.4. The best detection results for JPHide are obtained with a sensitivity value of 6.2. The paper concludes that the sensitivity parameter of Stegdetect needs to be adjusted carefully in forensic activities when many images are analyzed to reduce false-negative rates.

Järpe and Wecksténpresent Velody 2 [11], a new musical steganographic scheme for the MIDI format by modifying the velocity parameter considering constraints in capacity and security. The major drawback of most MIDI steganographic schemes is their lack of resilience against steganalysis since most existing methods leave traces that do not appear naturally in MIDI files. The proposed scheme is based on embedding information into the velocities of the note-on events to mimic the behavior of some available digital audio software suites. Data embedding is carried out by setting velocities to values within a narrow interval to be specified which removes potential mood swings in the velocity parameter of the music. The use of the technique is restricted to organ and harpsichord music, which are naturally performed with constant or close to constant velocities, but the method can be used with little artificial effects on other types of music. Regarding resilience against steganalysis, Velody 2 is shown to leave very little traces and is comparable with the best MIDI steganographic methods in state-of-the-art methods. As audibility is concerned, it is shown that 30 listeners could not significantly guess which files contain embedded information. As far as embedding rate is concerned, Velody 2 outperforms the methods proposed in recent works.

Keller and Wendzel [12] present a work on reversible and plausibly deniable covert channels OTP based on hash chains. A covert channel (CC) is an unforeseen communication channel in a system design that enables several actions related to cybercrime, such as information theft, barely detectable channels for commanding and controlling botnets, and secret criminal communications. The paper presents a covert channel between two devices where one device authenticates itself with Lamport's OTP based on a cryptographic hash function. The proposed channel provides plausible deniability, i.e., the communicating parties can deny the existence of the covert channel and reversibility, i.e., the reconstruction of the original carrier message to the state before the steganographic data was embedded, and it can be applied in different contexts, such as traditional TCP/IP communications, Internet of Things (IoT) environments, blockchain-based systems, and local inter-process communications that rely on hash chains. Countermeasures to detect such a covert channel are also presented, but such detection is difficult because hash values appear to be random binary strings and deviations are hard to detect. Experimental results are presented to evaluate the channel's performance, to conduct statistical tests using the NIST suite, and to determine the channel's stealthiness (by running a test for matching hash values between legitimate and covert environments). The experiments show that the proposed channel might be detectable under realistic conditions only if no encryption is applied and authentication data are collected over a longer time span. The exact time spans depend on the deployed variant of the covert channel, which, in turn, is affected by the width of the selected hash function.

Finally, two other application scenarios are presented in the remaining papers of this special issue. First, an adaptive reversible data hiding scheme is proposed [13] and, second, a Machine Learning (ML)-based solution for the detection of propaganda and misinformation spread using mixed-code text is presented [14].

In [13], Chen et al. propose an adaptive reversible data hiding scheme using absolute moment block truncation coding (AMBTC) and Quantization Level Difference (QLD). Reversible data hiding makes it possible to recover the original (cover) object after data extraction in the receiving end, being a very valuable application field when images must be protected even from the slightest modification (such as in medical and military applications). The proposed method provides a large embedding capacity with a reduced quality loss for the modified images and uses QLD together with an interpolation technique to adaptively embed the secret information into pixels of AMBTC-compressed block, except for the positions of two replaced quantization levels. The proposed method obtains good performance for embedding capacity and still meets the requirement for better-modified image quality when the image is complex thanks to the use of QLD. The experimental results show that the proposed method outperforms the referenced approaches regarding distortion in terms of peak signal-to-noise ratio (PSNR) and hiding capacity.

Finally, Tundis et al. [14] present an algorithm for the detection of hidden propaganda in mixed-code text over the internet. The internet has become a widely used tool for spreading misinformation and propaganda. Although mechanisms to track potentially fake information exist, various ways have been found to avoid such kind of detection. An example of the approaches used to bypass detection is to use mixed-code language, which consists of text written in an unconventional way combining different languages, symbols, scripts, and shapes, often substituting the usual alphabet letters. The message is still readable by humans, but algorithms often fail in their detection. The article proposes a machine learning (ML) approach for character identification to detect and analyze whether some content includes propaganda or disinformation hidden using mixed-code text. The paper first proposes a possible categorization of different types of existing mixed code. The study is focused on the analysis of one type of *Text as Art Form* written on a single row by adopting a methodological approach centered on two main aspects, namely mixed code text analysis and hidden propaganda detection. Regarding the mixed code text analysis, a four-step algorithm that supports both the identification of mixed code in the text along with its normalization into natural language is proposed. As the hidden propaganda detection is concerned, a Convolutional Neural Network (CNN) classifier is designed. The overall performance of the tests is on a publicly available dataset containing a collection of 15,847 textual propaganda and nonpropaganda-related items. The experimental results are very remarkable in terms of performance (accuracy, precision, F1-score, and recall), overcoming the achievements of the reference works.

In general, this special issue covers recent trends in both traditional and emerging applications of data hiding and constitutes a good sample of the current state-of-the-art results in this field.

Author Contributions: The authors contributed equally to the different steps of this research. All authors have read and agreed to the published version of the manuscript.

Funding: The authors acknowledge the funding obtained from the EIG CONCERT-Japan call to the project Detection of fake newS on SocIal MedIa pLAtfoRms "DISSIMILAR" through grants PCI2020-120689-2 (Spanish Government), JPMJSC20C3 (Japanese Government) and EIG CONCERT-

JAPAN/05/2021 (National Centre for Research and Development, Poland). The first author also acknowledges the funding to the project RTI2018-095094-B-C22 "CONSENT" by the Spanish Ministry of Science and Innovation.

Institutional Review Board Statement: Not applicable.

Informed Consent Statement: Not applicable.

Data Availability Statement: Not applicable.

Acknowledgments: We acknowledge the authors of Refs. [3–14] for their valuable contributions to this special issue.

Conflicts of Interest: The authors declare no conflict of interest.

References

1. Cox, I.; Miller, M.; Jeffrey, A.; Fridrich, J.; Kalker, T. *Digital Watermarking and Steganography*, 2nd ed.; Morgan Kaufmann: Burlington, MA, USA, 2008. [CrossRef]
2. Megías, D. Data hiding: New opportunities for security and privacy? In Proceedings of the European Interdisciplinary Cybersecurity Conference (EICC 2020), Rennes, France, 18 November 2020; Article No.: 15. pp. 1–6. [CrossRef]
3. Qureshi, A.; Megías, D. Blockchain-Based Multimedia Content Protection: Review and Open Challenges. *Appl. Sci.* **2021**, *11*, 1. [CrossRef]
4. Caviglione, L. Trends and Challenges in Network Covert Channels Countermeasures. *Appl. Sci.* **2021**, *11*, 1641. [CrossRef]
5. Botta, M.; Cavagnino, D.; Gribaudo, M.; Piazzolla, P. Fragile Watermarking of 3D Models in a Transformed Domain. *Appl. Sci.* **2020**, *10*, 3244. [CrossRef]
6. Chen, W.; Ren, N.; Zhu, C.; Zhou, Q.; Seppänen, T.; Keskinarkaus, A. Screen-Cam Robust Image Watermarking with Feature-Based Synchronization. *Appl. Sci.* **2020**, *10*, 7494. [CrossRef]
7. Frattolillo, F. A Watermarking Protocol Based on Blockchain. *Appl. Sci.* **2020**, *10*, 7746. [CrossRef]
8. Jebreel, N.; Domingo-Ferrer, J.; Sánchez, D.; Blanco-Justicia, A. KeyNet: An Asymmetric Key-Style Framework for Watermarking Deep Learning Models. *Appl. Sci.* **2021**, *11*, 999. [CrossRef]
9. Wu, H.; Chen, L.; Ching, Y. Block-Based Steganography Method Using Optimal Selection to Reach High Efficiency and Capacity for Palette Images. *Appl. Sci.* **2020**, *10*, 7820. [CrossRef]
10. Aziz, B.; Jung, J.; Lee, J.; Chun, Y. A False Negative Study of the Steganalysis Tool Stegdetect. *Appl. Sci.* **2020**, *10*, 8188. [CrossRef]
11. Järpe, E.; Weckstén, M. Velody 2—Resilient High-Capacity MIDI Steganography for Organ and Harpsichord Music. *Appl. Sci.* **2021**, *11*, 39. [CrossRef]
12. Keller, J.; Wendzel, S. Reversible and Plausibly Deniable Covert Channels in One-Time Passwords Based on Hash Chains. *Appl. Sci.* **2021**, *11*, 731. [CrossRef]
13. Chen, Y.; Chang, C.; Lin, C.; Wang, Z. An Adaptive Reversible Data Hiding Scheme Using AMBTC and Quantization Level Difference. *Appl. Sci.* **2021**, *11*, 635. [CrossRef]
14. Tundis, A.; Mukherjee, G.; Mühlhäuser, M. An Algorithm for the Detection of Hidden Propaganda in Mixed-Code Text over the Internet. *Appl. Sci.* **2021**, *11*, 2196. [CrossRef]

Review

Blockchain-Based Multimedia Content Protection: Review and Open Challenges

Amna Qureshi * and David Megías Jiménez

Internet Interdisciplinary Institute (IN3), Universitat Oberta de Catalunya (UOC), CYBERCAT-Center for Cybersecurity Research of Catalonia, Castelldefels (Barcelona), 08860 Catalonia, Spain; dmegias@uoc.edu
* Correspondence: aqureshi@uoc.edu

Abstract: In this paper, we provide a holistic survey of multimedia content protection applications in which blockchain technology is being used. A taxonomy is developed to classify these applications with reference to the technical aspects of blockchain technology, content protection techniques, namely, encryption, digital rights management, digital watermarking and fingerprinting (or transaction tracking), and performance criteria. The study of the literature reveals that there is currently no complete and systematic taxonomy dedicated to blockchain-based copyright protection applications. Moreover, the number of successfully developed blockchain-based content protection systems is very low. This points towards a research gap. To fill this gap, we propose a taxonomy that integrates technical aspects and application knowledge and can guide the researchers towards the development of blockchain-based multimedia copyright protection systems. Furthermore, the paper discusses some technical challenges and outlines future research directions.

Keywords: blockchain; digital watermarking; digital rights management; digital fingerprinting; cryptography

1. Introduction

Content distribution is a process of digital distribution or delivery of multimedia content such as audio, text, animation and video. Traditionally, multimedia content was distributed through physical exchange of papers, compact discs, or DVDs. With the technological evolution and growth of the Internet, multimedia content in the form of digital formats can be published online through digital distribution channels, such as the Internet-based delivery platforms [1] or peer-to-peer (P2P) file distribution and sharing systems [2], among others. These online distribution platforms have become the de facto standards for content delivery ensuring great performance, wide availability, and cost efficiency. According to the 2019 Global Internet Phenomena Report [3], media streaming applications, and on-demand video [1,4] and audio [5] delivery platforms, constitute a large portion of Internet traffic. However, with the widespread use of these delivery platforms, the safety of the multimedia content, the preservation of copyright, the traceability of copyright violators, and the secure distribution of content have become increasingly ubiquitous problems for content owners, multimedia producers and distributors.

To prevent data from being illegally downloaded and shared, and to track and punish copyright violators, it is important that the multimedia content owners can prove their copyrights over the contents upon copyright infringement. Many traditional content protection technologies, such as encryption [6], Digital Rights Management (DRM) [7], watermarking [8,9], and forensic watermarking (digital fingerprinting) [10–14] have been designed to protect data copyright or content ownership. Though a few of the distribution systems [6–14] address the problems of copyright protection, traceability, and secure content distribution, there are several open issues to be addressed: (1) there does not exist an effective proof-of-delivery mechanism; (2) a deposit is required to place an order for the content before its delivery, which involves a certain risk that the customer may receive

Citation: Qureshi, A.; Megías, D. Blockchain-Based Multimedia Content Protection: Review and Open Challenges. *Appl. Sci.* 2021, 11, 1. https://dx.doi.org/10.3390/app11010001

Received: 28 November 2020
Accepted: 17 December 2020
Published: 22 December 2020

Publisher's Note: MDPI stays neutral with regard to jurisdictional claims in published maps and institutional affiliations.

Copyright: © 2020 by the authors. Licensee MDPI, Basel, Switzerland. This article is an open access article distributed under the terms and conditions of the Creative Commons Attribution (CC BY) license (https://creativecommons.org/licenses/by/4.0/).

tampered data; (3) the specific information of copyright and transaction is not public to the clients; (4) clients' identities need to be verified through multiple interactions; and (5) often these systems are dependent on centralized trusted third parties for payment, management of the licenses and keys, and generation and verification of the watermark or fingerprint. These trusted third parties are vulnerable to single point failures, compromise and hacking attacks.

The blockchain technology, which is widely known as a mechanism to provide transaction verification, can be used to design a decentralized and transparent multimedia distribution system. The blockchain [15] is a distributed digital ledger of cryptographically signed transactions that are grouped into blocks. Each block is cryptographically linked to the previous one after validation and undergoing a consensus decision. As new blocks are added, older blocks become more difficult to modify (i.e., creating resistance against tampering).

In recent years, the blockchain technology has become a source of new hope with its broad spectrum of applications, e.g., finance, health care, supply-chain management or intrusion detection, to name a few. Recently, its footprint can be observed in intellectual property or copyright protection applications. The main attributes of the blockchain technology—i.e., transparency, decentralization, reliable database, collective maintenance, trackability, security and credibility, digital cryptocurrency, and programmable contracts—provide innovative ideas for protecting digital intellectual property and ensuring traceability. In recent years, a rapid development of decentralized applications based on blockchain technology has been observed, but the combination of content protection and blockchain technologies has not received much attention from researchers. Apart from a few commercially available blockchain-based copyright protection platforms [16,17], one can find only a handful of blockchain-based copyright protection schemes in the literature. Recently, the authors in [18] investigated the use of blockchain technology in diverse online multimedia applications, such as music and advertising industries, healthcare, social media, and content delivery networks. Though the descriptive study analyzes the characteristics (target market, underlying platform technologies, consensus protocols and reward system) of the existing blockchain-based online media platforms, the research direction is not focused on addressing the problems related to integration of copyright protection mechanisms with the blockchain technology. Through this research work, we attempt to investigate how copyright infringement-related problems can be resolved using the blockchain technology.

The key contribution of this paper is to provide a holistic survey of multimedia content protection applications that use the blockchain technology. A taxonomy is developed to classify these applications based on technical blockchain characteristics, content protection mechanisms, and performance criteria. To the best of our knowledge, no systematic taxonomy has been defined in the literature to characterize the state-of-the-art of blockchain-based copyright protection schemes. The proposed taxonomy integrates technical aspects and application knowledge to address the challenges with feasible solutions and identify the possible research gaps in blockchain-based copyright protection applications. We believe that the current moment is opportune to present this survey due to recent emergence of copyright protection systems based on blockchain.

The rest of the paper is organized as follows. Section 2 presents the taxonomy of blockchain-based multimedia content protection applications. Section 3 surveys recent work on copyright protection schemes based on the blockchain technology. Additionally, we compared the schemes w.r.t. the attributes defined in the taxonomy. Section 4 provides an overall discussion and reveals a number of insights into the field of research. In addition, the future research directions are outlined. Finally, we present the conclusions of this research work in Section 5.

2. Taxonomy of Blockchain-Based Multimedia Content Protection Systems

This section presents the proposed taxonomy that allows the decomposition and comparison of blockchain-based multimedia content applications in the literature in a systematic manner. This taxonomy identifies the common dimensions and requirements of blockchain-based copyright protection systems. The proposed taxonomy defines seven categories that are further divided into sub-categories. A comprehensive and in-depth classification of the defined categories is graphically represented in Figure 1.

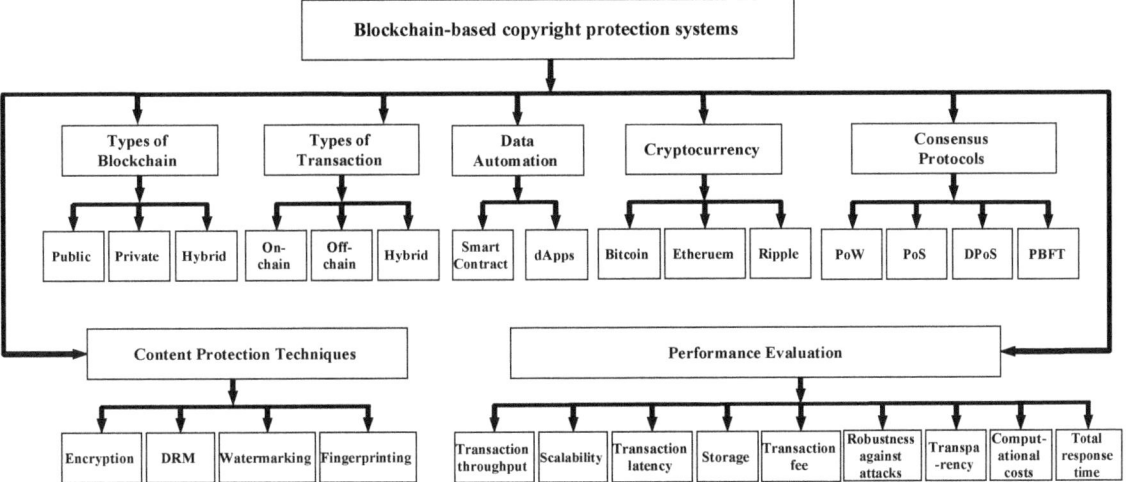

Figure 1. Taxonomy of Blockchain-based Copyright Protection Systems.

2.1. Types of Blockchain

The three possible types of blockchain are listed below:

- Public (permissionless) blockchain: A decentralized blockchain in which any node can join the network with read and write access permissions. It establishes trust through a consensus mechanism that makes the transaction immutable, once it is stored on the network. Since all nodes need to participate in the consensus process, the transaction speed is anomalously slow. Examples of a public blockchain are Bitcoin and Ethereum.
- Private (permissioned) blockchain: A partially decentralized blockchain in which only permissioned nodes can participate in the consensus, accounting and building blocks. It is managed by a trusted party and the encrypted database is commonly shared among the permissioned nodes. An example of this type is MultiChain.
- Hybrid (consortium) blockchain: A type of blockchain that combines "low-trust" offered by public blockchains and the "single highly-trusted entity" model of private blockchains. It has a multi-party consensus mechanism in which all operations are verified by special pre-approved nodes. A few examples include Quorum, Hyperledger, and Corda.

2.2. Types of Transaction

A transaction implies a state transition that changes data in the blockchain from one value to another. A blockchain transaction can involve cryptocurrency, smart contract, record, or data storage. The three different types of transactions on the blockchain are listed below:

- On-chain transactions: These are available on the distributed ledger and are visible to all participants on the network. Different details of this transaction are recorded

on the block and distributed to the entire blockchain, thus making the transaction irreversible as it cannot be altered. For the transaction to be complete, there has to be an agreed number of confirmations by miners. Moreover, the completion depends on network congestion. Consequently, sometimes transactions are delayed in case of a large volume of transactions waiting to be confirmed.
- Off-chain transactions: These occur outside of a main blockchain and are not published on the network. The involved parties can choose to have an agreement outside of the blockchain. In addition, it may involve a guarantor, who is responsible for confirming the completion of the transaction and certifying that the agreement has been honored. Upon agreement by the involved entities outside the blockchain, the actual transaction is then executed on the blockchain. These transactions can be carried out using different methods, e.g., multi-signature technologies, credit-based solutions, among others. Off-chain transactions are executed instantly as compared to on-chain transactions.
- Hybrid transactions: These transactions combine certain aspects of both on-chain and off-chain transactions. The separation of operations into on- and off-chain is based on different criteria, such as cost, decentralization, storage, privacy, etc.

2.3. Data Automation

A self-automated code, also known as a smart contract, consists of a program code, a storage file and an account balance. It is executed by miners that use consensus protocols to agree upon the sequence of actions resulting from the contract's code. Any user can create a contract by posting a transaction to the blockchain. The program code of a contract is fixed when the contract is created and cannot be changed, thus providing immutability. A contract's storage file is stored on the public blockchain. A smart contract can be invoked by entities within (other smart contracts) and outside (external data sources) the blockchain. While executing its code, the contract may read from or write to its storage file. Moreover, it can receive money into its account balance, and send money to other contracts or users. A smart contract is identified by a hash of 160 bits (a hexadecimal address used by many cryptocurrencies, e.g., Ethereum or LiteCoin, among others), and is operated within the environment that supports the use of a public-key cryptography. Smart contracts are widely used in most of the currently existing cryptocurrency networks and are the prominent features of Ethereum. A smart contract can be used to perform one type of transaction, while a distributed application (dApp) can bundle a set of smart contracts together to perform complex transactions. This dApp is a user-friendly interface (similar to a traditional website) that allows users to interact with the smart contracts stored on the blockchain.

Smart contracts could offer a number of benefits, such as accuracy (less prone to manual error), lower execution risk (automatic execution by the network), fewer intermediaries (reduced reliance on third-party intermediaries), lower cost (less human intervention and fewer intermediaries), speed and real-time updates (automated tasks), and new business models (from DRM and watermarking/fingerprinting of multimedia content to automated access to storage units).

2.4. Cryptocurrency

A cryptocurrency is a digital currency that uses cryptography to secure and verify transactions as well as to control the creation of new units of a particular cryptocurrency. The most attractive characteristic of cryptocurrency is its organic nature as it is not issued by any centralized authority (e.g., bank or financial intermediary). The main benefit of using cryptocurrency is that the funds are transferred more easily between any two parties in the transaction. All these transactions are facilitated through the use of public and private keys for security purposes, and are carried out with minimal processing costs. Bitcoin and Ethereum have been the two most popular cryptocurrencies since the emergence of the cryptocurrency phenomenon. Recently, Ripple has emerged as the third largest cryptocurrency in the trading market [19]. These three cryptocurrencies have a high market cap and a liquidity rate [20], and are the most traded cryptocurrencies on the mainstream trading platforms such as Plus500 [21]. A brief overview of top three cryptocurrencies is presented below:

- Bitcoin is the first P2P payment network of electronic cash based on the blockchain technology. The Bitcoin network adopts a hash-based proof-of-work (PoW) distributed consensus protocol. Bitcoin is pseudonymous, i.e., the funds are delivered to the Bitcoin addresses instead of the real-world identities. The average block creation time is 10 min, and the block size is limited to 1 MB [22], which constrains the network throughput. Moreover, the scalability is limited to 3–7 transactions/second [23]. Moreover, it is vulnerable to hacking attacks and theft, while being completely encrypted.
- Ethereum is an open-source, public, blockchain-based distributed computing platform that uses a proof-of-stake (PoS) consensus mechanism and allows programming of various types of smart contracts within the system. The transferable amount in Ethereum is ether. Any action in Ethereum requires gas, which is used as a fee instead of ether for ease of computations. The average block creation time is 17 s [24], and blocks are limited by a 6.7 million gas [25]. A simple Ethereum transaction can cost around 21,000 units of gas. However, a complicated smart contract can cost a lot more. The scalability of Ethereum is limited to 15–20 transactions/second [26]. Moreover, it is susceptible to security violations due to Solidity Language, causing compromise of stored data.
- Ripple is a for-profit technology platform that allows banks, payment providers, and digital asset exchanges to provide faster payment settlements and offers lower currency exchange costs. XRP is the cryptocurrency used by the Ripple payment network to make cross-border payments. Unlike blockchain mining, the Ripple network uses a unique distributed consensus protocol to validate transactions. This enables faster transactions without any centralized authority. The transactions in the Ripple network are confirmed instantly by the XRP gateways and take roughly 4 s. The Ripple network can process 1500 transactions/second [27]. Since Ripple is pre-mined, there exist little or no incentive for common nodes to work in the network, which subsequently leaves the corporations to provide the validator nodes.

2.5. Consensus Protocols

A consensus mechanism comprises protocols and algorithms, which establish the rules that the nodes (devices on the blockchain that maintain the blockchain and sometimes process transactions) must follow to validate the blocks. This mechanism solves data synchronization between the nodes that do not trust each other in a distributed system. The consensus protocol is a fault-tolerant mechanism that is used to achieve the necessary agreement on a single data value or a single state of the network. It consists of the following objectives: reaching an agreement, collaboration, cooperation, equal rights to every node, and mandatory participation of each node. Most blockchains use one of the following commonly used consensus protocols:

- PoW: The nodes (miners) involved in this process compete with each other to solve a complex mathematical puzzle. The first node to find a solution obtains the right to validate the block to create a new block that implements a transaction. Bitcoin and Ethereum 1.0 use the PoW [28]. However, PoW requires a lot of energy and computer power to reach a consensus, and therefore, it is a very expensive option.
- PoS: The miners in this process are required to prove the ownership of a certain amount of currency tokens to establish their stake. Hence, the more tokens a node has, the more likely it will validate the block, and thus, will determine the authenticity of the block. Dash and Neo use PoS [29]. Ethereum 2.0, an upgrade to the Ethereum blockchain, has switched to PoS [28] from PoW, in order to provide increased scalability and throughput. One of the major drawbacks of PoS is that it promotes "crypto-coin saving", rather than spending.

- Delegated proof-of-stake (dPoS): As a variation of the PoS, dPoS requires all token owners to select a group of delegates, who they trust to participate in the validation process. The nodes with the highest votes then authenticate the transactions. Lisk and BitShares use dPoS [30]. Though dPoS does not require much computing power, it is vulnerable to centralization as the number of witnesses is strictly limited.
- Practical Byzantine Fault Tolerance (PBFT): Byzantine fault tolerance (BFT) refers to reaching a consensus between two nodes communicating safely across a distributed network in the presence of malicious nodes. One of the examples of BFT, PBFT, is designed to be a high performance consensus algorithm that can rely on a set of trusted nodes in the network. PBFT can only tolerate faulty or malicious nodes until the number of such nodes is less than one-third of all the nodes. Since greater number of honest nodes will agree on a correct decision than a faulty or malicious nodes agreeing on an incorrect decision, false information will be rejected by the majority. This mechanism is currently being leveraged by Hyperledger Fabric and Zilliqa [31].

2.6. Multimedia Content Protection Techniques

Generally, a content protection technique can be defined as a measure to protect multimedia data against the threats arising from an unauthorized access to a user or a group of users. The protected properties generally include copy protection, traceability, authentication of content source and receivers, usage control, digital rights associated with the content, and secure distribution of content and access keys. According to Arnold et al. [32], any end-to-end content protection method should address all these basic security properties. Thus, an end-to-end copyright protection system is expected to provide security before and after transmission of the content, i.e., it ensures an authorized access of content, and controls the usage of the content once it is in the user's possession. In the following section, a brief overview of the most effective approaches for multimedia content protection is presented.

2.6.1. Multimedia Encryption

The process of encoding plaintext messages into ciphertext messages is called encryption, and the reverse process of transforming ciphertext back to plaintext is called decryption. This technique is expected to provide one or more of the following properties:

- Confidentiality: It refers to limiting data access or disclosure to authorized users and preventing access or disclosure to unauthorized ones.
- Integrity: It refers to protecting data against modification, or alteration, whether by accident or deliberately.
- Authenticity: It refers to enabling the receiver of data to ascertain its origin.

In the naïve approach, the entire multimedia content is encrypted using standard encryption methods such as symmetric (e.g., Advanced Encryption Standard (AES), Rivest Cipher (RC5), etc.) and asymmetric (Rivest–Shamir–Adleman (RSA), Digital Signature Algorithm (DSA), etc.) cryptographic algorithms. Since the multimedia content such as audio or video data is typically very large in size, the naïve approach becomes computationally demanding. Nowadays, many new encryption algorithms for audio and video have been proposed to avoid the naïve approach and gain better efficiency. These new algorithms can be divided into various categories: full encryption, selective encryption, joint compression and encryption, syntax-compliant encryption, scalable encryption and multi-access encryption.

Another important form of public-key cryptography is the homomorphic cryptosystem, which allows certain types of operations (addition/multiplication (partially homomorphic), or both (fully homomorphic) to be carried out over encrypted data while yielding the same encrypted results as if the operations were run on plaintext. Homomorphic cryptosystems are useful for copyright protection applications as they allow content owners to make computations directly to the ciphertext without exposing the keys. This property prevents the buyers' privacy-sensitive information from being exposed.

2.6.2. Digital Rights Management (DRM)

DRM systems have been developed to provide the secure delivery of digital content to an authorized receiver with restrictions (e.g., copying, printing or editing) on the usage of the content after delivery. A typical DRM system provides means for protecting content, creating and enforcing rights, identifying users, and monitoring of the content usage. A generic DRM architecture consists of three entities: content provider (responsible for generating the multimedia content, its metadata, and the corresponding content encryption keys, and encrypting the content), license provider (responsible for creating licenses and managing the content encryption keys), and a user (who has rights to access the content downloaded via a local software, called a DRM agent). DRM can be implemented as both software (Apple's FairPlay) and/or hardware (smart cards) solutions.

A DRM system is designed to satisfy the following security requirements:

- Unauthorized copying: It ensures that the digital asset is packaged in a secure manner so as to prevent unauthorized usage. This secure packaging is achieved by encryption.
- Secure distribution: It must securely distribute the digital asset to the authorized user.
- Conditional access: It must obtain the access conditions (licenses) specified by the owners of the protected content. The license consists of rights expression language, metadata or watermark, and a security mechanism to prevent users from circumventing DRM by modifying the access conditions.
- Tampering resistance: It must provide an effective tamper-resistant mechanism to process protected data and enforce content usage rights.

The core technologies used by DRM to fight piracy include encryption, passwords, watermarking, digital signature and payment systems. Encryption and password technologies are used to control who has access to the content and how it is used. Watermarks and digital signatures are used to protect the authenticity and integrity of the content, the copyright holders, and the users. Digital watermarking complements DRM to ensure that the digital rights of the copyright holders are not violated. Unlike traditional DRM schemes that compress and encrypt single multimedia content into multiple copies with each copy targeted at a specific application, and provide single access-control, modern DRM systems have been proposed to support encryption of scalable code streams with multiple keys to allow multiple accesses. Since a watermark can be used to identify the original content owner, it discourages a user from misrepresenting the content as if it was his/her own as well as unauthorized distribution or sharing it illegally with unauthorized parties.

2.6.3. Digital Watermarking

Unlike multimedia encryption, digital watermarking provides posterior protection when the multimedia content is decrypted by the authorized users. It imperceptibly alters the original content (host signal) by hiding the identification information (watermark) in it. This information can later prove ownership, and verify the authenticity of the carrier signal. A digital watermarking system generally includes two stages: watermark embedding and extracting. In the embedding algorithm, a watermark is embedded into the host signal to produce a watermarked signal, while in the extraction algorithm, the watermark is extracted from the manipulated/modified signal. If the signal was not modified during transmission, then the watermark is still present and it can be extracted. The watermark detection can only verify ownership, whereas watermark extraction can prove ownership. A secret key is used during the embedding and the extraction processes in order to prevent illegal access to the watermark.

Each of these following properties must be taken into consideration when applying a certain watermarking technique [33]:

- Imperceptibility: The perceptual similarity between the original and the watermarked versions of the digital content. The embedded watermark must not introduce distortion, which can cause quality degradation.

- Robustness: The ability to detect the watermark after common signal processing operations (such as cropping, compression or additive noise). A watermark must be robust enough to withstand all kinds of signal processing operations (at least below some distortion threshold). Depending on the robustness against attacks, digital watermarking can be categorized as robust, fragile and semi-fragile.
- Capacity: The number of bits a watermark encodes within a unit of time (or space in the case of still images).
- Security: The ability to resist intentional and/or malicious attacks. A watermarking algorithm must be secure in the sense that an attacker must not be able to detect the existence of embedded data or extract/remove it. Watermark information should only be accessible to the authorized parties.

Digital watermarking has been widely and successfully applied across a wide range of applications, such as copyright protection, transaction tracking, content authentication, broadcast monitoring, copy control, device control and legacy enhancement. The majority of the watermarking schemes proposed in recent years across the above mentioned range of applications focuses on producing image and video watermarked data, and very few focus on audio content.

2.6.4. Multimedia Fingerprinting

Unlike digital watermarking, which is incapable of tracing back the source of piracy, multimedia fingerprinting (also called transaction tracking) can trace back the identities of the pirates (colluders) upon finding an illegal copy. This traceability is achieved by embedding a unique user-specific information, known as a fingerprint, into different copies of the same content. A multimedia fingerprinting algorithm is a protocol between the content owner and the customer that involves three processes: fingerprint generation, embedding operation, and traceability of pirates from pirated/colluded copies.

A multimedia fingerprinting scheme is expected to address the following constraints [34]:

- Robustness: A fingerprint's robustness against signal processing operations is determined by the adopted watermark embedding method. Thus, a robust watermarking algorithm must be adopted so that the fingerprinting scheme can trace an illegal re-distributor after the digital content has been manipulated by common signal processing attacks.
- Collusion resistance: While digital fingerprinting may be effective at identifying a single adversary, multiple malicious buyers may collaborate to launch powerful collusion attacks against the fingerprinting system. By comparing their different versions, the colluders can attempt to identify the locations containing the fingerprint signal, remove the information from these locations and thereby create a copy that cannot be traced back to any of them. Thus, a fingerprinting scheme must be designed to withstand such collusion attacks.
- Quality tolerance: Fingerprinted content should have good visual quality and perceptual similarity to the original content.
- Embedding capacity: The capacity determines the length of fingerprint allocated to each user. The fingerprint is a binary string that can be long. Therefore, a digital fingerprint system should have a large enough embedding capacity to accommodate a full fingerprint.

From the customer's point of view, a traditional fingerprinting protocol between him/her and the content owner is unattractive, because during the embedding procedure, the content owner obtains the identity information of the customer. This enables a malicious content owner to embed the identity information of the customer into any content without the customer's consent, and subsequently, accuse him/her of illegal re-distribution. To eliminate this threat, anonymous fingerprinting protocols were developed based on cryptographic tools (such as homomorphic encryption, secure multiparty computation or zero-knowledge proof protocols). A complete and sound anonymous fingerprinting protocol [35] is expected to provide buyer frameproofness, traceability, collusion resistance, anonymity, non-repudiation, dispute resolution and unlinkability. Recently, a growing number of anonymous and collusion-resistant fingerprinting techniques have been proposed for multimedia content.

2.7. Performance Requirements

To evaluate the performance of blockchain-based copyright protection applications, several metrics should be taken into consideration. These are defined as follows:

- Transaction throughput: Throughput can be defined as the number of transactions/ second in each block, whereas transaction throughput can be defined as the rate at which valid transactions are committed by the blockchain in a defined time period.
- Scalability: The size and frequency of the blocks along with the number of transactions that the system can process to cope with the increased workload.
- Transaction latency: The amount of time required to add a block of transactions in the blockchain. This includes the propagation time and any settling time due to the consensus mechanism in place.
- Storage: On-chain storage of users' data (such as personal information, copyright information or keys) or off-chain mechanism (such as InterPlanetary File System (IPFS) or data lake) to store large amount of copyrighted data.
- Transaction fee: In Ethereum, an execution fee is used to compensate miners for the computational resources required to perform different smart contract functions (e.g., content registration or delivery). The gas price is measured in terms of ether. Hence, the total transaction fee is the gas consumed multiplied by the gas price. In Bitcoin, the transaction fee is the cost that a user incurs when he/she sends coins from one bitcoin wallet into another. This fee is based on the size (in bytes) of the transaction and the age of its inputs. The miners responsible for mining the block that includes the transaction are being paid with the transaction fee in BTC.
- Robustness of content protection schemes against different types of attacks: The copyright protection schemes (based on encryption, DRM, watermarking or fingerprinting) must be resistant against all possible threats, such as security, privacy, signal processing, tampering, communication and collusion attacks, among others. These threats are discussed in Section 2.6.
- Transparency of copyrighted multimedia content: In the copyright protection schemes based on watermarking/fingerprinting, the embedded watermark/fingerprint must be transparent and should not introduce distortion, which can cause quality degradation.
- Computational costs in generation of copyright content: These are on- or off-chain costs associated with the process of generating copyrighted content (encrypted with access control, watermarked or fingerprinted).
- Total response time: It includes the time taken by the content owner in registering the copyrighted content on the blockchain so as to make it available for the clients, and the time taken in delivering the content to the client upon final payment settlement.

3. State-of-The-Art of Blockchain-Based Content Protection Systems

Recently, both industry and academia have started to consider preservation of intellectual property rights using blockchain technologies. In the existing research, blockchain is considered to be a transparent and reliable ledger, which is used to solve the problems of copyright protection faced by the content owners and producers, e.g., the rights attribution certificate, data integrity, authenticity, piracy tracing and transparency, among others. In the remainder of this section, a brief overview of existing blockchain-based content protection systems is provided w.r.t. their main attributes and implementation details.

In Reference [36], the authors propose a blockchain-based framework that guarantees copyright compliance of multimedia objects by means of smart contracts. The proposed system uses an off-chain centralized storage solution, data lake, to store the transaction details of all the data added on the blockchain. The information stored on the data lake is encrypted and digitally signed to ensure the privacy and authenticity of the information. The stored data can only be accessed by the authorized users after verification of their digital signatures and access rights by the consent of the majority nodes. Although the decentralized data management framework ensures user data privacy and control, it is a proof-of-concept that has not been implemented and evaluated in the real world.

Peng et al. [37] propose an Ethereum-based digital copyright management system that enables content owners and customers to deal directly without the need of a centralized authority. In the proposed system, digital watermarking, the ElGamal cryptosystem, a perceptual hash function, the smart contract, and IPFS are used. However, the scheme incurs high overhead (memory and CPU time) due to use of ElGamal encryption for encrypting the whole multimedia content.

Chi et al. [38] introduce a secure and reliable blockchain-based real time eBook market system that allows users to publish themselves and receive direct payments from readers without any trusted party involvement. The proposed trading platform uses blockchain for protecting copyright of paid content and securely managing direct payments. It provides eBook ownership verification, data protection and confidentiality, permission to read the purchased ebook, authentication of a legitimate purchaser, non-forgeability and verifiability of both eBook contents and direct payment transactions, and prevention of eBook piracy and illegal distribution. The published encrypted (using Elliptic Curve Cryptography) eBook contents along with the book key are stored in a book repository.

Kishigami et al. [39] proposed a high-definition video copyright management system based on a decentralized blockchain to assist the content creators' demand for an efficient way to manage DRM. In the proposed scheme, the right holders themselves can control the system, which is based on the PoW mechanism. In this technique, the headers of ultra-high resolution video content (i.e., 4K or 8K) are encrypted and decrypted to balance the cryptographic costs associated with encryption/decryption operations. However, the system does not have an incentive mechanism for mining computation power. In addition, it does not provide cross-platform rendering and access policy control of the media file.

Zhao and O'Mahoney [40] proposed BMCProtector, a prototype implementation based on an Ethereum blockchain and smart contract technologies, for effective protection of music copyright and rights of copyright owners. BMCProtector uses the AES algorithm to encrypt the audio file, vector quantization (a watermarking technique) to track ownership of the music file off-chain, and an off-chain access control mechanism (DRM) to control the copyright of music during its distribution and usage. The deployed smart contract is responsible for sharing the copyright parameters of the music owners and automatic royalty payments distribution to the wallet addresses of the different copyright owners. However, BMCProtector provides the proof-of-concept design for a copyright management of audio files only. Moreover, it cannot redprovide copyright redprotection of music files in other formats, e.g., an audio file recorded during playing and then uploaded illegally.

In Reference [41], the Blockchain as a Service (BaaS) model is proposed for building a DRM platform that provides high-level credit and security to the content provider, the service provider, and the customers. The DRM platform provides core content rights information storage in the blockchain for tamper-resistant protection to prevent copyright from being violated or misused. The content consumers can use blockchain-based digital currency for content consumption payment. A cryptocurrency digital rights coin based on multi-signatures is proposed as a payment mechanism on the platform. Dynamic key agreement and session data encryption are used to ensure secure communications and data transfer. This scheme uses many modulo operations that significantly limit the cost-effectiveness of the generating a temporary shared key. Moreover, the scheme is based on the alliance chain, and thus has a centralized authority that prevents direct transactions between the content owner and the customer.

Ma et al. [42] proposed a Ethereum-based scheme, DRMChain, which ensures the correct usage of digital content by the authenticated users, and provides flexible external storage of decentralized digital content using IPFS. DRMchain employs two isolated blockchain application interfaces (BAI): BAI plain interface that stores the original content with its cipher summary, and BAI cipher interface, which stores the DRM-protected content service, such as content watermark, encryption, license and redviolation tracing, among others. DRMChain provides efficient and secure authentication, privacy protection, multi signature-based conditional traceability, and trusted and high-level credible content protection. However, DRMchain does not prevent the offline spread of the divulged copies. Moreover, the system lacks the diversified copyright management functions, such as copyright transaction. In addition, it lacks an effective punishment and reward mechanism.

Reference [43] proposed a blockchain-based DRM scheme for copyright protection of design works. The proposed system is categorized into two methods: copyright protection and trading. The copyright protection method performs copyright registration, information query and correlation verification, while the trading process encompasses design content protection and a proof-of-delivery method to guarantee fair trade. The enrolled buyer can purchase registered works from the content providers (sellers) through smart contracts. During the content delivery, the content is encrypted with the buyer's public key, and it is then delivered to the buyer through the application. Before receiving the content, the buyer needs to input his/her secret key to the application first, that performs decryption and makes it available to the buyer. However, the proposed scheme does not guarantee the security of the user's secret key submitted to the blockchain application for signing for the delivered content and the content decryption.

In Reference [44], a watermarking-based tamper-proof multimedia blockchain framework is proposed that provides security and integrity to the distributed image. The proposed blockchain model is based on a compressed sensing (CS)-based self-embedding watermarking algorithm in which the unique watermark information consists of a cryptographic hash and an image hash. The cryptographic hash comprises of transaction histories for retrieving the metadata of multimedia content from the multimedia blockchain, while the image hash is used for preserving retrievable original multimedia content.

The cryptographic hash can be used to retrieve the information of multimedia content (e.g., ownership and modification history) that is stored on the multimedia blockchain, and the image hash can be used to identify the tampered regions. The CS samples can be utilized for reconstructing the original image and locating the tampered regions. In the blockchain, a transaction is composed of the transaction information of the image containing transaction ID and the information of CS samples. Upon approval of the transaction by the validating nodes, the image is distributed and is then stored on a media database server. Though storing image verification information on the blockchain is a good strategy, the image is still stored in centralized manner or kept by the owner, which affects the availability of image management.

In Reference [45], an automated penalization of breach (APB) contract is proposed that consists of four main components: a claim-or-refund smart contract, a robust watermarking scheme, an oblivious-transfer scheme and a non-interactive zero knowledge (NIZK) proof for mutually distrusting parties. In this scheme, the sender and the receiver create a claim-or-refund transaction on Bitcoin, where an amount is deposited that can be spent at any time with a jointly signed transaction or spent after a period of time by a sender-only signed transaction. At the receiver's end, the received document consists of the receiver's secret key, which is embedded into it with a robust binary watermarking scheme. A two-party computation protocol is jointly performed by the parties to embed and ensure that the receiver's embedded key is retrievable for the sender in case of a content leakage.

Reference [46] proposes a blockchain-based data hiding method for digital video protection, which improves the integrity authentication of confidential data and videos. The proposed method consists of the following three parts: (1) on-chain data protection method that focuses on the integrity check and the security of the video by registering the signature of the video content on the blockchain; (2) off-chain data protection based on a data hiding algorithm that can achieve a good balance between visual distortion, embedding capacity and robustness; and (3) data protection management agreement based on a smart contract that consists of registration, inquiry and transfer contract models. However, in the proposed scheme, the users need to request data extraction from data hiding servers so as to enable multimedia playback.

In [47], the blockchain technology is used to store the watermark securely and to provide timestamp authentication for multiple watermarks. The proposed system uses the perceptual hash function for calculating a hash value of an image, the blockchain technology for recording metadata related to the copyright information, the QR code for generating a watermark, the digital watermarking algorithm for embedding the copyright information, the cryptographic hash function for calculating the hash values of both original and watermarked images, and the IPFS network for saving, managing and distributing the watermarked image and its related copyright information. The proposed scheme, however, provides the proof-of-concept design for copyright management of digital images only. Moreover, it can be observed that the perceptual hash values of modified/edited images (such as rotated or cropped) considerably differ from those of the original and the original image hash values recorded on the blockchain.

In [48], Fei proposes BDRM, a blockchain-based DRM system with the property of a fine-grained usage control. BDRM utilizes a smart contract to achieve copyright management related operations, such as copyright registration and copyright transactions. Moreover, a novel authorization tree is designed in the blockchain. Each time a user conducts a rights transaction, a usable digital watermark is embedded, and digital content distribution is performed under the encryption domain. The authorization tree is then updated and the transaction is recorded on the blockchain. The content is encrypted with the secret key of the content owner and is stored in the distributed file system (IPFS). However, BDRM is only applicable to copyright registration of a single content owner.

Reference [49] presents Y-DWMS, a digital watermark management system, based on a public smart contract platform to prevent digital rights infringement. The proposed system adopts non-repudiation of smart contracts and non-tampering of blockchain to implement a DRM mechanism that prevents users from sharing encryption keys or their accounts. The smart contract is designed to perform verification of watermarks in the disclosed copy, authentication of the informer's report, traceability of infringement, an act of rewarding informers and punishing infringers, and recovery of losses suffered by the copyright holders. However, Y-DWMS is still in an early stage of development and suffers from some security issues, such as account security and privacy.

Wu et al. [50] proposed a blockchain and smart contract-based data trading system with data tracking and illegal behavior detecting functions. It enables two trading scenarios with privacy protection against any unauthorized party, including the trading platform. An effective fingerprint method is designed to detect the manipulated image, thus protecting data copyright. A data fingerprint generator is designed to generate a fingerprint by concatenating multiple feature vectors extracted from the data. Upon finding an illegally distributed copy, the data fingerprint generator extracts an identifiable vector, which is then compared with the fingerprints recorded in all existing contracts. The generated fingerprint is resistant to minor data modifications, such as cropping, adding noise and changing brightness. However, the system does not satisfy the privacy and security properties of an anonymous fingerprinting protocol in a decentralized environment.

In Reference [51], the authors propose a P2P content distribution system based on the blockchain technology. The proposed system uses collusion-resistant fingerprinting (to provide collusion resistance), homomorphic and symmetric encryption schemes (to ensure content protection and data confidentiality), a perceptual hash function (to provide content authentication), an Ethereum-based smart contract (to execute atomic payment and provide proof-of-delivery) and the IPFS network (to store multimedia content). While the privacy and security properties of an anonymous fingerprinting protocol in a distributed environment are addressed by the proposed system, it is a proof-of-concept that has not been implemented and evaluated in the real world.

In Reference [52], Li proposes a blockchain-based novel fingerprint-related chaotic image encryption scheme that provides authentication, traceability, and resistance against security attacks (e.g., chosen plaintext attack or tampering). In this scheme, the content distributors' fingerprints embedded in the encrypted images are encoded with Tardos's collusion-resistant codes to record multiple fingerprints with fixed length of data and to provide traceability. Before content distribution, the original image is embedded with the signature of the sender and the fingerprints of all system distributors using a reversible watermarking scheme and a chaotic map. This fingerprinted image is then encrypted using Fridrich's structure, which consists of substitution, permutation and diffusion. The fingerprint, the data hiding key, and the encryption key are recorded on the blockchain. At the receiver's end, upon decryption, the fingerprinted image is obtained, and it contains the signature of the sender and all the fingerprints of the superior distributors (merged fingerprint), which can be extracted individually, and then compared with the recorded information on the blockchain for verification. Though the system provides collusion resistance, data integrity, and copyright protection, it does not satisfy all the privacy and security properties of an anonymous fingerprinting protocol in a decentralized environment.

Reference [53] presents a robust blockchain-based copyright protection system (RobustCPS) for audio content. RobustCPS consists of the following three parts: (1) the audio content is segmented into blocks; (2) content-based fingerprint is generated by applying the singular value decomposition (SVD) on each block; and (3) similarity detection is performed through an execution of a smart contract, which determines whether a similar fingerprint exists on the Ethereum blockchain. If a similar fingerprint is found on the blockchain, RobustCPS sends a warning to the copyright shareholder of the corresponding fingerprint so as to prevent copyright violation. In case a similar fingerprint is not found, the generated content-based fingerprint will be recorded on the blockchain. The content-based fingerprint is resistant to common signal processing attacks and de-synchronization attacks. Though the system is able to protect copyright across multiple online platforms, it does not provide security against collusion attacks. Additionally, it is a proof-of-concept that has not been implemented on the blockchain.

3.1. Comparative Analysis

This section presents a comparison and a fine-grained analysis of blockchain-based multimedia content protection schemes presented in Section 3 w.r.t. the attributes defined in the taxonomy (Section 2). The analysis is presented in the form of Tables 1 and 2, Figure 2, and an in-depth discussion on the systems' properties. The tables also allow a side-by-side comparison of the systems presented in Section 3.

Table 1 presents the comparison of the schemes w.r.t. types of blockchain, transaction types, data automation, cryptocurrency, consensus protocols, and content protection techniques, while Table 2 compares the performance of these scheme w.r.t. the performance evaluation metrics mentioned in Section 2.7. In Tables 1 and 2, a cell contains "–" when the corresponding attribute is not addressed by the scheme.

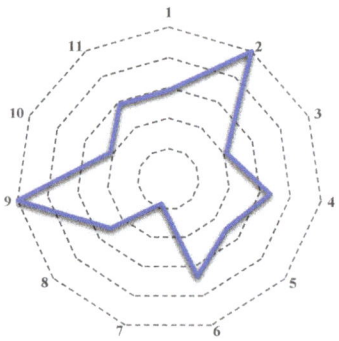

Figure 2. Analysis of security objectives of multimedia content protection techniques achieved by the analyzed systems.

Table 1. Comparison of blockchain-based copyright protection schemes with reference to the taxonomy.

References	Types of Content	Types of Blockchain	Types of Transaction	Data Automation	Crypto-currency	Consensus Protocols	Content Protection Techniques
Kishigami et al. (2015) [39]	HD video	Permissioned	On-chain	–	Bitcoin	PoW	DRM
Bhowmik & Feng (2017) [44]	Image	–	On-chain	Smart contract	Ethereum	–	Watermarking
Vishwa & Hussain (2018) [36]	–	Permissioned	Hybrid	dApp	Ethereum	–	Encryption
Zhao & Mahony (2018) [40]	Audio	Permissionless	Hybrid	dApp	Ethereum	PoW	Watermarking-based DRM
Ma et al. (2018) [41]	Video	Consortium	On-chain	dApp	Ethereum Token	PoW/PoS/PBFT	DRM
Ma et al. (2018) [42]	Video	Permissioned	Hybrid	dApp	Ethereum	PoW/PoS/PBFT	Watermarking-based DRM
Zhao et al. (2018) [46]	Video	Permissioned	Hybrid	Smart contract	Bitcoin	–	Watermarking
Meng et al. (2018) [47]	Image	Permissionless	Hybrid	–	–	–	Watermarking
Peng et al. (2019) [37]	Image	Permissioned	Hybrid	dApp	Ethereum	–	Encryption+Watermarking
Lu et al. (2019) [43]	Image	Consortium	On-chain	dApp	–	–	DRM
Mangipudi et al. (2019) [45]	Document	–	Hybrid	Smart contract	Bitcoin	–	Watermarking
Fei (2019) [48]	–	Consortium	Hybrid	Smart contract	Ethereum	Proof-of-Authority	Watermarking-based DRM
Zhao et al. (2019) [49]	–	Permissioned	On-chain	dApp	Ethereum	PBFT	Watermarking-based DRM
Wu et al. (2019) [50]	Image	–	Hybrid	dApp	–	–	Fingerprinting
Qureshi & Megías (2019) [51]	Image, Audio, Video	Permissioned	Hybrid	Smart contract	Ethereum	–	Fingerprinting
Chi et al. (2020) [38]	Document	Self-developed	Hybrid	–	Customized coin	PoW	ECC-based encryption
Li (2020) [52]	Image	–	On-chain	–	–	–	Encryption+Fingerprinting
Zhao (2020) [53]	Audio	Permissionless	On-chain	Smart contract	–	–	Content-based Fingerprinting

Table 2. Comparison of the blockchain-based multimedia content protection schemes with reference to the performance evaluation.

References	Transaction throughput	Scalability	Transaction Latency	Storage	Transaction Fee	Signal Processing	Communication	Collusion	Security	Transparency	Computational Costs	Total Response Time
						Performance Evaluation						
							Robustness against Attacks					
Kishigami et al. (2015) [39]	3–7 tps	–	10 min	On-chain	0.0001 BTC	–	–	–	Tampering resistance + Conditional access	–	–	–
Bhowmik & Feng (2017) [44]	15–20 tps	–	17 s	On-chain	0.00042 Ether	–	–	–	Tampering resistance	–	–	–
Vishwa & Hussain (2018) [36]	15–20 tps	–	17 s	On-chain + Data lake	–	–	–	–	Data confidentiality	–	–	–
Zhao & Mahony (2018) [40]	123k tps per day	–	17 s	On-chain + IPFS	–	Yes	Yes	–	Conditional access + Data confidentiality	–	–	–
Ma et al. (2018) [41]	– (HyperLedger fabric) 15–20 tps (Ethereum)	Yes (multi-sig)	– (HyperLedger fabric) 17 s (Ethereum)	On-chain	0.00042 Ether	–	Yes	–	Tampering resistance + Conditional access	–	1074 ms	987 ms
Ma et al. (2018) [42]	15–20 tps	Yes (multi-sig)	17 s	On-chain+ IPFS	0.00042 Ether	Yes	Yes	–	Tampering resistance + Conditional access + Traceability	38.96 dB	12,000 ms	45,000 ms
Zhao et al. (2018) [46]	3–7 tps	–	10 min	On-chain + Server	0.0001 BTC	Yes	Yes	–	Data integrity Tampering resistance	35.50 db	–	–
Meng et al. (2018) [47]	–	–	–	On-chain+ IPFS	–	–	–	–	Data integrity Tampering resistance	–	–	–
Peng et al. (2019) [37]	15–20 tps	–	17 s	On-chain + IPFS	0.00042 Ether	–	Yes	–	Data integrity Access control	–	–	–
Lu et al. (2019) [43]	–	–	–	On-chain + Personal equipment	–	–	Yes	–	Data confidentiality Proof-of-delivery Traceability	–	–	–
Mangipudi et al. (2019) [45]	3–7 tps	Yes (multi-sig)	10 min	On-chain + Server	–	Yes	Yes	Yes	Data integrity Fairness	–	–	–
Fei (2019) [48]	–	–	–	On-chain + IPFS	–	–	–	Yes	Conditional access Fine-grained usage control	–	–	97.077 ms
Zhao et al. (2019) [49]	–	Computationally intensive contract	–	On-chain	–	–	Yes	Yes	Traceability Rewards & Punishments Screen Record Prevention	–	–	–
Wu et al. (2019) [50]	–	–	–	On-chain + Server	–	Yes	Yes	–	Tamper proofness Traceability Frameproofness Non repudiation	–	–	–

Table 2. Cont.

References	Transaction throughput	Scalability	Transaction Latency	Storage	Transaction Fee	Signal Processing	Communication	Collusion	Security	Transparency	Computational Costs	Total Response Time
							Robustness against Attacks					
							Performance Evaluation					
Qureshi & Megías (2019) [51]	15–20 tps	–	17 s	On-chain+ IPFS	–	Yes	Yes	Yes	Proof-of-delivery Traceability Frameproofness Unlinkability	–	–	–
Chi et al. (2020) [38]	–	–	2.80 – 3.30 s	On-chain+ Server	–	–	Yes	–	Data confidentiality Non forgeability Verifiability	–	425.60ms (10 MB file)	11,386 ms (10 MB file)
Li (2020) [52]	–	–	–	On-chain	–	–	Yes	Yes	Data integrity Traceability	–	–	–
Zhao (2020) [52]	15–20 tps	–	17 s	On-chain	–	Yes	No	No	Authenticity	–	–	–

From Tables 1 and 2, we can make the following observations w.r.t. the attributes defined in the taxonomy:

- Most of the selected schemes [36,37,39,42,45,46,49,51] use a permissioned (private) blockchain, which implies a control layer on top of the blockchain that is governed by a trusted authority, who is responsible for permitting actions to be performed by the allowed system entities. Several other schemes [41,43,48] use consortium blockchain as a distributed ledger to retain control and privacy, while cutting down costs and increasing transaction speeds.
- The majority of the schemes [36–38,40,42,46–49,51,52] utilize hybrid transactions, which imply on-chain recording of data in a private or publicly accessible blockchain service, such as the content's metadata, copyright owners' or users' information, watermark or fingerprint of the user (in an encrypted form), DRM license and content obligation, among others, and off-chain mechanisms, such as generation and storage of copyrighted content, extraction of copyright information from the content or traceability protocol. The on-chain transactions are performed to achieve transparency, security, immutability and auditability, and are considered best for cryptocurrency transfers in a completely decentralized manner. The off-chain mechanisms allow the authorities to save on-chain costs as these do not have a transaction fee. In addition, these mechanisms are quite fast since these are not bound by the transactional speed limitations linked to on-chain transactions.
- In many schemes [36,37,40–43,49,50], multiple smart contracts are bundled together to create a blockchain-enabled dApp to automate the desired functionality between the copyright owner and the buyers. These contracts include a series of functions, such as data processing, value transfer, copyright protection, content distribution, and traceability. In other systems [44–46,48,51,53], a single smart contract is proposed to facilitate the purchase of the copyrighted content between the copyright owner and the clients (buyers).
- In the majority of the schemes [36,37,40,42,44,46,48,49,51,53], Ethereum, which is the second largest cryptocurrency platform by market capitalization behind Bitcoin, is used as a cryptocurrency for transactions. The Ethereum crypto token (Ether) transactions tend to be confirmed faster by the blockchain, and are much cheaper than most transactions on Bitcoin. Moreover, Ethereum not only allows Ether transfers between people, but can be used to create all types of other cryptocurrencies, such as in [41].
- Many schemes [38–42] use the most prominent consensus protocol, i.e., PoW, to confirm transactions and produce new blocks in the chain. PoW is the dominant choice in existing digital currencies due to its security features, which use cryptography that deters denial-of-service (DoS) and sybil attacks.
- The majority of the schemes guarantee content protection by using digital watermarking either as a standalone mechanism [44–47] or in combination with DRM [40,42,48,49] or encryption [37]. Only three schemes [50–53] used digital fingerprinting to provide copyright protection, while only two schemes, proposed in [39,41], used DRM techniques to ensure conditional access.
- From Table 2, we can make the following observations w.r.t. to the performance of the systems:
    - Since the majority of the schemes have utilized either Bitcoin or Ethereum for development or testing purposes, the average transaction throughput (3–7 tps for Bitcoin and 15–20 tps for Ethereum) and latency rates (10 min for Bitcoin and 17 s for Ethereum) have been considered. However, only a few schemes [37,39,41,42,44,46] consider the transaction fees per block per day.
    - Only a few schemes [41,42,45] address scalability by using the Schnorr's multi-signature technology, which also improves the privacy of the system and prevents spam attacks to a higher degree. In [49], a quite small number of miners

- are pseudo-randomly selected to execute off-chain computationally intensive smart contracts.
- The majority of the schemes use IPFS or data servers for storing and distributing the copyrighted content to the buyers upon a successful purchase.
- All schemes are based on different content protection mechanisms and satisfy the basic security requirements described in Section 2.6. Figure 2 illustrates the 11 identified individual security properties (excluding the common security properties) of four multimedia content protection techniques (encryption, DRM, watermarking and fingerprinting), and the analyzed systems (18) that satisfy each of these objectives.

  It can be observed that the majority of the systems provide data integrity (12 systems) and protection against communication attacks (12 systems). In terms of tamperproofness, we can observe that many systems guarantee tampering resistance (8 systems). This is to be expected since this property is provided by the blockchain technology. It can be observed that fewer schemes address data confidentiality (7 systems), traceability (7 systems), authenticity (6 systems), and conditional access (6 systems). In terms of security against attacks, only a few schemes are robust against common signal processing (7 systems) and collusion/coalition (5 systems) attacks. Considering the quality tolerance objective, we observe that transparency of the copyrighted (watermarked/fingerprinted) content is evaluated by many fewer schemes (2 systems).
- Most of the schemes presented in Table 2 are proof-of-concepts and have not been evaluated in a real-world scenario. In only three schemes [38,41,42], the total response time or the computational overhead in generating the copyrighted content is evaluated.

4. Limitations, Open Challenges and Future Research Directions

This section presents the limitations and research challenges that must often be faced when designing blockchain-based multimedia copyright protection applications. In addition, possible research directions are pointed out to be considered in future works.

4.1. Limitations and Research Challenges of Content Protection Techniques

The limitations and research challenges of the multimedia content protection techniques presented in Section 2.6 are discussed below:

- Encrypted content is only as secure as the key used for encrypting it. Thus, cryptographic keys must be carefully managed (e.g., transmission, storage or updating) to ensure data remains protected, yet accessible when needed among multiple users of a system.
- Encryption techniques cannot prevent a user from unauthorized usage and illegal distribution of the content upon decryption of the received content.
- Most of the research work involving DRM is non-interoperable, which does not constitute an efficient option for clients. For this reason, consumers may seek alternative options to obtain the content, such as P2P file-sharing applications. However, to make DRM systems interoperable, the content providers or vendors of multimedia players would need to know the sensitive information related to the DRM protection scheme, thus increasing the risk of leakage. In such a case, a single leakage (or "hack") has the potential to compromise not only one of several distribution channels, but the distribution of all interoperably DRMed content.
- DRM systems may give rise to a number of legal issues if not used correctly, e.g., the use of monitoring tools, either intentionally or unintentionally, to report and collect data pertaining to their consumers' habits and preferences (such as the type of content they enjoy, when they enjoy it and even where, by accessing users location details, among others). This may result in serious privacy implications, such as using these data for purposes unrelated to the platform or selling it to third parties.

- At the embedder's end in a digital watermarking scheme, maintaining an appropriate balance between robustness, capacity and imperceptibility properties is a challenging task, since these properties contradict one another, i.e., if one is increased, the other decreases.
- Security and complexity features have been given less priority in the development of the watermarking schemes. The more complex the watermarking scheme is, the higher the costs associated with the embedding and detection processes. The costs associated with the watermark embedding and detection should be minimal in order to meet the real-time requirements.
- In digital fingerprinting schemes based on collusion-resistant codes, there exists a trade-off among the size of a user base N, the collusion resilience c_0, and the codeword length m. With an increase in N or c_0, the length of m increases and vice versa. This trade-off may make the traceable code impractical because many applications require a large user base and collusion resistance. However, these requirements will result in long traceable codes.
- Most of the research work involving anonymous fingerprinting protocols assume the presence of a trusted third party that is responsible for generating the fingerprint and tracing the copyright violators. This trust implies a belief by the user that the trusted entity will behave in an expected manner in order to ensure security and anonymity. In a few other schemes that have avoided the use of such a party, the computational and communicational overheads are quite high due to the use of at least one of the following highly demanding technologies: homomorphic encryption, bit-commitment or secure multi-party computation.
- All types of attacks—internal and external—should be taken into consideration to evaluate the security and robustness of novel or existing watermarking and fingerprinting schemes.

4.2. Limitations and Research Challenges of the Blockchain Technology

In this section, we discuss the limitations and research challenges of the blockchain technology:

- The blockchain suffers from a scalability problem due to the limited block size, e.g., Bitcoin can reach 7 transactions per second due to the Bitcoin protocol restricting block sizes to 1 MB. A possible solution to this problem is to increase the block size, but it creates a strain on the security due to the fact that an increase in the probability of orphaned blocks would distinctly affect the bandwidth and validation costs. The higher the block size limit, the larger the transaction load, blockchain congestion, and transaction delays. Consequently, a decrease in the transaction fee would result in less security. Thus, a trade-off between security, scalability and decentralization is a challenge in the development of a blockchain.
- Permissionless blockchains establish that the recorded data is accessible, and thus, enable its public access to all participants. However, this may compromise data privacy. Furthermore, in the case that a sensitive or confidential data is uploaded mistakenly to the public blockchain, there is no way to rectify the damage.
- The codes of smart contracts are susceptible to the inclusion of bugs due to human error or incomplete information. Moreover, the self-executing nature of smart contracts implies reduced flexibility to give effect to the actual intentions of the parties.
- A programming language to implement smart contracts is an ongoing research field. Currently, the most used object-oriented and high-level language to implement complex smart contracts in Ethereum is Solidity (Turing-complete language), which is still evolving and has a number of limitations, such as lack of general purpose libraries, type checking and multi-threading support, among others. Other popular programming languages (Python, C++, Java) are also used to code smart contracts. However, making programs readable (human readable code and human readable execution) in each form remains a challenge. In the case of Bitcoin, the scripting language to write a

simple code is not Turing complete and does not support all possible programming structures, specifically loops.
- Blockchain could suffer from 51% attacks, where some nodes may attain the majority in a network and abuse it, e.g., they may reverse transactions to perform double spending and prevent other miners from confirming blocks.
- User's privacy can be breached within the blockchain, e.g., user's real IP address can be traced, transaction history can be linked to reveal his/her true identity or linkability through his/her connected set of nodes.
- Blockchain lacks interoperability due to the lack of universal standards. Existing blockchain networks have their own parameters, such as consensus models, transaction schemes, cryptocurrency, and smart contract functionality. Moreover, the uncertainty and speculative nature of cryptocurrency still prevent its widespread adoption.

4.3. Future Research Directions

In this section, we describe possible research directions that are identified during the fine-grained analysis of the 18 blockchain-based multimedia content protection systems. Future research works should address these research potentials to tackle the challenges identified in Sections 4.2 and 4.3, and to enhance the usability of the blockchain technology in copyright protection applications.

4.3.1. Designing an Efficient Blockchain-Based Framework to Satisfy the System Requirements of Copyright Protection Applications

- Scalability: Off-chain mechanisms such as Lightning Network (LN) for Bitcoin [54] and Plasma for Ethereum [55], or on-chain schemes like SegWit for Bitcoin [56] and Sharding [57] for Ethereum, can solve the blockchain's scalability problem. However, for LN, the main challenges are security and transparency per-transaction basis and centralization (presence of hubs), while in Plasma, long waiting periods (7–14 days) for withdrawal of funds and security risks are the open challenges. Similarly, the main challenges of SegWit are complexity, increased storage space and network bandwidth, while communication and security are the main issues in Sharding. The studies on addressing security, complexity, decentralization, performance, and communication strategies are expected to achieve significant research interest in the future.
- Validation of a framework: Many of the blockchain-based copyright protection applications solely focus on the technology's benefits, while leaving aside the details of their implementation. Therefore, it is important to design a practical blockchain-based framework that should address both technical and implementation details, e.g., assessing the advantages and disadvantages of permissioned and permissionless systems before opting for one of these solutions, the selection of the appropriate consensus mechanism depending on the requirements (e.g., transaction throughput, latency, minimum transaction fee, centralization/decentralization and security, among others), and the evaluation of the performance by implementing the proof-of-concepts to calculate computational overheads and the total response time.
- Standardization: The recognized technological standards establish specifications and procedures that are beneficial in terms of ensuring efficiency, reliability, and enhanced security. Through our fine-grained analysis, it can be deduced that there is a need of a universal standard that the multimedia content providers, producers and involved companies could follow to share new blockchain-based copyright protection solutions as well as to integrate these with the existing systems. Similarly, this standard should allow automatic conversion between different cryptocurrencies to enhance user experience.
- Privacy-aware design: Future research studies need to investigate possible privacy-aware solutions that could protect the privacy of the entities (content owner, buyer, and so on) involved in the transactions of the blockchain-based content protection applications. The privacy and security requirements should be defined at the initial stage of these schemes due to the fact that the data (e.g., information related to

the content owner, the public keys of the participants, pseudonyms and copyright information, among others) is visible to everyone on the network.
- Unlinkability: The privacy leakage issue in the blockchain needs to be addressed in order to prevent linkability and possible identification. Future research works could study the feasibility of incorporating anonymity mechanisms, such as CoinShuffle [58] (shuffle addresses), Zerocash [59] (hides the payment's origin, destination, and transferred amount) or differential privacy into the applications to meet the anonymity requirements.
- Smart contract security: All possible security and privacy attacks (e.g., eavesdropping, DDoS attack or impersonation) on the smart contract should be analyzed through formal security analysis. Moreover, smart contract transactions must be designed to be technically reversible in order to prove their long-term effectiveness. Furthermore, in order to modify or reverse a smart contract, the triggering event for the modification and its termination/extension should be anticipated by the code. Therefore, the problem of addressing security and privacy attacks on a smart contract needs further investigation.
- Dispute resolution: The immutability property of blockchain can act as a double-edged sword, since it removes the possibility of modifying/updating the content or the copyright information stored on it. Moreover, in the existence of immutability, the problem of resolving disputes over the copyright can be an interesting research topic.

4.3.2. Designing Multimedia Content Protection Systems to Support the Blockchain Technology

- Design improvements: The fine-grained analysis of the evaluated state-of-the-art systems sheds light on the need to improve traditional content protection mechanisms (encryption, DRM, watermarking/fingerprinting) so as to enable amicable integration with the blockchain technology. For example, key management, concurrent key acquisition and protection of keys can be explored in future studies for implementing blockchain-based multimedia encryption systems. Similarly, transfer of access rights to the consumers without a trusted third party, smooth execution of the transaction between the copyright provider and the client, and privacy-aware fine-grained usage control in blockchain-based DRM systems need further investigations. Likewise, in blockchain-based watermarking and fingerprinting schemes, low embedding and computational complexity, high robustness against possible security attacks, and acceptable transparency are a few mentionable open research challenges that the future research should tackle to enable widespread use of the blockchain-based copyright protection applications.
- Trustless systems: Fully decentralized content protection mechanisms had existed before the advent of blockchain. A key advantage that blockchain offers in addition to decentralization is trustlesness. The analyzed blockchain-based content protection systems are based on hybrid trust models that include presence of trusted third party or trusted users. Thus, there is a need to exploit the blockchain technology to its full potential and build truly trustless copyright protection systems.
- Security issues: The integration of the blockchain technology with an access control mechanism for off-chain sources needs to be investigated to ensure that only authorized parties can access the sensitive information. In addition, there is a need to address how to make the off-chain sources fault tolerant and prevent them becoming bottlenecks or single points of failure.
- Promoting adoption of blockchain in copyright applications: Most studies have yet to address the costs and limitations in deploying the content protection mechanisms on blockchain at the commercial level, and it would take considerable time to evolve, and require further technological advancements and security guarantees to be accepted by all the involved parties (such as copyright owners, multimedia producers, buyers, and others).

5. Conclusions

This study is aimed to present an overview of blockchain-based content protection applications. In this work, we have defined a taxonomy to classify the state-of-the-art blockchain-based copyright protection schemes w.r.t. technical characteristics of the blockchain technology, the most commonly used content protection mechanisms, and performance criteria. The discussion begins with some background knowledge of the blockchain technology and four commonly used content protection techniques. Then, a detailed review of blockchain-based copyright protection applications is presented. Moreover, these schemes are compared w.r.t. the defined taxonomy. In addition, some significant research challenges of content protection schemes and the blockchain technology are discussed. Finally, several future research directions are outlined.

For researchers, blockchain has an excellent potential to be broadly applied in copyright protection and management applications. The blockchain-based copyright protection applications allow copyright owners and consumers to interact without costly intermediaries. These applications allow the content owners to upload copyrighted content, control licensing/copyright options, manage distribution, trace sources of piracy, and receive payments upon content usage. However, there are still many open issues that need to be further researched and analyzed in order to create workable copyright protection applications that can fully benefit from the use of the blockchain technology. The success of such applications is however dependent on different factors related to the blockchain technology, such as scalability, reliability or market adoption, that are difficult to foresee. Researchers must consider all these aspects while designing and implementing a new blockchain-based content protection scheme. We hope that this survey will be considered a primary reference that can facilitate the process of finding the most relevant information w.r.t. integration between the content protection mechanisms and the blockchain technology.

Author Contributions: A.Q. and D.M.J. commonly finished the manuscript. Both authors have read and approved the final manuscript. Original draft preparation: both authors; Writing—review & editing: both authors. All authors have read and agreed to the published version of the manuscript.

Funding: The authors acknowledge the financial support received from the Spanish Government through grant RTI2018-095094-B-C22 "CONSENT".

Acknowledgments: The authors thank Alice Keefer Riva for proofreading the manuscript.

Conflicts of Interest: The authors declare no conflict of interest.

References

1. Valley, S. Netflix. 2007. Available online: http://www.netflix.com/ (accessed on 21 December 2020).
2. Cohen, B. BitTorrent. 2005. Available online: https://www.utorrent.com/ (accessed on 21 December 2020).
3. SANDVINE. 2019 Global Internet Phenomena Report. 2019. Available online: https://www.sandvine.com/global-internet-phenomena-report-2019 (accessed on 21 December 2020).
4. Amazon.com, Inc. Amazon Prime Video. 2006. Available online: https://www.primevideo.com/ (accessed on 21 December 2020).
5. Van Dijk, W. Streamit. 2003. Available online: https://www.streamit.eu/audio-distribution-platform/ (accessed on 21 December 2020).
6. Hamidouche, W.; Farajallah, M.; Sidaty, N.; Assad, S.E.; Deforges, O. Real-time selective video encryption based on the chaos system in scalable HEVC extension. *Signal Process. Image Commun.* **2017**, *58*, 73–86. [CrossRef]
7. Chen, Y.Y.; Jan, J.K.; Chi, Y.Y.; Tsai, M.L. A Feasible DRM Mechanism for BT-Like P2P System. In Proceedings of the International Symposium on Information Engineering and Electronic Commerce, Ternopil, Ukraine, 16–17 May 2009; pp. 323–327.
8. Pizzolante, R.; Castiglione, A.; Carpentieri, B.; Santis, A.D.; Castiglione, A. Reversible Copyright Protection for DNA Microarray Images. In Proceedings of the 10th International Conference on P2P, Parallel, Grid, Cloud and Internet Computing (3PGCIC), Krakow, Poland, 4–6 November 2015; pp. 707–712. [CrossRef]
9. Qiu, Y.; Gu, H.; Sun, J. Reversible watermarking algorithm of vector maps based on ECC. *Multimed. Tools Appl.* **2018**, *77*, 23651–23672. [CrossRef]
10. Qureshi, A.; Megías, D.; Rifà-Pous, H. Secure and Anonymous Multimedia Content Distribution in Peer-to-Peer Networks. In Proceedings of the 6th International Conference on Advances in Multimedia, Nice, France, 23–27 February 2014; pp. 91–96.
11. Megías, D. Improved Privacy-Preserving P2P Multimedia Distribution Based on Recombined Fingerprints. *IEEE Trans. Dependable Secur. Comput.* **2014**, *12*, 179–189. [CrossRef]

12. Qureshi, A.; Megías, D.; Rifà-Pous, H. PSUM: Peer-to-Peer Multimedia Content Distribution using Collusion-Resistant Fingerprinting. *J. Netw. Comput. Appl.* **2016**, *66*, 180–197. [CrossRef]
13. Megías, D.; Qureshi, A. Collusion-resistant and privacy-preserving P2P multimedia distribution based on recombined fingerprinting. *Expert Syst. Appl.* **2017**, *71*, 147–172. [CrossRef]
14. Kuribayashi, M.; Funabiki, N. Decentralized tracing protocol for fingerprinting system. *APSIPA Trans. Signal Inf. Process.* **2019**, *8*, 1–8. [CrossRef]
15. Nakamoto, S. Bitcoin: A Peer-To-Peer Electronic Cash System. 2008. Available online: http://www.bitcoin.org/bitcoin.pdf (accessed on 21 December 2020).
16. Michalko, M.; Kwan, W. DECENT, 2015. Available online: https://decent.ch/ (accessed on 21 December 2020).
17. Spotify USA, Inc. Mediachain, 2016. Available online: http://www.mediachain.io/ (accessed on 21 December 2020).
18. Shrestha, B.; Halgamuge, M.N.; Treiblmaier, H. Using Blockchain for Online Multimedia Management: Characteristics of Existing Platforms. In *Blockchain and Distributed Ledger Technology Use Cases: Applications and Lessons Learned*; Springer: Berlin/Heidelberg, Germany, 2020; pp. 289–303. [CrossRef]
19. Bambrough, B. Ripple's XRP Has More Than Doubled In Price This Week, Far Outpacing Bitcoin and Ethereum—Here's Why. 2020. Available online: https://www.forbes.com/sites/billybambrough/2020/11/24/ripples-xrp-has-more-than-doubled-in-price-this-week-far-outpacing-bitcoin-and-ethereum-heres-why/?sh=71901a8512e5 (accessed on 21 December 2020).
20. Statista. Distribution of Leading Cryptocurrencies from 2015 to 2020, by Market Capitalization. 2020. Available online: https://www-statista-com.biblioteca-uoc.idm.oclc.org/statistics/730782/cryptocurrencies-market-capitalization/ (accessed on 21 December 2020).
21. Machine, P.W.T. What Are the Most Traded Cryptocurrencies? 2020. Available online: https://www.plus500.com/Trading/CryptoCurrencies/What-are-the-Most-Traded-Cryptocurrencies~2 (accessed on 21 December 2020).
22. Kawase, Y.; Kasahara, S. Transaction-Confirmation Time for Bitcoin: A Queueing Analytical Approach to Blockchain Mechanism. In *Queueing Theory and Network Applications*; Springer: Berlin/Heidelberg, Germany, 2017; pp. 75–88.
23. Shahriar Hazari, S.; Mahmoud, Q. Improving Transaction Speed and Scalability of Blockchain Systems via Parallel Proof of Work. *Future Internet* **2020**, *12*, 125. [CrossRef]
24. Siriwardena, P. The Mystery Behind Block Time. 2017. Available online: https://medium.facilelogin.com/the-mystery-behind-block-time-63351e35603a (accessed on 21 December 2020).
25. Mitra, R. Bitcoin VS Ethereum: [The Ultimate Step-by-Step Comparison Guide]. 2020. Available online: https://blockgeeks.com/guides/bitcoin-vs-ethereum-ultimate-comparison-guide/ (accessed on 21 December 2020).
26. Terry, L. What Should We Expect From The Upcoming Release of Ethereum 2.0? 2020. Available online: https://hackernoon.com/what-should-we-expect-from-the-upcoming-release-of-ethereum-20-gc5m38hs (accessed on 21 December 2020).
27. Prut, A. Ripple (XRP)—Quick Introduction. 2019. Available online: https://medium.com/the-capital/ripple-xrp-quick-introduction-60b682375609 (accessed on 21 December 2020).
28. Won, D. Ethereum Proof of Stake Date: Date + What You Need to Know. 2020. Available online: https://www.exodus.io/blog/ethereum-proof-of-stake-date (accessed on 21 December 2020).
29. Won, D. Best Proof of Stake Coins 2020 for Easy Passive Income. 2020. Available online: https://www.exodus.io/blog/best-proof-of-stake-coins (accessed on 21 December 2020).
30. Staff, K. List Of DPOS Coins | DPOS Cryptocurrencies. 2018. Available online: https://kryptomoney.com/dpos-coins (accessed on 21 December 2020).
31. Fan, C.; Ghaemi, S.; Khazaei, H.; Musilek, P. Performance Evaluation of Blockchain Systems: A Systematic Survey. *IEEE Access* **2020**, *8*, 126927–126950. [CrossRef]
32. Arnold, M.; Schmucker, M.; Wolthusen, S.D. *Techniques and Applications of Digital Watermarking and Content Protection*, 2nd ed.; Artech House Publishers, Inc.: Norwood, MA, USA, 2003.
33. Cox, I.; Miller, M.; Bloom, J.; Fridrich, J.; Kalker, T. *Digital Watermarking and Steganography*, 2nd ed.; Morgan Kaufmann Publishers Inc.: San Francisco, CA, USA, 2007.
34. Katzenbeisser, S.; Petitcolas, F.A. *Information Hiding Techniques for Steganography and Digital Watermarking*, 1st ed.; Artech House, Inc.: Norwood, MA, USA, 2000.
35. Qureshi, A.; Megías, D.; Rifà-Pous, H. Framework for Preserving Security and Privacy in Peer-to-Peer Content Distribution Systems. *Expert Syst. Appl.* **2015**, *42*, 1391–1408. [CrossRef]
36. Vishwa, A.; Hussain, F.K. A Blockchain based approach for multimedia privacy protection and provenance. In Proceedings of the IEEE Symposium Series on Computational Intelligence, Bangalore, India, 18–21 November 2018; pp. 1941–1945. [CrossRef]
37. Peng, W.; Yi, L.; Fang, L.; XinHua, D.; Ping, C. Secure and Traceable Copyright Management System Based on Blockchain. In Proceedings of the IEEE 5th International Conference on Computer and Communications, Chengdu, China, 6–9 December 2019; pp. 1243–1247. [CrossRef]
38. Chi, J.; Lee, J.; Kim, N.; Choi, J.; Park, S. Secure and reliable blockchain-based eBook transaction system for self-published eBook trading. *PLoS ONE* **2020**, *15*, e0228418. [CrossRef] [PubMed]
39. Kishigami, J.; Fujimura, S.; Watanabe, H.; Nakadaira, A.; Akutsu, A. The Blockchain-Based Digital Content Distribution System. In Proceedings of the IEEE 5th International Conference on Big Data and Cloud Computing, Dalian, China, 26–28 August 2015; pp. 187–190. [CrossRef]

40. Zhao, S.; O'Mahony, D. BMCProtector: A Blockchain and Smart Contract Based Application for Music Copyright Protection. In Proceedings of the International Conference on Blockchain Technology and Application, Xi'an, China, 10–12 December 2018; pp. 1–5. [CrossRef]
41. Ma, Z.; Huang, W.; Gao, H. Secure DRM Scheme Based on Blockchain with High Credibility. *Chin. J. Electron.* **2018**, *27*, 1025–1036. [CrossRef]
42. Ma, Z.; Jiang, M.; Gao, H.; Wang, Z. Blockchain for digital rights management. *Future Gener. Comput. Syst.* **2018**, *89*, 746–764. [CrossRef]
43. Lu, Z.; Shi, Y.; Tao, R.; Zhang, Z. Blockchain for Digital Rights Management of Design Works. In Proceedings of the IEEE 10th International Conference on Software Engineering and Service Science, Beijing, China, 18–20 October 2019; pp. 596–603. [CrossRef]
44. Bhowmik, D.; Feng, T. The Multimedia Blockchain: A distributed and tamper-proof media transaction framework. In Proceedings of the 22nd International Conference on Digital Signal Processing (DSP), London, UK, 23–25 August 2017; pp. 1–5. [CrossRef]
45. Mangipudi, E.V.; Rao, K.; Clark, J.; Kate, A. Towards Automatically Penalizing Multimedia Breaches (Extended Abstract). In Proceedings of the IEEE European Symposium on Security and Privacy Workshops (EuroS PW), Stockholm, Sweden, 17–19 June 2019; pp. 340–346. [CrossRef]
46. Zhao, H.; Liu, Y.; Wang, Y.; Wang, X.; Li, J. A Blockchain-Based Data Hiding Method for Data Protection in Digital Video. In *Smart Blockchain*; Springer International Publishing: Berlin/Heidelberg, Germany, 2018; pp. 99–110. [CrossRef]
47. Meng, Z.; Morizumi, T.; Miyata, S.; Kinoshita, H. Design Scheme of Copyright Management System Based on Digital Watermarking and Blockchain. In Proceedings of the IEEE 42nd Annual Computer Software and Applications Conference, Tokyo, Japan, 23–27 July 2018; Volume 2, pp. 359–364. [CrossRef]
48. Fei, X. BDRM: A Blockchain-based Digital Rights Management Platform with Fine-grained Usage Control. *Int. J. Sci.* **2019**, *6*, 54–63.
49. Zhao, B.; Fang, L.; Zhang, H.; Ge, C.; Meng, W.; Liu, L.; Su, C. Y-DWMS—A digital watermark management system based on smart contracts. *Sensors* **2019**, *19*, 3091. [CrossRef] [PubMed]
50. Wu, Z.; Zheng, H.; Zhang, L.; Li, X. Privacy-friendly Blockchain Based Data Trading and Tracking. In Proceedings of the 5th International Conference on Big Data Computing and Communications, QingDao, China, 9–11 August 2019; pp. 240–244. [CrossRef]
51. Qureshi, A.; Megías, D. Blockchain-based P2P multimedia content distribution using collusion-resistant fingerprinting. In Proceedings of the 11th Asia-Pacific Signal and Information Processing Association (APSIPA) Annual Summit and Conference, Lanzhou, China, 18–21 November 2019; pp. 1606–1615. [CrossRef]
52. Li, R. Fingerprint-related chaotic image encryption scheme based on blockchain framework. *Multimed. Tools Appl.* **2020**, 1–21. [CrossRef]
53. Zhao, J.; Zong, T.; Xiang, Y.; Gao, L.; Beliakov, G. Robust Blockchain-Based Cross-Platform Audio Copyright Protection System Using Content-Based Fingerprint. In *Web Information Systems Engineering*; Springer: Berlin/Heidelberg, Germany, 2020; pp. 201–212. [CrossRef]
54. Poon, J.; Dryja, T. The bitcoin lightning network: Scalable off-chain instant payments. *Draft Version 0.5* **2016**, *9*, 14.
55. Poon, J.; Lee, J.H. Plasma: Scalable autonomous smart contracts. *Work. Draft* **2017**, *9*, 1–14.
56. Xie, J.; Tang, H.; Huang, T.; Yu, F.R.; Xie, R.; Liu, J.; Liu, Y. A Survey of Blockchain Technology Applied to Smart Cities: Research Issues and Challenges. *IEEE Commun. Surv. Tutor.* **2019**, *21*, 2794–2830. [CrossRef]
57. Kokoris-Kogias, E.; Jovanovic, P.; Gasser, L.; Gailly, N.; Syta, E.; Ford, B. OmniLedger: A Secure, Scale-Out, Decentralized Ledger via Sharding. In Proceedings of the IEEE Symposium on Security and Privacy (SP), San Francisco, CA, USA, 20–24 May 2018; pp. 583–598. [CrossRef]
58. Ruffing, T.; Moreno-Sanchez, P.; Kate, A. CoinShuffle: Practical Decentralized Coin Mixing for Bitcoin. In *Computer Security—ESORICS 2014*; Kutylowski, M., Vaidya, J., Eds.; Springer International Publishing: Berlin/Heidelberg, Germany, 2014; pp. 345–364. [CrossRef]
59. Sasson, E.B.; Chiesa, A.; Garman, C.; Green, M.; Miers, I.; Tromer, E.; Virza, M. Zerocash: Decentralized Anonymous Payments from Bitcoin. In Proceedings of the IEEE Symposium on Security and Privacy, San Jose, CA, USA, 18–21 May 2014; pp. 459–474. [CrossRef]

Article
Trends and Challenges in Network Covert Channels Countermeasures

Luca Caviglione

Institute for Applied Mathematics and Information Technologies, 16149 Genova, Italy; luca.caviglione@ge.imati.cnr.it

Abstract: Network covert channels are increasingly used to endow malware with stealthy behaviors, for instance to exfiltrate data or to orchestrate nodes of a botnet in a cloaked manner. Unfortunately, the detection of such attacks is difficult as network covert channels are often characterized by low data rates and defenders do not know in advance where the secret information has been hidden. Moreover, neutralization or mitigation are hard tasks, as they require to not disrupt legitimate flows or degrade the quality perceived by users. As a consequence, countermeasures are tightly coupled to specific channel architectures, leading to poorly generalizable and often scarcely scalable approaches. In this perspective, this paper investigates trends and challenges in the development of countermeasures against the most popular network covert channels. To this aim, we reviewed the relevant literature by considering approaches that can be effectively deployed to detect general injection mechanisms or threats observed in the wild. Emphasis has been put on enlightening trajectories that should be considered when engineering mitigation techniques or planning the research to face the increasing wave of information-hiding-capable malware. Results indicate that many works are extremely specialized and an effective strategy for taming security risks caused by network covert channels may benefit from high-level and general approaches. Moreover, mechanisms to prevent the exploitation of ambiguities should be already considered in early design phases of both protocols and services.

Keywords: network covert channels; detection; stegomalware; traffic sanitization; normalization

1. Introduction

Information hiding and steganographic techniques are becoming widely used by attackers to avoid detection and remain unnoticed for a large amount of time [1]. For instance, they have been used to conceal the presence of a malware within innocent looking pictures, to hide malicious code or additional functionalities with the aim of implementing covert multi-stage loading architectures, as well as to exfiltrate secret information in Advanced Persistent Threats (APTs) [2,3]. As a consequence of the versatility of information hiding mechanisms, a new-wave of malware endowed with steganographic capabilities (named *stegomalware*) has been observed in the wild and the trend is expected to grow in the near future [1,4]. One of the most popular and effective uses of information hiding to support insecurity concerns the creation of *covert channels*, i.e., hidden communication paths allowing two peers to exchange data. According to Lampson, covert channels are "*not intended for information transfer at all, such as the service program's effect on the system load*" [5]. Literature proposes a wide array of scenarios and mechanisms for creating hidden communication paths between a variety of software and hardware entities. As possible examples of endpoints wanting to secretly exchange data, we mention: cloud-based and softwarized services, containers and virtual machines and multi-core or multi-CPU frameworks. Despite the nature of the specific target, a covert channel can be generally linked to an imperfect isolation, i.e., state information or a specific behavior of a software or hardware element is leaked outside the intended functional perimeter [6].

To create a covert channel, the two secret endpoints must agree on a steganographic/hiding scheme, which acts as the pre-shared secret. The secret information is then embedded into a *carrier*. To this aim, different methodologies can be used and various hardware or software artifacts can be exploited for storing arbitrary data. For instance, the secret can be directly embedded in the metadata of a file or properly encoded by manipulating some temporal evolution such as the load offered to the CPU. Even if complex encoding and embedding strategies exist, the totality of covert channels can be reduced to a set of well-defined patterns, such as the modulation of some structural properties (e.g., the size of a file) or the introduction of artificial transmission errors [7]. Concerning carriers that can contain the secret information, network flows are becoming quickly the most preferred one used by attackers. Accordingly, the produced hidden communication paths are named *network covert channels*. As possible examples, channels can be built by injecting data in unused protocol fields as well as by modulating some behaviors of the flow like the throughput or the inter packet time (see, e.g., [8] for a survey on the topic).

As a consequence, the investigation of security risks caused by network covert channels has quickly become of paramount importance. In fact, network covert channels have proven to be an effective tool to support several malicious activities. Specifically, they have been used for exfiltrating stolen confidential data (e.g., login credentials), to orchestrate nodes of a botnet, to implement multi-stage loading architectures to retrieve attack routines (e.g., by embedding malicious code in innocent-looking images), to launch commands for configuring backdoors and to support industrial espionage campaigns [1,2,9]. Unfortunately, modern scenarios offer a wide range of protocols, software entities and hardware devices that can be used to contain secret information [7,8]. This grants the attacker huge advantages over the defender and the deployment of countermeasures against a specific steganographic threat seldom happens a priori. Therefore, covert channels are often addressed as a by-product outcome of the mitigation of apparently unrelated anomalous behaviors, the analysis and reverse engineering of a malware sample or the direct disclosure from the attacker [1–4]. Thus, recognizing that a given deployment is exposed to steganographic communication attempts may be a challenging and poorly generalizable process. Nevertheless, development of countermeasures may lead to inefficient solutions based on the "needle in the haystack" principle possibly accounting for the indiscriminate penalization of traffic flows, the disruption of some protocol functionalities or the introduction of performance bottlenecks in the network.

Despite the number of threats exploiting information hiding principles and covert channels to implement the various phases of an attack, the majority of research efforts focused on the investigation of how protocol ambiguities, poor design choices and flawed implementations of computing and communication frameworks can be used to covertly move information through the Internet. As a consequence, several reviews have been prepared (see, e.g., [1,2,8]) also by considering attacks targeting well-defined technological segments such as modern smartphones [9]. Alas, the specificities of the various embedding methods hindered the development of a coherent literature on countermeasures against network covert channels. In this perspective, the detection and neutralization of this class of threats have been never systematically organized or reviewed, with the notable exception of a partial discussion in [8], which dates back to 2007.

Therefore, this paper aims at investigating trends and challenges characterizing the development of countermeasures against network covert channels, with the wide acceptation of tools, methodologies and algorithms aiming at detecting hidden communication attempts. We also include approaches intended for limiting or completely neutralizing the transmission capability of hidden communication paths laying within a network flow. The goals of this investigation are multiple. First, we want to understand if it is possible to delineate a clear trajectory in the literature aiming at counteracting network covert channels, or if the topic is addressed in a split and heterogeneous manner. Second, we aim at deriving some general guidelines or gaps to be filled to face challenges arising from the diffusion of stegomalware. Third, we intend to define some tradeoffs to be considered when designing countermeasures. Last, we want to show that, even if a relevant corpus of works on the topic exists, the attacker can easily evade preexistent mitigation approaches by moving to another protocol or slightly changing the injection method. To answer such research questions, we carried out a systematic review of the literature also by considering attacks and threats observed in the wild. The limit of this investigation is rooted within the very carrier-centric nature of hiding methods and countermeasures. In fact, the majority of works only proposes channel-specific mitigation mechanisms without further deepening generalizability aspects. Another consequence is that the research is balkanized over different areas (e.g., information security, engineering and networking) often having incongruent definitions and thus accounting for overlaps or difficulties in retrieving ideas.

Summing up, the main contributions of the paper are: (i) a review of the most recent approaches for counteracting network covert channels; (ii) the identification of the major research challenges and the most promising development trends; (iii) the discussion of advancements needed for elaborating a more coherent and unified framework for taming network covert channels and stegomalware.

The remainder of the paper is structured as follows. Section 2 briefly introduces the background on network covert channels, while Section 3 discusses aspects to be considered when designing a mitigation approach. Section 4 showcases detection techniques and methodologies, while Section 5 deals with approaches devoted to limiting and eliminating network covert channels. Section 6 discusses trends and challenges and Section 7 concludes the paper and portraits possible future research directions.

2. Background

As hinted, the adoption of some form of steganography to endow malware with stealthy capabilities has started more than a decade ago, mainly with threats using digital media as a diffusion vector or to exchange data containing configuration details (e.g., a list of IP addresses to be inspected or attacked) [1]. Instead, network covert channels have become popular more recently, as they offer to the attacker a wider palette of opportunities. First, a traffic flow is somewhat boundless, thus providing a carrier with few constraints compared to other software artifacts or digital media. Second, it is not uncommon to have network infrastructures with flows that last hours or days, thus allowing the malware to implement permanent hidden communication paths, for instance to support APTs or to orchestrate botnets [10]. In this perspective, Figure 1 depicts the reference scenario when addressing network covert channels and their detection. In more detail, we consider two covert endpoints (named as covert sender and covert receiver, respectively) wanting to remotely communicate in a hidden manner. To this aim, the legitimate, overt network flow is used as the carrier for containing the secret information. We point out that the two covert endpoints can be located in different portions of the network, thus implementing channels with different scopes. They can act in a Man-in-the-Middle manner as depicted in Figure 1 by eavesdropping a preexistent flow, or they can be colocated within the end nodes generating the overt traffic flow. Despite the placement of the communicating endpoints, two core classes of covert channels can be be created. They are characterized according to the steganographic approach used to embed the secret information. Specifically:

- if the injection mechanism *directly embeds* data within the carrier, a *storage network covert channel* is created;
- if the injection mechanism manipulates the *timing* of events or the *temporal evolution* of the carrier, a *timing network covert channel* is created.

A general representation of the aforementioned approaches is depicted in Figure 1. A possible example of a storage channel is the one where the secret sender directly writes data in the unused bits available in the TCP header. For the case of a timing channel, the sender could encode information by modulating the delay experienced by two consecutive packets composing the flow, e.g., a delay greater than a given threshold value denotes a 1, otherwise a 0. As discussed in [11], the TCP/IP protocol architecture can be targeted with a variety of methods also by using many techniques or protocols simultaneously.

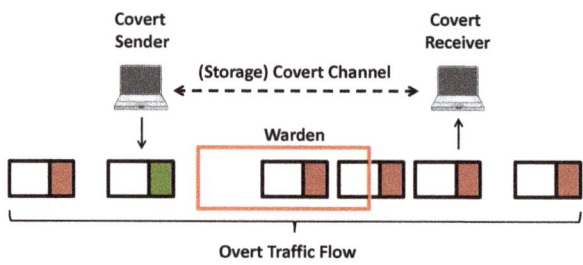

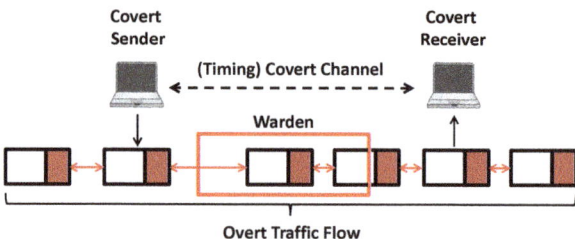

Figure 1. Reference scenario for the usage of network covert channels and their detection.

Similar to other applications of steganography and information hiding, network covert channels are also characterized by the following three core metrics:

- *steganographic bandwidth* or *capacity*: the volume of secret data that can be sent per time unit by using a given embedding method;
- *undetectability*: the inability to detect the secret data within a certain carrier;
- *robustness*: the number of alterations that the hidden message can withstand before being destroyed.

Obviously, the "best" covert channel should be robust and hard to detect, as well as able to provide the highest bandwidth. Unfortunately, it is not possible to maximize such properties at once, as they are tightly coupled via a *magic triangle* rule [9,12], i.e., it is not feasible to increase a performance index without lowering the remaining two. As an intuitive example, let us consider using some bits of an image as a method to embed secrets. Each alteration will lead to some noise, which must be kept under a suitable threshold to avoid detection or that the visual system can notice that some manipulations happened. In fact, the more bits that are used for the secret (the bandwidth increases), the more would be the noise or visual alterations, thus making the method more evident (detectable) [9]. Concerning network covert channels, embedding secrets directly in the unused bits of the TCP could lead to a channel with a capacity of up to 4 bits/segment. Clearly, the more bits are used, the higher will be the impact on the statistical distribution of bits composing the header, hence making the channel more detectable. Yet, the channel can be easily disrupted as it is sufficient to overwrite unused fields with random values or revert them to a standard configuration. This can be mitigated by using a more sophisticated embedding method, but paying something in terms of complexity and channel capacity. By contrast, a channel modulating the secret information in the inter packet time exploits a less obvious hiding scheme, but it is also slower and weaker since natural delays of the networks (e.g., due to queuing and competing with other flows) can completely destroy the information.

An additional metric, is the *steganographic cost*, which evaluates the degradation experienced by the carrier due to the application of a steganographic method. For instance, for a network covert channel living within a VoIP flow, the steganographic cost can represent the impact on the quality of the conversation experienced by users (e.g., additional delays, reduced SNR performances of the codec or audible artifacts) [13].

3. Development of Countermeasures

The magic triangle relation can be considered as a prime conceptual device for driving the development of countermeasures against the various flavors of covert channels. In this vein, the seminal work of G. J. Simmons introduced the notion of *warden*, i.e., an entity responsible of spotting hidden communication attempts [14]. Specifically, Simons modeled the threat by considering two prisoners wanting to orchestrate an escape plan by covertly exchanging details. The jail warden monitors such an exchange: if the attempt is spotted, prisoners will be confined. For the case of network covert channels, a warden can be a software or hardware entity able to collect and inspect network packets. Figure 1 depicts an intermediate node (denoted with a red box) acting as a warden.

According to [15], different wardens exist and they can be classified by considering the type of information they use to detect the covert channel as well as their structure. Literature sill not agree on a unique taxonomy, but three main traits can be used to describe middleboxes and techniques for detecting hidden communication attempts exploiting network artifacts:

- *functionality*: it denotes how the warden counteracts the covert channel. As it happens for other tools enforcing network security (e.g., firewalls or intrusion detection systems), a warden can be *stateless* or *stateful* depending on its ability of considering a packet at time or a burst of traffic, respectively. While the longer correlation of information can lead to improved performances, storing and processing huge traffic footprints may lead to unfeasible storage or computing requirements. If a warden only captures the traffic and acts on a private copy, it is considered *passive*. Otherwise, if it can manipulate, alter or drop packets, it is considered *active*. Lastly, a warden can be *static* or *dynamic*, according to the ability of changing its policies during time or adapting against specific threats or network conditions. We point out that a warden can simultaneously have multiple functionalities, e.g., it can be static and stateless.
- *knowledge*: it defines the type of information used by the warden to spot the presence of the channel. For instance, the warden can be aware of the exploited traffic or service (in this case, it is defined as *network-aware*) or totally *agnostic*. Moreover, it can know a priori the type of used embedding process or steganographic technique, or be engineered to only react against some specific patterns or threats.
- *localization*: it defines where the warden has been placed to intercept the traffic and to monitor the network usage. Due to the evolution of devices and deployments, modern wardens should be capable to protect large network trunks and interact with multiple replicas as to provide scalability and detect the most sophisticated threats. Thus, a warden can act on a *local* basis (e.g., on the device of the end user or his/her local network perimeter) or cover a vast geographical area. An emerging trend concerns the adoption of *distributed* wardens, i.e., nodes able to gather the traffic in different portions of the network and cooperate to spot the covert channel.

In the perspective of developing countermeasures against network cover channels, the ultimate goal of a warden is to neutralize steganographic threats laying within the legitimate traffic. To this aim, the first step is to perform the *detection*, i.e., become aware and identify the hidden communication path. This is a prerequisite for performing some further actions aimed at guaranteeing the security of network and computing infrastructures. Ideally, a warden should completely *eliminate* the channel, but this is not always possible. For instance, this happens when impeding a specific channel will also disrupt some legitimate network services or penalize too much the quality perceived by users. Therefore, it is not uncommon that the covert communication can be only partially impaired or *limited*, e.g., the steganographic bandwidth is reduced leading to a channel not usable or appealing for a specific attack.

A warden could be also considered as a tool for implementing some form of threat intelligence. Specifically, it can not be able to counteract an attack, but can provide suitable knowledge to prevent the creation of a network covert channel. This can be done by teaming with other tools (e.g., by driving the definition of packet filtering rules to be deployed in firewalls) or to support security-by-design approaches.

4. Covert Channel Detection

In this section, we present the main detection techniques with emphasis on the limits and the challenges to be faced in order to be deployed in real-world scenarios. First we will present mechanisms targeting the two fundamental injection families at the basis of a wide range of hidden communication paths (i.e., those allowing the creation of timing and storage channels). Then, we will address techniques intended for specific protocols. In more detail, we will investigate the detection of covert channels targeting IPv6, which will be expected to become widespread in the near future and thus appealing from the viewpoint of an attacker. In addition, we will also investigate the various methodologies used to reveal hidden communication paths in VoIP conversations as well as DNS and HTTP tunnels. Such protocols have in common a great popularity and the ubiquitous availability, hence their presence in a network is seldom perceived as an anomaly and defenders typically need to deals with non-negligible traffic volumes.

4.1. Timing Channels

The majority of timing channels injects secret information by modulating the inter-packet time of IP datagrams, thus leading to protocol-agnostic methods, i.e., the encoding happens at the network level, despite the used higher protocols and applications responsible of generating and manipulating the stream. Popular transmission schemes are: *on-off switching*, i.e., if the sender transmits a packet within an agreed time frame it signals a 1, otherwise a lack of transmissions represents a 0; *jitterbug*-like, i.e., the information is encoded by changing the inter-packet arrival time of keystrokes within normal keystroke traffic (this algorithm can be generalized to be applied to other traffic sources).

The detection of network timing channels is primarily based on the computation of a statistical indicator or a general performance metric to assess the regularity of the temporal evolution of the traffic flow. Thus, the decision is performed when the timing statistics of the flow deviate too much, e.g., from a threshold [16]. Unfortunately, as discussed in [17], such a class of covert channels can not be easily spotted if the attacker frequently changes the encoding scheme and the protocol, or injects a suitable amount of noise (e.g., via additional delays or by randomly starting and stopping the injection of data within the transmission window). This trait can be mitigated by using more sophisticated statistical tests, but at the price of more complex and memory consuming computations (e.g., over 2000 timing values needed to be processed for up to 400 iterations of an algorithm [18]). As a consequence, when in the presence of large-scale networks or multiple flows characterized by a high throughput the implementation of an effective warden could be not a trivial task. Moreover, traffic composed of small protocol data units can exacerbate performance bottlenecks or the presence of non-optimized implementations.

A key challenge to be faced concerns the ability of the attacker of applying obfuscation or changing the encoding scheme used to map the information on the timing of packets. In this vein, literature showcases several techniques that can be used to avoid the detection from a warden or a firewall (see, e.g., [8,16] and references therein for a detailed discussion). As a workaround, machine learning can be considered for developing more general and efficient classifiers able to reveal relationships difficult to capture via network analysis approaches based on the common sense. For instance, in [19] support vector machines are used to spot different covert communications exploiting a timing scheme. Unfortunately, as it happens for other traffic classification problems, this requires to have enough data for training the decision maker. In addition, the attacker can also adopt more advanced techniques like encrypting the hidden message or apply an obfuscation algorithm to the overt traffic. A promising approach is presented in [17], where authors propose to exploit possible correlation between the content of the memory and the information injected in the traffic flow. Alas, the limit of the idea is that the warden should reside on the node hosting the covert sender or the covert receiver as well as rethink the general detection principle could be required.

Another class of timing channels targets TCP segments, which offer a more fine array of possibilities for encoding the information. For instance, steganographic schemes may exploit sequences of ACK/SYN, patterns of segments containing information and artificial reordering. Detection can still be done via general network analysis frameworks, but there is also the need of considering specific behaviors of the TCP. For instance, analyzing the size of the various bursts composing a stream can reveal the presence of a secret sender modulating the stream (in general, the size of bursts are solely ruled by the congestion control behavior of the TCP) [20]. A further idea could be developed by considering the timing statistics of segments containing an acknowledgment.

Typically, the elimination of a network timing channel can be considered simple in some network scenarios or under some hypotheses (e.g., the absence of traffic with real-time constraints) and possible optimizations can be borrowed from the literature dealing with timing channels targeting the single node (see [21] for a comprehensive survey on timing channels not limited to the network case). However, an attacker could be able to slow the rate of the covert channel as to make the attack not detectable or the communication impossible to disrupt without impacting legitimate traffic. When designing a warden against timing network covert channels, the detection may be more desirable than limiting or eliminating the threat [16] as identifying compromised hosts or the range of contacted IP addresses could lead to neutralize some "assets" of a cybercriminal, such as a botnet.

Lastly, when in the presence of methods reordering the sequence of packets or messages (e.g., IP datagrams, TCP segments or HTTP requests), a promising trend is to borrow techniques for data mining and apply them to the captured traffic [22]. This can be also done for implementing distributed wardens able to perform detection by considering observations gathered in different portions of the network. Moreover, being able to implement protocol-agnostic schemes is an important requirement, since the attacker can use different layers of the network stack to exfiltrate information. For instance, [23] proposes a protocol-independent approach and demonstrates that the detectability of a channel is proportional to the number of packets altered by the secret sender.

4.2. Storage Channels

As hinted, each network storage covert channel targets a specific part of the protocol data unit [11]. Therefore, the detection is seldom generalizable and requires the development of ad-hoc solutions or methodologies. A complementary approach exploits malware analysis to isolate and reverse engineer the executable to identify the carriers used for establish the channel [24]. To some extent, storage channels represent the perfect synecdoche of the application of steganographic techniques to network traffic, since they highlight that the defender often has to grope in the dark.

In this perspective, development of countermeasures could follow two paths. The first concerns the ability of developing wardens able to inspect in an efficient manner multiple protocols via frameworks that can be easily extended. In this manner, the defender can try to gain ground owing to the inspection of multiple protocol fields without deteriorating performances or having to rewrite relevant portions of the code each time. For instance, [25] proposes to use code augmentation techniques offered by the Linux kernel to efficiently gather data that can be used to spot covert channels. The main advantage of the idea is that multiple "filters" can be stacked without causing too many degradations and very different protocol and software entities can be accessed via a unique programming interface. Data gathering is important not only for performing detection of network covert channels and stegomalware. In fact, being able to implement a warden to efficiently collect information on traffic flows is the prime requirement for populating datasets to be jointly used with machine-learning-capable mechanisms. Unfortunately, the very composite set of features exploited by storage channels highly limits the performances of AI-based methods [26], but a possible improvement can be achieved by searching for well-known, recurrent embedding patterns [27]. Similarly, application-layer firewalls (e.g., entities able to inspect traffic to perform keyword-based analysis) can spot a hidden communication but paying in terms of capabilities and engineering efforts [28]. To develop successful detection mechanisms, the second path relies upon the design of high-level methods or approaching the detection problem in a more general manner. As possible examples, Ref. [29] showcases the use of visualization tools to ease the development of countermeasures by helping professionals working in threat intelligence with the specific aim of spotting network steganography attacks.

4.3. Packet Length and Inter-Protocol Interdependencies

Modulation of the length of packets is another popular approach used to implement network covert channels and can be applied to different protocols (e.g., IPv6 datagrams [30] or packets containing audio conversations [31]). Additionally in this case, there is not a one-fits-all approach, but the development of some high-level indicators can be the basis to design universal detectors, e.g., by exploiting ubiquitous machine learning classifiers [32] or frameworks able to spot statistical anomalies [33]. In this perspective, the major challenge concerns the ability of engineering an effective dataset for training and tuning the warden.

Additionally, advanced channels exploiting inter-protocol relationships are emerging [34]. Even if the work addresses real-time services, such principles can be also extended to embedding schemes leveraging packet lengths. To perform detection of such a complex method using multiple/different protocols at the same time, a promising mechanism exploits traffic coloring.

4.4. IPv6

The advent of IPv6 opens to many potential covert channels. Specifically, the attacker can exploit new features offered by the protocol or the various transitional and tunneling mechanisms designed to allow IPv4 and IPv6 to coexist. Despite the rich set of features offered by IPv6, real network deployments scale back the different types of covert channels that can be used to launch a real attack [30]. In fact, the amount of IPv6 traffic is still limited (compared to IPv4) and its statistical variability can make some channels highly detectable. For instance, when using the `Traffic Class` field to contain secrets, real traces are characterized only by three different values, thus limiting the bandwidth of the covert channel to few bit/s. A further constraint is due to the Explicit Congestion Notification feature, which is rarely used in real-world nodes, thus causing the alteration of the field as highly suspicious.

As a consequence, the development of detection techniques targeting IPv6 traffic seldom necessitates of additional hardware/software and can be implemented on top of normal traffic inspection frameworks. Similar to many other threats, another emerging approach leverages machine learning. As an example, the work in [35] demonstrates the use of fuzzy logic and genetic algorithms to achieve high detection rates of covert channels targeting the IPv6 header. We point out that both methods require to employ deep packet inspection principles, thus impacting on the scalability of the approach.

Transitional mechanisms can be also abused to create network covert channels or exfiltrate information. According to [36], modern intrusion detection systems are affected by major drawbacks when handling IPv6 traffic. For instance, covert channels targeting transition methods using both IPv4 and IPv6 traffic are difficult to detect compared to other attacks exploiting DNS or SSH tunneling.

4.5. VoIP

Owing to its ubiquitous availability and the potential capacity when used as a carrier, many works concentrated on the detection of covert channels targeting VoIP traffic. Alas, VoIP streams can be exploited in different parts, e.g., in the vocal payload or in the resulting network traffic. Specifically, many techniques use some form of audio steganography or digital watermarking for blending an arbitrary message within the audio of the talker. In general, a common approach for detecting the presence of secret information requires the warden to compute some audio quality metric to reveal the hidden data [37]. However, this could not be a simple task, as the attacker may take advantage of specific features of the used codec, or transcode the conversation to free space in packets to embed information while maintaining the same level of quality [38]. Therefore, the performance of the detection can be influenced by the original codec both in terms of performance and scalability. A possible improvement could exploit information provided by the network traffic in order to reveal "misuse patterns" [39]. For instance, the warden can identify a covert channel within a VoIP flow by using statistical metrics like the variance of inter-arrival time of packets composing the Real-time Transport Protocol (RTP) stream. The idea of using simple metrics and calculations for spotting the presence of the channel has not been considered only to optimize performances and extendability of a warden. Specifically, computing metrics on the audio signal could be unfeasible due to encryption or to not break the privacy of users. In this vein, lower-level and simpler approaches should be carefully evaluated. As an example, in [40] a scheme exploiting a matrix containing sketches of packets is presented. Another challenge concerns the ability of detecting short communications or channels transferring a restricted amount of information. In this case, the adoption of some form of artificial intelligence looks very promising [41] but at the price of being able to collect suitable data for training the detection framework.

Lastly, if the VoIP stream exploits some form of standard technologies like the Session Initiation Protocol (SIP), the warden can try to detect the hidden communication by analyzing anomalous distributions of values in the headers, bursts of methods or deviation in the traffic statistics of the resulting RTP and SIP flows [31,42]. A major challenge concerns the development of a suitable warden able to perform detection without disrupting the real-time, interactive nature of VoIP communications and SIP signaling. Emerging approaches exploit the use of application-agnostic parameters (e.g., the size of the protocol data units) and deep the detection at the codec or audio level only if packets are considered potentially suspicious. Moreover, algorithms used for traffic coloring can offer an effective foundation to reveal hidden data within RTP and Realtime Transport Control Protocol streams [34].

4.6. DNS and HTTP Tunnels

A class of threats often exploited in the perspective of developing network covert channels is the one relying upon the creation of tunnels. Put briefly, the attacker could try to exfiltrate data or establish abusive communications by injecting malicious traffic within legitimate traffic flows. Even if not strictly related to network steganography or network covert channels, many threats demonstrated the risk of not performing any detection attempts against tunneling approaches. Literature on tunneling often deviates from the one belonging to covert channels but, at the same time, exhibits important overlaps. As a consequence, we also present major ideas and some research questions on DNS and HTTP tunnels, which are the most popular. Observations presented in this paper can be extended straightforwardly to other similar approaches, for instance malware abusing SSH connections.

Concerning the detection of DNS tunnels, the work in [43] presents a method based on uni-bi-tri-grams frequencies of characters of domains resolved via DNS queries. Specifically, since the domain names are mostly characterized by distributions and patterns similar to those describing natural languages, discrepancies or deviations can be used as effective indicators to reveal the presence of hidden data. A different approach, leveraging Markov decision process, is presented in [44]. Tunnels leveraging DNS traffic can be also detected by using a more network-oriented approach. For instance, the throughput of DNS flows can be considered a valid indicator to detect anomalous usages [45]. The importance of being able to reveal the presence of DNS tunnels within a network infrastructure is expected to increase in the future. In fact, many APTs are progressively using domain fronting techniques (i.e., the generation of synthetic domain names and related DNS queries to exfiltrate data or orchestrate a botnet), which can be efficiently spotted via ad-hoc classifiers [46]. Flux/DNS fronting techniques require a sufficient amount of data to train classifiers and non-negligible computing power to deploy such frameworks in real networks without impacting the quality experienced by end users.

Indeed, being able to identify HTTP tunnels is also important since HTTP is typically used to develop custom signaling protocols or to retrieve additional malware components [1,2]. Owing to such a popularity, many security appliances operating at the application layer can already inspect or filter HTTP traffic. However, in the perspective of making the detection of covert channels, using more general and technology-independent mechanisms could be beneficial. For instance, in [47] authors show how evaluating the inter arrival time, size and ordering of the packets can be adopted to discriminate between legitimate HTTP traffic and tunneled contents. The aforementioned quantities can be used to compute metrics and train machine learning mechanisms [48], possibly via approaches extracting features in an automated manner [49]. However, the tight coupling of the method creating the covert communication path with the protocol internals still remains the major challenge to face. Specifically, an attacker could attempt to evade detection or reduce the performance of a classifier by altering information like the User-Agent [50]. Another aspect to be considered when engineering a warden to spot HTTP-based covert channels is the ability of an attacker of evading network-based detection deliberately. For instance, it can encode data in the number of hyperlinks and manipulate referrals [51].

5. Covert Channel Limitation, Elimination and Prevention

As discussed, upon detecting the covert channel, further actions to be performed can have different functional goals (e.g., limitation or elimination). Usually, applying a countermeasure to a class of covert channels requires to choose among different tradeoffs. Specifically:

- **security vs. quality**: the limitation or elimination capacity could require reducing the quality perceived by users. For instance, to prevent an attack, the entity in charge of performing the sanitization of the network traffic may delay or drop packets in an unacceptable manner;
- **accuracy vs. performance**: despite the used hardware and software architecture, the processing capacity of the warden (including various middleboxes for enforcing network security) could impact on the behavior of the traffic (i.e., by altering its quality parameters) or require an amount of resources not feasible (e.g., computing and storage capacity). Therefore, the accuracy of the limitation and elimination process should be carefully evaluated especially in terms of overheads;
- **complexity vs. cost**: the degree of sophistication of a covert channel may account for complex mitigation methods. This usually leads to software being developed, hardware resources, or alteration of the network infrastructure, for instance to duplicate traffic flows or to avoid performance bottlenecks. Clearly, such requirements lead to economical expenditures and maintenance costs, which should be carefully evaluated;
- **blockage vs. functionalities**: with the term blockage, we intend the ability of impeding that a given network protocol is used as a carrier. This typically requires to block a protocol for a network or host, or reduce some functionalities. Even if "mutilating" the protocol stack can be admissible in scenarios with high security constraints, this tradeoff should be carefully evaluated, especially for networks operating not in a local manner;
- **security vs. risk**: being able to completely eliminate a channel could not be mandatory or possible in terms of the aforementioned tradeoffs. Thus, according to the considered scenario, it could be more convenient to only limit the steganographic bandwidth of the channel. For instance, a channel of few bit/s could be enough to activate or configure a backdoor, but not sufficient to exfiltrate an industrial secret. Usually, this is at the basis of the "arms race" between defender and attacker, trying to slow the data exfiltration rate or the steganographic bandwidth to remain under the radar [52].

We point out that the aforementioned tradeoffs also apply in the case of detection, but the limitation of a channel and the sanitization of network traffic usually require greater amounts of resources to avoid performance bottlenecks or impair some network functionalities.

5.1. Elimination and Limitation

One of the first ideas to tame covert channels is the Network Pump, theorized and designed by Kang, Moskowitz and Lee in a paper published in 1996 [53,54]. The Pump has been originally designed to prevent the possibilities of using a fraction of the traffic (e.g., ACKs) to build covert channels between processes with different security levels (i.e., high and low in the original work). In essence, it can be used to connect different portions of the networks and data are "pumped" upon proper queuing and ACKs are sent in a probabilistic manner as to reduce the possibility that an attacker can create a covert channel. An important contribution of the Pump is making clear that it is only capable of limiting the risk of setting up a covert channel.

In general, the complete elimination of the chance that a network can be used for setting up a covert channel is an inefficient and unrealistic goal [55]. For instance, guaranteeing that HTTP will not be used to tunnel information can be only achieved by completely blocking its utilization in a given scenario, which is mostly unfeasible. Instead, it would be possible to design a countermeasure to pursue a *tradeoff* between the security risk and the functioning of the network both in terms of performances and functionalities. Always referring to the HTTP case, a possible approach tries to "sanitize" the various flows in order to reduce the carriers that can be used to contain secret information [56]. In this case, the semantic of the protocol is evaluated and restored as close as possible to the one prescribed by the RFCs. Thus, the countermeasure mainly acts by reducing the ambiguities (e.g., the use of capitalized strings within the protocol to encode data) to make the channel less attractive by the attacker or limiting its bandwidth. Alas, objects exchanged via HTTP can still contain hidden data. In this case, ad-hoc proxies can be deployed to check inline objects against steganographic contents and sanitize them [57]. This requires a non-negligible amount of computing resources and also accounts for the presence of specific detectors/sanitizers for each considered inline object (e.g., protocol headers, images, audio, video and additional plugins). Similar consideration can be done for other applications, e.g., for the VoIP. For instance, network-related protocols can be restored, whereas random noise can be added to the voice information as to disrupt or reduce the performances of the covert channel [37]. The examples allow to underline the magnitude of the problem space to be faced for completely eliminating a channel, especially when there is the need of operating at higher levels of the protocol architecture. We point out that, this sort of pseudo-proxying could break the end-to-end semantics of the overt traffic flow, thus leading to additional security and privacy issues.

For the case of storage channels, classical approaches aim at restoring unused fields within header to default values whenever possible or to insert specific padding sequences to overwrite manipulation attempts [9]. An interesting aspect to be considered regards how protocols designed decades ago now behave in the modern Internet. Taking as a paradigmatic example IPv6, the investigation in [30] highlights that the diffuse lack of networks supporting Quality of Service guarantees permits an attacker to use the `Traffic Class` to embed data. Instead, in some circumstances, the network could protect itself. In fact, the presence of transitional mechanisms or middleboxes (e.g., network address translation) account for manipulations of the header and buffering operations, which can disrupt the most fragile covert channels. A further aspect to consider is the increasing use of encryption and secure variant of protocols. This multiplies the opportunities for an attacker to have additional carriers but also boost the design of "more secure" implementations to mitigate the risks of being abused to set covert channels. To illustrate this concept, we consider the case of IPSec [58], which can be natively endowed with padding for preventing covert channels modulating the packet size, and techniques for adding random errors for disrupting mechanisms embedding data by artificially manipulating packet losses. The limit of such an approach is the need of updating implementations and perform such optimizations on a per-protocol basis. Instead, it could be beneficial centralizing such workarounds in a unique network entity.

Timing channels appears to be more easy to limit or prevent, at least those manipulating inter packet statistics. In this case, buffering and adding random delays can be sufficient. The drawback of this class of countermeasures is rooted in the indiscriminate penalization of all traffic flows. When in the presence of traffic with real-time constraints, buffering can not be too aggressive, thus leaving the attacker with chances of creating a channel. In this case, the goal is to reduce its steganographic bandwidth in order to render the channel unsuitable for the attack. Literature offers different techniques for timing channels. We mention the use entropy-based schemes to make the detection more robust to prevent the attacker from limiting his/her rate to evade the detection [59], and addressing in a more detail timing channels mimicking realistic patterns [60].

5.2. Prevention

An important aspect to consider to fully asses the security of network/computing infrastructures concerns how to completely prevent the possibility of setting up a network covert channel. As hinted, protocols known to be prone to steganographic attacks should be completely blocked [1,8,55]. Unfortunately, this is unfeasible in many scenarios and use cases. Since covert channels are the prime consequence of imperfect isolation, prevention mechanisms should aim at restoring the protocol data units to their basic form, in order to reduce the chance of leaking states or embedding additional information. In this vein, reverting fields to default values or inserting padding (or trimming messages) are the methodologies at the basis of many countermeasures [9].

However, the increasing sophistication of exfiltration attempts as well as the complexity of modern network architectures require to consider covert channels from the early stage of the design phase. Thus, prevention should be considered an "offline" process and handled in a *security-by-design* manner. To this extent, standardization surely plays a major role and security considerations on potential covert channels should be always present. Enforcing a flow to adhere to its standard implementation can be also exploited at runtime to sanitize the behavior of the protocol and disrupt secret messages, if present. Covert channels can be also impeded by selectively blocking some protocol features while pursuing functional tradeoffs acceptable for the specific scenario or application.

6. Trends and Challenges

The growing adoption of covert channels as a paradigm to empower stegomalware and support data exfiltration is expected to persist in the future [1]: new attacks will be more sophisticated, cross-layer and able to leverage the complex interplay of hardware and software components [52]. This will magnify the gap between the attacker and the defender, especially in terms of uncertainty of what to inspect and where to place wardens within the overall network architecture. Reviewed countermeasures as well as tools deployed in the wild seem only partially trying to mitigate such an aspect. Thus, the main trends in the development of countermeasures observed and the challenges to be faced are:

- **generalization**: data gathering as well as detection and sanitization of network covert channels may require to deploy a wide range of collection techniques and to inspect several heterogeneous carriers [2]. As regards the collection phase, literature showcased the use of in-kernel mechanisms to analyze the various carriers exploited to set local covert channels (see, e.g., [25] for the use of the extended Berkeley Packet Filter to spot stealth data exchange via alteration of Unix file permissions). Future wardens should be able to exploit similar techniques to have general filters that can be stacked up when the used carrier is uncertain or impossible to isolate a priori. Moreover, performing kernel-level analysis could help in avoiding bottlenecks or mitigating overheads causing legitimate flows to experience additional delays;
- **abstraction**: future channels are expected to target different parts of modern network ecosystems, such as appliances and IoT nodes. In this vein, network covert channels will be able to use a multitude of carriers, mainly characterized by a very composite set of protocols, sensors and architectural blueprints. In this perspective, an interesting

approach concerns the development of more abstract metrics, which can be used to spot the steganographic attack despite the used carrier. Literature demonstrated that process correlation [61] or anomalous energy consumption and drains [62,63] are excellent candidates to make the detection more threat-independent. To pursue such a vision, the detection could need to be shifted towards the border of the network or close to users. This poses several challenges, for instance in terms of avoiding performance degradation of devices of end users and additional security requirements;

- **cloud**: without doubts, cloud infrastructures will remain a relevant component of the future Internet. There are many works highlighting that covert channels are progressively used to attack virtualized environments mainly to let virtual machines to collude and evade security frameworks (see [64] for a review on the topic). Concerning network covert channels, recent investigations showcased how cloud architectures can be abused to set up Internet-wide communication paths [65]. As a consequence, cloud and virtualized environments should be protected against information-hiding-capable threats [66] and data breaches orchestrated via network covert channels;

- **everything-as-a-service**: as shown, being able to detect covert channels may require a non-negligible amount of storage (e.g., to store traffic dumps or datasets) and computing power (e.g., to compute metrics or run machine-learning-capable frameworks). Being able to deploy wardens for protecting large-scale networks or running sophisticated detection software while delivering satisfactory performances could be unfeasible for small-medium actors. Therefore, a relevant effort should be done to explore Warden-as-a-Service approaches [3,4];

- **reversibility**: in reversible network covert channels, the two secret endpoints communicating are able to "restore" the traffic to its original form (i.e., before the injection of the hidden data) in order to avoid detection [67,68]. To spot this class of emerging threats, the warden should collect the traffic in different portions of the network and do some form of comparison. This poses several challenges, not only limited to technical aspects. For instance, the needed traffic could be collected in environments of different operators leading to technical and legal issues;

- **resistance by design**: the ability of storing arbitrary data or manipulating a protocol are usually consequence of an ambiguous design or an imperfect implementation. An interesting research activity deals with the identification of patterns at the basis of the creation of network covert channels [7] and should be considered when designing the next-generation of secure-by-design protocols. Nevertheless, the application of formal methods to endow a warden with the ability of performing runtime checks or model unknown threats is another promising trend to explore.

7. Conclusions

In this paper, we have presented a thorough review on countermeasures against network covert channels. We have addressed the different steps needed to enforce security when in the presence of hidden communications. In more detail, we have considered works dealing with the detection, limitation and elimination of network covert channels. We have also addressed methodologies to prevent hidden communications. Even if comprehensive, the investigation revealed some imperfections. For instance, the complex continuum of computing and networking platforms leads to a problem space not well delimited. Thus, it has been difficult tracing a clear line between network covert channels and other types of threats. For instance, covert channels targeting cloud scenarios could be quickly become relevant for the network case (and vice versa).

As shown, the majority of frameworks and ideas handles security issues caused by stegomalware and network covert channels in an almost unique threat-dependent flavor, mainly due to the strict dependency of the behavior of the channel on the used carrier or injection mechanism. This magnifies the asymmetry between the attacker and the defender. To partially recover to this, future research should focus on the development of more general indicators and frameworks, as well as methodologies to inspect multiple carriers at once. Such a trend is partially observable in the literature (see, e.g., energetic indicators to abstract the underlying threat) but, to be effective, should be consolidated. Another interesting path to pursue, which requires long term research efforts, concerns increasing the awareness of developers and engineers of risks caused by network covert channels. In this case, different research areas (e.g., networking and software engineering) could find a common "playground" and do not duplicate efforts or develop overlapped solutions. Moreover, awareness should lead to adopt methodologies for preventing the exploitation of ambiguities already in early design phases both of protocols, services and architectures.

Funding: This research was funded by EU Project SIMARGL—Secure Intelligent Methods for Advanced Recognition of Malware and Stegomalware (Grant Agreement No 833042) and the EU Project ASTRID—AddreSsing ThReats for virtuaIIzeD services (Grant Agreement No 786922).

Conflicts of Interest: The authors declare no conflict of interest.

References

1. Mazurczyk, W.; Caviglione, L. Information Hiding as a Challenge for Malware Detection. *IEEE Secur. Priv.* **2015**, *13*, 89–93. [CrossRef]
2. Mazurczyk, W.; Wendzel, S. Information hiding: Challenges for forensic experts. *Commun. ACM* **2017**, *61*, 86–94. [CrossRef]
3. Cabaj, K.; Caviglione, L.; Mazurczyk, W.; Wendzel, S.; Woodward, A.; Zander, S. The new threats of information hiding: The road ahead. *IT Prof.* **2018**, *20*, 31–39. [CrossRef]
4. Caviglione, L.; Wendzel, S.; Mazurczyk, W. The future of digital forensics: Challenges and the road ahead. *IEEE Secur. Priv.* **2017**, *15*, 12–17. [CrossRef]
5. Lampson, B.W. A Note on the Confinement Problem. *Commun. ACM* **1973**, *16*, 613–615. [CrossRef]
6. Falzon, K.; Bodden, E. Towards a Comprehensive Model of Isolation for Mitigating Illicit Channels. In Proceedings of the International Conference on Principles of Security and Trust, Eindhoven, The Netherlands, 4–5 April 2016; pp. 116–138.
7. Wendzel, S.; Zander, S.; Fechner, B.; Herdin, C. Pattern-based survey and categorization of network covert channel techniques. *ACM Comput. Surv. (CSUR)* **2015**, *47*, 1–26. [CrossRef]
8. Zander, S.; Armitage, G.; Branch, P. A survey of covert channels and countermeasures in computer network protocols. *IEEE Commun. Surv. Tutor.* **2007**, *9*, 44–57. [CrossRef]
9. Mazurczyk, W.; Caviglione, L. Steganography in modern smartphones and mitigation techniques. *IEEE Commun. Surv. Tutorials* **2014**, *17*, 334–357. [CrossRef]
10. Caviglione, L.; Mazurczyk, W.; Wendzel, S. Advanced Information Hiding Techniques for Modern Botnets. In *Botnets: Architectures, Countermeasures, and Challenges*; CRC Press: Boca Raton, FL, USA, 2019; pp. 165–199.
11. Mileva, A.; Panajotov, B. Covert channels in TCP/IP protocol stack - extended version. *Cent. Eur. J. Comput. Sci.* **2014**, *4*, 45–66. [CrossRef]
12. Fridrich, J.; Pevný, T.; Kodovský, J. Statistically undetectable jpeg steganography: Dead ends challenges, and opportunities. In Proceedings of the 9th Workshop on Multimedia & Security, Dallas, TX, USA, 20–21 September 2007; pp. 3–14.
13. Mazurczyk, W. VoIP steganography and its detection a survey. *ACM Comput. Surv. (CSUR)* **2013**, *46*, 1–21. [CrossRef]
14. Simmons, G.J. The prisoners' problem and the subliminal channel. In *Advances in Cryptology*; Springer: Boston, MA, USA, 1984; pp. 51–67.
15. Mazurczyk, W.; Wendzel, S.; Chourib, M.; Keller, J. Countering adaptive network covert communication with dynamic wardens. *Future Gener. Comput. Syst.* **2019**, *94*, 712–725. [CrossRef]
16. Cabuk, S.; Brodley, C.E.; Shields, C. IP covert timing channels: Design and detection. In Proceedings of the 11th ACM Conference on Computer and Communications Security, Washington, DC, USA, 25–29 October 2004; pp. 178–187.
17. Stillman, R.M. Detecting IP covert timing channels by correlating packet timing with memory content. In Proceedings of the IEEE SoutheastCon 2008, Huntsville, AL, USA, 3–6 April 2008; pp. 204–209.
18. Rezaei, F.; Hempel, M.; Sharif, H. Towards a reliable detection of covert timing channels over real-time network traffic. *IEEE Trans. Dependable Secur. Comput.* **2017**, *14*, 249–264. [CrossRef]
19. Shrestha, P.L.; Hempel, M.; Rezaei, F.; Sharif, H. A support vector machine-based framework for detection of covert timing channels. *IEEE Trans. Dependable Secur. Comput.* **2015**, *13*, 274–283. [CrossRef]
20. Luo, X.; Chan, E.W.; Chang, R.K. TCP covert timing channels: Design and detection. In Proceedings of the 2008 IEEE International Conference on Dependable Systems and Networks with FTCS and DCC (DSN), Anchorage, AK, USA, 24–27 June 2008; pp. 420–429.
21. Biswas, A.K.; Ghosal, D.; Nagaraja, S. A survey of timing channels and countermeasures. *ACM Comput. Surv. (CSUR)* **2017**, *50*, 1–39. [CrossRef]
22. Nowakowski, P.; Zórawski, P.; Cabaj, K.; Mazurczyk, W. Network covert channels detection using data mining and hierarchical organisation of frequent sets: An initial study. In Proceedings of the 15th International Conference on Availability, Reliability and Security, Dublin, Ireland, 17–20 August 2020; pp. 1–10.

23. Wendzel, S. Protocol-independent Detection of "Messaging Ordering" Network Covert Channels. In Proceedings of the 14th International Conference on Availability, Reliability and Security, Canterbury, UK, 26–29 August 2019; pp. 1–8.
24. Chakkaravarthy, S.S.; Sangeetha, D.; Vaidehi, V. A Survey on malware analysis and mitigation techniques. *Comput. Sci. Rev.* **2019**, *32*, 1–23. [CrossRef]
25. Carrega, A.; Caviglione, L.; Repetto, M.; Zuppelli, M. Programmable Data Gathering for Detecting Stegomalware. In Proceedings of the 2020 6th IEEE Conference on Network Softwarization (NetSoft), Ghent, Belgium, 29 June–3 July 2020; pp. 422–429.
26. Cho, D.; Thuong, D.; Dung, N. A Method of Detecting Storage Based Network Steganography Using Machine Learning. *Procedia Comput. Sci.* **2019**, *154*, 543–548. [CrossRef]
27. Ayub, M.A.; Smith, S.; Siraj, A. A Protocol Independent Approach in Network Covert Channel Detection. In Proceedings of the 2019 IEEE International Conference on Computational Science and Engineering (CSE) and IEEE International Conference on Embedded and Ubiquitous Computing (EUC), New York, NY, USA, 1–3 August 2019; pp. 165–170.
28. Gilbert, P.A.; Bhattacharya, P. An approach towards anomaly based detection and profiling covert TCP/IP channels. In Proceedings of the 2009 7th International Conference on Information, Communications and Signal Processing (ICICS), Macau, China, 8–10 December 2009; pp. 1–5.
29. Mazurczyk, W.; Szczypiorski, K.; Jankowski, B. Towards steganography detection through network traffic visualisation. In Proceedings of the 2012 IV International Congress on Ultra Modern Telecommunications and Control Systems, St. Petersburg, Russia, 3–5 October 2012; pp. 947–954.
30. Mazurczyk, W.; Powójski, K.; Caviglione, L. IPv6 covert channels in the wild. In Proceedings of the Third Central European Cybersecurity Conference, Munich, Germany, 14–15 November 2019; pp. 1–6.
31. Saenger, J.; Mazurczyk, W.; Keller, J.; Caviglione, L. VoIP network covert channels to enhance privacy and information sharing. *Future Gener. Comput. Syst.* **2020**, *111*, 96–106. [CrossRef]
32. Nair, A.S.; Sur, A.; Nandi, S. Detection of packet length based network steganography. In Proceedings of the 2010 International Conference on Multimedia Information Networking and Security, Nanjing, China, 4–6 November 2010; pp. 574–578.
33. Sur, A.; Nair, A.S.; Kumar, A.; Jain, A.; Nandi, S. Steganalysis of network packet length based data hiding. *Circuits Syst. Signal Process.* **2013**, *32*, 1239–1256. [CrossRef]
34. Lehner, F.; Mazurczyk, W.; Keller, J.; Wendzel, S. Inter-protocol steganography for real-time services and its detection using traffic coloring approach. In Proceedings of the 2017 IEEE 42nd Conference on Local Computer Networks (LCN), Singapore, 9–12 October 2017; pp. 78–85.
35. Salih, A.; Ma, X.; Peytchev, E. Implementation of hybrid artificial intelligence technique to detect covert channels attack in new generation internet protocol IPv6. In *Leadership, Innovation and Entrepreneurship as Driving Forces of the Global Economy*; Springer: Berlin/Heidelberg, Germany, 2017; pp. 173–190.
36. Blumbergs, B.; Pihelgas, M.; Kont, M.; Maennel, O.; Vaarandi, R. Creating and detecting IPv6 transition mechanism-based information exfiltration covert channels. In Proceedings of the Nordic Conference on Secure IT Systems, Oulu, Finland, 2–4 November 2016; pp. 85–100.
37. Takahashi, T.; Lee, W. An assessment of VoIP covert channel threats. In Proceedings of the 2007 Third International Conference on Security and Privacy in Communications Networks and the Workshops-SecureComm 2007, Nice, France, 17–21 September 2007; pp. 371–380.
38. Janicki, A.; Mazurczyk, W.; Szczypiorski, K. Steganalysis of transcoding steganography. *Ann. Telecommun. Ann. Télécommun.* **2014**, *69*, 449–460. [CrossRef]
39. Pelaez, J.C. Using misuse patterns for voip steganalysis. In Proceedings of the 2009 20th International Workshop on Database and Expert Systems Application, Linz, Austria, 31 August–4 September 2009; pp. 160–164.
40. Garateguy, G.; Arce, G.R.; Pelaez, J. Covert channel detection in VoIP streams. In Proceedings of the 2011 45th Annual Conference on Information Sciences and Systems, Baltimore, MD, USA, 23–25 March 2011; pp. 1–6.
41. Lin, Z.; Huang, Y.; Wang, J. RNN-SM: Fast steganalysis of VoIP streams using recurrent neural network. *IEEE Trans. Inf. Forensics Secur.* **2018**, *13*, 1854–1868. [CrossRef]
42. Zhao, H.; Zhang, X. Sip steganalysis using chaos theory. In Proceedings of the 2012 International Conference on Computing, Measurement, Control and Sensor Network, Taiyuan, China, 7–9 July 2012; pp. 95–100.
43. Born, K.; Gustafson, D. Detecting dns tunnels using character frequency analysis. *arXiv* **2010**, arXiv:1004.4358.
44. Mc Carthy, S.M.; Sinha, A.; Tambe, M.; Manadhata, P. Data exfiltration detection and prevention: Virtually distributed pomdps for practically safer networks. In Proceedings of the International Conference on Decision and Game Theory for Security, New York, NY, USA, 2–4 November 2016; pp. 39–61.
45. Himbeault, M. A Novel Approach to Detecting Covert dns Tunnels Using Throughput Estimation. Master's Thesis, University of Manitoba, Department of Electrical and Computer Engineering, Winnipeg, MB, Canada, 2014.
46. Antonakakis, M.; Perdisci, R.; Nadji, Y.; Vasiloglou, N.; Abu-Nimeh, S.; Lee, W.; Dagon, D. From throw-away traffic to bots: detecting the rise of DGA-based malware. In Proceedings of the 21st {USENIX} Security Symposium ({USENIX} Security 12, Bellevue, WA, USA, 11–13 August 2021; pp. 491–506.
47. Crotti, M.; Dusi, M.; Gringoli, F.; Salgarelli, L. Detecting http tunnels with statistical mechanisms. In Proceedings of the 2007 IEEE International Conference on Communications, Glasgow, UK, 24–28 June 2007; pp. 6162–6168.

48. Ding, Y.j.; Cai, W.d. A method for HTTP-tunnel detection based on statistical features of traffic. In Proceedings of the 2011 IEEE 3rd International Conference on Communication Software and Networks, Xi'an, China, 27–29 May 2011; pp. 247–250.
49. Davis, J.J.; Foo, E. Automated feature engineering for HTTP tunnel detection. *Comput. Secur.* **2016**, *59*, 166–185. [CrossRef]
50. Schwenk, G.; Rieck, K. Adaptive detection of covert communication in http requests. In Proceedings of the 2011 Seventh European Conference on Computer Network Defense, Gothenburg, Sweden, 6–7 September 2011; pp. 25–32.
51. Luo, X.; Zhou, P.; Chan, E.W.; Chang, R.K.; Lee, W. A combinatorial approach to network covert communications with applications in web leaks. In Proceedings of the 2011 IEEE/IFIP 41st International Conference on Dependable Systems & Networks (DSN), Hong Kong, China, 27–30 June 2011; pp. 474–485.
52. Caviglione, L.; Choraś, M.; Corona, I.; Janicki, A.; Mazurczyk, W.; Pawlicki, M.; Wasielewska, K. Tight Arms Race: Overview of Current Malware Threats and Trends in Their Detection. *IEEE Access* **2020**, *9*, 5371–5396. [CrossRef]
53. Kang, M.H.; Moskowitz, I.S.; Lee, D.C. A network pump. *IEEE Trans. Softw. Eng.* **1996**, *22*, 329–338. [CrossRef]
54. Kang, M.H.; Moskowitz, I.S.; Chincheck, S. The pump: A decade of covert fun. In Proceedings of the 21st Annual Computer Security Applications Conference (ACSAC'05), Tucson, AZ, USA, 5–9 December 2005; p. 7.
55. Zander, S.; Armitage, G.; Branch, P. Covert channels and countermeasures in computer network protocols [reprinted from ieee communications surveys and tutorials]. *IEEE Commun. Mag.* **2007**, *45*, 136–142. [CrossRef]
56. Schear, N.; Kintana, C.; Zhang, Q.; Vahdat, A. Glavlit: Preventing exfiltration at wire speed. Irvine Burn. In Proceedings of Fifth Workshop on Hot Topics in Networks (Hot-Nets), Irvine, CA, USA, 29–30 November 2006; Volume 133.
57. Blasco, J.; Hernandez-Castro, J.C.; de Fuentes, J.M.; Ramos, B. A framework for avoiding steganography usage over HTTP. *J. Netw. Comput. Appl.* **2012**, *35*, 491–501. [CrossRef]
58. Schulz, S.; Varadharajan, V.; Sadeghi, A.R. The silence of the LANs: efficient leakage resilience for IPsec VPNs. *IEEE Trans. Inf. Forensics Secur.* **2013**, *9*, 221–232. [CrossRef]
59. Walls, R.J.; Kothari, K.; Wright, M. Liquid: A detection-resistant covert timing channel based on IPD shaping. *Comput. Netw.* **2011**, *55*, 1217–1228. [CrossRef]
60. Gianvecchio, S.; Wang, H.; Wijesekera, D.; Jajodia, S. Model-based covert timing channels: Automated modeling and evasion. In Proceedings of the International Workshop on Recent Advances in Intrusion Detection, Cambridge, MA, USA, 15–17 September 2008; pp. 211–230.
61. Urbanski, M.; Mazurczyk, W.; Lalande, J.F.; Caviglione, L. Detecting local covert channels using process activity correlation on android smartphones. *Int. J. Comput. Syst. Sci. Eng.* **2017**, *32*, 71–80.
62. Caviglione, L.; Gaggero, M.; Lalande, J.F.; Mazurczyk, W.; Urbański, M. Seeing the unseen: revealing mobile malware hidden communications via energy consumption and artificial intelligence. *IEEE Trans. Inf. Forensics Secur.* **2015**, *11*, 799–810. [CrossRef]
63. Caviglione, L.; Gaggero, M.; Cambiaso, E.; Aiello, M. Measuring the energy consumption of cyber security. *IEEE Commun. Mag.* **2017**, *55*, 58–63. [CrossRef]
64. Betz, J.; Westhoff, D.; Müller, G. Survey on covert channels in virtual machines and cloud computing. *Trans. Emerg. Telecommun. Technol.* **2017**, *28*, e3134. [CrossRef]
65. Caviglione, L.; Podolski, M.; Mazurczyk, W.; Ianigro, M. Covert channels in personal cloud storage services: The case of Dropbox. *IEEE Trans. Ind. Inform.* **2016**, *13*, 1921–1931. [CrossRef]
66. Liu, A.; Chen, J.; Yang, L. Real-time detection of covert channels in highly virtualized environments. In Proceedings of the International Conference on Critical Infrastructure Protection, Hanover, NH, USA, 23–25 March 2011; pp. 151–164.
67. Mazurczyk, W.; Szary, P.; Wendzel, S.; Caviglione, L. Towards reversible storage network covert channels. In Proceedings of the 14th International Conference on Availability, Reliability and Security, Canterbury, UK, 26–29 August 2019; pp. 1–8.
68. Szary, P.; Mazurczyk, W.; Wendzel, S.; Caviglione, L. Design and performance evaluation of reversible network covert channels. In Proceedings of the 15th International Conference on Availability, Reliability and Security, Dublin, Ireland, 25–28 August 2020; pp. 1–8.

Article

Fragile Watermarking of 3D Models in a Transformed Domain

Marco Botta [1,*], Davide Cavagnino [1], Marco Gribaudo [2] and Pietro Piazzolla[3]

1. Dipartimento di Informatica, Università di Torino, 10100 Torino, Italy; davide.cavagnino@unito.it
2. Dipartimento di Elettronica, Informazione e Bioingegneria—Politecnico di Milano, 20100 Milano, Italy; marco.gribaudo@polimi.it
3. Dipartimento di Ingegneria Gestionale e della Produzione—DIGEP—Politecnico di Torino, 10100 Torino, Italy; pietro.piazzolla@plm.polito.it
* Correspondence: marco.botta@unito.it

Received: 7 April 2020; Accepted: 2 May 2020; Published: 7 May 2020

Abstract: This paper presents an algorithm aimed at the integrity protection of 3D models represented as a set of vertices and polygons. The proposed method defines a procedure to perform a fragile watermarking of the vertices' data, namely 3D coordinates and polygons, introducing a very small error in the vertices' coordinates. The watermark bit string is embedded into a secret vector space defined by the Karhunen–Loève transform derived from a key image. Experimental results show the good performance of the method and its security.

Keywords: 3D model; integrity protection; fragile watermarking; data hiding; genetic algorithm; Karhunen–Loève transform

1. Introduction

Digital watermarking refers to a family of methods that embed a signal into a digital object. For example, visible logos in a TV broadcast or on a picture for sale on the web are two applications of visible watermarking. Nonetheless, digital technology allows for more complex applications of the general idea of watermarking, also allowing invisible (to humans) watermarks to be embedded into digital objects. Copyright protection, tracking origin, authentication, and integrity protection are examples of the application of this technology.

It is possible to classify watermarking algorithms according to various characteristics [1]: the main properties of digital watermarking algorithms will be discussed in the following.

A first, trivial, subjective property of watermarks is imperceptibility, that is the inability of a human being to recognize the presence of a watermark embedded into an object.

A digital watermark may be robust, semi-fragile, or fragile. Robust watermarking refers to the embedding of a signal with the purpose of resisting malicious attempts aimed at its removal, maintaining the possibility to show the presence of the signal; a typical application of this kind of watermarking algorithms is copyright protection. On the other hand, fragile watermarks have the purpose of being altered by minimal modification of the digital object containing them; fields of application are integrity protection and authentication. The class of semi-fragile watermarking algorithms contains those methods that accept a minimal level of modification without flagging a tampering alarm.

On the detection side, watermarking methods may be grouped as informed (non-blind) or blind depending on the necessity or not of the original host object. Moreover, if an algorithm can recover the original data, it is called reversible; otherwise, it is called lossy or non-reversible.

The values of the watermark signal w may be embedded into the host object by modifying the object features in different domains; the most widely used are the spatial domain and the frequency domain (or transformed domain). The spatial domain refers to the values that describe and represent the object; as examples, for an image, they may be the pixel intensities; for a 3D model, they may be the vertices' (spatial) coordinates. Instead, in the case of embedding in the frequency domain, the object's data are first transformed with a linear transform, like the discrete Fourier transform, the wavelet transform, the singular value decomposition or the Karhunen–Loève Transform (KLT), then the watermark signal is applied to alter the transform coefficients; after that, the inverse transformation is applied to compute the modified values, which represent the watermarked object. In general, embedding in the frequency domain requires satisfying non-linear constraints (like obtaining integer pixel values or modifying only some parts of the transformed coefficient); thus, computational intelligence algorithms which look for almost optimal solutions in non-linear domains can be a possible embedding method.

Most of the 3D model watermarking works are focused on copyright protection (by inserting robust watermarks), while there are fewer works on integrity protection and authentication. Moreover, existing approaches to fragile watermarking introduce high distortion and/or might require extra information for verification. In this paper, we present a blind, non-reversible fragile watermarking algorithm that adds an extra level of security (by defining a secret embedding space through the KLT transform) and protects the integrity of 3D models, with negligible alterations to the host model vertices' coordinates.

The host model original file format may be both textual or binary, but the watermarked model file is binary (as in many graphics file formats, like Blender).

The following section recalls some related works in the field of 3D model watermarking. Sections 3 and 4 present two fundamental tools used by the proposed algorithm, discussed in Section 5, to embed in a secure way a watermark in a 3D model. Section 6 reports numerical results from experiments applying the method to publicly available models. The results are discussed in Section 7, and some conclusions are drawn in Section 8.

2. Related Works

The field of digital watermarking has seen a large development of methods for images and audio, but also the protection of 3D models has received attention from researchers. Several algorithms for robust (see Table 1) and fragile (see Table 2) watermarking of 3D models have been developed in recent years. Here, we report a list of the properties declared by the authors, along with their pros and cons.

Table 1. Summary of related works on robust watermarking: main properties, pros, and cons.

Reference	Embedding Space	Verification Type	Pros	Cons
[2]	Spread spectrum	Non-blind	Watermark process as matrix operation	Requires original for detection, low quality
[3]	Spread spectrum	Blind	Redundant watermark embedding in sub-meshes for improved robustness	Complexity in computing eigenvectors
[4]	Spread spectrum	Blind	More efficient eigenvalue decomposition, more robustness	Low quality
[5]	Coarse, low resolution approximation	Blind	Pretty robust to attacks	Tampering detection relies on a simple correlation
[6]	Vertices' space	Non-blind	Redundant watermark embedding for robustness	Requires original for detection, low quality
[7]	Spherical harmonic transform space	Blind	Embeds in the transform space, robust	Low quality
[8]	Vertex norms distribution histogram bins	Blind	Robust against distortionless and distortion attacks	Not applicable to very small models and vulnerable to center of gravity alteration
[9]	Sparse quantization index modulation space	Blind	Uses a neural network to choose embedding vertices	Only robust to deletion of vertices

Table 2. Summary of related works on fragile watermarking: main properties, pros, and cons. KLT, Karhunen–Loève Transform.

Reference	Embedding Space	Verification Type	Pros	Cons
[10]	Vertices' space	Blind, semi-fragile	Resists unintentional changes (like compression, transformation, and random noise)	False positives possible
[11]	Vertices' space	Blind	Protection against cropping	Need inserted watermark for verification
[12]	Vertices' space	Blind	Addresses causality and convergence problems, users can control distortion level	Low quality
[13]	Mantissa of vertices' coordinates	Blind	Numerically stable, solves causality problem, immune to vertex renumbering, can control watermark intensity	Sensitive to parameter selection
[14]	Model connection points	Blind, semi-fragile	Watermark depends on model topological features	Can only authenticate and verify the topology integrity
[15]	Spherical coordinate space	Non-blind	Immune to vertex reordering, causality, convergence, and synchronization problems	Requires the center of gravity for detection
[16]	Hash transform space	Blind	Capable of detecting object cropping	Fails to localize changes and proved weak against vertex reordering
[17]	Vertices' space	Blind	Immune to vertex reordering	Low quality
[18]	Watermark digest	Blind	Computes a message digest of the model	Watermark requires extra space
[19]	Vertices' space	Blind	Robust to translation, rotation, and uniform scaling, but is fragile and sensitive to other operations	Low quality
[20]	Vertices' space	Non-blind	Robust to translation, rotation, and uniform scaling	Medium quality
Proposed Method	Secret KLT transform space	Blind	Imperceptible, highly secure, very fragile	False negatives

Our proposed method shares a number of features with the literature and differs substantially in others: the main and more significant difference is the embedding space, which is secret and allows an extra level of security, as it is unfeasible for an attacker to reproduce such a space. Most of the related works in the literature are actually robust watermarking schemes, while our method is an extremely fragile method whose watermark is broken by negligible alterations to the 3D models it protects. Similarly to [13], we modify the binary float representation of the vertices' coordinates, but our watermark is not directly inserted into them, as done in [13]. Moreover, the proposed method is immune to vertex reordering and can tolerate affine transformations to the model when these transformations are stored separately from the vertex coordinates in the output file format (such as done in Blender). Finally, similarly to [20], we use a genetic algorithm to compute a (quasi)optimal solution to the embedding problem, but again, our watermark is embedded into a secret space and not directly into the vertices' coordinates.

3. The Karhunen–Loève Transform

The discrete Karhunen–Loève Transform (KLT) (also called Hotelling transform or Principal Component Analysis (PCA)) is a linear transformation that maps vectors from one n-dimensional vector space to another vector space of the same dimension: this mapping is defined by a square matrix of size $n \times n$, called the kernel.

Differently from other linear transformations like the discrete cosine transform or the Fourier transform, one of the characteristics of the KLT is having a kernel that is not fixed a priori, i.e., its transformation matrix is computed from a set of vectors that must be given to define the mapping.

This characteristic of the KLT is exploited in the present algorithm to have a compact, secure, and efficient way to define a secret space of embedding: if the set of vectors used in computing the KLT kernel is kept secret, then also the kernel will be secret, defining a transformed domain in which to embed the watermark securely; for example, using a secret image's pixel values to define these vectors, then only the entities possessing this image will be able to verify the integrity of the 3D model. Moreover, lacking knowledge of the embedding space does not allow modifying the 3D model without altering the fragile watermark.

Consider a set of vectors $\{\mathbf{x}_1, \mathbf{x}_2, \ldots, \mathbf{x}_r\}$ of an n-dimensional vector space, and compute their mean vector $\mathbf{m} = E\{\mathbf{x}_i\}$. Then, evaluate the covariance matrix of the centered vectors $\mathbf{C} = E\{(\mathbf{x}_i - \mathbf{m})(\mathbf{x}_i - \mathbf{m})'\}$, where $\mathbf{z}'$ represents the conjugate transpose of $\mathbf{z}$. The eigenvectors $\mathbf{e}_i, i = 1, 2, \ldots, n$, of the covariance matrix $\mathbf{C}$, computed as:

$$\mathbf{C}\mathbf{e}_i = \lambda_i \mathbf{e}_i \tag{1}$$

define an orthonormal basis for the n-dimensional vector space; the λ_is are the associated eigenvalues. Thus, arranging the eigenvectors as rows of a matrix $\mathbf{A}$ in descending sort order of the respective eigenvalues, the KLT $\mathbf{y}$ of a vector $\mathbf{x}$ is computed as:

$$\mathbf{y} = \mathbf{A}(\mathbf{x} - \mathbf{m}). \tag{2}$$

Each element of the vector $\mathbf{y}$ is called the coefficient of the transform; the position of every coefficient in the vector $\mathbf{y}$ is called the order of the coefficient.

It is possible to reverse the transformation process through the inverse KLT:

$$\mathbf{x} = \mathbf{A}^{-1}\mathbf{y} + \mathbf{m} \tag{3}$$

which, by the orthonormality of $\mathbf{A}$, may be also written as:

$$\mathbf{x} = \mathbf{A}'\mathbf{y} + \mathbf{m}. \tag{4}$$

One property of the eigenvectors is that they define the directions of maximum data spread in the data sample, and sorting them according to their associated eigenvalues allows exploiting the energy compaction property of the KLT transform, useful when expressing the elements of the vector space with a reduced number of coefficients: it may be shown that the eigenvalues represent the variance of the coefficients in each dimension.

For more details on the KLT, see [21].

4. Genetic Algorithms

A Genetic Algorithm (GA) is a computing paradigm that simulates, in a simplified manner, the evolution and selection processes of natural species.

It may be used in solving non-linear optimizations problems when they may be coded in a set of parameters, and it is possible to define a function, called the fitness (function), that measures how close a solution is to the optimum.

A set of instantiated parameters describing the problem at hand is called the individuals: these parameters are put in a sequence similar to a chromosome, which is distinctive for its individual and defines it. Moreover, a fitness function is defined to evaluate the quality of the individual in terms of approximating the optimal solution.

A set of individuals, i.e., a population, is evolved in a way similar to the development of natural species. They mate, reproduce, and possibly have random modifications of their genes.

A chromosome codes a sequence of parameters, typically binary or integer numbers or a mix of them (but any type of data could be used in principle) with the constraint that the operations on them keep the data types consistent in the resulting chromosomes.

A population of individuals is created and (randomly) initialized; in general, a population of a hundred chromosomes is considered adequate.

Then, the GA goes through an iterative process, and in every cycle, the population is evolved according to the following steps:

- selection: pairs of individuals are mated for the following reproduction operation; individuals may be selected randomly or given priority depending on fitness; many strategies can be adopted, like roulette wheel or tournament selection [22];
- crossover: the previously selected pairs of chromosomes are mated by exchanging some (homologous) parts of their chromosomes with probability p_c; one or more "cutting" points are randomly chosen, and the genes between pairs of such points are exchanged to define two new offspring;
- mutation: with the aim of better exploring the solution space, each chromosome is mutated with probability p_m; mutation is performed by choosing at random one of the parameters coded in the chromosome and altering it by a random quantity;
- population update: to generate a new population and to keep the number of individuals constant, a selection among the individuals in the set composed by the old population and the new offspring should be performed; many different strategies could be adopted, e.g., two individuals in the set are randomly chosen, and the one with the best fitness is moved to the new population, repeating this process until the output population reaches the desired cardinality.

The described cycle is performed until a termination condition is met. In general, to avoid infinite cycles, an upper limit to the number of generations is fixed. Furthermore, the cycle may be terminated when at least one of the individual's fitness drops below (in this case, the lower the fitness, the better the individual) a pre-defined threshold. In both cases, the GA returns the best individual, representing the near-optimal solution it was able to find. For a deeper insight into GAs, see [22,23].

As will be shown in the following Section 5, to minimize the embedding noise due to watermark embedding, the watermark bits are stored, modifying the less significant part of the floating point numbers representing the 3D model vertex coordinates. This is obtained by considering the bytes encoding these floating point numbers as unsigned integers and changing the less significant bytes. This mode of operation results in a minimization problem in a non-linear space, a task where GAs, among other algorithms, are flexible and efficient to implement and apply.

5. The Proposed Algorithm

The developed algorithm has the objective to protect the shape and the structure of a 3D model, defined in terms of a mesh of polygons, providing a verification that allows for identification and localization of modifications to the model. In particular, the algorithm that will be presented in this section will protect:

- vertex coordinates (i.e., the geometry of the model);
- the polygon structure, as defined by the corresponding vertex connections (that is, the topology).

In the present embodiment, vertices' normal vectors are not considered because it was found that some 3D modeling software (e.g., Blender) alter them according to vertices' positions; thus, authentication data would be obsoleted by the modeling software at saving or loading time, inducing our verification procedure to flag vertices as forged. Nonetheless, protecting vertices will have as a side effect the protection of normals computed from them.

To allow modifications that maintain the structure of the 3D model to the file representing it, the proposed method permits order alterations to the vertices and to the polygons as they are stored in the file. This provides independence, to some extent, from the particular file format.

The method is composed of two main modules, namely an embedder and an extractor, and three companion modules, which are a key generator, a watermark generator, and a verifier. The interactions between the modules and the main data interchanged are shown in Figure 1.

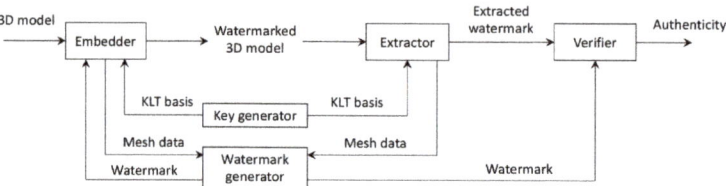

Figure 1. A high level scheme of the proposed method.

Each vertex is considered an Embedding Unit (EU); in the present embodiment, the vertex is defined by three spatial coordinates (x, y, z) and by the polygons to which the vertex belongs; a detailed description of this structure and of the embedding procedure will be given at the end of this section and in Section 5.2. The use of the EU concept solves the problem in 3D models that is not present in audio and image samples, that is the lack of the total order of the vertices.

A bird's eye-view of the various modules is the following:

- Key generator: defines a secret KLT basis to specify an embedding space;
- Watermark generator: creates the watermark bit string to be stored in each EU;
- Embedder: stores the watermark in the 3D model, one vertex at a time, using the KLT basis and the watermark provided by the respective modules; a computational intelligence technique, described in Section 4, is used to alter the vertex components so that the KLT coefficients of the vertex data contain the watermark; the output is a 3D model storing the fragile watermark;
- Extractor: extracts the watermark present in a 3D model using the secret KLT basis provided by the key generator module;
- Verifier: compares the extracted watermark with the one that should be contained in the vertices, providing the localization of tampered areas.

The input data are a 3D model composed of a set of vertices and a set of polygons. Each vertex is defined by three coordinates (x, y, z); every component value is considered in binary format, float representation (four bytes) in the IEEE 754 format. Every polygon is defined by the sequence of the indexes of its vertices. The watermark Embedding Unit (EU) is defined by the vertex data (x, y, z) along with a combined fingerprint of the t polygons to which the vertex belongs.

The fingerprint of a polygon is computed as follows: for every pair of vertices $(\mathbf{v}_i, \mathbf{v}_{i+1})$ encountered on the perimeter, a cryptographic hash (c. h.) function H is computed, $H(\mathbf{v}_i, \mathbf{v}_{i+1}) = h_{i,i+1}$; thus, for a polygon of n vertices, n cryptographic hashes will be obtained $h_{1,2}, h_{2,3}, \ldots, h_{n,1}$. To be independent from the starting vertex, these hashes are XORed $q = h_{1,2} \oplus h_{2,3} \oplus \ldots \oplus h_{n,1}$, then a c. h. is computed on the result q; the value $H(q)$ is the fingerprint of a polygon. Finally, a combined fingerprint F is obtained by XORing (to be independent from the order of the polygons considered) the fingerprints $H(q_i)$ of the t polygons the vertex belongs to:

$$F = H(q_1) \oplus H(q_2) \oplus \ldots \oplus H(q_t). \tag{5}$$

The c. h. function H used is MD5, whose hash length is 16 bytes.

Thus, the EU is composed of x, y, z (all floats, each one occupying four bytes) and a fingerprint F (bit string, 16 bytes), making 28 bytes in total (see Figure 2).

In Figure 2, note the bytes marked with vertical stripes: they are the least significant bytes of the mantissa of each float value. The watermark is embedded altering only those bytes; it follows that the polygon hashes do not take into account those bytes in the computation, i.e., if $[.]_3$ is the operator that extracts the three most significant bytes, then given two vertices $\mathbf{v}_i = (x_i, y_i, z_i)$ and $\mathbf{v}_j = (x_j, y_j, z_j)$, the c. h. $h_{i,j}$ is:

$$h_{i,j} = H([x_i]_3 \mid [y_i]_3 \mid [z_i]_3 \mid [x_j]_3 \mid [y_j]_3 \mid [z_j]_3), \tag{6}$$

where the symbol | means string concatenation.

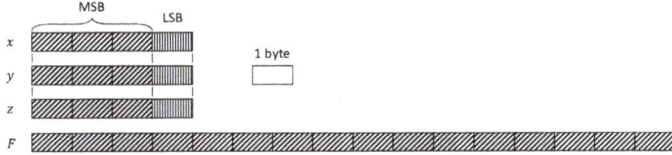

Figure 2. The fields and structure of an Embedding Unit (EU).

Note that the algorithm can cope with more data related to each vertex, for example uv coordinates: it is sufficient to add them to the EU and modify the KLT basis size.

5.1. Key Generation

The key generator module has the objective to create a secret orthonormal basis to define a secret space of embedding. This space must be known to the embedder and to the extractor; thus, the key generator must provide the basis to both of them during their operations.

In principle, any secret orthonormal basis of the required dimension (in the present embodiment, 28) would suffice; nonetheless, the KLT provides a method to define a basis starting from a set of vectors, so we found that using a secret image to derive a set of vectors from which to compute a KLT basis was a flexible and viable solution.

5.2. Watermark Embedding

The watermark string w to be embedded into an EU is derived by the key generator module from the fixed part of the EU itself, i.e., the diagonal striped bytes in Figure 2. This string can be computed as the MD5 hash of the aforementioned data: from the resulting 128 bits, a predefined subset is extracted for embedding. Note that this step is not strictly necessary because the watermark is embedded into a secret space, as will be discussed in the following; thus, also a constant w bit string would suffice; nonetheless, a variable w further improves security.

A high level description of the algorithm is the following.

The fragile watermark is stored in the coefficients of every EU KLT: the 28 bytes of the EU are considered as 28 non-negative integer pixel values, which are KLT transformed, producing 28 coefficients. If m is the payload in bpv (bits-per-vertex), i.e., m is the length of the watermark w for every EU, then a subset of m KLT coefficients is chosen a priori to store the watermark bits. In the present implementation, a coefficient c is considered as carrying a watermark bit b in position p (the p value is a parameter of the algorithm) iff:

$$b = \mathrm{round}(2^{-p}c) \bmod 2 \tag{7}$$

(see [24] for a deeper discussion on various methods for embedding the watermark bits into a set of coefficients).

The GA alters the values of the vertical striped bytes in Figure 2 until the watermark is embedded into the EU KLT coefficients, i.e., if $\mathbf{g} = (g_1, g_2, \ldots, g_{28})$ is the EU, the GA alters g_4, g_8, g_{12} (the vertical striped bytes) so that the predefined coefficients in $(c_1, c_2, \ldots, c_{28}) = \text{KLT}(g_1, g_2, \ldots, g_{28})$ contain the respective m bits watermark. The reason for using a GA in this task is its ability to find the solution of a non-linear problem (bytes representing integer values) looking for the (local) minima of the error w.r.t. the original data.

Referring to Equation (7), the present implementation of the algorithm considers the first m coefficients among the 28 transform coefficients and embeds into the bit in position $p = -2$.

When all the EUs have been processed by the GA, the 3D model with the new modified coordinates contains the fragile watermark allowing for the integrity check by the modules presented in the following section.

5.3. Watermark Extraction and Verification

The extraction of the watermark starts with building the EU for every vertex. Using the KLT basis from the key generator module, 28 coefficients are extracted from every EU: from the subset of coefficients used for watermark embedding, the watermark bits are computed using Equation (7) and stored in a string w_e. Note that this operation requires the computation of a forward KLT; the inverse KLT is not used in the proposed algorithm.

After that, the watermark generator module is called for every EU, producing a watermark string w for each of them.

At this point, the verifier module compares the two strings w_e and w for every vertex: if the strings are equal, then the vertex is marked as authentic; otherwise, it is flagged as potentially forged.

The possible forging of a 3D model represented as a set of vertices connected to form polygons may be done by altering or modifying:

- at least one of the coordinates of a vertex, or
- removing, replacing, or adding a vertex to a polygon, or
- shuffling the order of the vertices on the perimeter of a polygon.

According to the integrity protection provided by the proposed algorithm, a vertex can be detected as tampered if:

1. at least one of the coordinates x, y, z has been altered: in this case, if only the lower part (the vertical striped bytes in Figure 2) of one of the values is modified, then the vertex alone will be flagged as tampered; if the higher part is altered, then the vertex itself and all the vertices belonging to the polygons containing the vertex will be detected as tampered.
2. one of the polygons containing it is altered, that is:
   - one of its vertices has been modified in the higher part of the coordinates, or
   - at least one of its vertices has been substituted by another vertex, or
   - the order of the vertices on the perimeter has been changed (comprising the clockwise or anti-clockwise order), or
   - the number of vertices has been changed;
3. it has been removed from one of the polygons it belongs to, or
4. it has been added to a polygon (even duplicating a polygon).

6. Experimental Results

This section summarizes the results of a number of experiments we executed to test the performance of the proposed algorithm. In order to measure the resulting quality, we considered four objective parameters, namely the sensitivity, the Mean Absolute Error (MAE), the Root Mean Squared Error (RMSE), and the Peak Signal-to-Noise Ratio (PSNR). Indeed, the sensitivity gives a measure of the capability of the algorithm to detect tampering attacks. Thus, the meanings of the parameters used to measure the performance of the proposed algorithm are:

- Sensitivity (defined as in [24]): the sensitivity of level $\pm\delta$ is defined as the fraction of vertices that are detected as tampered in the verification phase when one byte of each EU is modified by $\pm\delta$; this is a very powerful fragility measure, in particular for small values of δ as one or two, because it is actually the least tampering an attacker can perform: any other attack, such as noise addition, adding, removing, or shifting vertices or surfaces, etc., would modify the mantissa values of the vertex coordinates of more than just $\pm\delta$;
- Mean Absolute Error (MAE): measures the average absolute difference between vertex attributes of the host and the watermarked model,

$$\text{MAE} = \frac{\sum_{\mathbf{v} \in Y} \sum_{c \in \Omega} |\mathbf{v}_c - \mathbf{v}_{c'}|}{\text{card}(Y)\,\text{card}(\Omega)}, \tag{8}$$

where $\mathbf{v}$ scans the set Y of all vertices, c scans the set Ω of the attributes that can be modified by the embedder (i.e., in the present embodiment x, y, z), the $'$ symbol refers to the modified attribute in the watermarked model, and the function $\text{card}()$ returns the cardinality of a set;

- Root Mean Squared Error (RMSE): measures the distortion between vertex coordinates of the host and the watermarked model,

$$\text{RMSE} = \sqrt{\frac{\sum_{\mathbf{v} \in Y} \|\mathbf{v} - \mathbf{v}'\|^2}{\text{card}(Y)}}, \tag{9}$$

where $\mathbf{v}'$ represent the modified vertices and the operator $\|.\|$ computes the Euclidean distance;

- Peak Signal-to-Noise Ratio (PSNR): measures the distortion with respect to the maximum elongation of the vertices from the centroid of the model,

$$\text{PSNR} = 10 \log_{10} \frac{\left(\max_{\mathbf{v} \in Y} \|\mathbf{v} - \mathbf{c}\|\right)^2}{\frac{1}{\text{card}(Y)} \sum_{\mathbf{v} \in Y} \|\mathbf{v} - \mathbf{v}'\|^2}, \tag{10}$$

where $\mathbf{v}'$ represent the modified vertices, $\mathbf{c}$ is the centroid of the host model, and the operator $\|.\|$ computes the Euclidean distance.

We chose a setting for the genetic algorithm to be used in all experiments; in particular, we derived the setting values from many experiments devised to have fast convergence to a solution resulting in a high quality watermarked model. The settings were population size = 300, $p_c = 0.9$, $p_m = 0.25$, maximum generations = 2000.

We ran the embedding algorithm on ten 3D models (shown in Figure 3), and the objective results are reported in Table 3. The payload in all experiments was set to 5 bpv.

From Table 3, it can be seen that, given the very high values of sensitivity for small modifications (more than 99% of vertices detected when altering them by only ± 2 in one of the bytes of their coordinates), the proposed algorithm is highly reliable in tampering detection, i.e., it is very fragile. Moreover, the very small values of MAE and RMSE and the very high values of PSNR proved that the 3D models underwent a negligible modification, which may be generally accepted apart from specific applications, in which case we think that a reversible algorithm should be applied (but this is not the objective of the present proposal).

As concerns the complexity of the proposed method, let us consider separately the preprocessing phase, the embedding phase, and the verification phase. During preprocessing, for every vertex, a signature of the polygons to which it belongs is computed. In the worst case scenario, a vertex is connected to all other vertices, so this computation would take $O(n^2)$ time, where n is the number of vertices. The embedding phase, instead, is linear in the number of vertices of the model, and it is upper bounded because the GA is run for a given predefined number of generations. Finally, the verification phase is very fast, and again, it is linear in the number of vertices (it usually takes a few hundreds of milliseconds on a standard laptop).

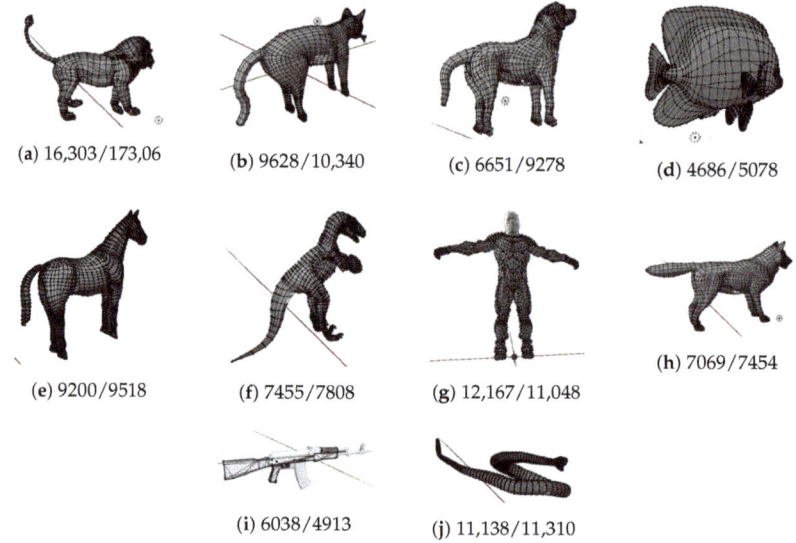

Figure 3. Original models used in the experiments along with [number of vertices]/[number of polygons]composing them: (**a**) lion, (**b**) cat, (**c**) dog, (**d**) fish, (**e**) horse, (**f**) raptor, (**g**) suit, (**h**) wolf, (**i**) AK, and (**j**) snake.

Table 3. Performance of the proposed algorithm on a set of ten publicly available 3D models.

3D Model	Sensitivity ±1 (%)	Sensitivity ±2 (%)	MAE ×10^{-6}	RMSE ×10^{-6}	PSNR (dB)
lion	93.85	99.82	0.65	2.76	312.85
cat	93.68	99.84	0.63	2.74	310.07
dog	93.83	99.81	0.75	3.08	310.85
fish	93.71	99.85	0.50	2.30	311.03
horse	93.79	99.84	2.30	2.96	306.21
raptor	93.82	99.83	0.69	2.95	314.29
suit	93.71	99.84	0.071	0.36	299.61
wolf	94.01	99.88	0.63	2.80	309.04
AK	93.94	99.83	1.52	8.85	317.46
snake	93.81	99.85	0.73	3.10	302.39
Average	93.82 ± 0.20	99.84 ± 0.02	0.43 ± 0.35	3.19 ± 2.04	309.36 ± 5.12

One of the original models (lion) is shown in Figure 4a. To present how the algorithm operates on the model from a subjective point of view, in Figure 4b, the same model after the fragile watermark embedding is reported.

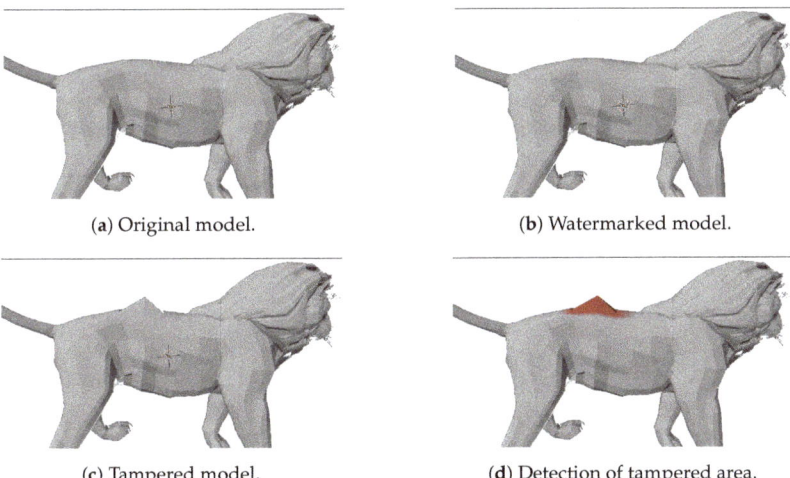

(**a**) Original model. (**b**) Watermarked model.

(**c**) Tampered model. (**d**) Detection of tampered area.

Figure 4. Application of the proposed algorithm to a model (lion).

An example of tampering is shown in Figure 4c, and the resulting tamper detection highlights the modified vertices in red color, as can be seen in Figure 4d.

To give more insights into how the algorithm detects tampering, we report a simple model in Figure 5a and show how the removal of a single vertex (Figure 5c) from the watermarked model (Figure 5b) results in a detection (Figure 5d) that highlights all the vertices contiguous to the removed one; these vertices are marked as forged because, as said in Item 2. of Section 5.3, the polygons containing them were altered: indeed, they were removed, deleting the vertex in the cone apex.

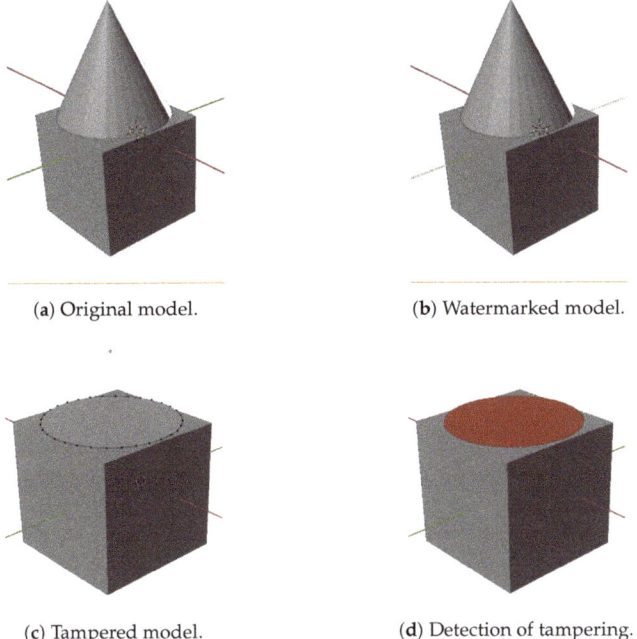

(**a**) Original model. (**b**) Watermarked model.

(**c**) Tampered model. (**d**) Detection of tampering.

Figure 5. Application of the proposed algorithm to a simplified model.

Comparison with Related Works

Among the related works, we selected for comparison the ones that reported numerical (objective) measures of distortion introduced by their algorithms, as there were no visible modifications to the model after watermark embedding. It should be pointed out that an exact comparison was not really possible as every paper used different sets of models with respect to one another, so we only compared with the best results they reported. Moreover, we emphasize that there were not many works on fragile watermarking reporting parameters to compare to in a fair way.

All in all, we can say that our proposed method was superior to all the compared methods in terms of quality (in many cases, more than two orders of magnitude of the considered measure) of the resulting models and the fragility of the watermark.

In [14], the authors reported the best PSNR value of 84.47 dB, which was far less than the smallest PSNR (>299 dB) our algorithm produced.

In [12], the authors reported distortion (the same as our MAE values) for various settings of their method's parameters; again, an exact comparison was difficult for two main reasons. First, the set of models they used was different from our set, and the model precision was 10^{-6}, whereas the precision of our models was 10^{-4}. Anyway, their best result was 1.3×10^{-5}, which was worse than our worst result (horse, 2.30×10^{-6}) by one order of magnitude. In [18], the same authors reported a distortion of 0.01, four orders of magnitude worse than our distortion results.

In [10], the authors reported a mean distance error (averaged over five models) of 2.33×10^{-4}, which was two orders of magnitude greater than the mean distance error (averaged over 10 models) computed by our models (1.92×10^{-6}).

In [15], the authors reported an average RMS error (3.74×10^{-4}) that was two orders of magnitude greater than our reported RMSE (3.19×10^{-6}), while our *RMSRatio* (1.07×10^{-7}) was comparable with theirs. It should be pointed out, anyway, that our payload (five bits per vertex) was five times that of [15], but the distortion induced was the same. Moreover, the work in [15] had the disadvantage of requiring the centroid of the original model to perform the integrity verification, thus requiring out-of-band information to be kept per-model.

In [20], the authors reported an average (over five models) SNR of 124.24 dB that was far smaller than our average (over 10 models) SNR of 231.14 dB.

Finally, we performed several other experiments on the same models with different precisions, and in general, we could say that the proposed method resulted in a distortion that was in the order of $1/100^{\text{th}}$ of the precision of the original model.

7. Discussion

The proposed fragile watermarking algorithm for 3D models performed a watermark bit string embedding by modifying the least significant part of some vertices' attributes (in the present embodiment, coordinates): the watermark was stored in a secret space defined by a secret KLT basis and protected the integrity of the structure of the 3D model, that is the polygon mesh and the vertices of these polygons. Thus, the security of the method lied in the secrecy of the vectors used to derive the KLT kernel.

The main advantages of the method were:

- the proposed method was very general because it worked on single vertices and may be extended to protect any number of vertex attributes (like normals, texture properties, etc.), even without modifying the KLT basis size: for example, by applying the cryptographic hash function also on these attributes and XORing the result to the fingerprint F;
- the watermark was embedded into the vertices without tying to a particular representation of the model, i.e., vertices could be changed in order as long as the polygons were updated accordingly;
- modifications to the data were limited to the least significant bits of the mantissa value, so keeping the relative error as small as possible;

- affine transformations to the 3D models were allowed (no tampering was shown), as long as they were represented and stored as matrix operations to be applied to vertex coordinates (this is the default Blender behavior).

At the same time, the disadvantages of the method were:

- a slight change to the vertices' coordinates was performed;
- if a vertex was duplicated in the 3D model, after watermark embedding, two vertices with different coordinates and/or normal components would be created; thus, small holes or changes in illumination in the vertex area were created; this issue could be solved by recognizing coincident vertices and modifying them in the same manner during watermark embedding; it was possible to perform this action because it was highly probable that both vertices allowed for an equal modification embedding different watermark strings.

7.1. Security Considerations

The security of the method was based on the secrecy of the KLT basis. Thus, this set of orthonormal vectors constituted the secret key. This basis may be derived from any sample of vectors belonging to a vector space of the right dimension: in our case, the EU was composed of 28 bytes; thus, the vector space should be of dimension 28.

For example, considering a grayscale image and building vectors from pixel values taken in raster scan order allowed the computation of a covariance matrix from which to derive an orthonormal basis (as shown in Section 3): if the image were kept secret, so would be the KLT basis and consequently the embedding space of the watermark bit string. This prevented an attacker from creating forged vertices embedding a correct watermark given that she/he would not know the kernel basis of the transform.

If the length of the watermark stored in each EU were m bits (i.e., the payload was m bpv), then the probability that a forged vertex would not be detected as such would be $1/2^m$. Nonetheless, as previously said, if the modification were in the higher part of the vertex data, then all the polygons sharing that vertex would detect the modification: given that for each polygon, the probability to fail detection would be $1/2^m$, if the forged vertex were shared amongst k polygons, then the probability that the tampering went undetected by all polygons would be $1/2^{mk}$.

8. Conclusions

The proposed method performed an integrity protection of 3D models in a more secure embedding space of the watermark while reducing the distortion induced to the model. It applied a small modification to some attributes of the vertices of the model (in the current implementation, vertices' coordinates, but it could be extended to other vertex features). The error introduced w.r.t. the original attribute values was in the order of 4.3×10^{-7} (average MAE for the models analyzed in Table 3) and was not noticeable from the rendered model (as subjectively judged from a sample of 10 observers).

The security of the whole process lied in the secrecy of the KLT basis, which, in turn, was based on the secrecy of the vectors used to compute it. Public parameters of the algorithm were the cryptographic hash function, the payload m (in bpv), the orders of the m KLT coefficients, and the embedding position p.

As future work, we plan to extend the algorithm to protect other vertex attributes, like uv coordinates and normals.

Author Contributions: Conceptualization: M.B., D.C. and M.G.; Methodology: M.B. and D.C.; Software: M.B.; Data Curation: P.P.;writing—original draft preparation, M.B., D.C., M.G. and P.P.; writing—review, M.B., D.C., M.G. and P.P. All authors have read and agreed to the published version of the manuscript.

Funding: This research received no external funding.

Conflicts of Interest: The authors declare no conflict of interest.

References

1. Cox, I.; Miller, M.; Bloom, J.; Fridrich, J.; Kalker, T. *Digital Watermarking and Steganography*, 2nd ed.; Morgan Kaufmann: San Francisco, CA, USA, 2007.
2. Praun, E.; Hoppe, H.; Finkelstein, A. Robust mesh watermarking. In *Proceedings of the 26th Annual Conference on Computer Graphics and Interactive Techniques, SIGGRAPH '99*; ACM Press/Addison-Wesley Publishing Co.: New York, NY, USA, 1999; pp. 49–56. [CrossRef]
3. Ohbuchi, R.; Takahashi, S.; Miyazawa, T.; Mukaiyama, A. Watermarking 3D Polygonal Meshes in the Mesh Spectral Domain. In Proceedings of the Graphics Interface 2001 Conference, Ottawa, ON, Canada, 7–9 June 2001; pp. 9–18.
4. Ohbuchi, R.; Mukaiyama, A.; Takahashi, S. A Frequency-Domain Approach to Watermarking 3D Shapes. *Comput. Graph. Forum* **2002**, *21*, 373–382. [CrossRef]
5. Barni, M.; Bartolini, F.; Cappellini, V.; Corsini, M.; Garzelli, A. Digital watermarking of 3D meshes. Mathematics of Data/Image Coding, Compression, and Encryption VI, with Applications. *Int. Soc. Opt. Photonics* **2004**, *5208*, 68–79.
6. Yu, Z.; Ip, H.H.; Kwok, L. A robust watermarking scheme for 3D triangular mesh models. *Pattern Recognit.* **2003**, *36*, 2603–2614. [CrossRef]
7. Li, L.; Zhang, D.; Pan, Z.; Shi, J.; Zhou, K.; Ye, K. Watermarking 3D mesh by spherical parameterization. *Comput. Graph.* **2004**, *28*, 981–989. [CrossRef]
8. Cho, J.W.; Prost, R.; Jung, H.Y. An Oblivious Watermarking for 3-D Polygonal Meshes Using Distribution of Vertex Norms. *IEEE Trans. Signal Process.* **2007**, *55*, 142–155. [CrossRef]
9. Vasic, B.; Raveendran, N.; Vasic, B. Neuro-OSVETA: A Robust Watermarking of 3D Meshes. In *International Telemetering Conference Proceedings*; International Foundation for Telemetering: San Diego, CA, USA, 2019; Volume 55.
10. Wang, Y.P.; Hu, S.M. A New Watermarking Method for 3D Models Based on Integral Invariants. *IEEE Trans. Vis. Comput. Graph.* **2009**, *15*, 285–294. [CrossRef]
11. Yeung, M.; Yeo, B.L. Fragile watermarking of Three-Dimensional Objects. In Proceedings of the International Conference on Image Processing, ICIP98, Chicago, IL, USA, 7 October 1998; Volume 2, pp. 442–446.
12. Chou, C.M.; Tseng, D.C. A Public Fragile Watermarking Scheme for 3D Model Authentication. *Comput.-Aided Des.* **2006**, *38*, 1154–1165. [CrossRef]
13. Wang, W.B.; Zheng, G.Q.; Yong, J.H.; Gu, H.J. A Numerically Stable Fragile Watermarking Scheme for Authenticating 3D Models. *Comput.-Aided Des.* **2008**, *40*, 634–645. [CrossRef]
14. Su, Z.; Li, W.; Kong, J.; Dai, Y.; Tang, W. Watermarking 3D CAPD models for topology verification. *Comput.-Aided Des.* **2013**, *45*, 1042–1052. [CrossRef]
15. Huang, C.C.; Yang, Y.W.; Fan, C.M.; Wang, J.T. A Spherical Coordinate Based Fragile Watermarking Scheme for 3D Models. In *International Conference on Industrial, Eengineering and other Applications of Applied Intelligent Systems*; Springer: Berlin/Heidelberg, Germany, 2013; pp. 566–571.
16. Yeo, B.L.; Yeung, M.M. Watermarking 3D objects for verification. *IEEE Comput. Graph. Appl.* **1999**, *19*, 36–45.
17. Lin, H.Y.S.; Liao, H.Y.M.; Lu, C.S.; Lin, J.C. Fragile watermarking for authenticating 3-D polygonal meshes. *IEEE Trans. Multimed.* **2005**, *7*, 997–1006. [CrossRef]
18. Chou, C.M.; Tseng, D.C. Affine-Transformation-Invariant Public Fragile Watermarking for 3D Model Authentication. *IEEE Comput. Graph. Appl.* **2009**, *29*, 72–79. [CrossRef] [PubMed]
19. Wu, H.T.; Cheung, Y.M. A Fragile Watermarking Scheme for 3D Meshes. In Proceedings of the 7th Workshop on Multimedia and Security, New York, NY, USA, 1–2 August 2005; ACM: New York, NY, USA, 2005; pp. 117–124. [CrossRef]
20. Motwani, M.; Motwani, R.; Frederick Harris, J. Fragile Watermarking of 3D Models Using Genetic Algorithms. *J. Electron. Sci. Technol.* **2010**, *8*, 244–250.
21. Gonzalez, R.C.; Wintz, P. *Digital Image Processing*, 2nd ed.; Addison-Wesley Publishing Co., Inc.: Reading, MA, USA, 1987.
22. Goldberg, D.E. *Genetic Algorithms in Search, Optimization and Machine Learning*; Addison-Wesley Longman Publishing Co., Inc.: Boston, MA, USA, 1989.

23. Hassanien, A.E.; Abraham, A.; Kacprzyk, J.; Peters, J.F. Computational intelligence in multimedia processing: Foundation and trends. In *Computational Intelligence in Multimedia Processing: Recent Advances*; Springer: Berlin/Heidelberg, Germany, 2008; pp. 3–49.
24. Botta, M.; Cavagnino, D.; Pomponiu, V. A modular framework for color image watermarking. *Signal Process.* **2016**, *119*, 102–114. [CrossRef]

© 2020 by the authors. Licensee MDPI, Basel, Switzerland. This article is an open access article distributed under the terms and conditions of the Creative Commons Attribution (CC BY) license (http://creativecommons.org/licenses/by/4.0/).

Article

Screen-Cam Robust Image Watermarking with Feature-Based Synchronization

Weitong Chen [1,2,3], Na Ren [1,2,3,*], Changqing Zhu [1,2,3], Qifei Zhou [1,2,3], Tapio Seppänen [4] and Anja Keskinarkaus [4]

1. Key Laboratory of Virtual Geographic Environment (Nanjing Normal University), Ministry of Education, Nanjing 210023, China; 171301018@njnu.edu.cn (W.C.); 09322@njnu.edu.cn (C.Z.); 181301014@njnu.edu.cn (Q.Z.)
2. State Key Laboratory Cultivation Base of Geographical Environment Evolution, Nanjing 210023, China
3. Jiangsu Center for Collaborative Innovation in Geographical Information Resource Development and Application, Nanjing 210023, China
4. Physiological Signal Analysis Team, Center for Machine Vision and Signal Analysis, University of Oulu, 90014 Oulu, Finland; Tapio.Seppanen@oulu.fi (T.S.); Anja.Keskinarkaus@oulu.fi (A.K.)
* Correspondence: 09359@njnu.edu.cn; Tel.: +86-136-1157-8959

Received: 23 September 2020; Accepted: 22 October 2020; Published: 25 October 2020

Abstract: The screen-cam process, which is taking pictures of the content displayed on a screen with mobile phones or cameras, is one of the main ways that image information is leaked. However, traditional image watermarking methods are not resilient to screen-cam processes with severe distortion. In this paper, a screen-cam robust watermarking scheme with a feature-based synchronization method is proposed. First, the distortions caused by the screen-cam process are investigated. These distortions can be summarized into the five categories of linear distortion, gamma tweaking, geometric distortion, noise attack, and low-pass filtering attack. Then, a local square feature region (LSFR) construction method based on a Gaussian function, modified Harris–Laplace detector, and speeded-up robust feature (SURF) orientation descriptor is developed for watermark synchronization. Next, the message is repeatedly embedded in each selected LSFR by an improved embedding algorithm, which employs a non-rotating embedding method and a preprocessing method, to modulate the discrete Fourier transform (DFT) coefficients. In the process of watermark detection, we fully utilize the captured information and extract the message based on a local statistical feature. Finally, the experimental results are presented to illustrate the effectiveness of the method against common attacks and screen-cam attacks. Compared to the previous schemes, our scheme has not only good robustness against screen-cam attack, but is also effective against screen-cam with additional common desynchronization attacks.

Keywords: screen-cam process; local square feature region; synchronization; DFT; robust watermarking

1. Introduction

Currently, the ubiquity of the computer office and the development of communication technology render digital image storage, copying, and transmission convenient and fast. Security problems involving digital images, such as leakage, malicious theft, and illegal dissemination, still frequently occur. In order to protect the data on the computer side, data encryption [1–6] and software watermarking [7,8] schemes are proposed. Similarly, some scholars have also investigated access control technology [9–11] to prevent illegal copying and transmission of data by restricting internal operations. Although these methods can effectively prevent the illegal acquisition of digital data directly from a computer, they cannot prohibit using a camera to take a photo of sensitive information displayed on the screen. In particular, the popularization of smartphones has made data leakage by capturing on-screen content much easier and common. However, verifying the copyright of a camera-captured image that is published without permission is still challenging. Digital image watermarking technology has been widely used for copyright protection and leakage tracking [12–16]. To hold someone accountable for the behavior of sneak shots, an invisible screen-cam robust watermark can be embedded in images. In this circumstance, the embedded watermark will survive in a camera-captured image.

To design a screen-cam robust watermarking scheme that can extract watermark information from a single screen-captured photo, we need to analyze the screen-cam process first. The screen-cam process can be considered a compound attack containing moiré noise, luminance distortion, and geometric distortion. Consequently, most traditional watermarking methods are not applicable to the screen-cam process. The process of generating a new image by camera capture is referred to as a cross-media information transfer process that contains analog-to-digital and digital-to-analog conversion attacks. Thus, the print-scan and print-cam processes have certain similarities with the screen-cam process.

Many researchers have focused on extracting watermark information from printed images. Based on embedding domains, these methods can be divided into spatial domain-based and frequency domain-based methods. The spatial domain-based algorithms primarily employed watermark patterns as watermark information. Nakamura et al. [17] proposed a sinusoidal watermark pattern-based adaptive additive embedding algorithm. The pattern-based method was continuously improved with a frame detection method [18] to achieve autocorrection during extraction, a new pattern design [19–21] to achieve better imperceptibility and robustness, or a combination with computational photography technology [22,23] to solve the lens focusing problem.

However, these pattern-based watermark methods are weak to cropping attacks, and the performance of watermark detection will decrease if an image is zoomed-out before it is printed. The frequency domain-based algorithms include Fourier domain-based methods and wavelet domain-based methods. The Fourier domain-based algorithms can be subdivided into two categories. The first category is transform-invariant domain-based methods [24,25], which employed log-polar mapping (LPM) and discrete Fourier transform (DFT) to achieve robustness to rotation, scaling, and translation (RST) distortions. The second category uses the selected magnitude coefficients of the DFT domain as the message carrier [26–29]. Researchers have improved the method by choosing the optimal radius of the implementation to minimize quality degradation [28] or by color correction to enhance the extraction accuracy [29]. For the wavelet domain-based algorithms, messages are embedded by modulating the coefficients of the wavelet transform. These algorithms commonly combine with another domain-based watermark to achieve robustness to affine distortion attacks [30], to rotation and scale attacks [31], or implement fragile watermarking [32]. Similarly, because the frequency domain-based methods are global watermarks, they are also weak to cropping attacks. Furthermore, the experiments in [33] show that these print-scan and print-cam robust watermarking methods have a relatively higher bit error rate that cannot be directly applied to the screen-cam process.

Considering the particularity of the screen-cam process, Fang et al. [33] proposed an effective screen-cam robust image watermark algorithm with an intensity-based scale-invariant feature transform (I-SIFT)-based synchronization. The message is embedded in the discrete cosine transform (DCT) domain of each feature region. However, this method needs to record the four vertices of the image in advance, which means it cannot cope with the situations where the image's original size is unknown. Besides, this method cannot address orientation or scale desynchronization attacks.

However, normal user operations may cause watermark desynchronization inevitably. For example, the image displayed on the screen is blocked by other application windows or the image has been zoomed, rotated, and cropped for usage. Because the spy may just capture the content displayed on the screen, if we do not know the original information of the captured image, we may not be able to restore the image to its original orientation and scale. Therefore, to address possible desynchronization attacks besides screen-cam attack, a screen-cam, RST, and cropping invariant watermark synchronization method need to be further investigated.

To solve these issues, a feature and Fourier-based screen-cam robust watermarking scheme is proposed in this paper. The main contributions are as follows:

- We analyze the performance of commonly used feature operators and the variation rules of DFT magnitude coefficients during the screen-cam process.
- We designed an orientation and scale invariant local square feature region (LSFR) construction method, which can achieve watermark synchronization against screen-cam attack and also common desynchronization attacks.
- We employ a non-rotating embedding algorithm based on the properties of the DFT coefficients, which can avoid further distortions that may be caused by orientation normalization.
- We present a preprocessing method for message embedding. By working in combination with the proposed local statistical feature-based message extraction method, it can improve the extraction accuracy.

The remainder of the paper is organized as follows: Section 2 summarizes different distortions in the screen-cam process. Section 3 describes the implementation details of the proposed method. The selection of parameters and experiment results are presented in Sections 4 and 5. Finally, Section 6 concludes the paper.

2. Screen-Cam Process Analysis

The screen-cam process contains various distortions [34]. The subprocesses of the screen-cam process produce different types of distortions, as shown in Figure 1, and cause severe image quality degradation. This section aims to provide a basis for the design of screen-cam robust watermarking schemes by analyzing the different types of distortions generated in each step of the screen-cam process.

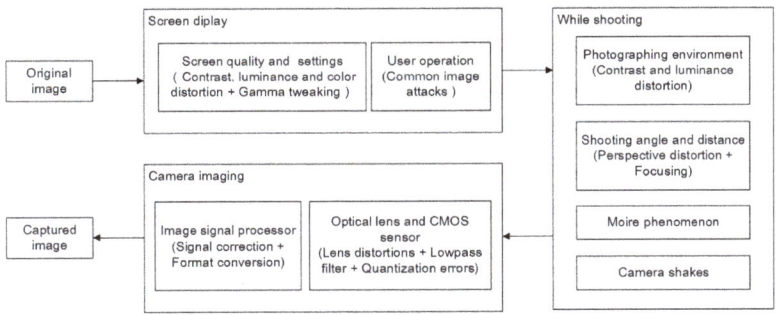

Figure 1. Various processes and corresponding distortions in screen-cam process.

The screen-cam process can be divided into three subprocesses: screen display, while shooting, and camera imaging.

In the screen display process, the main factors that affect image signal are the quality of different monitors and their settings. Regular user operations will also cause distortions.

With regard to the while shooting process, the main factors are the shooting environment, the relative position of screen and camera, and the moiré phenomenon. If shooting at a large angle, the focusing problem cannot be disregarded [23]. Besides, camera shake may occur when pressing the shutter.

The camera imaging process of a mobile phone is the process of converting optical signals to digital image signals and processing them. The main types of equipment in the process are the optical lens, the CMOS sensor [35], and the digital signal processor (DSP). With regard to CMOS sensors, the most important components are the photoelectric sensor and analog-to-digital sensor in receiving and processing signals. Therefore, the factors can be divided into hardware parts and software parts.

The hardware part is related to the quality of the cameras' hardware devices. The software part is related to the image processing algorithm performed by the image signal processor (ISP). This part contains signal correction and format conversion before storage.

Assuming an original image is displayed on a screen, and it is well captured by a camera, the distortions created during this screen-cam process can be divided into five categories.

Linear distortion: The luminance, contrast, and color distortions caused by the quality and settings of the monitor can be approximated as a linear change. Linear distortion can also occur through linear correction of the image by the ISP.

Gamma tweaking: To fit the human vision, the monitor performs gamma correction on the digital image, which is a nonlinear distortion. The ISP of the mobile phone performs a gamma compensation according to the algorithms on the digital image. The effect of gamma compensation may be amplified by other previous attacks.

Geometric distortion: (1) Different degrees of perspective distortion are caused by the distance and angle of capturing, which will generate an uneven scaling attack on the digital image. (2) Another perspective distortion, such as pincushion distortion and barrel distortion, is caused by lens distortion of the optical lens. By controlling the photographer, the effects of these attacks can be reduced to a certain extent.

Noise attack: Noise attacks are important factors that cause a sharp reduction in image quality during the screen-cam process. Noise attacks can be divided into four categories: moiré noise, noise caused by the external environment, hardware, and software. (1) In physics, moiré noise is a phenomenon of beat noise, which is the wave interference that occurs between two different objects [36]. During the screen-cam process, the light-sensitive elements in a camera emit high-frequency electromagnetic waves and the object being photographed, such as a liquid crystal display (LCD), emits some electromagnetic interference. When the two electromagnetic waves intersect, the waveforms are superimposed and cause electronic fluctuations of the acquiring device. The original waveforms are changed to form a new waveform that is moiré. Generally, the moiré phenomenon is most severe when the two wave frequencies are similar or in a multiple relationship. (2) External noise is caused by unstable external light interference and screen reflections while shooting. (3) Hardware devices such as sensor material properties, electronic components, and circuit structures can cause different noise. The most typical is the quantization error noise caused in the process of digitizing the captured signal by the CMOS processor, where the actual continuous signal is quantized to the pixel values of the digital image signal. (4) The ISP corrects the captured signal, which is independent of the original image to some extent, so the noise reduction correction process also produces new noise.

Low-pass filtering attack: Although a camera has a high resolution and the number of pixels in the captured image is commonly larger than that of the original image, during the process of capturing an optical signal, the signal acquisition does not record each pixel of an image independently. Interference that occurs between the lights causes blurring of the adjacent pixels, which approximates a low-pass filtering attack. Blurring caused by unfocused pixels is similar.

3. Proposed Watermarking Scheme

This section is dedicated to present the watermark embedding and detection procedures of the proposed watermarking scheme, and it explains the reasons for doing so. In the process of watermark embedding, we first construct LSFRs as message embedding regions. After that, a watermark message is embedded in each LSFR repeatedly with the proposed algorithm. In the process of watermark detection, we first perform perspective correction on the captured image. Then, we find out all the candidate regions and perform message extraction on these candidate regions one by one. Therefore, this section is organized as follows: In Section 3.1, we analyze the selection of feature operators and present the detailed procedures of the proposed LSFR construction method. In Section 3.2, we analyze the embedding operations and present the detailed procedures of the proposed embedding method. The corresponding watermark detection method is given in Section 3.3.

3.1. Local Square Feature Region Construction

Due to the desynchronization attacks caused by the screen-cam process and user operations, we need to develop an appropriate synchronization method to locate the watermark. We test the feasibility of the Harris–Laplace, SIFT, and SURF operators, which are extensively employed to construct local scale-invariant feature regions (LFRs) as message embedding areas [37–45], in the screen-cam process. To select the most suitable operators for LFRs construction, the variations of feature point coordinates, feature scale, and feature direction are quantitatively analyzed under different shooting distances. The images we used here are shown in Figure 2. All host images are 1024 × 1024 pixels. Because of the blurring of the image edges caused by the low-pass filtering attack and the lens distortion, it is difficult to restore the captured image to exactly correspond to the original image. Inevitably, there will be a displacement between the coordinates of the corresponding pixels. Therefore, the feature points are considered to be repeated when the offsets of their coordinates are smaller than five pixels. Besides, considering the requirements of watermark synchronization, the feature scale variation should be below 10% at the same time. Furthermore, the feature points at the edge of the image are excluded. In order to reduce the impact of noise, we perform a Gaussian filter on both the original images and the captured images. As shown in Figure 3a, after a Gaussian function, we discover that the middle- and high-scale, which means the feature scale is greater than 15, feature points of the Harris–Laplace or SIFT operators can achieve high repeatability. The repeatability here refers to the ratio of the number of feature points extracted after a screen-cam attack and satisfying the above-mentioned pixel offset and scale variation criteria, compared to the original number of feature points. We also note that although the SIFT operator has a better performance at a long shooting distance, it does not work well at a close shooting distance, which indicates that it is more sensitive to moiré noise. Comparatively, the Harris–Laplace operator is more stable at different shooting distances, which is more suitable for watermark synchronization. Regarding the feature orientation descriptors, we note that the SURF orientation descriptor is more robust than the SIFT to the screen-cam process, where the orientation variations of repeated SURF feature points are predominantly less than five degrees, as shown in Figure 3b. We considered that the integral image and Haar wavelet-based SURF orientation descriptor is more robust to the blurring and luminance change in the screen-cam process than a Gaussian image and histogram-based SIFT orientation descriptor.

Figure 2. Host images: Lena, Baboon, Airplane, Peppers, Building, Pentagon, White House, and Naval Base.

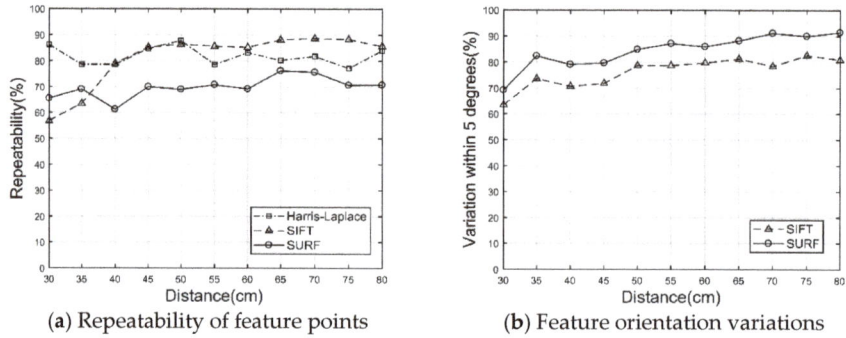

(a) Repeatability of feature points

(b) Feature orientation variations

Figure 3. The variations of feature points in screen-cam process.

Therefore, in our method, a modified Harris–Laplace detector and SURF orientation descriptor are integrated to construct the RST invariant LFRs. To increase the detection rate of feature points during the screen-cam process, we also employ a Gaussian function.

In previous LFR-based methods, circular feature regions are commonly constructed. These regions will involve zero-padding [43] or rearrangement [46] to a square region before message embedding, which will cause further distortions [47]. Therefore, we directly construct LSFRs. Figure 4 illustrates the subprocesses. The details are as follows.

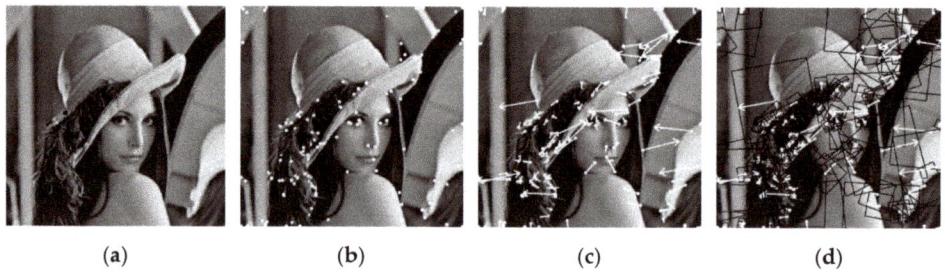

(a) (b) (c) (d)

Figure 4. The construction process of local square feature regions in 1024 × 1024 Lena image. (a) Luminance image of Lena after a Gaussian function. (b) The extracted feature points by modified Harris–Laplace. (c) The associated orientation. (d) The associated LSFRs.

3.1.1. Gaussian Function Preprocess

In the embedding and extraction processes, the detection of feature points will be performed on the Gaussian filtered images. A two-dimensional Gaussian function $G(x,y)$ is obtained by the product of two one-dimensional Gaussian functions and can be defined as:

$$G(x,y) = \frac{1}{2\pi\sigma^2} e^{-\frac{x^2+y^2}{2\sigma^2}} \quad (1)$$

where σ is the standard deviation. The Gaussian kernel H_G, whose sigma is set to 2 and window size to 7, is employed here. The image convolution process is defined as:

$$I'(x,y) = H_G * I(x,y) \quad (2)$$

where I is the input image and I' is the convolution result. $*$ denotes the convolution operator.

3.1.2. Modified Harris–Laplace Detector

The Harris–Laplace detector proposed by Mikolajczyk and Schmid [48,49] has been extensively employed in different watermarking schemes. Therefore, here we give a brief description of it, and the modified part will be explained in detail.

First, Harris points are detected in the scale space. To obtain the invariance to scale variation, we built a scale-space representation with the Harris function for preselected scales. The Harris detector is based on a specific image descriptor, which is referred to as the second moment matrix, and reflects the local distribution of gradient directions in the image [50]. To make the matrix independent of the image resolution, the scale-adapted second moment matrix is defined by:

$$M(x,y,\sigma_I,\sigma_D) = \sigma_D^2 G(\sigma_I) * \begin{bmatrix} L_x^2(x,y,\sigma_D) & L_xL_y(x,y,\sigma_D) \\ L_xL_y(x,y,\sigma_D) & L_y^2(x,y,\sigma_D) \end{bmatrix} \quad (3)$$

where σ_I and σ_D are the integration scale and local scale, respectively, and L is the derivative computed in an associated direction by a Gaussian. Given σ_D, the uniform Gaussian multiscale space representation L is defined by:

$$L(x,y,\sigma_D) = G(x,y,\sigma_D) * I' \quad (4)$$

where G is the associated uniform Gaussian kernel with a standard deviation σ_D and a mean of zero.

Given σ_I and σ_D, the scale-adapted Harris corner strength *cornerness* used to quantitatively describe the stability under variations in imaging conditions can be computed. The original *cornerness* measure function needs an empirical parameter, which may float for different images. Therefore, in this paper, we will adopt another *cornerness* measure function, that is, the Alison Noble measure [51]:

$$cornerness(x,y,\sigma_I,\sigma_D) = \det(M(x,y,\sigma_I,\sigma_D))/(\text{trace}(M(x,y,\sigma_I,\sigma_D)) + eps) \quad (5)$$

where $\det(\cdot)$ and $\text{trace}(\cdot)$ denote computation of the determinant of the matrix and the trace of the matrix, respectively. *eps* is the smallest integer to ensure that the denominator is nonzero. The feature points obtained by this method are more robust under variations in imaging conditions [51].

At each level of the scale space, the candidate points are extracted as follows:

$$\begin{cases} cornerness(x,y,\sigma_I,\sigma_D) > cornerness(\hat{x},\hat{y},\sigma_I,\sigma_D) & \forall (\hat{x},\hat{y}) \in A \\ cornerness(x,y,\sigma_I,\sigma_D) > t_n \end{cases} \quad (6)$$

where A represents the points within the $3\sigma_I$ radius neighborhood, and t_n is the threshold, which is $0.1 \cdot \max(cornerness_I)$.

The automatic scale selection of the feature points is performed. To select the characteristic scale of the local structure, a scale-normalized derivative LoG operator is defined as:

$$\text{LoG}(x,y,\sigma_I) = \sigma_I^2 |L_{xx}(x,y,\sigma_I) + L_{yy}(x,y,\sigma_I)| \quad (7)$$

where L_{xx} and L_{yy} are second partial derivatives with respect to x and y, respectively.

For each candidate point, we apply an iterative method to determine the location and scale of the feature points. Given the initial point p with the scale σ_I, the iteration steps are presented as follows.

Step (1) Find the local extremum over the scale of LoG for the point p_k; otherwise, reject the point. The investigated range of scales is limited to $\sigma_I^{(k+1)} = t \cdot \sigma_I^{(k)}$ with $t \in [0.7,\ldots,1.4]$.

Step (2) Detect the spatial point p_{k+1} of a maximum of the SHCS closest to p_k for the selected $\sigma_I^{(k+1)}$.

Step (3) Go to step 1 if $\sigma_I^{(k+1)} \neq \sigma_I^{(k)}$ or $p_{k+1} \neq p_k$.

3.1.3. SURF Orientation Descriptor

To obtain the invariance to the rotation, each feature point will be assigned a direction based on the SURF orientation descriptor. We calculate the Haar wavelet response on the selected circle region of the integral image, which is centered at the feature points and is six times the feature scale as the radius. The Gaussian weighting function, for which σ is two times the feature scale, is used to Gaussian weight the response of the Haar wavelet.

To obtain the dominant orientation, we calculate the sum of all responses within a sliding orientation window of size $\pi/3$. By summing the horizontal and vertical responses within the window, the vector (m_w, θ_w) can be obtained, which is defined as:

$$m_w = \sum_w \mathrm{d}\,x + \sum_w \mathrm{d}\,y \tag{8}$$

$$\theta_w = \arctan\left(\sum_w \mathrm{d}\,x / \sum_w \mathrm{d}\,y\right) \tag{9}$$

where m_w is the summarized responses, and θ_w is the associated orientation. The dominant orientation θ is defined as:

$$\theta = \theta_w | \max\{m_w\} \tag{10}$$

3.1.4. LSFRs for Watermarking

Considering the severe distortion during the screen-cam process, the constructed LSFRs should have a sufficient range to ensure that information can survive. Thus, the feature points with appropriate scale and location are selected, and the side length L_0 of LSFR is designed as:

$$L_0 = 2 \cdot \mathrm{floor}(k_1 \cdot s) + 1 \tag{11}$$

where k_1 is a constant coefficient, and s is the feature scale value.

In Figure 5, are shown the LSFRs for the 8-image test set. Because the watermark information will be embedded in the DFT coefficients, according to its characteristics, the following two situations are also feasible. When a small part of the candidate LSFR exists outside the image, shown in Figure 5f, or when a small part of the two LSFRs overlapped, shown in Figure 5g, these LSFRs can also be utilized as embedding areas.

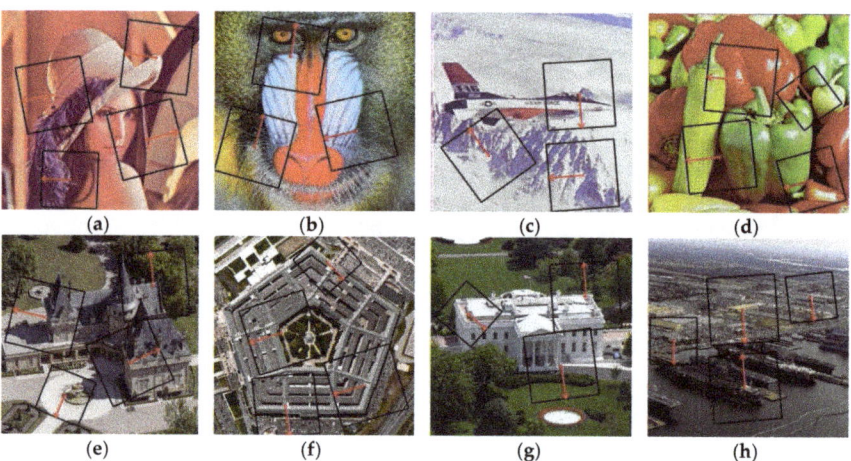

Figure 5. The selected local square feature regions (LSFRs) for watermark embedding of eight host images.

3.2. Watermark Embedding

3.2.1. Selection of Embedding Operations

As discussed in Section 3.1, there is an inevitable shift in the corresponding positions between the corrected image and the original image. Fortunately, due to the nature of DFT coefficients in image translation, the coefficients of captured images can be corrected to correspond to the original image, if the four corners are carefully selected to avoid too much rotation and scaling distortions after perspective rectification. Therefore, it is advantageous to select the DFT domain for embedding a watermark message.

In order to use DFT coefficients as a watermark carrier, we need to analyze their variation rules in the screen-cam process first. The variations of the DFT magnitude coefficients with different shooting conditions were analyzed in detail. As mid-frequency coefficients are commonly employed as watermark carriers, we take the mid-frequency spectrum of 512 × 512 sized Lena image and the variation after screen-cam as an example to illustrate the details of their variation rules, as shown in Figure 6. The axis scale value is the coordinate in the spectrum of the original image.

We find that most of the magnitude coefficients with high values are well preserved. For example, (301, 299), (301, 300), (302, 304), and other points of deep warm color in Figure 6. Furthermore, the magnitude coefficients with low values commonly vary to become higher values. In general, the more blurred the image is, the higher the magnitude coefficients with low values will increase. Examples of this are the points (297, 305), (300, 296), and (302, 303) in Figure 6.

The changes can be summarized as blew. In the mid-frequency bands, the magnitude coefficients with high values are well preserved during the screen-cam process, while those with low values commonly become higher values to approximate their adjacent magnitude values. Therefore, we choose mid-frequency bands and embed the message by modifying the selected magnitude coefficients to higher values.

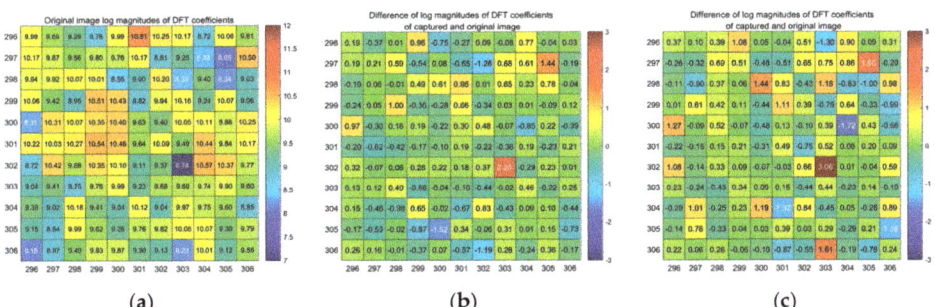

Figure 6. Detailed variations of discrete Fourier transform (DFT) coefficient magnitudes during screen-cam process. (**a**): Original image spectrum in the log domain. (**b**,**c**): Difference in log DFT magnitudes of original image and captured image at a vertical distance of 30 and 50 cm.

3.2.2. Message Embedding

Figure 7 illustrates the embedding process. Each selected LSFR is treated as an independent communication channel, and the same watermark message will be embedded in every LSFR. Compared with the DCT-based method in [33], which embeds the message in the sub-blocks of feature regions, the proposed DFT-based method takes each LSFR as a whole, it has better robustness against cropping attacks.

To avoid the LSFR from being further distorted during the rotation process of orientation normalization, we designed a non-rotating embedding method based on the properties of the DFT coefficients. Furthermore, to improve extraction accuracy, a preprocessing method of DFT magnitude coefficients is proposed. Specific steps are as follows.

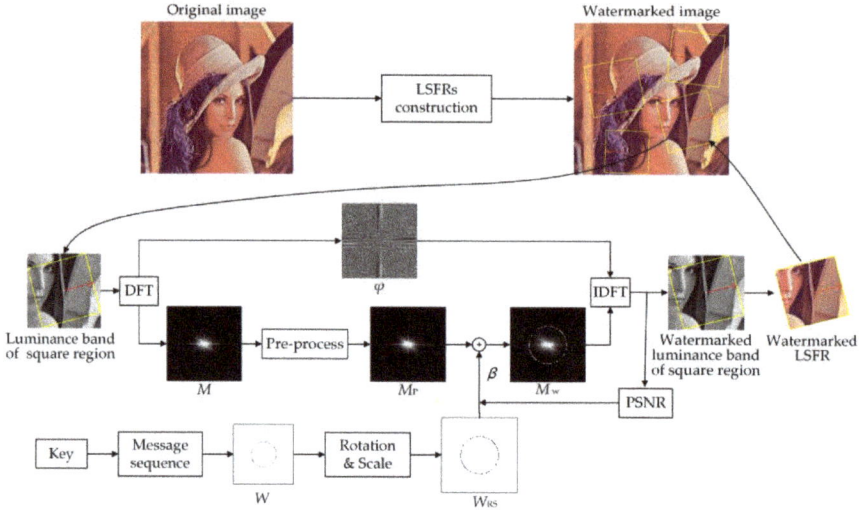

Figure 7. Framework of watermark embedding process.

First, the minimum square regions that contain the LSFRs to be embedded are extracted in order. The luminance band of this area is converted to the DFT domain.

Second, for the watermark information, the pseudorandom sequence $W = \{w(i) | w(i) \in \{-1, 1\}, t = 0, \ldots, l-1\}$ is generated by the secret key, where l is the size of the sequence. In order to achieve blind detection that can cope with the situation where the original size is unknown, the embedding radius R of W is set to a fixed value. Correspondingly, the embedding radius R_1 of W_{RS} is defined as:

$$R_1 = \text{round}\left(\frac{L_1}{L_0} \cdot R\right) \qquad (12)$$

where R_1 is the embedded radius of the square region and L_1 is the side length of the square region. According to the characteristics of the DFT coefficients, which is centrosymmetric, we can have 180 degrees as embedding region. The coordinates $W_{RS}(x_i, y_i)$ of the message embedding position in the square region are defined as:

$$\begin{aligned} x_i &= \tfrac{L_0+1}{2} + \text{floor}\left[R_1 \cdot \cos\left(\tfrac{j}{l} \cdot \pi + \theta_d\right)\right] \\ y_i &= \tfrac{L_0+1}{2} + \text{floor}\left[R_1 \cdot \sin\left(\tfrac{j}{l} \cdot \pi + \theta_d\right)\right] \end{aligned} \qquad (13)$$

where j is the j-th element of W. Therefore, the elements of the message $W(x_i, y_i)$ are equally spaced around the center of the embedding region. θ_d defines the angle between the feature orientation of the LSFR and the normalized orientation.

Third, to obtain a better detection rate, the magnitudes M need to be preprocessed before the signal embedding. In theory, the more obvious the difference between the magnitudes, where the watermark embedded information is "1" and "−1", the better the message extraction results. Considering the various rules of the magnitudes during the screen-cam process, we need to avoid high magnitude values at the positions that represent the watermark information "−1". Therefore, some extreme high magnitude values of these positions and their neighborhoods need to be reduced. For a normal distribution, nearly 84% of the values are less than the sum of the mean and one standard deviation. Hence, the preprocess is defined as follows:

$$m_p(x,y) = \begin{cases} \overline{m}_p + \sigma_p & if \ m_p(x,y) > \overline{m}_p + \sigma_p \\ no\ change & otherwise \end{cases} \quad (14)$$

where $m_p(x,y)$ defines all magnitudes of the positions that represent the watermark information "−1" and their eight neighbor magnitudes, and $\overline{m}_p$ and σ_p define the mean value and the standard deviation of these magnitudes, respectively.

The watermark signal is embedded in preprocessed magnitudes M_P using the following equation:

$$M_w(x,y) = \begin{cases} \overline{m}_p + \beta \cdot \sigma_p & if \ W_{RS}(x,y) = 1 \\ no\ change & if \ W_{RS}(x,y) = -1 \end{cases} \quad (15)$$

where $M_w(x,y)$ define the watermarked magnitudes and β the embedding strength. We provide an initial value $\beta = 0.1R$, which is set based on experience and adjust the value by the calculated peak signal to noise ratio (PSNR) index. If the PSNR value is less than 42 dB, the β will be reduced by 0.2. Iterate this process until the PSNR value is higher than 42 dB.

Last, M_W is combined with φ, which is converted to the watermarked luminance band of the square region and then transformed to the spatial domain. Only the pixel values within the LSFR are replaced. The result is a watermarked LSFR.

After all selected LSFRs are embedded, the embedding process is completed.

3.3. Watermark Detection

Figure 8 illustrates the watermark detection process, which can be divided into the following three steps: perspective correction, candidate regions locating, and message extraction.

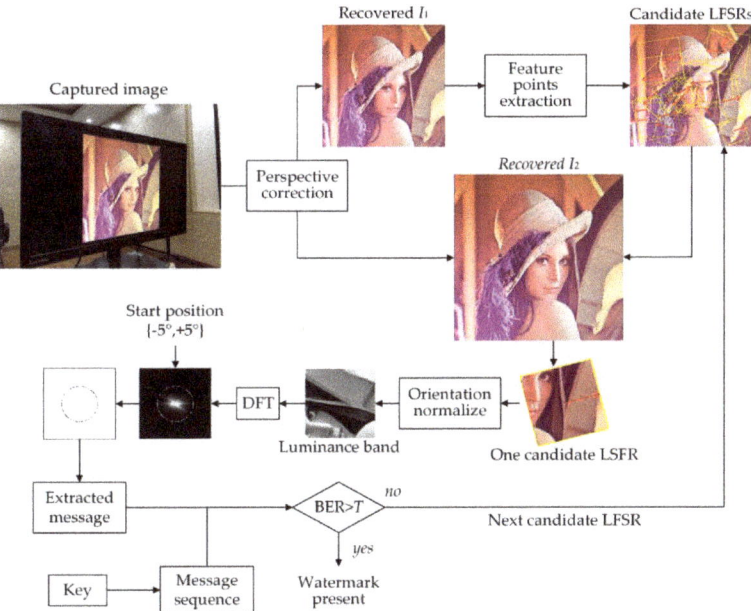

Figure 8. Framework of watermark detection process.

3.3.1. Perspective Correction

Because different shooting angles and distances will cause perspective distortion, we need to correct it and extract the needed portion from the captured images. The perspective correction function can be written as:

$$\begin{bmatrix} x' \\ y' \\ 1 \end{bmatrix} = H \begin{bmatrix} x \\ y \\ 1 \end{bmatrix}, \text{ where } H = \begin{bmatrix} m_{11} & m_{12} & m_{13} \\ m_{21} & m_{22} & m_{23} \\ m_{31} & m_{32} & m_{33} \end{bmatrix} \qquad (16)$$

where $[x', y', 1]^T$ and $[x, y, 1]^T$ define the homogeneous point coordinates of the corrected image and the photo, respectively. H defines a nonsingular 3×3 homogeneous matrix. According to the formula, the matrix has eight degrees of freedom (DOF). Therefore, at least four sets of points are required to calculate H.

We manually select the four needed vertices from the captured image. As the proposed watermarking scheme is designed for leak tracking, manual selection is acceptable. Since the watermark synchronization method is robust to scaling, the images do not have to be recovered to the original pixel size. In theory, without knowing the original size of the image or if the image has been cropped, we can also choose to use the four vertices of the screen to help with perspective correction, as shown in Figure 9. We at least need to know the size or aspect ratio of the screen, or the aspect ratio of the image if it has not been cropped.

Because smartphones have high-megapixel cameras, the pixels of the captured image are commonly substantially larger than the original image. To fully utilize the captured information, a judgment based on the shortest distance between the four points is made before the correction. If it is larger than 1500 pixels, the image will be recovered to two different sizes. By recovering to the original size, if known, or a relatively minor size, the recovered image I_1 is used to calculate the candidate LSFRs, which also accelerates the calculation. The image is recovered based on the shortest distance between two of the four vertices, as shown in Figure 9. The recovered image I_2 is used for message extraction. Otherwise, only one image will be recovered.

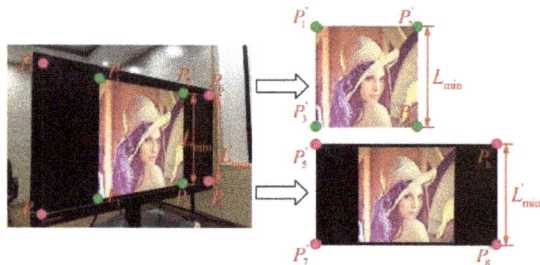

Figure 9. Schematic diagram of correction process.

3.3.2. Candidate Regions Locating

The calculation process of the candidate LSFRs is the same as the embedding process, which will be performed on I_1. The Gaussian function is performed first to reduce the impact of a noise attack. The feature points and associated orientation are calculated. To avoid missing detection, all feature points that may be used for watermark synchronization are selected based on scale and spatial location. We obtain the candidate LSFR set of I_1. The corresponding regions are extracted from I_2 for message extraction.

3.3.3. Message Extraction

Watermark detection is an iterative search for candidate LSFRs. As long as watermark information is detected in one LSFR, the watermark detection of the captured image is completed. Each time, one candidate LFSR is orientation normalized and discrete Fourier transformed. According to the nature of the DFT coefficients, although we do not know the original size, the radius of watermark locations will not vary as long as the area corresponding to the feature scale has not varied. However, the feature scale and its corresponding area will vary slightly, resulting in a slight variation in the radius of watermark locations. Therefore, the searching area will be between $R_i \in (R-10, R+10)$ at a step of 1 pixel. Besides, we also need to consider the variation in the feature orientation. As we have investigated in Section 3.1, the orientation variation is primarily less than five degrees. Therefore, the starting position is between $\left(-5°, +5°\right)$ of the initial position at each radius R_i at a step of one degree.

The correction of perspective distortion will inevitably cause some shift of the coefficients and imperfections in resampling. This results in a variation in the coefficient of the adjacent point. An example is shown in Figure 10. In addition, because the feature orientation will vary, the starting position cannot be located directly. Therefore, each time, the maximum magnitude value of the candidate positions and their neighborhoods are extracted to obtain the message V.

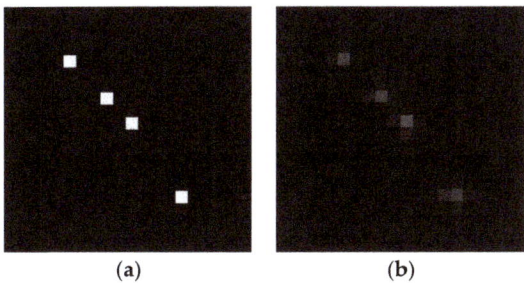

Figure 10. Magnitude coefficients before (**a**) and after (**b**) screen-cam.

Based on local statistical feature, the extracted message w is defined as:

$$w(i) = \begin{cases} 1 & if\ V(i) \geq \overline{M}_w + k_2 \sigma_w \\ -1 & if\ V(i) < \overline{M}_w + k_2 \sigma_w \end{cases} \quad (17)$$

where $\overline{M}_w$ and σ_w define the mean value and the standard deviation of all the magnitudes in the range of $\{R_i - 2, R_i + 2\}$. $V(i)$ is the extracted maximum value within 3×3 magnitudes, k_2 is a parameter used to determine the threshold for message extraction.

The extracted w is compared with the pseudorandom sequence W generated by the secret key to calculate the number of erroneous bits. The watermark detection is positive if the number of erroneous bits is below the predefined threshold T. If the detection is negative, the iterative process continues.

4. Parameter Settings

For demonstration and experimental purposes, the watermark length l is set to 60, which can be considered a reasonable message length for real use cases. Based on this, we designed a series of experiments to select the most appropriate values for the parameters mentioned above.

4.1. The Selection of Embedding Radius

The magnitudes at different embedding radii R have different variation rules which affect the robustness of the algorithm. Considering the imperceptibility of the algorithm, the embedding strength β can vary according to different embedding radii.

To select the most suitable embedding radius for the algorithm, we designed an experiment. The eight host images are resized to 241 × 241, which can be treated as an LSFR. We generate the watermark information with the key K_1, where totality of 32 watermark bits is "1".

Based on the discussion in Section 3.3.3, the embedding radius should be no less than 55 to avoid the watermark bits being too close affecting each other. According to the method in Section 3.2.2, the DFT magnitudes of the experiment images are preprocessed first. Then, watermark information is embedded at different radii for all images based on Equation 15. The PSNR value of the watermarked images is controlled to be around 42 dB by adjusting the embedding strength. The relationship between embedding radius R and the average embedding strength β is shown in Figure 11a. With the increase in the embedding radius, the embedding strength can be increased.

In order to compare the variation of the watermarked magnitudes in different radii and at different shooting distances, we designed an index $K_{r,d}$ as an evaluation indicator to describe the significance of watermark information. Because only the magnitudes of the positions where watermark bit is "1" are modified, $K_{r,d}$ only need to consider the modified magnitudes. According to Equation (17), it is defined as:

$$K_{r,d} = \frac{\sum_1^{32}\left(m_{c(r,i)} - \overline{M_w}\right)}{32 \cdot \sigma_w} \tag{18}$$

where $K_{r,d}$ defines the index of the image captured at the distance of d with embedding radius r. $m_{c(r,i)}$ defines the magnitude in i-th position where watermark bit is "1" in the captured image with embedding radius r.

The relationship between the average of calculated $K_{r,d}$ and different shooting distances with different embedding radii is shown in Figure 11b. When the shooting distance is close to the screen, the watermark information with a larger embedding radius is more significant due to the higher embedding strength. However, the captured details of the watermark will be less and less as the shooting distance increases, so the higher frequency band coefficients will be poorly preserved. When the embedding radius is 56 and 60, the watermark information can be better preserved at different shooting distances. Considering the real scene, in order to better capture the image displayed on the screen, we usually shoot at 40 to 60 cm. At these distances, results with an embedding radius of 60 are better. Therefore, R is set to 60 in our experiment.

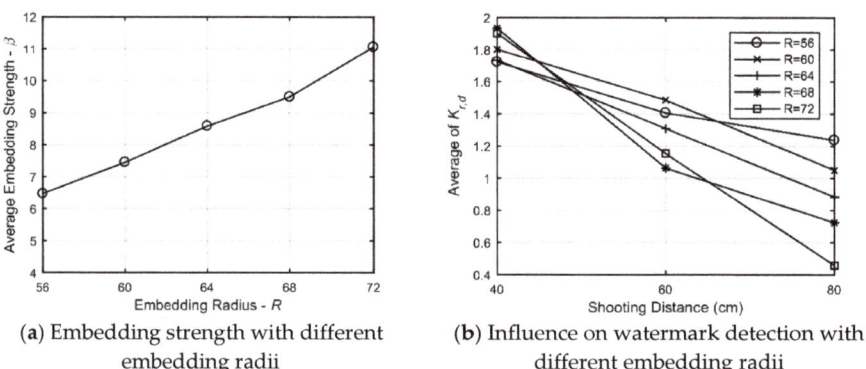

(a) Embedding strength with different embedding radii

(b) Influence on watermark detection with different embedding radii

Figure 11. Influence of different embedding radii.

4.2. The Selection of the Size and Number of LSFRs

The size and number of LSFRs determine the robustness of the proposed algorithm. Besides, the size of the constructed LSFRs determines the number of them. According to Equation (11), the size and number of constructed LSFRs in our experiment are determined by k_1.

The 60 images from the database [52] are resized to 1024 × 1024 as experiment images here. We statistically analyzed the average number of constructed LSFRs with different k_1. In theory, the larger and the greater the number of LSFRs, the better the robustness of the algorithm. Therefore, we also count the number of constructed LSFRs with side lengths of 240–300 and the number of constructed LSFRs with side lengths greater than 300, as shown in Table 1. When k_1 is set to 6 and 6.5, the most LSFRs with side lengths greater than 300 can be constructed, and the total number can also satisfy the requirements. Therefore, k_1 is set to 6.5 in our experiment.

Table 1. Average number of constructed LSFRs with a different k_1.

k_1	4.5	5	5.5	6	6.5	7	7.5	8	8.5	9
Side length between 240 and 300	3.78	3.62	3.53	0.88	0.88	1.32	1.77	1.77	0.88	0.88
Side length over 300	0.00	0.00	0.00	2.65	2.65	2.20	1.77	1.77	1.77	1.77
Total	3.78	3.62	3.53	3.53	3.53	3.52	3.53	3.53	2.65	2.65

4.3. The Selection of the Threshold for Message Extraction

According to Equation (17), k_2 determines the threshold for message extraction, which will affect the success rate and validity of watermark information extraction. We performed a statistical analysis of the extraction results of the 29 LSFRs constructed from the eight host images with and without watermarks to select the most appropriate threshold. The experiment was set at a shooting angle of 0, 15, and 30 degrees and a shooting distance from 40 to 110 cm at intervals of 10 cm. Therefore, each LSFR was captured 24 times with different shooting conditions.

Based on the extraction method in Section 3.3.3, a total of 696 results of watermarked LSFRs and 648 results of unwatermarked LSFRs were obtained. The average erroneous bits with a different k_2 is shown in Figure 12a. The extraction results of watermarked LSFRs achieve the minimum erroneous bits when k_2 is set to 1. The distributions of erroneous bits with $k_2 = 1$ are shown in Figure 12b. The average of detected erroneous bits of unwatermarked LSFRs is around nineteen which is independent of k_2. Therefore, k_2 is set to 1 in our experiment.

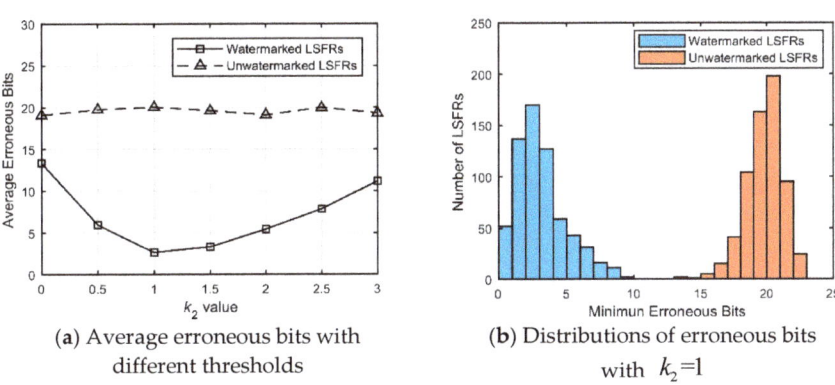

(a) Average erroneous bits with different thresholds
(b) Distributions of erroneous bits with $k_2=1$

Figure 12. Erroneous bits corresponding to different message extraction thresholds.

4.4. The Selection of the Threshold for Watermark Detection

The selection of the threshold T determines the false-positive rate and the true-positive rate. T needs to be set low enough to ensure that the watermark can be detected from watermarked LSFRs and high enough to ensure that the watermark cannot be detected from unwatermarked LSFRs.

Messages extracted from an unwatermarked image can be considered as independent random variables [43]. Therefore, the probability that a single bit match is 0.5. The relationship between the false-positive rate of single detection P_f and the threshold T is:

$$P_f = \sum_{i=l-T}^{l} (0.5)^l \cdot \left(\frac{l!}{i!(l-i)!} \right) \tag{19}$$

As mentioned in Section 3.3.3, each LSFR will be iteratively detected at different radii and angles. The maximum number of iterations is 231 times. Suppose we complete all iterative detection, the false-positive rate of the detection of one LSFR P'_f is:

$$P'_f = 1 - \left(1 - P_f\right)^{231} \tag{20}$$

The false-positive rate curve with different thresholds is shown in Figure 13a. In order to choose an appropriate threshold, we further analyzed the influence of different secret keys and different host images on the positive detection rate. The eight host images were all embedded with other three different keys: K_2, K_3, K_4. Each watermarked image was captured 24 times with different shooting conditions. The experimental setting is the same as in Section 4.3.

Based on the 768 detection results of watermarked images with four different keys, eight different host images, and 24 different shooting conditions, we can calculate the true-positive rate with different thresholds. The true-positive rate curves between different keys and different host images are shown in Figure 13b,c. The true-positive rate can be seen to be stable for different embedding messages. However, different images have different variations during screen-cam, so the true-positive rate is also different when T is below 10.

According to the result, we set threshold T to 8, which means when the number of erroneous bits is below 8, the detection is successful. According to Formula 20, the false-positive rate of the detection of one LSFR is 8.86×10^{-8}. The true-positive rate with K_1, K_2, K_3 and K_4 is 98.44%, 96.88%, 97.40%, and 96.35%, respectively. Furthermore, the true-positive rate of the eight host images is 100%, 92.71%, 97.92%, 100%, 94.79%, 100%, 93.75%, and 98.96%, respectively.

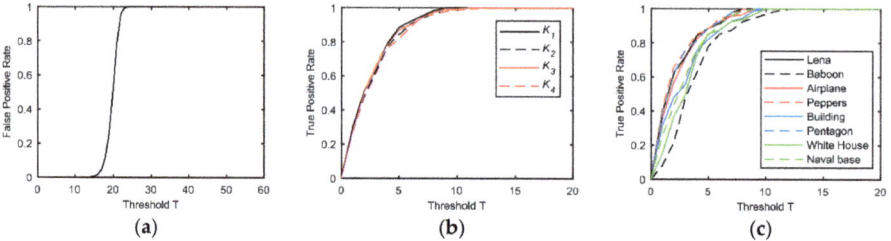

Figure 13. Influence of different thresholds on (**a**) false-positive rate of one LSFR and on true-positive rate between different (**b**) keys and (**c**) images.

5. Experimental Results and Analysis

We conducted a series of experiments to verify the robustness of the algorithm. Robustness refers to the ability to detect the watermark after the designated class of transformations [53]. Bit Error Ratio (BER) is a commonly used metrics to measure the robustness of watermarking methods. BER is defined as:

$$\text{BER}(W, w) = \frac{n_e}{l} \tag{21}$$

where n_e is the number of erroneous bits. A lower BER indicates the extracted results are closer to the original watermark information, which means the better robustness. Since the threshold T for watermark detection is set to 8, and the watermark length *l* is set to 60 in our method, this means that watermark detection is successful when BER is below 0.1333.

In Section 5.1, the robustness to common image attacks is discussed. In Section 5.2, the proposed scheme is compared with two state-of-the-art schemes and the performance against screen-cam attack is analyzed in detail. In Section 5.3, considering real-life scenarios, some hypothetical scenarios were designed to verify the robustness of the algorithm.

The experimental instruments are as follows: The display device in this scenario is a 23-inch monitor with 1920 × 1080 pixels. Since the ordinary users' monitors are not accurately corrected, to mimic a real-world scenario, the monitors are not explicitly calibrated. An iPhone X with dual 12 MP pixels is used as the photography equipment. The lens is well focused while shooting, and shooting quality is controlled as much as possible.

The host images are the eight images in Figure 2. The PSNR values of each square region that contains an LSFR are controlled to be no less than 39 dB in our experiment. Figure 14 shows the corresponding watermarked images generated by the proposed method.

Figure 14. Watermarked images.

5.1. Robustness against Common Image Attacks

To prove that the algorithm also has excellent robustness against common image attacks without screen-cam attack, we performed corresponding experiments. The results are shown in Table 2, and the PSNR and mean structural similarity index (MSSIM) [54] values are also listed.

The robustness primarily depends on whether feature points and watermarking information can be simultaneously detected. As shown in Table 2, the algorithm is robust to JPEG attacks, which can mostly survive at a JPEG of 20%. Because scale attacks cause the frame to shrink, we restore the scaled images before detection. The algorithm works when under a scaling 0.5 attack and basically works when under a scaling 0.4 attack. For cropping-off attacks, which refer to a continuous crop from the right in this section, assuming more than one relatively complete embedded LSFR exists, the detection can be successful in theory. Due to the fact that the watermark is repeatedly embedded in each LSFR, we can detect the watermark information at a cropping-off 50% attack in the experiments. The rotation attack may cause the loss of feature points since we only need at least one successful detection, and the algorithm is also effective. The algorithm also works at a median filter 3 × 3 attack. Thus, our watermarking scheme has excellent robustness to common image attacks.

Table 2. Performance of image quality and robustness against common attacks.

	Host Image	Lena	Baboon	Airplane	Peppers	Building	Pentagon	White House	Naval Base
	PSNR (dB)	42.3166	44.0559	43.7674	43.0367	42.4984	43.4840	44.1091	42.7127
	MSSIM	0.9544	0.9831	0.9659	0.9564	0.9733	0.9890	0.9839	0.9894
	JPEG 40%	0	0.0667	0	0.0833	0.0667	0.0333	0.0333	0.1000
	JPEG 30%	0	0.0833	0	0.1167	0.0833	0.0500	0.0500	0.0833
	JPEG 20%	0	0.0667	0	0.2833	0.0500	0.0333	0.1167	0.1167
	JPEG 10%	0.0667	0.2333	0.1500	0.4167	0.1333	0.1000	0.2500	0.2167
	Scaling 0.6	0	0.0500	0	0.0333	0.0833	0.0500	0.0333	0.0333
	Scaling 0.5	0	0.0500	0	0.0500	0.0500	0.0667	0.0333	0.0500
	Scaling 0.4	0	0.0333	0	0.2167	0.1167	0.0500	0.0333	0.0833
	Scaling 0.3	0.1667	0.4000	0.3500	0.4500	0.4500	0.4667	0.4667	0.3500
BER	Cropping-off 20%	0	0	0	0	0	0	0	0
	Cropping-off 30%	0	0	0	0	0	0	0	0
	Cropping-off 40%	0	0	0	0	0	0	0	0
	Cropping-off 50%	0	0	0	0	0	0	0	0
	Rotation 15°	0	0	0	0	0	0	0	0
	Rotation 30°	0	0	0	0	0	0	0	0
	Rotation 45°	0	0	0	0	0	0	0	0
	Rotation 90°	0	0	0	0	0	0	0	0
	Median filter 3 × 3	0	0.0667	0	0.0333	0.0333	0.0333	0.0333	0.0667
	Median filter 5 × 5	0.0667	0.1500	0.0500	0.4500	0.2667	0.3000	0.4000	0.2833

Note: The underlined coefficient represents failed detection.

5.2. Robustness against Screen-Cam

In this section, we verify the robustness against a screen-cam attack. First, we compare the proposed method with two existing algorithms [21,33]. Since the size of the host images used in their articles is different from this one, we use the same host images here. In order to improve the independence of the experimental results to the host images, we use additional twelve images from the database [52] to verify the performance. The PSNR values of the images generated by the proposed method are controlled to be not lower than by other methods, which are at around 42 dB. An example of Lena embedded with different methods is shown in Table 3. All the watermarked images are displayed on the screen at the original resolution. The comparison of BER for different shooting conditions is shown in Figure 15. The result shows method [21] designed for print-cam is not applicable for screen-cam process, and the proposed method and method [33] both have good robustness against screen-cam attack.

Table 3. Images generated by different methods.

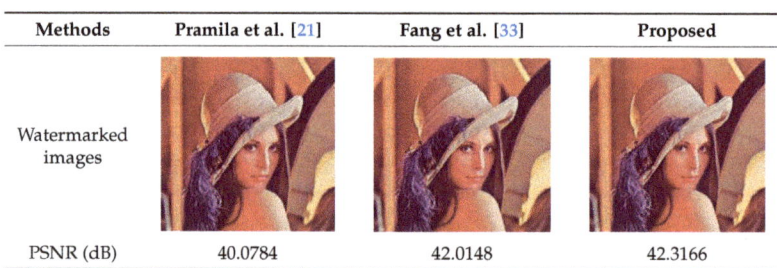

Methods	Pramila et al. [21]	Fang et al. [33]	Proposed
Watermarked images			
PSNR (dB)	40.0784	42.0148	42.3166

In theory, without considering external interference, the distortion caused by shooting from the horizontal left and horizontal right is similar. Shooting at different vertical angles is also similar to shooting at different horizontal angles with a 90-degree rotation of the image. Therefore, as shown in Figure 16, the shooting angle is set from being perpendicular to the screen up to 60 degrees of horizontal left at intervals of fifteen degrees. The shooting distance is set from 40 to 110 cm at intervals of 10 cm. When the shooting angle is 45 or 60, the shooting distance of 40 cm is too small to capture the entire image. Therefore, the distance is selected to be over 50 cm.

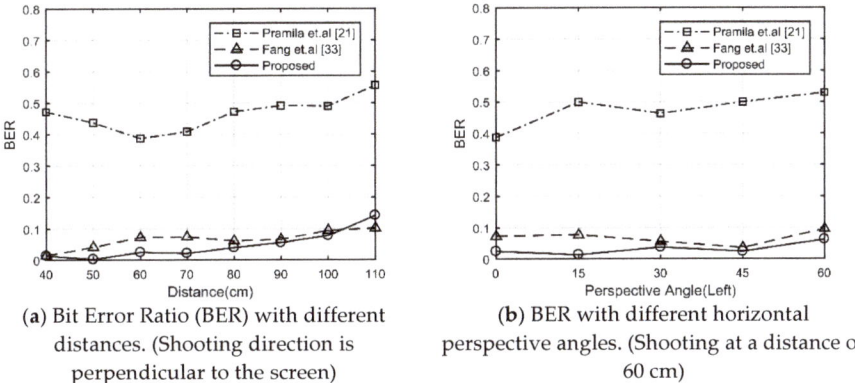

(a) Bit Error Ratio (BER) with different distances. (Shooting direction is perpendicular to the screen)

(b) BER with different horizontal perspective angles. (Shooting at a distance of 60 cm)

Figure 15. Comparison of different methods for different shooting conditions.

The example of Lena images recovered from captured images with different angles and distances and their detected BER by the secret key K_1 are shown in Table 4. The detection results of eight images are shown in Figure 16, where the red mark indicates the camera position relative to the screen and the dotted straight line indicates the shooting direction.

Table 4. Examples of Lena recovered from different captured images.

Horizontal Angle (Left)	Distance							
	40 cm	50 cm	60 cm	70 cm	80 cm	90 cm	100 cm	110 cm
0°								
BER	0	0	0	0	0.0333	0.0500	0.0500	0.1167
15°								
BER	0.0167	0	0	0	0.0333	0.0167	0.0167	0.0500
30°								
BER	0.0167	0	0	0.0167	0	0.0167	0.0167	0.0667
45°								
BER		0	0	0	0.1000	0.1167	0.1167	0.1833
60°								
BER		0.1000	0.0500	0.0667	0.2000	0.1667	0.3333	0.2833

As shown in Figure 16, when the horizontal shooting angle is lower than 30 degrees, watermarks are mostly detected successfully. When the horizontal shooting angle is 45 degrees, the watermark can be detected within a shooting distance of 90 or 100 cm. For a large shooting angle of 60 degrees, the image cannot be well focused. Thus, the watermark information can commonly be detected within a closer shooting distance, which is approximately 70 or 80 cm.

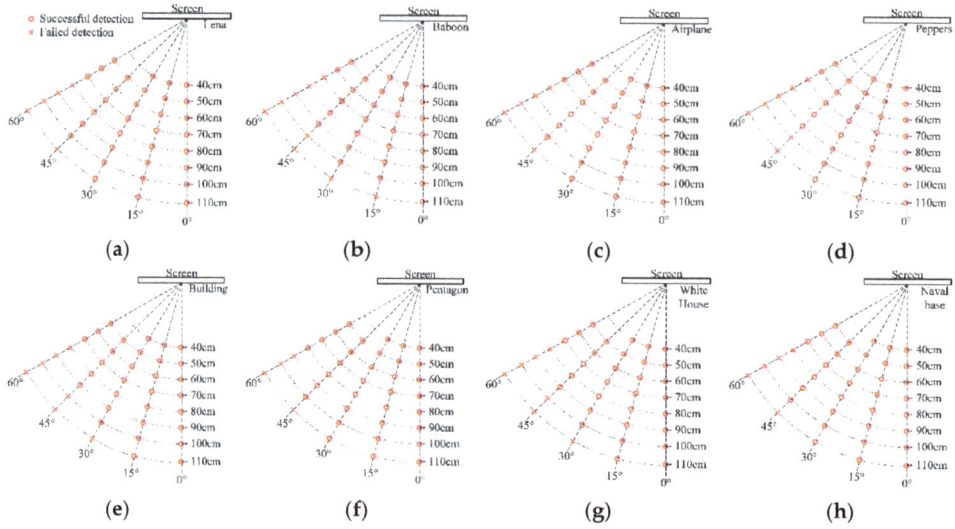

Figure 16. Watermark detection results against screen-cam attack. (**a**) Lena. (**b**) Baboon. (**c**) Airplane (**d**) Peppers. (**e**) Building. (**f**) Pentagon. (**g**) White House. (**h**) Naval base.

We also tested the performance at other tilt shooting angles with a handhold shooting, as shown in Table 5; it also has excellent performance. Therefore, the proposed algorithm is robust to a screen-cam attack.

Table 5. Examples of Handhold Shooting.

Handhold Scenarios	Example 1	Example 2	Example 3	Example 4
Captured image				
Recovered image				
BER	0.0167	0	0.0667	0.0833

5.3. Robustness against Screen-Cam with Additional Common Attacks

The scheme in [33] needs to record the four vertices, which means it needs to know the original size. Furthermore, the scheme in [21] cannot deal with the cropping attack. However, in a real-life scenario, images may under common image processing attacks caused by normal user operations. Therefore, we experimented with several hypothetical scenarios to verify the effectiveness of the proposed algorithm for screen-cam with additional common attacks. We designed four realistic application scenarios where method [21,33] are not applicable: (a) the Lena image is blocked by the window at 20 percent, which is equal to being cropped; (b) the Peppers image is rotated five degrees and cropped; (c) the Building image is scaled by 80%; (d) the Pentagon image is scaled by 80% and rotated 90 degrees counterclockwise. An example of the four scenarios is shown in Table 6. When doing the watermark detection, assume that we do not know the specifics of the attacks, which means we do not correct the image to its original scale or original orientation manually. The coordinate points that are used for perspective correction are denoted in Table 6 as red dots.

Table 6. Examples of Four Hypothetical Scenarios.

Hypothetical Scenario	Scenario (a)	Scenario (b)	Scenario (c)	Scenario (d)
Captured image				
Recovered image				

Figure 17 shows the detection results of the four scenarios. The construction of Figure 17 is the same as Figure 16. Furthermore, due to the different sizes of the experimental images, the shooting distance was adjusted accordingly. Because Scenario (a) and Scenario (b) use the four corner points of the screen for perspective correction, the experiment shooting distance starts from 50 cm. In these two scenarios, the performance of watermark detection is the same as the detection results of the same host images in Section 5.2. In Scenario (c) and Scenario (d), because the images are scaled, the test starting shooting distance can be shortened, and the effective detection distance is also shortened. When the shooting angle is 15 and 30 degrees, the watermark information can be detected at all shooting distances in the experiments. As the shooting angle increases, the detectable shooting distance is substantially reduced. Watermark information can be detected within a shooting distance of 50 cm when the horizontal shooting angle is 60 degrees. Thus, the scaling of the images has a considerable influence on the watermark detection of the large angle captured image, but it can still meet the actual needs. These results verified the fact that the proposed scheme can handle screen-cam with common attacks.

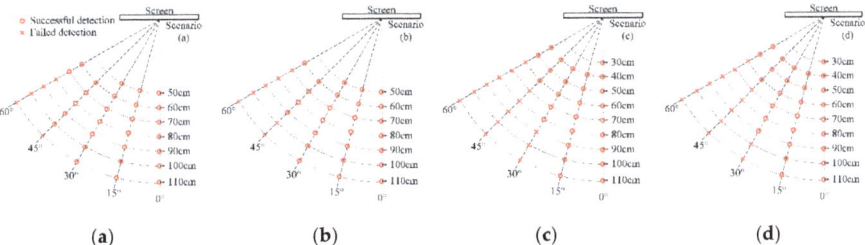

Figure 17. Watermark detection results against screen-cam with common attacks. (**a**–**d**) represent scenarios (**a**–**d**), respectively.

5.4. Applicability and Limitations Analysis

The proposed scheme works well for most types of images, but it inevitably has limitations. Feature point-based algorithms are limited by the feature point operator itself. For images with simple texture, the feature points are often unstable when under a severe image quality degradation. Therefore, for images with simple texture, the proposed method may not achieve accurate watermark synchronization, which will probably cause watermark detection to fail.

Another limitation is that the proposed scheme is not applicable to this situation, where the image displayed on the screen is greatly zoomed out before we capture it with a camera. Because in this case, the image displayed on the screen is resampled, which will cause a massive loss of image details. Unfortunately, the screen-cam process will amplify this distortion. Especially for high-resolution images, the users are most likely to zoom out to view the entire image. Therefore, the proposed scheme could be used with access control systems or other specific applications to avoid this situation.

Furthermore, because the motivation of this method is to hold accountability for leakage behavior, the time complexity of algorithm is not a very important consideration. However, in other words, time complexity is also one of our limitations. The computation time of watermark embedding includes two parts: LSFRs construction and message embedding. Based on a personal computer, which CPU is Intel Core i7–9700 CPU and RAM is 32 GB, the average computation time of LSFRs construction and message embedding for the host images are 7.041 s and 0.106 s, respectively. The Harris–Laplace operation involves multiscale and iterative calculations, which cost most of the computation time. Based on the algorithm, the time complexity of embedding algorithm is $O(Length \cdot Width)$, where $Length$ and $Width$ define the length and width of the image, respectively. Hence, for high-resolution images, the computation time will vary according to their size. With respect to watermark detection, the process of finding candidate LSFRs is similar to the process of constructing LSFRs. Although the message extraction process iterates the message extraction algorithm within our defined detection range, the computation time is still insignificant compared with the process of finding candidate LSFRs. Hence, after the manual perspective correction process, the time complexity of watermark detection is similar to watermark embedding. Therefore, considering the user experience, the algorithm is not recommended for real-time applications for now.

6. Conclusions

In this paper, a novel feature and Fourier-based screen-cam robust watermarking scheme is proposed. The distortions during the screen-cam process are analyzed. To resist possible desynchronization attacks caused by user operations and the screen-cam process, an LSFR construction method, based on the modified Harris–Laplace detector and SURF orientation descriptor, is designed to achieve watermark synchronization. In the proposed message embedding scheme, we repeatedly embed the message sequence in the DFT domain of each selected LSFR to achieve robustness against the screen-cam process. To decrease the quality degradation after embedding and improve the extraction accuracy, we employ a non-rotating embedding method and a preprocessing method to modulate the DFT magnitude coefficients. On the extraction side, we restore the captured image based on the size of the image itself to help improve the detection accuracy. The experiment shows that the proposed scheme has high robustness for common image attacks and screen-cam attacks. Compared with existing methods, the proposed scheme can further achieve robustness against screen-cam with additional common attacks.

In future research, we aim to investigate automatic detection methods, which is a more practical application foreground. To achieve this goal, screen-cam robust invariants should be further investigated to help design novel local feature-based watermark synchronization methods or develop novel synchronization watermark message embedding and automatic detection methods.

Author Contributions: Conceptualization, W.C. and N.R.; methodology, W.C., N.R. and C.Z.; software, W.C. and Q.Z.; data curation, W.C., T.S. and A.K.; writing—original draft preparation, W.C. and N.R.; writing—review and editing, Q.Z., T.S. and A.K.; funding acquisition, C.Z. All authors have read and agreed to the published version of the manuscript.

Funding: This research was funded by the National Natural Science Foundation of China, grant number 42071362 and 41971338, the Natural Science Foundation of Jiangsu Province, grant number BK20191373.

Conflicts of Interest: The authors declare no conflict of interest.

References

1. Abd El-Latif, A.A.; Abd-El-Atty, B.; Talha, M. Robust Encryption of Quantum Medical Images. *IEEE Access* **2018**, *6*, 1073–1081. [CrossRef]
2. Abd El-Latif, A.A.; Li, L.; Wang, N.; Han, Q.; Niu, X. A new approach to chaotic image encryption based on quantum chaotic system, exploiting color spaces. *Signal Process.* **2013**, *93*, 2986–3000. [CrossRef]
3. Abd El-Latif, A.A.; Yan, X.; Li, L.; Wang, N.; Peng, J.-L.; Niu, X. A new meaningful secret sharing scheme based on random grids, error diffusion and chaotic encryption. *Opt. Laser Technol.* **2013**, *54*, 389–400. [CrossRef]
4. Belazi, A.; Abd El-Latif, A.A.; Belghith, S. A novel image encryption scheme based on substitution-permutation network and chaos. *Signal Process.* **2016**, *128*, 155–170. [CrossRef]
5. Belazi, A.; Abd El-Latif, A.A.; Diaconu, A.-V.; Rhouma, R.; Belghith, S. Chaos-based partial image encryption scheme based on linear fractional and lifting wavelet transforms. *Opt. Lasers Eng.* **2017**, *88*, 37–50. [CrossRef]
6. Abd El-Latif, A.A.; Li, L.; Niu, X. A new image encryption scheme based on cyclic elliptic curve and chaotic system. *Multimed. Tools Appl.* **2012**, *70*, 1559–1584. [CrossRef]
7. Alrehily, A.; Thayananthan, V. Computer Security and Software Watermarking Based on Return-oriented Programming. *Int. J. Comput. Netw. Inf. Secur.* **2018**, *10*, 28–36. [CrossRef]
8. Wang, Y.; Gong, D.; Lu, B.; Xiang, F.; Liu, F. Exception Handling-Based Dynamic Software Watermarking. *IEEE Access* **2018**, *6*, 8882–8889. [CrossRef]
9. Jha, S.; Sural, S.; Atluri, V.; Vaidya, J. Specification and Verification of Separation of Duty Constraints in Attribute-Based Access Control. *IEEE Trans. Inf. Forensics Secur.* **2018**, *13*, 897–911. [CrossRef]
10. Xu, G.; Li, H.; Dai, Y.; Yang, K.; Lin, X. Enabling Efficient and Geometric Range Query With Access Control Over Encrypted Spatial Data. *IEEE Trans. Inf. Forensics Secur.* **2019**, *14*, 870–885. [CrossRef]
11. Castiglione, A.; De Santis, A.; Masucci, B.; Palmieri, F.; Castiglione, A.; Huang, X. Cryptographic Hierarchical Access Control for Dynamic Structures. *IEEE Trans. Inf. Forensics Secur.* **2016**, *11*, 2349–2364. [CrossRef]
12. Carpentieri, B.; Castiglione, A.; De Santis, A.; Palmieri, F.; Pizzolante, R. One-pass lossless data hiding and compression of remote sensing data. *Future Gener. Comput. Syst.* **2019**, *90*, 222–239. [CrossRef]
13. Liu, X.; Lou, J.; Fang, H.; Chen, Y.; Ouyang, P.; Wang, Y.; Zou, B.; Wang, L. A novel robust reversible watermarking scheme for protecting authenticity and integrity of medical images. *IEEE Access* **2019**, *7*, 76580–76598. [CrossRef]
14. Yu, X.; Wang, C.; Zhou, X. A Robust Color Image Watermarking Algorithm Based on APDCBT and SSVD. *Symmetry* **2019**, *11*, 1227. [CrossRef]
15. Zhou, K.; Zhang, Y.; Li, J.; Zhan, Y.; Wan, W. Spatial-Perceptual Embedding with Robust Just Noticeable Difference Model for Color Image Watermarking. *Mathematics* **2020**, *8*, 1506. [CrossRef]
16. Lee, J.-E.; Seo, Y.-H.; Kim, D.-W. Convolutional Neural Network-Based Digital Image Watermarking Adaptive to the Resolution of Image and Watermark. *Appl. Sci.* **2020**, *10*, 6854. [CrossRef]
17. Nakamura, T.; Katayama, A.; Yamamuro, M.; Sonehara, N. Fast watermark detection scheme for camera-equipped cellular phone. In *Proceedings of the 3rd International Conference on Mobile and Ubiquitous Multimedia*; Association for Computing Machinery: New York, NY, USA, 2004; pp. 101–108.
18. Katayama, A.; Nakamura, T.; Yamamuro, M.; Sonehara, N. New high-speed frame detection method: Side Trace Algorithm (STA) for i-appli on cellular phones to detect watermarks. In *Proceedings of the 3rd International Conference on Mobile and Ubiquitous Multimedia*; Association for Computing Machinery: New York, NY, USA, 2004; pp. 109–116.
19. Keskinarkaus, A.; Pramila, A.; Seppänen, T. Image watermarking with feature point based synchronization robust to print–scan attack. *J. Vis. Commun. Image Represent.* **2012**, *23*, 507–515. [CrossRef]
20. Kim, W.-G.; Lee, S.H.; Seo, Y.-S. Image fingerprinting scheme for print-and-capture model. In *Proceedings of Pacific-Rim Conference on Multimedia*; Springer: Berlin/Heidelberg, Germany, 2006; pp. 106–113.
21. Pramila, A.; Keskinarkaus, A.; Seppänen, T. Toward an interactive poster using digital watermarking and a mobile phone camera. *Signal Image Video Process.* **2011**, *6*, 211–222. [CrossRef]
22. Pramila, A.; Keskinarkaus, A.; Takala, V.; Seppänen, T. Extracting watermarks from printouts captured with wide angles using computational photography. *Multimed. Tools Appl.* **2016**, *76*, 16063–16084. [CrossRef]
23. Pramila, A.; Keskinarkaus, A.; Seppänen, T. Increasing the capturing angle in print-cam robust watermarking. *J. Syst. Softw.* **2018**, *135*, 205–215. [CrossRef]

24. Kang, X.; Huang, J.; Zeng, W. Efficient general print-scanning resilient data hiding based on uniform log-polar mapping. *IEEE Trans. Inf. Forensics Secur.* **2010**, *5*, 1–12. [CrossRef]
25. Lin, C.-Y.; Wu, M.; Bloom, J.A.; Cox, I.J.; Miller, M.L.; Lui, Y.M. Rotation, scale, and translation resilient watermarking for images. *IEEE Trans. Image Process.* **2001**, *10*, 767–782. [CrossRef] [PubMed]
26. Gourrame, K.; Douzi, H.; Harba, R.; Ros, F.; El Hajji, M.; Riad, R.; Amar, M. Robust Print-cam Image Watermarking in Fourier Domain. In *Proceedings of International Conference on Image and Signal Processing*; Springer International Publishing: Cham, Switzerland, 2016; pp. 356–365.
27. Gourrame, K.; Douzi, H.; Harba, R.; Riad, R.; Ros, F.; Amar, M.; Elhajji, M. A zero-bit Fourier image watermarking for print-cam process. *Multimed. Tools Appl.* **2019**, *78*, 2621–2638. [CrossRef]
28. Poljicak, A.; Mandic, L.; Agic, D. Discrete Fourier transform-based watermarking method with an optimal implementation radius. *J. Electron. Imaging* **2011**, *20*, 033008. [CrossRef]
29. Riad, R.; Harba, R.; Douzi, H.; Ros, F.; Elhajji, M. Robust fourier watermarking for id images on smart card plastic supports. *Adv. Electr. Comput. Eng.* **2016**, *16*, 23–30. [CrossRef]
30. Keskinarkaus, A.; Pramila, A.; Seppänen, T.; Sauvola, J. Wavelet domain print-scan and JPEG resilient data hiding method. In *Proceedings of International Workshop on Digital Watermarking*; Springer: Berlin/Heidelberg, Germany, 2006; pp. 82–95.
31. Pramila, A.; Keskinarkaus, A.; Seppänen, T. Multiple domain watermarking for print-scan and JPEG resilient data hiding. In *Proceedings of International Workshop on Digital Watermarking*; Springer: Berlin/Heidelberg, Germany, 2008; pp. 279–293.
32. Jassim, T.; Abd-Alhameed, R.; Al-Ahmad, H. A new robust and fragile watermarking scheme for images captured by mobile phone cameras. In Proceedings of the 1st International Conference on Communications, Signal Processing, and Their Applications ICCSPA 2013, Sharjah, UAE, 12–14 February 2013; pp. 1–5.
33. Fang, H.; Zhang, W.; Zhou, H.; Cui, H.; Yu, N. Screen-shooting resilient watermarking. *IEEE Trans. Inf. Forensics Secur.* **2018**, *14*, 1403–1418. [CrossRef]
34. Schaber, P.; Kopf, S.; Wetzel, S.; Ballast, T.; Wesch, C.; Effelsberg, W. CamMark: Analyzing, modeling, and simulating artifacts in camcorder copies. *ACM Trans. Multimed. Comput. Commun. Appl. Tomm* **2015**, *11*, 1–23. [CrossRef]
35. Bigas, M.; Cabruja, E.; Forest, J.; Salvi, J. Review of CMOS image sensors. *Microelectron. J.* **2006**, *37*, 433–451. [CrossRef]
36. Kong, L.; Cai, S.; Li, Z.; Jin, G.; Huang, S.; Xu, K.; Wang, T. Interpretation of moiré phenomenon in the image domain. *Opt. Express* **2011**, *19*, 18399–18409. [CrossRef]
37. Niu, P.-P.; Wang, X.-Y.; Liu, Y.-N.; Yang, H.-Y. A robust color image watermarking using local invariant significant bitplane histogram. *Multimed. Tools Appl.* **2017**, *76*, 3403–3433.
38. Seo, J.S.; Yoo, C.D. Image watermarking based on invariant regions of scale-space representation. *IEEE Trans. Signal Process.* **2006**, *54*, 1537–1549. [CrossRef]
39. Su, P.-C.; Chang, Y.-C.; Wu, C.-Y. Geometrically resilient digital image watermarking by using interest point extraction and extended pilot signals. *IEEE Trans. Inf. Forensics Secur.* **2013**, *8*, 1897–1908. [CrossRef]
40. Thanh, T.M.; Tanaka, K.; Dung, L.H.; Tai, N.T.; Nam, H.N. Performance analysis of robust watermarking using linear and nonlinear feature matching. *Multimed. Tools Appl.* **2018**, *77*, 2901–2920. [CrossRef]
41. Tsai, J.-S.; Huang, W.-B.; Kuo, Y.-H. On the selection of optimal feature region set for robust digital image watermarking. *IEEE Trans. Image Process.* **2010**, *20*, 735–743. [CrossRef] [PubMed]
42. Wang, C.; Zhang, Y.; Zhou, X. Robust image watermarking algorithm based on ASIFT against geometric attacks. *Appl. Sci.* **2018**, *8*, 410. [CrossRef]
43. Wang, X.; Wu, J.; Niu, P. A new digital image watermarking algorithm resilient to desynchronization attacks. *IEEE Trans. Inf. Forensics Secur.* **2007**, *2*, 655–663. [CrossRef]
44. Wang, X.-Y.; Hou, L.-M.; Wu, J. A feature-based robust digital image watermarking against geometric attacks. *Image Vis. Comput.* **2008**, *26*, 980–989. [CrossRef]
45. Wang, X.-Y.; Niu, P.-P.; Yang, H.-Y.; Chen, L.-L. Affine invariant image watermarking using intensity probability density-based Harris Laplace detector. *J. Vis. Commun. Image Represent.* **2012**, *23*, 892–907. [CrossRef]
46. Hsu, P.H.; Chen, C.C. A robust digital watermarking algorithm for copyright protection of aerial photogrammetric images. *Photogramm. Rec.* **2016**, *31*, 51–70. [CrossRef]

47. Solanki, K.; Madhow, U.; Manjunath, B.; Chandrasekaran, S.; El-Khalil, I. Print and scan'resilient data hiding in images. *IEEE Trans. Inf. Forensics Secur.* **2006**, *1*, 464–478. [CrossRef]
48. Mikolajczyk, K.; Schmid, C. An affine invariant interest point detector. In *Proceedings of European Conference on Computer Vision*; Springer: Berlin/Heidelberg, Germany, 2002; pp. 128–142.
49. Mikolajczyk, K.; Schmid, C. Scale & affine invariant interest point detectors. *Int. J. Comput. Vis.* **2004**, *60*, 63–86.
50. Harris, C.G.; Stephens, M. A combined corner and edge detector. In Proceedings of the Alvey Vision Conference, Manchester, UK, 31 August–2 September 1988; pp. 147–151.
51. Noble, J.A. Finding corners. *Image Vis. Comput.* **1988**, *6*, 121–128. [CrossRef]
52. Related Images of the Experiments. Available online: http://decsai.ugr.es/cvg/dbimagenes/c512.php (accessed on 6 September 2020).
53. Kumar, C.; Singh, A.K.; Kumar, P. A recent survey on image watermarking techniques and its application in e-governance. *Multimed. Tools Appl.* **2018**, *77*, 3597–3622. [CrossRef]
54. Wang, Z.; Bovik, A.C.; Sheikh, H.R.; Simoncelli, E.P. Image quality assessment: From error visibility to structural similarity. *IEEE Trans. Image Process.* **2004**, *13*, 600–612. [CrossRef] [PubMed]

Publisher's Note: MDPI stays neutral with regard to jurisdictional claims in published maps and institutional affiliations.

© 2020 by the authors. Licensee MDPI, Basel, Switzerland. This article is an open access article distributed under the terms and conditions of the Creative Commons Attribution (CC BY) license (http://creativecommons.org/licenses/by/4.0/).

Article

A Watermarking Protocol Based on Blockchain

Franco Frattolillo

Department of Engineering, University of Sannio, Corso Garibaldi 107, 82100 Benevento, Italy; frattolillo@unisannio.it

Received: 27 September 2020; Accepted: 30 October 2020; Published: 2 November 2020

Abstract: Digital watermarking can be used to implement mechanisms aimed at protecting the copyright of digital content distributed on the Internet. Such mechanisms support copyright identification and content tracking by enabling content providers to embed perceptually invisible watermarks into the distributed copies of content. They are employed in conjunction with watermarking protocols, which define the schemes of the web transactions by which buyers can securely purchase protected digital content distributed by content providers. In this regard, the "buyer friendly" and "mediated" watermarking protocols can ensure both a correct content protection and an easy participation of buyers in the transactions by which to purchase the distributed content. They represent a valid alternative to the classic "buyer and seller" watermarking protocols documented in the literature. However, their protection schemes could be further improved and simplified. This paper presents a new watermarking protocol able to combine the "buyer friendly" and "mediated" design approach with the blockchain technology. The result is a secure protocol that can support a limited and balanced participation of both buyers and content providers in the purchase transactions of protected digital content. Moreover, the protocol can avoid the direct involvement of trusted third parties in the purchase transactions. This can reduce the actual risk that buyers or sellers can violate the protocol by illicitly interacting with trusted third parties. In fact, such peculiarities make the proposed protocol suited for the current web context.

Keywords: watermarking protocols; digital copyright protection; blockchain

1. Introduction

Social networks and user-generated content platforms have turned common web users into actual producers of multimedia digital content. Such content can be easily duplicated without reducing their perceptual quality. They can be also maliciously modified and/or re-distributed, thus damaging the reputation of their legitimate owners, or revealing their private information, or causing economic loss. In addition, current mechanisms implemented to protect the copyright of multimedia digital content cannot adequately meet the protection requirements needed to solve piracy problems on the Internet.

One of the technologies proposed to protect the users' copyrights on their multimedia digital content is "digital watermarking" [1,2] used in conjunction with "watermarking protocols" [3–5].

Digital watermarking makes it possible to insert hidden information, such as, for example, a "fingerprint" [6–8], within any copy of content that has to be protected. Such information, called a "watermark", can be used to identify the user who possesses the content, and makes the copy of the content unique and personalized.

However, to combat the unauthorized sharing of multimedia digital content on the Internet, it is necessary to distribute the watermarked content according to specific interaction schemes defined by watermarking protocols. Thus, whenever a copy of watermarked content is found in a suspicious location, such as in file repositories shared by peer-to-peer applications, the embedded watermark can be used as a proof of ownership to establish who has initially obtained the copy and then illegally shared it on the Internet.

The most relevant watermarking protocols documented in the literature enable the implementation of mechanisms for copyright protection based on content tracking by fingerprinting [3–5,8,9]. They mainly involve two parties: the "buyer" and the "seller". The former wishes to get content from a web content provider, whereas the latter wishes to release it in a digitally protected form obtained by inserting a watermark. In particular, the early experiences also involve specific trusted third parties (TTPs), called "watermark certification authorities" (WCAs), whose main function is to guarantee the correct execution of the protocols [4,10–15]. However, the introduction of WCAs can reduce the security level of the protocols, since TTPs can give rise to potential collusive behaviors with buyers or sellers [2,16]. As a consequence, a number of watermarking protocols are based on "simplified" interaction schemes that do not exploit WCAs [17–21]. Such approaches appear to be more secure, but they turn out to be impracticable in the current web context, since they are characterized by interaction schemes that force buyers to perform complex security actions to complete content purchase transactions [22].

The watermarking protocols described in [22–24] attempt to overcome the drawbacks affecting previous solutions existing in the literature by proposing a new "buyer friendly" and "mediated" design approach. Such an approach reintroduces the TTP, but its role is carefully limited to a restricted part of the protocol, so as to enable a simplified participation of buyers in the content purchase transactions without reducing the security level of the protocol.

Although such experiences represent a good balance between security and easy participation of buyers in the protocol, further efforts are needed to simplify the interaction schemes of such watermarking protocols, so as to make them best suited to the current web context that does not like the presence of TTPs. In this regard, it is worth noting that blockchain technology has begun to be employed in the area of digital copyright protection [25–29]. In fact, blockchain belongs to the category of distributed ledger technologies that enable commercial or network transaction data to be recorded in cryptographic chained blocks by employing several security technologies, such as cryptographic hash, digital signature, and distributed consensus mechanism. When they are appended to a chain, blocks are timestamped and linked in a way that makes them resilient to modifications. Therefore, they are considered to be trusted for transactions among web entities, and can be verified in a decentralized way by exploiting multiple web nodes to form a consensus on whether a transaction is valid or not. In addition, blockchain supports the so-called "smart contracts", which represent a way to automatically execute the terms of an agreement reached between distinct web entities. More precisely, a smart contract encapsulates a number of preset rules in the form of code, and sets corresponding trigger events under specific conditions: when the conditions are met, the terms of the agreement are automatically executed without control from a central authority [26–31].

This paper presents a new watermarking protocol based on blockchain technology. The protocol is built on the experiences previously conducted with the protocols documented in [22–24], and follows the buyer friendly and mediated design approach. The main aim is to simplify the interaction scheme of the protocol by exploiting the blockchain technology, which makes it possible to better control the involvement of the TTP in the protocol. In fact, such an involvement has been further restricted in order to reduce the possibility of collusive actions from the TTP, making the developed protocol more secure and suited to the current web context.

The paper is organized as follows. Section 2 reports on related work. Section 3 introduces the main challenges faced in developing the proposed protocol. Section 4 reports the basics of the proposed protocol, whereas Section 5 describes the protocol in detail. Section 6 analyzes the proposed protocol. Section 7 focuses on the main implementation aspects of the watermarking protocol. The final remarks are in Section 8.

2. Related Work

Most of the watermarking protocols documented in the literature do not exploit blockchain technology, but they are based on the well-known "buyer and seller" protection schemes and their variants characterized by the absence of TTPs. They are widely described and discussed in [5,22–24]. Some of them also inspire the so-called DRM (digital rights management) systems, which are complex web platforms that adopt specific technologies and interaction schemes to enable the copyright protection of digital content on the Internet [32,33]. More precisely, DRM systems do not actually define watermarking protocols, but they still implement mechanisms by which to prevent the unauthorized use of protected digital content without payment. To achieve such a goal, DRM systems use technologies based on encryption and key management [34]. However, such technologies cannot inhibit legitimate users from illegally sharing their purchased content on the Internet.

To overcome the drawbacks reported above, a number of DRM systems implement protection schemes based on "trusted computing". They prevent the sharing of illegal keys and protected content by enabling the access to such content on the basis of the web users' biometric features [35,36]. In fact, such systems appear to be very promising, but they lack flexibility, since they need particular hardware, such as "trusted platform modules" (TPMs) or fingerprint recognizers, and cannot defend against specific attacks, such as screen recording or I/O monitoring.

The blockchain technology, in conjunction with digital watermarking, is employed in a number of DRM systems to provide some copyright management services, such as to keep track of possible and required content modifications, copyright transfers or other transaction trails related to the managed digital content [37–39]. In particular, digital watermarking is mainly used to provide content tracking by fingerprinting. However, such DRM systems do not implement protection schemes able to address the peculiar problems that affect watermarking protocols, such as the "customer's right problem" or the "unbinding problem" [4,11,22]. As a consequence, once content is downloaded and tampered, there is no legal way to prove the ownership of the content and to trace who should be responsible for copyright infringement. In fact, such considerations motivate the design of innovative watermarking protocols able to exploit the blockchain technology to overcome the limitations described above.

3. Main Challenges

One of the main challenges in designing watermarking protocols consists of accurately defining the role played by TTPs in the purchase transactions, since TTPs could collude with the other parties involved in the protocols [17,20,40] so as to impair them. In this regard, the best solution would be to totally eliminate TTPs from protocols. However, such a solution is not always possible, since protocols often need TTPs to validate specific data, or some phases of the protocol, or, for example, the plug-ins that have to be downloaded and installed in the buyers' web browsers to complete the purchase transactions [22,23]. Furthermore, when TTPs play a limited role in the protocols, buyers end up being forced to perform complex security actions to complete the purchase transactions, and this makes the protocols impractical for the web context [17–21,40–44].

The watermarking protocols presented in [22–24] do not completely eliminate the TTP, but they carefully exploit it without assigning it a central role in order to simplify the buyer participation in the protocols. In particular, the TTP participates only in the initial phase of the protocols and restricts its role to the generation of a number of tokens needed to unambiguously bind the chosen content to the buyer, the seller and the ongoing purchase transaction.

Although the role of the TTP is rather restricted in the protocols described in [22–24], it has to be further limited if the main goal is to develop an innovative watermarking protocol suited for the current web context. In this regard, blockchain technology represents a challenge to achieve such a goal. In fact, it can be exploited in the proposed protocol with the aim of securely tracking the purchase transactions in a public ledger that can be updated by automatically executing smart contracts without resorting to the control of a TTP [26–29]. Thus, the TTP involved in the proposed protocol can act as a simple and trusted web distributor of secure tokens needed to complete the purchase transactions of protected digital content. In fact, it is not a WCA, even though it has to behave as a TTP in the sense of a common certification authority (CA) [45–47].

The adoption of blockchain technology to strongly restrict the role of TTP makes it necessary to accurately design and code the smart contract that controls the execution of the proposed watermarking protocol and validates each purchase transaction. In fact, this represents a relevant practical challenge well documented in the literature, since the code that implements the contract, once it has been released, can no longer be modified or updated. Therefore, if the code of the contract is incorrect or gives rise to a problem during use, it ends up impairing the entire protocol [48].

4. Basics of the Protocol

The proposed watermarking protocol is based on a limited set of well-known security facilities: public key infrastructure (PKI), homomorphic cryptosystem [49], encrypted and signed tokens [4,5,22], and blind and readable watermarking scheme [1]. Furthermore, it exploits the public key and secure communication support implemented by the SSL/TLS protocol for all the messages exchanged among the web entities involved in the protocol [46].

In more detail, if a piece of content and a watermark can be described according to a block-wise representation in the form of $X = \{x_1, x_2, \ldots x_l\}$ and $W = \{w_1, w_2, \ldots w_l\}$ respectively, the watermark insertion adopted by the proposed protocol, denoted as $\oplus$, results in the following expression:

$$X \oplus W = \{x_1 \oplus w_1, x_2 \oplus w_2, \ldots x_l \oplus w_l\} = \tilde{X}$$

since such an insertion is assumed to be based on linear watermarks [1,10,17,50]. Furthermore, if $X = \{x_1, x_2 \ldots x_l\}$ is a digital content, its encryption by means of the function $\mathbb{E}$ results in the following expression:

$$\mathbb{E}_{pk}(X) = \mathbb{E}_{pk}(x_1, x_2 \ldots x_l) = (\mathbb{E}_{pk}(x_1), \mathbb{E}_{pk}(x_2) \ldots \mathbb{E}_{pk}(x_l))$$

since $\mathbb{E}$ is assumed to be a block-wise function [10,50].

Finally, the encryption function $\mathbb{E}$ is assumed to be "homomorphic" with respect to the watermark insertion. This means that any linear watermark can be embedded directly into the encrypted domain according to the following expression [10,50]:

$$\mathbb{E}_{pk}(X \oplus W) = \mathbb{E}_{pk}(X) \oplus \mathbb{E}_{pk}(W) = \mathbb{E}_{pk}(\tilde{X})$$

In fact, a cryptosystem $\mathbb{E}$ is homomorphic with respect to an operation $\odot$ if

$$\mathbb{E}_{pk}(m_1 \odot m_2) = \mathbb{E}_{pk}(m_1) \odot \mathbb{E}_{pk}(m_2)$$

for any two plain messages m_1 and m_2 [49]. As a consequence, homomorphic encryption makes it possible to perform operations by directly working on encrypted data.

5. Watermarking Protocol

The proposed watermarking protocol is an enhancement of the buyer friendly and mediated protocols presented in [22–24]. It has been designed and developed according to what is reported in Section 3. Therefore, it exploits the blockchain technology to avoid the participation of a TTP in the core of the protection phase so as to simplify and secure the basic interaction scheme characterizing the protocols described in [22–24]. The result is an innovative watermarking protocol in which the blockchain is employed to lock in a public ledger the main tokens characterizing purchase transactions. In fact, such tokens are collected and controlled by executing a specific smart contract: if they turn out to be correct, the ongoing purchase transaction is automatically validated and completed without the direct intervention of a TTP.

Even though the proposed protocol can run without a centralized control, it still needs a TTP acting as a trusted web distributor of security tokens, such as one-time public and private key pairs and encrypted "nonces" [51], needed to complete the purchase transactions of protected digital content according to the original buyer friendly and mediated approach [22]. Moreover, the proposed protocol needs a further TTP, called "judge". It does not participate in the phase of the protocol that applies the protection to the digital content distributed on the Internet. It only participates in the subsequent "identification and arbitration phase" needed to determine the identity of an illegal distributor of a copy of a protected digital content [22–24]. In fact, the TTP and the judge could even coincide, but conventional certification authorities do not usually implement the service performed by the judge [17,22].

More precisely, the proposed watermarking protocol is characterized by a protection scheme in which: (1) the seller or content provider $\mathcal{CP}$ releases content in an encrypted and watermarked form; (2) the buyer $\mathcal{B}$ can obtain the protected content by simply decrypting it; (3) the purchase transaction of a protected digital content occurring between the buyer and the content provider is validated by automatically executing a smart contract within a blockchain $\mathcal{BC}$, which takes charge of controlling all the tokens generated by the transaction; (4) buyer and content provider take part in transactions that employ security tokens guaranteed by a "registration authority" $\mathcal{RA}$ [22–24]; (5) a judge $\mathcal{J}$ guarantees the dispute resolution protocol and determines if a buyer is guilty of having released pirated copies [22–24].

The protocol consists of two subprotocols: the *protection protocol* and the *identification and arbitration protocol*. The meanings of the symbols used to describe the protocol are reported in Table 1.

Table 1. Meanings of the symbols used to describe the proposed protocol.

Symbol	Meaning
$\mathcal{B}$	buyer
$\mathcal{CP}$	content provider or seller
$\mathcal{RA}$	registration authority
$\mathcal{BC}$	blockchain
$\mathcal{J}$	judge
X	digital content purchased by $\mathcal{B}$
X_d	information used by $\mathcal{CP}$ to unambiguously identify X
T_X	timestamp referred to the transaction by which $\mathcal{B}$ buys X
B_{id}	information used to identify $\mathcal{B}$
B_{ad}	destination address provides by $\mathcal{B}$
N	nonce used to mark the watermarking transaction
W	watermark
$W_{Ent.}$	part of the watermark W generated by the entity $Ent.$
$\bar{X}$	watermarked X
$pk_{Ent.}$	public key of the entity $Ent.$
$sk_{Ent.}$	secret key of the entity $Ent.$
$pk_{Ent.}^X$	one time public key generated by the entity $Ent.$ in the transaction to watermark X
$sk_{Ent.}^X$	one time secret key generated by the entity $Ent.$ in the transaction to watermark X
$E_{key}(\ldots)$	token encrypted using the key *key* and a public key cryptosystem
$\mathbb{S}_{key}(\ldots)$	token digitally signed using the secret key *key* and the SHA-1 secure hash algorithm
$\mathbb{E}_{key}(\ldots)$	token encrypted using the key *key* and a cryptosystem that is privacy homomorphic with respect to the watermark insertion
$\mathbb{D}_{key}(\ldots)$	decryption function corresponding to the encryption function $\mathbb{E}_{key}(\ldots)$

5.1. Protection Protocol

The protocol, whose scheme is reported in Table 2, starts when $\mathcal{B}$ visits the $\mathcal{CP}$'s web site, chooses the content X, and sends the purchase request to $\mathcal{CP}$ in the message m_1.

Table 2. Protection protocol.

$\mathcal{B}$	: visits the $\mathcal{CP}$'s web site and chooses the content X
$\mathcal{B} \to \mathcal{CP}$	: $m_1 = \{\text{request for } X\}$
$\mathcal{CP} \to \mathcal{RA}$	: $m_2 = \{\text{request for security tokens}\}$
$\mathcal{RA} \to \mathcal{CP}$	: $m_3 = \{pk_{\mathcal{RA}}^X, \mathbb{E}_{pk_{\mathcal{RA}}^X}(N), \mathbb{S}_{\mathcal{RA}}(pk_{\mathcal{RA}}^X, \mathbb{E}_{pk_{\mathcal{RA}}^X}(N))\}$
$\mathcal{CP} \to \mathcal{B}$	: $m_4 = \{X_d, T_X, pk_{\mathcal{RA}}^X, \mathbb{S}_{\mathcal{RA}}(pk_{\mathcal{RA}}^X, \mathbb{E}_{pk_{\mathcal{RA}}^X}(N)),$
	$\mathbb{S}_{\mathcal{CP}}(X_d, T_X, pk_{\mathcal{RA}}^X, \mathbb{S}_{\mathcal{RA}}(pk_{\mathcal{RA}}^X, \mathbb{E}_{pk_{\mathcal{RA}}^X}(N)))\}$
$\mathcal{CP}$	: generates $W_{\mathcal{CP}}, \mathbb{E}_{pk_{\mathcal{RA}}^X}(W_{\mathcal{CP}}), \mathbb{E}_{pk_{\mathcal{RA}}^X}(X)$
$\mathcal{CP}$	: generates $\mathbb{E}_{pk_{\mathcal{RA}}^X}(W) = \mathbb{E}_{pk_{\mathcal{RA}}^X}(W_{\mathcal{CP}}) \| \mathbb{E}_{pk_{\mathcal{RA}}^X}(N)$
$\mathcal{CP}$	: generates $\overline{\mathbb{E}_{pk_{\mathcal{RA}}^X}(X)} = \mathbb{E}_{pk_{\mathcal{RA}}^X}(X) \oplus \mathbb{E}_{pk_{\mathcal{RA}}^X}(W)$
$\mathcal{CP} \to \mathcal{B}$	: $m_5 = \{\overline{\mathbb{E}_{pk_{\mathcal{RA}}^X}(X)}\}$
$\mathcal{CP} \to \mathcal{BC}$	: $m_6 = \{X_d, T_X, pk_{\mathcal{RA}}^X, \mathbb{E}_{pk_{\mathcal{RA}}^X}(N), \mathbb{S}_{\mathcal{RA}}(pk_{\mathcal{RA}}^X, \mathbb{E}_{pk_{\mathcal{RA}}^X}(N)),$
	$\mathbb{S}_{\mathcal{CP}}(X_d, T_X, pk_{\mathcal{RA}}^X, \mathbb{E}_{pk_{\mathcal{RA}}^X}(N), \mathbb{S}_{\mathcal{RA}}(pk_{\mathcal{RA}}^X, \mathbb{E}_{pk_{\mathcal{RA}}^X}(N)))\}$
$\mathcal{B} \to \mathcal{BC}$	: $m_7 = \{X_d, T_X, pk_{\mathcal{RA}}^X, \mathbb{S}_{\mathcal{RA}}(pk_{\mathcal{RA}}^X, \mathbb{E}_{pk_{\mathcal{RA}}^X}(N)), B_{id}, B_{ad}\}$
$\mathcal{BC}$	: activates the smart contract
$\mathcal{BC}$	: compares the tokens and verifies the signatures included in m_6 and m_7
$\mathcal{BC}$	: generates a node in the blockchain by which to publish $X_d, T_X,$
	$pk_{\mathcal{RA}}^X, \mathbb{E}_{pk_{\mathcal{RA}}^X}(N), \mathbb{S}_{\mathcal{RA}}(pk_{\mathcal{RA}}^X, \mathbb{E}_{pk_{\mathcal{RA}}^X}(N)),$
	$\mathbb{S}_{\mathcal{CP}}(X_d, T_X, pk_{\mathcal{RA}}^X, \mathbb{E}_{pk_{\mathcal{RA}}^X}(N), \mathbb{S}_{\mathcal{RA}}(pk_{\mathcal{RA}}^X, \mathbb{E}_{pk_{\mathcal{RA}}^X}(N)))$
$\mathcal{BC}$	: implements the payment phase
$\mathcal{BC} \to \mathcal{RA}$	: $m_8 = \{B_{ad}, pk_{\mathcal{RA}}^X\}$
$\mathcal{BC}$	: $\mathbb{E}_{pk_{\mathcal{RA}}}(B_{id}, pk_{\mathcal{RA}}^X, \mathbb{E}_{pk_{\mathcal{RA}}^X}(N))$
$\mathcal{BC} \to \mathcal{CP}$	: $m_9 = \{\mathbb{E}_{pk_{\mathcal{RA}}}(B_{id}, pk_{\mathcal{RA}}^X, \mathbb{E}_{pk_{\mathcal{RA}}^X}(N))\}$
$\mathcal{CP}$	: saves a new entry in its databases composed of $X_d, T_X, pk_{\mathcal{RA}}^X, \mathbb{E}_{pk_{\mathcal{RA}}^X}(N),$
	$\mathbb{S}_{\mathcal{RA}}(pk_{\mathcal{RA}}^X, \mathbb{E}_{pk_{\mathcal{RA}}^X}(N))$, and $\mathbb{E}_{pk_{\mathcal{RA}}}(B_{id}, pk_{\mathcal{RA}}^X, \mathbb{E}_{pk_{\mathcal{RA}}^X}(N))$
	whose search key is $W_{\mathcal{CP}}$
$\mathcal{RA} \to \mathcal{B}$	: $m_{10} = \{sk_{\mathcal{RA}}^X\}$
$\mathcal{B}$	: $\bar{X} = \mathbb{D}_{sk_{\mathcal{RA}}^X}(\overline{\mathbb{E}_{pk_{\mathcal{RA}}^X}(X)})$

Upon receiving the purchase request, $\mathcal{CP}$ contacts $\mathcal{RA}$, by sending the message m_2, in order to obtain the security tokens to complete the purchase transaction. In fact, $\mathcal{RA}$ is a TTP that publishes a list of pairs, each including a public key $pk_{\mathcal{RA}}^X$ and an encrypted token $\mathbb{E}_{pk_{\mathcal{RA}}^X}(N)$. In particular, $pk_{\mathcal{RA}}^X$ corresponds to the secret key $sk_{\mathcal{RA}}^X$. They represent a one-time key pair that can be used only in the current transaction [52]. N is a "nonce" represented by a binary string. It is encrypted by employing the public key $pk_{\mathcal{RA}}^X$ and a cryptosystem that is "privacy homomorphic" [49] with respect to the subsequent watermark insertion. In fact, the resulting token $\mathbb{E}_{pk_{\mathcal{RA}}^X}(N)$ will be then used to generate the watermark to be inserted into the content X.

The chosen pair $(pk_{\mathcal{RA}}^X, \mathbb{E}_{pk_{\mathcal{RA}}^X}(N))$ is returned by $\mathcal{RA}$ in the message m_3 together with the signature $\mathbb{S}_{\mathcal{RA}}(pk_{\mathcal{RA}}^X, \mathbb{E}_{pk_{\mathcal{RA}}^X}(N))$.

Upon receiving m_3, $\mathcal{CP}$ can confirm the purchase request made by $\mathcal{B}$. In fact, $\mathcal{CP}$ generates two tokens, X_d and T_X. The former is a string that identifies the requested content X. It includes the name of the content and further data that can unambiguously describe it. The latter is a timestamp that is referred to the ongoing transaction. Then, $\mathcal{CP}$ generates the signature $\mathbb{S}_{\mathcal{CP}}(X_d, T_X, pk_{\mathcal{RA}}^X, \mathbb{S}_{\mathcal{RA}}(pk_{\mathcal{RA}}^X, \mathbb{E}_{pk_{\mathcal{RA}}^X}(N)))$ and sends the message m_4 to $\mathcal{B}$, which includes X_d, T_X, $pk_{\mathcal{RA}}^X$, $\mathbb{S}_{\mathcal{RA}}(pk_{\mathcal{RA}}^X, \mathbb{E}_{pk_{\mathcal{RA}}^X}(N))$, and $\mathbb{S}_{\mathcal{CP}}(X_d, T_X, pk_{\mathcal{RA}}^X, \mathbb{S}_{\mathcal{RA}}(pk_{\mathcal{RA}}^X, \mathbb{E}_{pk_{\mathcal{RA}}^X}(N)))$.

After having confirmed the purchase request, $\mathcal{CP}$ can apply the protection to X. Therefore, $\mathcal{CP}$ generates its part of watermark, denoted by $W_{\mathcal{CP}}$, which is a fingerprinting binary code obtained as an anti-collusion code [6,7,16] concatenated with an error correcting code used to address the problems of bit errors that can arise during the watermark verification process. Then, $\mathcal{CP}$ encrypts $W_{\mathcal{CP}}$ and X using the public key $pk_{\mathcal{RA}}^X$ and the same homomorphic cryptosystem used by $\mathcal{RA}$ to encrypt N, thus generating $\mathbb{E}_{pk_{\mathcal{RA}}^X}(W_{\mathcal{CP}})$ and $\mathbb{E}_{pk_{\mathcal{RA}}^X}(X)$.

Then, according to the basics reported in Section 4, $\mathcal{CP}$ concatenates $\mathbb{E}_{pk_{\mathcal{RA}}^X}(W_{\mathcal{CP}})$ and $\mathbb{E}_{pk_{\mathcal{RA}}^X}(N)$ to generate the encrypted watermark $\mathbb{E}_{pk_{\mathcal{RA}}^X}(W)$ according the following expression:

$$\mathbb{E}_{pk_{\mathcal{RA}}^X}(W) = \mathbb{E}_{pk_{\mathcal{RA}}^X}(W_{\mathcal{CP}}) \| \mathbb{E}_{pk_{\mathcal{RA}}^X}(N) = \mathbb{E}_{pk_{\mathcal{RA}}^X}(W_{\mathcal{CP}} \| N) \qquad (1)$$

Moreover, $\mathcal{CP}$ can embed the encrypted watermark $\mathbb{E}_{pk_{\mathcal{RA}}^X}(W)$ directly into the encrypted content $\mathbb{E}_{pk_{\mathcal{RA}}^X}(X)$ according to the following expression:

$$\overline{\mathbb{E}_{pk_{\mathcal{RA}}^X}(X)} = \mathbb{E}_{pk_{\mathcal{RA}}^X}(\tilde{X}) = \mathbb{E}_{pk_{\mathcal{RA}}^X}(X \oplus W) = \mathbb{E}_{pk_{\mathcal{RA}}^X}(X) \oplus \mathbb{E}_{pk_{\mathcal{RA}}^X}(W) \qquad (2)$$

since encryption is homomorphic with respect to watermark insertion [10,49,50]. The encrypted and watermarked content $\overline{\mathbb{E}_{pk_{\mathcal{RA}}^X}(X)}$ can be thus sent by $\mathcal{CP}$ to $\mathcal{B}$ in the message m_5.

At this point, $\mathcal{CP}$ and $\mathcal{B}$ can activate the smart contract in the blockchain $\mathcal{BC}$ by sending the messages m_6 and m_7, respectively.

In particular, the message m_6 is sent by $\mathcal{CP}$ to $\mathcal{BC}$, and contains X_d, T_X, $pk_{\mathcal{RA}}^X$, $\mathbb{E}_{pk_{\mathcal{RA}}^X}(N)$, $\mathbb{S}_{\mathcal{RA}}(pk_{\mathcal{RA}}^X, \mathbb{E}_{pk_{\mathcal{RA}}^X}(N))$, and the signature $\mathbb{S}_{\mathcal{CP}}(X_d, T_X, pk_{\mathcal{RA}}^X, \mathbb{E}_{pk_{\mathcal{RA}}^X}(N), \mathbb{S}_{RA}(pk_{\mathcal{RA}}^X, \mathbb{E}_{pk_{\mathcal{RA}}^X}(N)))$.

The message m_7 is sent by $\mathcal{B}$ to $\mathcal{BC}$, and includes X_d, T_X, $pk_{\mathcal{RA}}^X$, and $\mathbb{S}_{\mathcal{RA}}(pk_{\mathcal{RA}}^X, \mathbb{E}_{pk_{\mathcal{RA}}^X}(N))$. In addition, $\mathcal{B}$ also sends B_{id} and B_{ad} to $\mathcal{BC}$ in the message m_7: the former is a token that unambiguously identifies $\mathcal{B}$, whereas the latter represents his/her destination address. In particular,

- B_{id} is generated depending on the specific "negotiation mechanism" chosen by $\mathcal{B}$ among those ones supported by $\mathcal{BC}$ [4,5]. In this regard, in the proposed protocol $\mathcal{BC}$ is assumed to provide multiple negotiation mechanisms, which enable $\mathcal{B}$ to be identified, for example, using an anonymous digital certificate or a personal digital certificate or a credit card [4,5]. In fact, the last two mechanisms enable $\mathcal{B}$ to be directly identified. However, they are assumed to be implemented according to the concept of "multilateral security" applied to web transactions [53,54].
- B_{ad} is the $\mathcal{B}$'s shipping address that will enable him/her to receive the secret key $sk_{\mathcal{RA}}^X$ corresponding to the public key $pk_{\mathcal{RA}}^X$.

When the messages m_6 and m_7 are received by $\mathcal{BC}$, the code associated to a specific smart contract is automatically executed. The code of the contract mainly compares the tokens, verifies the signatures contained in the two received messages, and checks whether the tokens $pk_{\mathcal{RA}}^X$ and $\mathbb{E}_{pk_{\mathcal{RA}}^X}(N)$, generated by $\mathcal{RA}$, have been already used in a previous purchase transaction or not. In fact, this means to check whether $pk_{\mathcal{RA}}^X$ and $\mathbb{E}_{pk_{\mathcal{RA}}^X}(N)$ have been already published in a node of the blockchain or not. If all data turn out to be correct, match, and the tokens generated by $\mathcal{RA}$ have not been used in previous transactions, the code enables the generation of a new node in $\mathcal{BC}$, which makes some of the tokens identifying the ongoing transactions, such as X_d, T_X, $pk_{\mathcal{RA}}^X$, $\mathbb{E}_{pk_{\mathcal{RA}}^X}(N)$, $\mathbb{S}_{\mathcal{RA}}(pk_{\mathcal{RA}}^X, \mathbb{E}_{pk_{\mathcal{RA}}^X}(N))$, and $\mathbb{S}_{\mathcal{CP}}(X_d, T_X, pk_{\mathcal{RA}}^X, \mathbb{E}_{pk_{\mathcal{RA}}^X}(N), \mathbb{S}_{\mathcal{RA}}(pk_{\mathcal{RA}}^X, \mathbb{E}_{pk_{\mathcal{RA}}^X}(N)))$, public. Moreover, the execution of the smart contract within $\mathcal{BC}$ takes also charge of implementing the payment phase. It ends by sending two messages, m_8 and m_9, to $\mathcal{RA}$ and $\mathcal{CP}$, respectively.

The message m_8 includes B_{ad} and $pk_{\mathcal{RA}}^X$, and enables $\mathcal{RA}$ to send the secret key $sk_{\mathcal{RA}}^X$ to $\mathcal{B}$ in the message m_{10}. $\mathcal{B}$ can thus decrypt $\overline{\mathbb{E}_{pk_{\mathcal{RA}}^X}(X)}$ and obtain the final protected content according to the following equalities:

$$\overline{\mathbb{E}_{pk_{\mathcal{RA}}^X}(X)} = \mathbb{E}_{pk_{\mathcal{RA}}^X}(\bar{X}), \qquad \bar{X} = \mathbb{D}_{sk_{\mathcal{RA}}^X}(\overline{\mathbb{E}_{pk_{\mathcal{RA}}^X}(X)}) \tag{3}$$

The message m_9 contains the security token $E_{pk_{\mathcal{RA}}}(B_{id}, pk_{\mathcal{RA}}^X, \mathbb{E}_{pk_{\mathcal{RA}}^X}(N))$. It is stored by $\mathcal{CP}$ in a new entry in its databases, whose search key is the watermark $W_{\mathcal{CP}}$. The entry also includes the following tokens: X_d, T_X, $pk_{\mathcal{RA}}^X$, $\mathbb{E}_{pk_{\mathcal{RA}}^X}(N)$, and $\mathbb{S}_{\mathcal{RA}}(pk_{\mathcal{RA}}^X, \mathbb{E}_{pk_{\mathcal{RA}}^X}(N))$. Such tokens are needed to prove that $\mathcal{B}$ is the legitimate owner of the protected content $\bar{X}$ sold by $\mathcal{CP}$ through a transaction registered by a node published in the blockchain $\mathcal{BC}$.

5.2. Identification and Arbitration Protocol

The protocol is run by $\mathcal{CP}$ to identify the responsible distributor of a pirated copy of $\bar{X}$, who was the legitimate copyright owner of $\bar{X}$, with undeniable evidence [4,5].

As shown in Table 3, the first step of the protocol consists of extracting the watermark W' from the pirated copy of $\bar{X}$, denoted as X'. After the extraction of $W' = W'_{\mathcal{CP}} \| N'$, $\mathcal{CP}$ can access its databases and use $W'_{\mathcal{CP}}$ to search them for a match. If a possible match is found [11], $\mathcal{CP}$ can retrieve the tokens saved during the purchase transaction of $\bar{X}$, which are X_d, T_X, $pk_{\mathcal{RA}}^X$, $\mathbb{E}_{pk_{\mathcal{RA}}^X}(N)$, $\mathbb{S}_{\mathcal{RA}}(pk_{\mathcal{RA}}^X, \mathbb{E}_{pk_{\mathcal{RA}}^X}(N))$, and $E_{pk_{\mathcal{RA}}}(B_{id}, pk_{\mathcal{RA}}^X, \mathbb{E}_{pk_{\mathcal{RA}}^X}(N))$. Then, $\mathcal{CP}$ can send the tokens, together with W', to $\mathcal{J}$ in the message m_1.

Table 3. Identification and arbitration protocol.

$\mathcal{CP}$	:	finds X' in the market and extracts $W' = W'_{\mathcal{CP}} \| N'$
$\mathcal{CP}$	:	searches its databases for a possible match on $W'_{\mathcal{CP}}$
$\mathcal{CP} \to \mathcal{J}$	:	$m_1 = \{W', X_d, T_X, pk_{\mathcal{RA}}^X, \mathbb{E}_{pk_{\mathcal{RA}}^X}(N), \mathbb{S}_{\mathcal{RA}}(pk_{\mathcal{RA}}^X, \mathbb{E}_{pk_{\mathcal{RA}}^X}(N)),$ $E_{pk_{\mathcal{RA}}}(B_{id}, pk_{\mathcal{RA}}^X, \mathbb{E}_{pk_{\mathcal{RA}}^X}(N))\}$
$\mathcal{J}$	:	searches $\mathcal{BC}$ for a node including $pk_{\mathcal{RA}}^X$ and $\mathbb{E}_{pk_{\mathcal{RA}}^X}(N)$
$\mathcal{J}$	:	retrieves the tokens published in the node of $\mathcal{BC}$, which are X_d, T_X, $pk_{\mathcal{RA}}^X$, $\mathbb{E}_{pk_{\mathcal{RA}}^X}(N)$, $\mathbb{S}_{\mathcal{RA}}(pk_{\mathcal{RA}}^X, \mathbb{E}_{pk_{\mathcal{RA}}^X}(N))$, $\mathbb{S}_{\mathcal{CP}}(X_d, T_X, pk_{\mathcal{RA}}^X, \mathbb{E}_{pk_{\mathcal{RA}}^X}(N), \mathbb{S}_{\mathcal{RA}}(pk_{\mathcal{RA}}^X, \mathbb{E}_{pk_{\mathcal{RA}}^X}(N)))$
$\mathcal{J}$	:	verifies if the tokens retrieved from $\mathcal{BC}$ match those ones received from $\mathcal{CP}$
$\mathcal{J} \to \mathcal{RA}$	:	$m_2 = \{pk_{\mathcal{RA}}^X, \mathbb{E}_{pk_{\mathcal{RA}}^X}(N), E_{pk_{\mathcal{RA}}}(B_{id}, pk_{\mathcal{RA}}^X, \mathbb{E}_{pk_{\mathcal{RA}}^X}(N))\}$
$\mathcal{RA}$	:	decrypts $E_{pk_{\mathcal{RA}}}(B_{id}, pk_{\mathcal{RA}}^X, \mathbb{E}_{pk_{\mathcal{RA}}^X}(N))$
$\mathcal{RA} \to \mathcal{J}$	:	$m_3 = \{B_{id}, N\}$
$\mathcal{J}$	:	compares N' with N and adjudicates

$\mathcal{J}$ receives m_1 and verifies the signature $\mathbb{S}_{\mathcal{RA}}(pk_{\mathcal{RA}}^X, \mathbb{E}_{pk_{\mathcal{RA}}^X}(N))$. Then, it searches the blockchain $\mathcal{BC}$ for a node using $pk_{\mathcal{RA}}^X$ and $\mathbb{E}_{pk_{\mathcal{RA}}^X}(N)$ as search keys. If a node is found, $\mathcal{J}$ can access the tokens published by the node, which are reported in Table 2, and compare them with those one received by $\mathcal{CP}$. If all the tokens match, $\mathcal{J}$ can send $pk_{\mathcal{RA}}^X$, $\mathbb{E}_{pk_{\mathcal{RA}}^X}(N)$, and $E_{pk_{\mathcal{RA}}}(B_{id}, pk_{\mathcal{RA}}^X, \mathbb{E}_{pk_{\mathcal{RA}}^X}(N))$ to $\mathcal{RA}$ in the message m_2.

$\mathcal{RA}$ decrypts $E_{pk_{\mathcal{RA}}}(B_{id}, pk_{\mathcal{RA}}^X, \mathbb{E}_{pk_{\mathcal{RA}}^X}(N))$ and verifies the received tokens. If all data are correct, $\mathcal{RA}$ decrypts $\mathbb{E}_{pk_{\mathcal{RA}}^X}(N)$ and sends B_{id} and N to $\mathcal{J}$ in the message m_3.

Upon receiving m_3, $\mathcal{J}$ compares N' and N. If $N' = N$, the identity of the buyer B_{id} is revealed, and $\mathcal{J}$ can adjudicate him/her to be a traitor, thus closing the case. Otherwise, the protocol ends without exposing any identity.

6. Protocol Analysis

In the conducted analysis, the ideal behavior of the proposed watermarking protocol can be modeled as follows: a content provider $\mathcal{CP}$ sells the digital content X to a buyer $\mathcal{B}$; $\mathcal{B}$ obtains the protected digital content $\tilde{X}$ from $\mathcal{CP}$; a blockchain $\mathcal{BC}$ is a ledger that publishes the tokens that identify each purchase transaction of digital content distributed on the web; a registration authority $\mathcal{RA}$ generates some specific data that have to be used by $\mathcal{CP}$ to protect X; a judge $\mathcal{J}$ decides whether $\mathcal{B}$ is guilty of releasing pirated copies.

The ideal behavior is modeled under the following assumptions:

- $\mathcal{J}$ and $\mathcal{RA}$ cannot be corrupted.
- $\mathcal{CP}$ and $\mathcal{B}$ can be only corrupted "statically", i.e., the set of the corrupt entities is decided at the beginning of the protocol execution and cannot be modified throughout the execution [55].
- $\mathcal{BC}$ is assumed to be characterized by an "honest-but-curious" behavior [55]. As a consequence, $\mathcal{BC}$ is obliged to follow the rules of the protocol, even though it can try its best to get information from the executed actions. This means that $\mathcal{BC}$ cannot collude with $\mathcal{B}$ or $\mathcal{CP}$, and this is a reasonable assumption, since $\mathcal{BC}$ is assumed to limit its action to automatically executing a smart contract whose code is approved and accepted in advance and cannot be modified during the life of the blockchain [26–30].
- Uncorrupt buyers and content providers are assumed to never release pirated copies.

The assumptions reported above ensure that, if $\mathcal{CP}$ and $\mathcal{B}$ are uncorrupt, $\mathcal{B}$ receives a unique and personalised protected content $\tilde{X}$ during the purchase transaction. Therefore, if a pirated copy of $\tilde{X}$ is found on the web, it can be always traced back to $\mathcal{B}$ and to the purchase transaction. On the contrary, if $\mathcal{CP}$ is corrupt, $\mathcal{B}$ receives a protected content $\tilde{X}$ that cannot be correctly tied to any buyer. As a consequence, nobody can be adjudicated to be a traitor, and the corruption of $\mathcal{CP}$ ends up being useless and pernicious just for $\mathcal{CP}$. Likewise, if $\mathcal{B}$ is corrupt, $\mathcal{CP}$ can abort the purchase transaction without releasing any content.

6.1. Assumptions

The proposed protocol assumes that the watermark insertion technique employed to protect a digital content is robust against the most common and nonmalevolent manipulations, and survives the most relevant and intentional attacks, such as signal processing based attacks, geometric attacks, or collusion attacks [6,7,56–60]. In fact, such an assumption is realistic since there is a vast literature on watermark insertion techniques that documents the existence of increasingly robust and secure watermarking algorithms [1,20,21,61–65] together with a promising and increasing research activity in the development of new techniques and algorithms.

The protocol also assumes that the digital encryption applied within the context of a PKI is characterized by indistinguishability under chosen plaintext attack (IND-CPA). As a consequence, an adversary cannot get any knowledge about a plaintext message m from the corresponding ciphertext c.

Finally, the protocol assumes that the adopted cryptosystem is privacy homomorphic with respect to watermark insertion according to what is specified in Section 4 [49].

6.2. Analysis

The security analysis follows the scheme adopted in [22–24], and examines the behavior of the proposed watermarking protocol when corrupt entities make their strongest attacks [46,47,66,67]. Therefore, the analysis is restricted to two main attacks, which represent the two worst cases for security: (1) when $\mathcal{CP}$ is corrupt and tries to cheat $\mathcal{B}$; (2) when $\mathcal{B}$ is corrupt and attempts to cheat $\mathcal{CP}$. In both cases, according to what is reported in Sections 3 and 5, the analysis is conducted by assuming the presence of an honest-but-curious $\mathcal{BC}$ [55,68] and of a TTP $\mathcal{RA}$.

6.2.1. $\mathcal{CP}$ is Corrupt

Consider the execution of the proposed protocol when a corrupt party $\mathcal{CP}^c$ and an honest $\mathcal{B}$ are involved.

$\mathcal{B}$ chooses the content X and communicates the wish to buy it to $\mathcal{CP}^c$. $\mathcal{CP}^c$ interacts with $\mathcal{RA}$ and obtains $pk_{\mathcal{RA}}^X$ and $\mathbb{E}_{pk_{\mathcal{RA}}^X}(N)$. During this preliminary phase, no corrupting actions may occur.

Lemma 1 (Basic Lemma). *Under the basic assumptions reported in Section 6.1, if $\mathcal{CP}^c$ tries to embed a corrupt watermark W^c into X in order to accuse an innocent buyer of illegal content distribution, such a corruption is disclosed by running the identification and arbitration protocol.*

Proof. Since the watermark W is composed of N and $W_{\mathcal{CP}}$ (see Expression (1)), $\mathcal{CP}^c$ can embed a corrupt watermark into X only if it can corrupt the part N of W. Therefore, consider the case in which $\mathcal{CP}^c$ wants to embed a corrupt N^c into the content X purchased by $\mathcal{B}$. To achieve such a goal, $\mathcal{CP}^c$ has to be able to:

1. embedd the watermark $W^c = W_{\mathcal{CP}} || N^c$ into the content X directly in the encrypted domain, according to the Expressions (1) and (2);
2. obtain the generation of a node in the blockchain $\mathcal{BC}$, which occurs only if $\mathcal{BC}$ can certify consistency between the security tokens sent in the messages m_6 and m_7 by $\mathcal{CP}^c$ and $\mathcal{B}$ respectively (see Table 2).

The former condition is needed because $\mathcal{B}$ obtains the final and protected version of the purchased content $\tilde{X}$ by decrypting the content $\overline{\mathbb{E}_{pk_{\mathcal{RA}}^X}(X)}$ with the secret key received by $\mathcal{RA}$ in the message m_{10} (see Table 2), according to the Expression (3). This also means that, if $\mathcal{CP}^c$ wants to use a corrupt key $pk_{\mathcal{RA}}^{X^c}$ to encrypt the nonce N^c, it has also to control the corresponding secret key sent by $\mathcal{RA}$ to $\mathcal{B}$ in the message m_{10}, which has to necessarily become $sk_{\mathcal{RA}}^{X^c}$.

The latter condition implies that $\mathcal{CP}^c$ can obtain or generate a valid and verifiable signature $\mathbb{S}_{\mathcal{RA}}(pk_{\mathcal{RA}}^X, \mathbb{E}_{pk_{\mathcal{RA}}^X}(N^c))$ on the corrupt token $\mathbb{E}_{pk_{\mathcal{RA}}^X}(N^c)$. Furthermore, if $\mathcal{CP}^c$ decides to also employ a corrupt key $pk_{\mathcal{RA}}^{X^c}$ to encrypt N^c, then the corrupt signature to obtain or generate becomes $\mathbb{S}_{\mathcal{RA}}(pk_{\mathcal{RA}}^{X^c}, \mathbb{E}_{pk_{\mathcal{RA}}^{X^c}}(N^c))$.

In this regard, it is worth noting that, under the assumptions reported in Section 6.1, $\mathcal{CP}^c$ cannot generate a valid signature $\mathbb{S}_{\mathcal{RA}}(\ldots)$ on corrupt tokens. This means that $\mathcal{CP}^c$ cannot choose an arbitrary nonce N^c or key pair $(pk_{\mathcal{RA}}^{X^c}, sk_{\mathcal{RA}}^{X^c})$ to conduct a purchase transaction, but it could only attempt to reuse tokens generated by $\mathcal{RA}$ in previous purchase transactions. However, the following considerations have to be taken into account:

1. When a key pair $(pk_{\mathcal{RA}}^X, sk_{\mathcal{RA}}^X)$ and an encrypted nonce $\mathbb{E}_{pk_{\mathcal{RA}}^X}(N)$ are employed in a valid purchase transaction, they are included and published in a node of $\mathcal{BC}$, and can no longer be re-used, as reported in Section 5.1.
2. Once the public key $pk_{\mathcal{RA}}^X$ has been chosen and sent to $\mathcal{B}$ in the message m_4, it can no longer be corrupted by $\mathcal{CP}^c$, since it has to correspond to the secret key $sk_{\mathcal{RA}}^X$ released by $\mathcal{RA}$ in the message m_{10}. Therefore, if $\mathcal{CP}^c$ encrypts the watermark to be inserted into X using the corrupt key $pk_{\mathcal{RA}}^{X^c}$, it ends up generating the content $\mathbb{E}_{pk_{\mathcal{RA}}^{X^c}}(X)$. However, $\mathcal{B}$ will employ the secret key $sk_{\mathcal{RA}}^X$ to decrypt the received content $\overline{\mathbb{E}_{pk_{\mathcal{RA}}^{X^c}}(X)}$ according to the Expression (3), thus generating a protected content containing an unknown and unpredictable watermark. In fact, this just damages $\mathcal{CP}^c$, which ends up releasing a piece of content including a watermark that cannot be linked to any buyer.
3. If $\mathcal{CP}^c$ receives the key $pk_{\mathcal{RA}}^X$ from $\mathcal{RA}$ in the message m_3 and forwards the corrupt key $pk_{\mathcal{RA}}^{X^c}$ to $\mathcal{B}$ in the message m_4, the key exchange is always disclosed by $\mathcal{BC}$ unless $\mathcal{CP}^c$ generates a valid signature $\mathbb{S}_{\mathcal{RA}}(pk_{\mathcal{RA}}^{X^c}, \ldots)$, which, as reported above, is impossible. This is because $\mathcal{BC}$ compares

the tokens received in the messages m_6 and m_7, and generates a new node in the blockchain only if the tokens turn out to be consistent.

4. For the same reason reported at the previous point, if $\mathcal{CP}^c$ receives the encrypted nonce $\mathbb{E}_{pk_{\mathcal{RA}}^X}(N)$ from $\mathcal{RA}$ in the message m_3 and forwards the corrupt nonce $\mathbb{E}_{pk_{\mathcal{RA}}^X}(N^c)$ to $\mathcal{BC}$ in the message m_6, the nonce exchange is always disclosed by $\mathcal{BC}$ unless $\mathcal{CP}^c$ generates a valid signature $\mathbb{S}_{\mathcal{RA}}(pk_{\mathcal{RA}}^X, \mathbb{E}_{pk_{\mathcal{RA}}^X}(N^c))$, which, as reported above, is impossible.

Therefore, suppose that $\mathcal{B}$ starts a purchase transaction and that $\mathcal{CP}^c$ receives the message m_3 containing $pk_{\mathcal{RA}}^X$, $\mathbb{E}_{pk_{\mathcal{RA}}^X}(N)$, and $\mathbb{S}_{\mathcal{RA}}(pk_{\mathcal{RA}}^X, \mathbb{E}_{pk_{\mathcal{RA}}^X}(N))$ (see Table 2). Suppose also that $\mathcal{CP}^c$ inserts a corrupt watermark $W^c = W_{\mathcal{CP}} || N^c$ into the content X, thus creating the protected copy $\bar{X}^c$, and suppose that $\bar{X}^c$ is found in the market. $\mathcal{CP}^c$ starts the identification and arbitration protocol by extracting the watermark W^c from $\bar{X}^c$ and by sending to $\mathcal{J}$ all the tokens existing in its databases and associated to W^c, according to what is reported in Section 5.2.

Suppose that $\mathcal{CP}^c$ wants to cheat $\mathcal{J}$ in order to accuse a buyer of illegal content distribution. To achieve such a goal, $\mathcal{CP}^c$ has to send, among the others, the following corrupt tokens $pk_{\mathcal{RA}}^X$, $\mathbb{E}_{pk_{\mathcal{RA}}^X}(N^c)$, $\mathbb{S}_{\mathcal{RA}}(pk_{\mathcal{RA}}^X, \mathbb{E}_{pk_{\mathcal{RA}}^X}(N^c))$, $E_{pk_{\mathcal{RA}}}(B_{id}, pk_{\mathcal{RA}}^X, \mathbb{E}_{pk_{\mathcal{RA}}^X}(N^c))$ to $\mathcal{J}$ (see Table 3), which have to be all coherent with N^c. However, according to what is reported above and under the assumptions of Section 6.1, the following constraints have to be considered:

- $\mathcal{CP}^c$ cannot generate a valid signature $\mathbb{S}_{\mathcal{RA}}(\ldots)$ on arbitrary security tokens;
- the security tokens that can be employed in a valid purchase transaction have to be among those ones generated by $\mathcal{RA}$;
- $\mathcal{CP}^c$ cannot reuse security tokens employed in previous purchase transactions and already published in the nodes of $\mathcal{BC}$;

As a consequence, if $\mathcal{CP}^c$ attempts to accuse an innocent buyer of illegal content distribution by generating corrupt tokens coherent with the corrupt watermark $W^c = W_{\mathcal{CP}} || N^c$ embedded into the content X^c found in the market, the attempt ends up being revealed by the execution of the identification and arbitration protocol, and this prevents the protocol from adjudicating anybody to be a traitor. □

Lemma 2. *Under the assumptions reported in Section 6.1, if $\mathcal{CP}^c$ tries to alter the tokens that are managed during the protection phase in order to accuse an innocent buyer of illegal content distribution, such a corruption is disclosed by the identification and arbitration protocol.*

Proof. The basic lemma proves that the security tokens, such as $pk_{\mathcal{RA}}^X$, $\mathbb{E}_{pk_{\mathcal{RA}}^X}(N)$, and $\mathbb{S}_{\mathcal{RA}}(pk_{\mathcal{RA}}^X, \mathbb{E}_{pk_{\mathcal{RA}}^X}(N))$, generated by $\mathcal{RA}$ and associated to a valid purchase transaction registered by a node of $\mathcal{BC}$, cannot be coherently corrupted by $\mathcal{CP}^c$ to insert an arbitrary watermark into the content purchased by $\mathcal{B}$ without such a corruption being disclosed by running the identification and arbitration protocol. More precisely, the impossibility of corrupting the security tokens has been proved be the basic lemma independently of the corruption of the watermark to be inserted into X. In fact, the proof is mainly based on the general incapacity of $\mathcal{CP}^c$ to alter or regenerate or reuse the tokens generated by $\mathcal{RA}$ for a given purchase transaction [22–24]. Therefore, the attempts of $\mathcal{CP}^c$ to alter the tokens generated by $\mathcal{RA}$ can be always disclosed by running the identification and arbitration protocol, since such tokens either have been generated and employed during previous, valid purchase transactions by $\mathcal{RA}$ or are directly generated by $\mathcal{CP}^c$ and so they cannot be registered in a node of $\mathcal{BC}$. □

The lemmas reported above prove that $\mathcal{CP}^c$ cannot frame an innocent buyer, because every attempt to corrupt the security tokens that have to be registered in the nodes of $\mathcal{BC}$ is disclosed by the identification and arbitration protocol, and this prevents the watermarking protocol from adjudicating anybody to be a traitor.

6.2.2. $\mathcal{B}$ is Corrupt

Consider the execution of the proposed protocol when the involved parties are a corrupt buyer $\mathcal{B}^c$ and an honest $\mathcal{CP}$.

Suppose that $\mathcal{B}^c$ contacts $\mathcal{CP}$ in order to buy the content X. $\mathcal{B}^c$ receives the confirmation message m_4 from $\mathcal{CP}$, which contains the following tokens: X_d, T_X, $pk_{\mathcal{RA}}^X$, $\mathbb{S}_{\mathcal{RA}}(pk_{\mathcal{RA}}^X, \mathbb{E}_{pk_{\mathcal{RA}}^X}(N))$, $\mathbb{S}_{\mathcal{CP}}(X_d, T_X, pk_{\mathcal{RA}}^X, \mathbb{S}_{\mathcal{RA}}(pk_{\mathcal{RA}}^X, \mathbb{E}_{pk_{\mathcal{RA}}^X}(N)))$ (see Table 2).

Lemma 3 (Basic Lemma). *Under the basic assumptions reported in Section 6.1, if $\mathcal{B}^c$ tries to complete the purchase transaction by employing a corrupt content identifier X_d^c in order to impair the piracy tracing mechanism implemented by $\mathcal{CP}$, such a corruption is disclosed and the purchase transaction is aborted.*

Proof. Suppose that $\mathcal{B}^c$ wants to use a corrupt identifier X_d^c to conduct the purchase transaction. Under the assumptions reported in Section 6.1, such a goal can be achieved only if $\mathcal{B}^c$ can obtain the generation of a node in the blockchain $\mathcal{BC}$ which contains X_d^c. This occurs only when $\mathcal{BC}$ can certify consistency between the security tokens sent by $\mathcal{CP}$ and $\mathcal{B}^c$ in the messages m_6 and m_7 respectively (see Table 2). This also means that, if $\mathcal{B}^c$ wishes to include the corrupt identifier X_d^c in the message m_7, the buyer must ensure that the corresponding signature $\mathbb{S}_{\mathcal{CP}}(X_d, \ldots)$ is included in the message m_6. However, it is worth noting that, under the assumptions reported in Section 6.1:

1. $\mathcal{B}^c$ cannot autonomously generate a valid and verifiable signature $\mathbb{S}_{\mathcal{CP}}(\ldots)$ on corrupt tokens.
2. X_d is generated by $\mathcal{CP}$ to unambiguously identify the content X requested by the buyer. Therefore, $\mathcal{CP}$ uniquely accepts the content identifiers that it has generated during the initial phase of the protection protocol. No other identifiers can be accepted.
3. X_d is always sent by $\mathcal{CP}$ to $\mathcal{BC}$ in the message m_6, together with the corresponding signature $\mathbb{S}_{\mathcal{CP}}(\ldots)$. Therefore, if the content identifiers included in the messages m_6 and m_7 do not coincide or do not match with the signature $\mathbb{S}_{\mathcal{CP}}(\ldots)$, $\mathcal{BC}$ does not complete the purchase transaction.

As a consequence, $\mathcal{B}^c$ cannot employ arbitrary content identifiers in the protection protocol, but he/she can, at the most, exploit pairs $(X_d, \mathbb{S}_{\mathcal{CP}}(X_d, \ldots))$ generated by $\mathcal{CP}$ in other previous, incomplete purchase transactions. In fact, such pairs must not be already included in nodes of the blockchain.

Suppose that $\mathcal{B}^c$ can get two distinct content identifiers Y_d and Z_d, together with the corresponding signatures $\mathbb{S}_{\mathcal{CP}}(Y_d, \ldots)$ and $\mathbb{S}_{\mathcal{CP}}(Z_d, \ldots)$, from $\mathcal{CP}$. The two identifiers refer to the content Y and Z distributed by $\mathcal{CP}$.

Suppose that $\mathcal{B}^c$ starts a transaction with $\mathcal{CP}$ to purchase X. $\mathcal{B}^c$ receives X_d and $\mathbb{S}_{\mathcal{CP}}(X_d, \ldots)$ from $\mathcal{CP}$ in the message m_4. This also means that $\mathcal{BC}$ will receive X_d and $\mathbb{S}_{\mathcal{CP}}(X_d, \ldots)$ from $\mathcal{CP}$ in the subsequent message m_6, and this will prevent $\mathcal{B}^c$ from using any other pair of content identifier and signature in the message m_7. In fact, if this happens, $\mathcal{BC}$ can always disclose the mismatch between the tokens included in the message m_6 and those ones included in the message m_7, according to what is reported above. As a consequence, every attempt of $\mathcal{B}^c$ to conduct a purchase transaction by employing corrupt content identifiers causes the purchase transaction to abort. □

Lemma 4. *Under the assumptions reported in Section 6.1, if $\mathcal{B}^c$ tries to corrupt the tokens needed to run the protection protocol in order to impair the piracy tracing mechanism implemented by the watermarking protocol, such a corruption is directly disclosed by $\mathcal{BC}$ and the purchase transaction is aborted.*

Proof. This lemma is an extension of the basic lemma, which has proved that $\mathcal{B}^c$ cannot deceive $\mathcal{BC}$ by proposing arbitrary content identifiers or identifiers that are incoherent with the corresponding signatures. The trivial reason is that $\mathcal{BC}$ accepts the tokens sent by $\mathcal{B}^c$ in the message m_7 only if they are consistent with those ones sent by $\mathcal{CP}$ in the message m_6. Therefore, every attempt of $\mathcal{B}^c$ to corrupt the tokens generated by $\mathcal{CP}$ during a purchase transaction causes the protection protocol to abort without releasing any protected content. □

The lemmas reported above prove that the corrupt entity $\mathcal{B}^c$ cannot cheat $\mathcal{CP}$ in order to release a piece of content not tied to any buyer, because every attempt to corrupt the tokens managed by the protection protocol is always disclosed by $\mathcal{BC}$, which can thus abort the purchase transaction.

7. Implementation

The first prototype implementation of the proposed protocol is mainly based on the experiences documented in [22,24]. It consists of two parts.

The former comprises the same set of C++ separate programs that implement $\mathcal{B}, \mathcal{CP}, \mathcal{RA},$ and $\mathcal{J}$ in [22,24]. The programs run on Linux operating system and communicate via TCP implemented by standard socket library. They implement the encryption/decryption and watermark insertion algorithms by exploiting the NTL library and the GNU Multi Precision Arithmetic library. In particular, watermark insertion is based on the "Quantization Index Modulation" algorithm [61] extended to the homomorphic cryptosystem proposed by Paillier [69] according to the main ideas reported in [9,63]. It follows the indications reported in [42], which successfully address a number of problems that tend to make watermark insertion directly into the encrypted domain inefficient. In this regard, in order to reduce both the number of encryptions and the operations performed on encrypted values, watermark insertion is carried out in the encrypted domain by exploiting the specific technique of the "composite signal representation" described in [42], also called "efficient composite embedding" [50].

The latter implements the blockchain $\mathcal{BC}$ according to the Figure 1. In particular, the blockchain can be classified as "public", with a fully decentralized architecture, and based on the classic "proof of work" consensus algorithm [27]. Furthermore, the nodes of the blockchain are implemented in Ethereum [70], whereas the smart contract employed by the proposed protocol is written in Solidity [71].

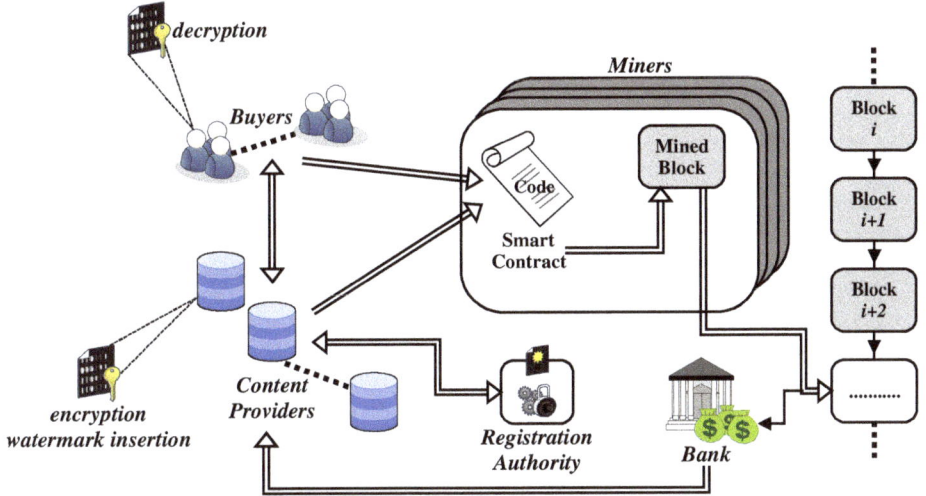

Figure 1. The blockchain within the proposed watermarking protocol.

The performance of the proposed prototype implementation mainly depends on both the basic operations characterizing watermarking protocols and the overhead induced by the blockchain management. In fact, the former are the classic encryption/decryption and watermark insertion operations. Their performances are omitted because, as reported above, they are well documented by the results published in [22,24]. On the contrary, the latter depends on a number of factors, such as, for example, the Ethereum node implementation, the adopted consensus algorithm, and the number of nodes averagely involved in the blockchain, which are essentially independent of proposed watermarking protocol [28,29]. In this regard, it is worth noting that an Ethereum, public and decentralized blockchain, based on the "proof of work" consensus algorithm, is characterized by undoubted advantages, such as decentralization, lack of trusted third parties, and immutability [27–29], but it is also affected by low performance and efficiency levels caused by the time needed for propagating, processing, and validating the purchase transactions [72]. In fact, the higher the number of nodes participating in the blockchain is, the more limiting power consumption and block generation rate become. However, the main goals of the proposed protocols are to achieve high levels of robustness and security without reducing simplicity of the protection scheme. After all, it is not wrong to think that the proposed watermarking protocol will be able to take advantage of the next generation blockchains, which promise to achieve higher performance and efficiency levels, particularly in terms of power consumption, due the development of new consensus algorithms. Nevertheless, such performance aspects have not been investigated because they are out of the scope of this paper.

8. Conclusions

The main goal in developing the proposed protocol has been to simplify the basic interaction scheme that characterizes the previous protocols that adopt a "buyer friendly" and "mediated" design approach without compromising on their relevant achievements [22–24]. The solution has been found in the smart contracts to be exploited within the blockchain technology. In fact, a smart contract has been employed to simply validate the security tokens generated during purchase transactions and then published as immutable purchase information in the blocks maintained by the blockchain [27–29,31]. It has made it possible to avoid the direct involvement of a TTP in the protection scheme without forcing buyers to carry out complex actions to participate in the purchase transactions. In this way, the interaction scheme turns out to be simple while, at the same time, it strongly reduces the possibility of collusion actions among the parties participating in the protocol, thus making the protocol secure and suited to the current web context.

The proposed protocol also confirms the security achievements characterizing the previous similar protocols [22–24]: (1) $\mathcal{CP}$ keeps control on the content that it distributes on the Internet, since it never releases them in unprotected forms; (2) $\mathcal{B}$ is the only entity that gets access to the final watermarked content $\tilde{X}$, and this makes it possible to trace back pirated copies of $\tilde{X}$ to $\mathcal{B}$; (3) X is never released in a partially protected form, thus solving the specific problem arisen in the watermarking protocol proposed in [11] and discussed in [22,23]; (4) a suspected buyer is not required to cooperate in the "identification and arbitration protocol" to make appropriate adjudications.

Finally, it is worth noting that the adoption of blockchain technology represents a relevant step in the direction of secure and simplified buyer friendly and mediated watermarking protocols. Moreover, the performance achieved by the prototype implementation of the proposed protocol is overall good, even though it is penalised by the adopted consensus algorithm. However, this cannot be considered an actual problem, since next generations of blockchains will be able to implement improved algorithms and to provide better and better performances [73,74].

Funding: This research received no external funding.

Acknowledgments: The author wishes to thank Domenico Di Pietro for his good advice.

Conflicts of Interest: The author declares no conflict of interest.

References

1. Cox, I.; Miller, M.; Bloom, J.; Fridrich, J.; Kalker, T. *Digital Watermarking and Steganography*; Morgan Kaufmann: Burlington, MA, USA, 2007.
2. Barni, M.; Bartolini, F. Data Hiding for Fighting Piracy. *IEEE Signal Process. Mag.* **2004**, *21*, 28–39. [CrossRef]
3. Gopalakrishnan, K.; Memon, N.; Vora, P.L. Protocols for watermark verification. *IEEE Multimed.* **2001**, *8*, 66–70. [CrossRef]
4. Frattolillo, F. Watermarking protocol for web context. *IEEE Trans. Inf. Forensics Secur.* **2007**, *2*, 350–363. [CrossRef]
5. Frattolillo, F. Watermarking Protocols: Problems, Challenges and a Possible Solution. *Comput. J.* **2015**, *58*, 944–960. [CrossRef]
6. Trappe, W.; Wu, M.; Wang, Z.J.; Liu, K.J.R. Anti-collusion fingerprinting for multimedia. *IEEE Trans. Signal Process.* **2003**, *41*, 1069–1087. [CrossRef]
7. Liu, K.J.R.; Trappe, W.; Wang, Z.J.; Wu, M.; Zhao, H. *Multimedia Fingerprinting Forensics for Traitor Tracing*; Hindawi Publishing Corporation: New York, NY, USA, 2005.
8. Pehlivanoglu, S. An Asymmetric Fingerprinting Code for Collusion-resistant Buyer-seller Watermarking. In Proceedings of the 1st ACM Workshop on Information Hiding and Multimedia Security, Montpellier, France, 17–19 June 2013; ACM: New York, NY, USA, 2013; pp. 35–44.
9. Kuribayashy, M.; Tanaka, H. Fingerprinting Protocol for Images Based on Additive Homomorphic Property. *IEEE Trans. Image Process.* **2005**, *14*, 2129–2139. [CrossRef] [PubMed]
10. Memon, N.; Wong, P.W. A buyer-seller watermarking protocol. *IEEE Trans. Image Process.* **2001**, *10*, 643–649. [CrossRef]
11. Lei, C.L.; Yu, P.L.; Tsai, P.L.; Chan, M.H. An Efficient and Anonymous Buyer-Seller Watermarking Protocol. *IEEE Trans. Image Process.* **2004**, *13*, 1618–1626. [CrossRef] [PubMed]
12. Fan, C.I.; Chen, M.T.; Sun, W.Z. Buyer-Seller Watermarking Protocols with Off-line Trusted Parties. In Proceedings of the IEEE Int. Conf. on Multimedia and Ubiquitous Engineering, Seul, Korea, 26–28 April 2007; IEEE Computer Society: Washington, DC, USA, 2007; pp. 1035–1040.
13. Das, V.V. Buyer-Seller Watermarking Protocol for an Anonymous Network Transaction. In Proceedings of the 1st Int. Conf. on Emerging Trends in Engineering and Technology, Nagpur, India, 16–18 July 2008; IEEE Computer Society: Washington, DC, USA, 2008; pp. 807–812.
14. Laxmi, V.; Khan, M.N.; Kumar, S.S.; Gaur, M.S. Buyer seller watermarking protocol for digital rights management. In Proceedings of the 2nd Int. Conf. on Security of information and networks, Famagusta, North Cyprus, 6–10 October 2009; ACM: New York, NY, USA, 2009; pp. 298–301.
15. Hu, D.; Li, Q. A secure and practical buyer-seller watermarking protocol. In Proceedings of the Int. Conf. on Multimedia Information Networking and Security, Hubei, China, 18–20 November 2009; IEEE Computer Society: Washington, DC, USA, 2009; pp. 105–108.
16. Zhao, H.V.; Liu, K.J.R. Traitor-within-Traitor Behavior Forensics: Strategy and Risk Minimization. *IEEE Trans. Inf. Forensics Secur.* **2006**, *1*, 440–456. [CrossRef]
17. Rial, A.; Deng, M.; Bianchi, T.; Piva, A.; Preneel, B. A Provably Secure Anonymous Buyer–Seller Watermarking Protocol. *IEEE Trans. Inf. Forensics Secur.* **2010**, *5*, 920–931. [CrossRef]
18. Rial, A.; Balasch, J.; Preneel, B. A Privacy-Preserving Buyer–Seller Watermarking Protocol Based on Priced Oblivious Transfer. *IEEE Trans. Inf. Forensics Secur.* **2011**, *6*, 202–212. [CrossRef]
19. Xu, Z.; Li, L.; Gao, H. Bandwidth Efficient Buyer-seller Watermarking Protocol. *Int. J. Inf. Comput. Secur.* **2012**, *5*, 1–10. [CrossRef]
20. Bianchi, T.; Piva, A. TTP-free asymmetric fingerprinting based on client side embedding. *IEEE Trans. Inf. Forensics Secur.* **2014**, *9*, 1557–1568. [CrossRef]
21. Bianchi, T.; Piva, A.; Shullani, D. Anticollusion solutions for asymmetric fingerprinting protocols based on client side embedding. *Eurasip J. Inf. Secur.* **2015**, *2015*, [CrossRef]
22. Frattolillo, F. A Buyer–Friendly and Mediated Watermarking Protocol for Web Context. *ACM Trans. Web.* **2016**, *10*, 1–8. [CrossRef]
23. Frattolillo, F. Watermarking protocols: An excursus to motivate a new approach. *Int. J. Inf. Secur.* **2018**, *17*, 587–601. [CrossRef]

24. Frattolillo, F. A multiparty watermarking protocol for cloud environments. *J. Inf. Secur. Appl.* **2019**, *47*, 246–257. [CrossRef]
25. Tapscott, D.; Tapscott, A. *Blockchain Revolution: How the Technology Behind Bitcoin Is Changing Money, Business, and the World*; Portfolio-Penguin: New York, NY, USA, 2016.
26. Mougayar, W. *The Business Blockchain: Promise, Practice, and Application of the Next Internet Technology*; Wiley: Hoboken, NJ, USA, 2016.
27. Zheng, Z.; Xie, S.; Dai, H.N.; Chen, X.; Wang, H. Blockchain challenges and opportunities: A survey. *Int. J. Web Grid Serv.* **2018**, *14*, 352–375. [CrossRef]
28. Casino, F.; Dasaklis, T.K.; Patsakis, C. A systematic literature review of blockchain-based applications: Current status, classification and open issues. *Telemat. Inform.* **2019**, *36*, 55–81. [CrossRef]
29. Aggarwal, S.; Chaudhary, R.; Aujla, G.S.; Kumar, N.; Choo, K.K.R.; Zomaya, A.Y. Blockchain for smart communities: Applications, challenges and opportunities. *J. Netw. Comput. Appl.* **2019**, *144*, 13–48. [CrossRef]
30. Tresise, A.; Goldenfein, J.; Hunter, D. What Blockchain Can and Can't Do for Copyright. *Aust. Intellect. Prop. J.* **2018**, *28*, 144–157.
31. Macrinici, D.; Cartofeanu, C.; Gao, S. Smart contract applications within blockchain technology: A systematic mapping study. *Telemat. Inform.* **2018**, *35*, 2337–2354. [CrossRef]
32. Ku, W.; Chi, C.H. Survey on the Technological Aspects of Digital Rights Management. In Proceedings of the 7th Int. Information Security Conference, Lecture Notes in Computer Science, Palo Alto, CA, USA, 27–29 September 2004; Zhang, K., Zheng, Y., Eds.; Springer: Berlin, Germany, 2004; Volume 3225, pp. 391–403.
33. Zhang, Z.; Pei, Q.; Ma, J.; Yang, L. Security and Trust in Digital Rights Management: A Survey. *Int. J. Netw. Secur.* **2009**, *9*, 247–263.
34. Abdalla, H.; Hu, X.; Wahaballa, A.; Abdalla, A.; Ramadan, M.; Zhiguang, Q. Integrating the Functional Encryption and Proxy Re-cryptography to Secure DRM Scheme. *Int. J. Netw. Secur.* **2017**, *19*, 27–38.
35. Barbareschi, M.; Cilardo, A.; Mazzeo, A. A partial FPGA bitstream encryption enabling hardware DRM in mobile environment. In Proceedings of the ACM Int. Conf. on Computing Frontiers, Como, Italy, 16–18 May 2016; ACM: New York, NY, USA, 2016; pp. 443–448.
36. Lee, C.C.; Li, C.T.; Chen, Z.W.; Lai, Y.M.; Shieh, J.C. An improved E-DRM scheme for mobile environments. *J. Inf. Secur. Appl.* **2018**, *39*, 19–30. [CrossRef]
37. Bhowmik, D.; Feng, T. The multimedia blockchain: A distributed and tamper-proof media transaction framework. In Proceedings of the 22nd Int. Conf. on Digital Signal Processing, London, UK, 23–25 August 2017; IEEE Computer Society: Washington, DC, USA, 2017; pp. 1–5.
38. Meng, Z.; Morizumi, T.; Miyata, S.; Kinoshita, H. Design Scheme of Copyright Management System Based on Digital Watermarking and Blockchain. In Proceedings of the IEEE 42nd Annual Computer Software and Applications Conference, Tokyo, Japan, 23–27 July 2018; IEEE Computer Society: Washington, DC, USA, 2018; pp. 359–364.
39. Zhaofeng, M.; Weihua, H.; Hongmin, G. A new blockchain-based trusted DRM scheme for built-in content protection. *Eurasip J. Image Video Process.* **2018**, *2018*, 91. [CrossRef]
40. Deng, M.; Preneel, B. Attacks On Two Buyer-Seller Watermarking Protocols and An Improvement for Revocable Anonymity. In Proceedings of the IEEE Int. Symp. on Electronic Commerce and Security, Guangzhou, China, 3–5 August 2008; IEEE Computer Society: Washington, DC, USA, 2008; pp. 923–929.
41. Deng, M.; Preneel, B. On secure and anonymous buyer-seller watermarking protocol. In Proceedings of the 3rd Int. Conf. on Internet and Web Applications and Services, Athens, Greece, 8–13 June 2008; IEEE Computer Society: Washington, DC, USA, 2008; pp. 524–529.
42. Deng, M.; Bianchi, T.; Piva, A.; Preneel, B. An efficient buyer-seller watermarking protocol based on composite signal representation. In Proceedings of the 11th ACM Workshop on Multimedia and Security, Princeton, NJ, USA, 7–8 September 2009; ACM: New York, NY, USA, 2009; pp. 9–18.
43. Wen, Q.; Wang, Y. Improvement of the Digital Watermarking Protocol based on the Zero-Watermark Method. In Proceedings of the 3rd Annual Summit and Conf. of Asia Pacific Signal and Information Processing Association, Xi'an, China, 18–21 October 2011; APSIPA Publisher: Xi'an, China, 2011.
44. Terelius, B. Towards transferable watermarks in buyer-seller watermarking protocols. In Proceedings of the IEEE Int. Work. on Information Forensics and Security, Guangzhou, China, 18–21 November 2013; IEEE Computer Society: Washington, DC, USA, 2013; pp. 197–202.

45. Qiao, L.; Nahrstedt, K. Watermarking schemes and protocols for protecting rightful ownership and customer's rights. *J. Vis. Commun. Image Represent.* **1998**, *9*, 194–210. [CrossRef]
46. Poh, G.S.; Martin, K.M. Classification Framework for Fair Content Tracing Protocols. In Proceedings of the 8th Int. Workshop on Digital Watermarking, Guildford, UK, 24–26 August 2009; Ho, A.T.S., Shi, Y.Q., Kim, H.J., Barni, M., Eds.; Lecture Notes in Computer Science; Springer: Berlin, Germany, 2009; Volume 5703, pp. 252–267.
47. Poh, G.S. Design and Analysis of Fair Content Tracing Protocols. Ph.D. Thesis, Department of Mathematics, Royal Holloway, University of London, Egham, Surrey, UK, 2009.
48. Cong, L.W.; He, Z. Blockchain Disruption and Smart Contracts. *Rev. Financ. Stud.* **2019**, *32*, 1754–1797. [CrossRef]
49. Fontaine, C.; Galand, F. A Survey of Homomorphic Encryption for Nonspecialists. *Eurasip J. Inf. Secur.* **2007**, *2007*. [CrossRef]
50. Bianchi, T.; Piva, A. Secure Watermarking for Multimedia Content Protection: A Review of its Benefits and Open Issues. *IEEE Signal Process. Mag.* **2013**, *30*, 87–96. [CrossRef]
51. Ellison, C.; Frantz, B.; Lampson, B.; Rivest, R.; Thomas, B.; Ylonen, T. *SPKI Certificate Theory*; RFC 2693; RFC Editor: Marina del Rey, CA, USA, 1999.
52. Williams, D.M.; Treharne, H.; Ho, A.T.S. On the Importance of One-time Key Pairs in Buyer-seller Watermarking Protocols. In Proceedings of the Int. Conf. on Security and Cryptography, Athens, Greece, 26–28 July 2010; IEEE Computer Society: Washington, DC, USA, 2010; pp. 441–446.
53. Rannenberg, K. Multilateral Security. A Concept and Examples for Balanced Security. In Proceedings of the 9th ACM Workshop on New Security Paradigms, Ballycotton, County Cork, Ireland, 18–21 February 2001; ACM: New York, NY, USA, 2001; pp. 151–162.
54. Rannenberg, K.; Royer, D.; Deuker, A. *The Future of Identity in the Information Society—Challenges and Opportunities*; Springer: Berlin, Germany, 2009.
55. Canetti, R. Security and Composition of Cryptographic Protocols: A Tutorial. *ACM SIGACT News.* **2006**, *37*, 67–92. [CrossRef]
56. Hartung, F.; Su, J.K.; Girod, B. Spread Spectrum Watermarking: Malicious Attacks and Counterattacks. In Proceedings of the SPIE Security and Watermarking of Multimedia Contents, San Jose, CA, USA, 23–27 January 1999; Delp, E.J., Wong, P.W., Eds.; SPIE: Bellingham, WA, USA, 1999; Volume 3657, pp. 147–158.
57. Katzenbeisser, S.; Veith, H. Securing Symmetric Watermarking Schemes Against Protocol Attacks. In Proceedings of the SPIE Security and Watermarking of Multimedia Contents IV, San Jose, CA, USA, 19 January 2002; Delp, E.J., Wong, P.W., Eds.; SPIE: Bellingham, WA, USA, 2002; Volume 4675, pp. 260–268.
58. Petitcolas, F.A.P. Watermarking schemes evaluation. *IEEE Signal Process. Mag.* **2000**, *17*, 58–64. [CrossRef]
59. Petitcolas, F.A.P.; Steinebach, M.; Raynal, F.; Dittmann, J.; Fontaine, C.; Fates, N. A public automated web-based evaluation service for watermarking schemes: StirMark Benchmark. In Proceedings of the SPIE Electronic Imaging 2001, Security and Watermarking of Multimedia Contents, San Jose, CA, USA, 22–25 January 2001; Wong, P.W., Delp, E.J., Eds.; SPIE: Bellingham, WA, USA, 2001; Volume 4314, pp. 575–584.
60. Barni, M.; Bartolini, F. *Watermarking Systems Engineering: Enabling Digital Assets Security and Other Applications*; CRC Press: Boca Raton, FL, USA, 2004.
61. Chen, B.; Wornell, G. Quantization index modulation: A class of provably good methods for digital watermarking and information embedding. *IEEE Trans. Inf. Theory* **2001**, *47*, 1423–1443. [CrossRef]
62. Malvar, H.S.; Florêncio, D.A.F. Improved Spread Spectrum: A New Modulation Technique for Robust Watermarking. *IEEE Trans. Signal Process.* **2003**, *51*, 898–905. [CrossRef]
63. Prins, J.P.; Erkin, Z.; Lagendijk, R.L. Anonymous fingerprinting with robust QIM watermarking techniques. *Eurasip J. Inf. Secur.* **2007**, *2007*, [CrossRef]
64. Zebbiche, K.; Khelifi, F.; Loukhaoukha, K. Robust additive watermarking in the DTCWT domain based on perceptual masking. *Multimed. Tools Appl.* **2018**, *77*, 21281–21304. [CrossRef]
65. Begum, M.; Uddin, M.S. Analysis of Digital Image Watermarking Techniques through Hybrid Methods. *Adv. Multimed.* **2020**, *2020*, [CrossRef]
66. Bellare, M.; Rogaway, P. The Security of Triple Encryption and a Framework for Code-Based Game-Playing Proofs. In Proceedings of the 25th Int. Cryptology Conference, Saint Petersburg, Russia, 28 May–1 June 2006; Vaudenay, S., Ed.; Lecture Notes in Computer Science; Springer: Berlin, Germany, 2006; Volume 4004, pp. 409–426.

67. Williams, D.M.; Treharne, H.; Ho, A.T.S.; Waller, A. Formal Analysis of Two Buyer-Seller Watermarking Protocols. In Proceedings of the 7th Int. Workshop on Digital Watermarking, Lecture Notes in Computer Science, Busan, Korea, 10–12 November 2008; Kim, H.J., Katzenbeisser, S., Ho, A.T.S., Eds.; Springer: Berlin, Germany, 2008; Volume 5450, pp. 278–292.
68. Canetti, R. Universally Composable Security: A New Paradigm for Cryptographic Protocols. In Proceedings of the 42nd IEEE Int. Symp. on Foundations of Computer Science, Newport Beach, CA, USA, 8–11 October 2001; IEEE Computer Society: Washington, DC, USA, 2001; pp. 136–145.
69. Paillier, P. Public-key Cryptosystems Based on Composite Degree Residuosity Classes. In Proceedings of the Eurocrypt '99, Lecture Notes in Computer Science, Prague, Czech Republic, 2–6 May 1999; Springer: Berlin, Germany, 1999; Volume 1592, pp. 223–238.
70. Ethereum. Available online: https://ethereum.org (accessed on 1 November 2020).
71. Solidity. Available online: https://solidity.readthedocs.io (accessed on 1 November 2020).
72. Bamakan, S.M.H.; Motavali, A.; Bondarti, A.B. A survey of blockchain consensus algorithms performance evaluation criteria. *Expert Syst. Appl.* **2020**, *154*, 113385. [CrossRef]
73. Fernandez-Carames, T.M.; Fraga-Lamas, P. A Review on the Application of Blockchain to the Next Generation of Cybersecure Industry 4.0 Smart Factories. *IEEE Access* **2019**, *7*, 45201–45218. [CrossRef]
74. Palacios, R.C.; Gordon, M.S.; Aranda, D.A. A critical review on blockchain assessment initiatives: A technology evolution viewpoint. *J. Softw. Evol. Process.* **2020**, *2020*, [CrossRef]

Publisher's Note: MDPI stays neutral with regard to jurisdictional claims in published maps and institutional affiliations.

© 2020 by the author. Licensee MDPI, Basel, Switzerland. This article is an open access article distributed under the terms and conditions of the Creative Commons Attribution (CC BY) license (http://creativecommons.org/licenses/by/4.0/).

Article

KeyNet: An Asymmetric Key-Style Framework for Watermarking Deep Learning Models

Najeeb Moharram Jebreel *, Josep Domingo-Ferrer, David Sánchez and Alberto Blanco-Justicia

CYBERCAT-Center for Cybersecurity Research of Catalonia, UNESCO Chair in Data Privacy, Department of Computer Engineering and Mathematics, Universitat Rovira i Virgili, Av. Països Catalans 26, 43007 Tarragona, Catalonia, Spain; josep.domingo@urv.cat (J.D.-F.); david.sanchez@urv.cat (D.S.); alberto.blanco@urv.cat (A.B.-J.)
* Correspondence: najeebmoharramsalim.jebreel@urv.cat; Tel.: +34-977558270

Abstract: Many organizations devote significant resources to building high-fidelity deep learning (DL) models. Therefore, they have a great interest in making sure the models they have trained are not appropriated by others. Embedding watermarks (WMs) in DL models is a useful means to protect the intellectual property (IP) of their owners. In this paper, we propose *KeyNet*, a novel watermarking framework that satisfies the main requirements for an effective and robust watermarking. In *KeyNet*, any sample in a WM carrier set can take more than one label based on where the owner signs it. The signature is the hashed value of the owner's information and her model. We leverage multi-task learning (MTL) to learn the original classification task and the watermarking task together. Another model (called the private model) is added to the original one, so that it acts as a private key. The two models are trained together to embed the WM while preserving the accuracy of the original task. To extract a WM from a marked model, we pass the predictions of the marked model on a signed sample to the private model. Then, the private model can provide the position of the signature. We perform an extensive evaluation of *KeyNet*'s performance on the CIFAR10 and FMNIST5 data sets and prove its effectiveness and robustness. Empirical results show that *KeyNet* preserves the utility of the original task and embeds a robust WM.

Keywords: deep learning models; ownership; intellectual property; watermarking; security and privacy; private model

1. Introduction

Deep learning (DL) models are used to solve many complex tasks, including computer vision, speech recognition, natural language processing, or stock market analysis [1–3]. However, building representative and highly accurate DL models is a costly endeavor. Model owners, such as technology companies, devote significant computational resources to process vast amounts of proprietary training data, whose collection also implies a significant effort. For example, a conversational model from Google Brain contains 2.6 billion parameters and takes about one month to train on 2048 TPU cores [4]. Besides, designing the architecture of a DL model and choosing its hyperparameters require substantial ML experience and many preliminary tests. Thus, it is not surprising that the owners of DL models seek compensation for the incurred costs by reaping profits from commercial exploitation. They may monetize their models in Machine Learning as a Service (MLaaS) platforms [5] or license them for a financial return to their customers for a specific period of time [6].

Unfortunately, the high value of pretrained DL models is attractive for attackers who would like to steal those models and use them illegally. For example, a user may leak a pretrained model to an unauthorized party or continue to use it after the license period has expired. Furthermore, if a model is offered as MLaaS, many model theft techniques are available to steal it based on its predictions [7,8]. Due to the competitive nature of the technology market, a stolen or misused model is clearly detrimental to its owner on both economic and competitive terms.

As model theft cannot be prevented in advance, legitimate owners need a robust and reliable way to prove their ownership of DL models in order to protect their intellectual property (IP).

Digital watermarking techniques have been widely used in the past two decades as a means to protect the ownership of multimedia contents like photos, videos and audios [9–12]. The general idea of watermarking is to embed secret information into a data item (without degrading its quality) and then use the embedded secret to claim ownership of the item.

This concept of watermarking can also be extended to DL models. Several authors have proposed to use digital WMs to prove the ownership of models and address IP infringement issues [13–21]. The proposed methods fall into two main classes: (i) *white-box methods*, which directly embed the WM information into the model parameters and then extract it by accessing those parameters, and (ii) *black-box methods*, which embed WMs in the output predictions of DL models. The latter type of methods employ so-called trigger (or carrier) data samples that trigger an unusual prediction behavior: these unusual trigger-label pairs constitute the model watermark and they can be used by the model owner to claim her ownership.

As shown in Table 1, watermarking should fulfill a set of requirements to ensure its effectiveness and robustness [13,15,18,19,22]. Nonetheless, simultaneously satisfying all of these requirements is difficult to achieve [22].

Table 1. Requirements for watermarking of deep learning models.

Requirement	Description
Fidelity	The accuracy of the marked model on the original task shall not be degraded as a result of watermark embedding.
Robustness	The watermark shall be robust against model modifications such as model fine-tuning, model compression or WM overwriting.
Reliability	Watermark extraction shall exhibit a minimal false negative rate to allow legitimate owners to detect the WM with high probability.
Integrity	Watermark extraction shall result in a minimal amount of false positives; unmarked models must not be falsely claimed.
Capacity	It must be possible to include a large amount of watermark information in the target model.
Security	The watermark must not leave a detectable footprint on the marked model; an unauthorized party must not be able to detect the existence of a WM.
Unforgeability	An attacker must not be able to claim ownership of another party's watermark, or to embed additional watermarks into a marked model.
Authentication	A strong link between the owner and her watermark must be provided; reliable verification of the legitimate owner's identity shall be guaranteed.
Generality	The watermarking methodology must be applicable to different DL architectures and data sets.
Efficiency	Embedding and extracting WMs shall not entail a large overhead.
Uniqueness	The watermarking methodology must be able to embed a unique watermark for each user in order to distinguish each distributed marked model individually.
Scalability	Unique watermarking must scale to many users.

Contributions and Plan of This Article

We propose *KeyNet*, a novel watermarking framework that meets a wide range of desirable requirements for effective watermarking. In particular it offers fidelity, robustness, reliability, integrity, capacity, security, authentication, uniqueness, and scalability.

KeyNet depends on three components: the WM carrier set distribution, the signature, and the marked model and its corresponding private model. The private model is trained together with the original model to decode the WM information from the marked model's predictions. The WM information is only triggered by passing a sample from the WM carrier set signed by the legitimate owner to the corresponding marked model. The predictions of the marked model represent the encoded WM information that can be decoded only by the corresponding private model. The private model takes the predictions as input and decodes the WM information.

Unlike in previous works (discussed in Section 2), a watermarked input can take more than one label, which corresponds to the position of the owner's signature. Besides, the number of WM classes can be greater than the original task classes.

To successfully embed the WM and preserve the original task accuracy, the owner leverages multi-task learning (MTL) to learn both the original and the watermarking tasks together. After that, the owner distributes the marked original model, and keeps the private model secret. The owner uses the private model as a private key to decode the original model's outputs on the WM carrier set.

The main contributions of our work can be summarized as follows:

- *KeyNet* provides a strong link between the owner and her marked model by integrating two reliable authentication methods: a cryptographic hashing algorithm and a verification protocol. Furthermore, the use of a cryptographic hash improves the capacity of embedding WM information. Besides being robust against DL model modifications such as compression and fine-tuning, *KeyNet* does not allow the WM to be overwritten by attackers without losing the accuracy of the original task.
- We demonstrate the ability of our framework to scale and fingerprint different unique copies of a DL model for different users in the system. The information of a user is combined with the owner's information, the carrier is signed with the combined information, and then a unique pair of a pretrained model along with its corresponding private model is fine-tuned before being delivered to the user. After that, the owner can identify the point of leakage with a small number of queries.
- We conduct extensive experiments and evaluate the proposed framework on different DL model architectures. The results show that *KeyNet* can successfully embed WMs with reliable detection accuracy while preserving the accuracy of the original task. Moreover, it yields a small number of false positives when tested with unmarked models.

The remainder of the paper is organized as follows. Section 2 discusses related work. Section 3 describes the attack model to watermarking systems. Section 4 presents our framework in detail. Section 5 describes the experimental setup and reports the results on a variety of data sets. Finally, Section 6 gathers conclusions and proposes several lines of future research.

2. Related Work

The use of digital watermarking techniques has recently been extended from traditional domains such as multimedia contents to deep learning models. Related works can be categorized based on their application scenario as follows.

2.1. White-Box Watermarking

In this scenario, the model internal weights are publicly accessible. In [13], the authors embed an N-bit string WM into specific parameters of a target model via regularization. To this end, they add a regularizer term to the original task loss function that causes a statistical bias on those parameters and use this bias to represent the WM. To project the parameters carrying the WM information, they use an embedding parameter X for WM embedding and verification. Based on the same idea, the authors of [23] use an additional neural network instead of the embedding parameter to project the WM. The additional network is kept secret and serves for WM verification. Other works [24,25] also adopt the same approach for embedding the WM information in the internal weights of DL models.

2.2. Black-Box Watermarking

Assuming direct access to the weights of a DL model to extract the WM is often unrealistic, particularly when someone wishes to extract the WM to claim legitimate ownership of a seemingly stolen model in someone else's power. To overcome this problem, several black-box watermarking methods have been proposed. These methods assume access to the predictions of the model and, thus, embed the WM information into the model's outputs. The idea of these methods is to use some samples and assign each sample a specific label within the original task classes [14,15,17,19,26]. The trigger–label pairs form what is called a trigger set or a carrier set. The carrier set is then used to embed the WM into the target model by training the target model to memorize its trigger–label pairs along with learning the original task. As DL models are overparameterized, it is possible to make them memorize the trigger–label samples through overfitting [27]. Such embedding methods are known as backdooring methods [15]. The triggers are used later to query a remote model and compare its predictions with the corresponding labels. A high proportion of matches between the predictions and the labels is used to prove the ownership of the model.

Trigger set methods can be classified into several types. A first type of methods is based on assigning a random label to each trigger. The trigger samples themselves may be random samples from different distributions [15] or adversarial samples [17]. This approach has many drawbacks. Beyond its limited capacity regarding the number of triggers that can be used for verification, it does not establish a strong link between the owner and her WM. Thus, it is easy for an attacker to insert his WM by using a set of trigger–label pairs, giving them random labels, and then claim ownership of the owner's model. This type of attack is called the ambiguity attack [24].

A second type of methods relies on inserting the WM information into the original data. The inserted information may be a graphical logo [28], the owner's signature [26], a specific text string (which could be the company name) [14], or some pattern of noise [14]. These methods may affect the accuracy of the model in the original task. Besides, the WM may be vulnerable to model fine-tuning aimed at destroying the WM. That is possible because the WM samples will be close to their counterparts in the same class in the feature space. Therefore, fine-tuning may cause the WM pattern to be ignored and those samples to be classified into their original classes again [29].

Another type of black-box methods proposes to exploit the discarded capacity in the intermediate distribution of DL models' output to embed the WM information [21]. They use non-classification images as triggers and assign each trigger a serial number (SN) as label. SN is a vector that contains n decimal units where n is the number of neurons in the output layer. The value of SN serves as an identity bracelet that proves ownership of a marked model. To embed the WM information in the softmax layer predictions, they train the target model to perform two tasks simultaneously: the original task, which is a multi-class classification task, and the watermarking task, which is a regression task. They use the mean square error (MSE) as a loss function for the watermarking task to minimize the difference between the predicted value of a trigger and its corresponding SN. To link the owner with her marked model, they create an endorsement by a certification authority on the generated SNs. Ownership verification is performed by sending some trigger inputs, extracting their corresponding SNs, and having them verified by the authority. This method preserves the original task accuracy and also creates a link between the owner and her WM model. However, it has several drawbacks. The length of the SN depends on the size of the output layer in the model. This may prevent the owner from embedding a large WM. Moreover, by relying on values after the decimal point to express a specific symbol in the SN, if some decimal values are slightly changed, the entire SN will be corrupted. A modification like model fine-tuning would lead to destroying the WM information. In this respect, the authors do not evaluate two important types of modifications that could affect the WM: model fine-tuning and WM overwriting.

A recent paper [30] proposes to watermark DL models that output images. They force the marked model to embed a certain WM (e.g., logo) in any image output by that model.

They train two models together: the marked model and the extractor model. The latter extracts the WM from the output of the former. The marked model is distributed while the extractor is kept secret by the owner. The paper does not evaluate the robustness of the method against the basic attacks that may target the marked model, such as model fine-tuning, model compression, and WM overwriting. Besides, there is a high probability that the WM extractor has memorized the WM in its weights; as a result, when it receives images from models different from the marked one, it might generate the same WM each time.

A shortcoming of most of the aforementioned WM methods is that the WM is the same in all copies of the model [22]. Therefore, if the owner distributes more than one copy of a model, it is impossible for the legitimate owner to determine which of the authorized users has leaked it.

3. Attack Model

To ensure the robustness of a watermarking methodology, it should effectively overcome (at least) three potential attacks:

- **Model fine-tuning**. In this attack, an attacker who has a small amount of the original data retrains the WM model with the aim of removing the WM while preserving the accuracy in the original task.
- **Model compression**. The compression of a DL model's weights minimizes its size and speeds up its performance. Model compression may compromise the WM within the marked model, thereby affecting its detection and extraction.
- **Watermark overwriting**. This type of attack is a major threat to the WM because it might result in the attacker being able to overwrite the owner's WM, or also to embed another WM of his own and thus seize ownership of the WM model. We make the following assumptions about the attacker. First, the attacker is assumed to have a small amount of training data when compared to the owner. Otherwise, he can use his data to train a new model from scratch, or use the predictions of the WM model to create an unmarked copy of it by predictive model-theft techniques [7]. Second, the attacker is assumed to be aware of the methodology used to embed the WM but to be unaware of the carrier set distribution, the owner's signature, or the topology of the owner's private model. An attack is considered to be successful if the attacker manages to overwrite the WM without losing much accuracy in the original task. The goal is to prevent the attacker from overwriting the WM without significantly impairing the original task accuracy, proportional to the amount of data he knows. To make a realistic trade-off, the relationship between the size of the data known by the attacker and the loss in original task accuracy should be inversely proportional: the smaller the attacker data, the greater the accuracy loss is.

4. The *KeyNet* Framework

Instead of having the model memorize the WM through overfitting, in our approach we design the watermarking task as a standalone ML task with its logical context and rules. First, this task performs a one-vs.-all classification so that it can distinguish WMs from original samples with different distributions. Second, the watermarking task learns the features that enable it to identify the spatial information of the legitimate owner's signature. Third, it learns to distinguish the pattern of the owner's signature from the patterns of fake signatures. The purpose of designing the watermarking task in this way is (i) to increase the difficulty of the task so that an attacker with little training data cannot add his WM without losing the accuracy of the original task, (ii) to provide a reliable verification method that strengthens the owner's association with her marked model, (iii) to achieve greater security by keeping the private model in the hands of the owner, (iv) to embed a robust WM without affecting the accuracy of the original task, (v) to produce different unique copies of a DL model for different users of the system based on the same carrier by signing the carrier with the joint signature of the user/owner and (vi) to scale for a large number of users and identify the leakage point with high confidence and little effort.

KeyNet consists of two main phases: watermark embedding and watermark extraction and verification. Figure 1 shows the global workflow of *KeyNet*. The marked DL model is used as a remote service, so that the user can only obtain its final predictions. *KeyNet* passes the final predictions of the remote DL model to its corresponding private model, which uses them to decode the WM information. In the ownership verification protocol we exploit the fact that each sample in the owner's WM carrier set can take different labels based on the position of the owner's signature in it. We next briefly explain the workflow of each phase.

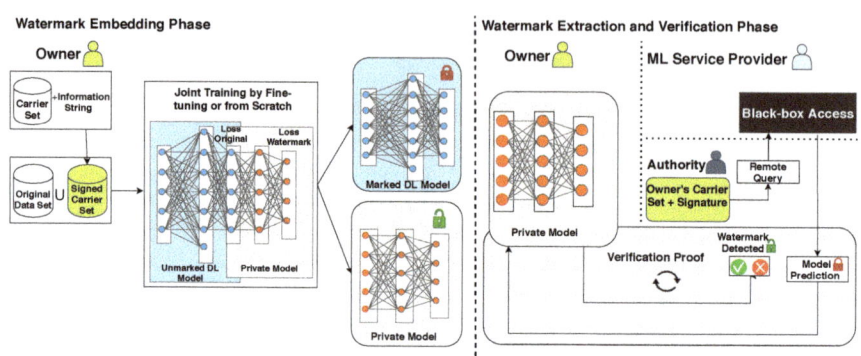

Figure 1. *KeyNet* global workflow.

Watermark embedding. *KeyNet* takes four main inputs in the WM embedding phase: the target model (pretrained or from scratch), the original data set, the owner's WM carrier set, and the owner's information string. The output is the marked model, its corresponding private model, and the owner's signature. The WM carrier set samples are signed using the owner's signature. After that, the signed WM carrier set is combined with the original data set and they are used to fine-tune (or train) the targeted model. The private model takes the final predictions of the original model as inputs and outputs the position of the owner's signature on the WM sample. To embed the WM information and preserve the main task accuracy at the same time, WM embedding leverages multi-task learning (MTL) to train the two models jointly.

MTL is an ML approach that allows learning multiple tasks in parallel by sharing the feature representation among them [31,32]. Many MTL methods [33–35] show that different tasks can share several early layers, and then have task-specific parameters in the later layers. MTL also helps the involved tasks to generalize better by adding a small amount of noise that helps them reduce overfitting [36,37].

In our framework, the original model parameters are shared among the original task and the watermarking task. When the marked model receives unmarked data samples, its predictions represent the classification decision on those samples. However, when it receives a watermarked sample, its output represents the features that the private model needs to distinguish the signature position on that sample. For this to be possible, the private model forces the shared layer (the original model parameters) to produce a different representation of the WM samples. We can see the private model as a private key held only by the owner that decodes the WM information from the original model predictions. More details about this phase are given in Sections 4.2 and 4.3.

Watermark extraction and verification. The owner can extract the WM information from a suspicious remote DL by taking a random sample from her WM carrier set, putting her signature on one of the predefined positions, and querying the remote model. After that, he/she passes the remote model's predictions to the private model. If the private model decodes the WM information and provides the position of the signature with high accuracy, then the owner can claim her ownership.

To verify the ownership of a remote black-box DL model, the owner first delivers the WM carrier set and her signature to the authority. He/she also tells the authority about the methodology used to sign the WM samples along with the predefined positions where the WM may be placed. The authority (i.e., the *verifier*) randomly chooses a sample from the carrier set, puts the signature in a random position, queries the remote DL model, and sends the model's predictions to the owner. The owner (i.e., the *prover*) takes the predictions, passes them to her private model, and tells the authority the position of her signature on the image. The authority repeats the proof as many times as he/she desires. After that, the owner's answer accuracy is evaluated according to a minimum threshold. If the owner surpasses the threshold, his/her ownership is regarded as proven by the authority. More details about this phase are given in Section 4.4.

The following subsections describe each phase in detail. First, we formalize the problem. Then, we describe the methodology for signing and labeling the WM carrier set using the hashed value of the owner's information. After that, we describe the WM embedding phase by training the original model and the private model on the original and the watermarking tasks jointly. Finally, we explain the WM extraction and verification phase.

4.1. Problem Formulation

The key idea of our framework is to perform two tasks at the same time: the original classification task T_{org} and the watermarking task T_{wm}. To do so, *KeyNet* leverages the multi-task learning (MTL) approach to achieve high accuracy in both tasks by sharing the parameters of the original model between the two tasks. *KeyNet* adds a private model to the original model. The original model's objective is to correctly classify the original data samples into their corresponding labels, while the private model's objective is to correctly predict the position of the owner's signature in a sample of the WM carrier set using the original model predictions. We can formally represent as follows the problem being tackled:

- **Representation of the original, private, and combined models.** Let $D_{org} = \{(x_i, y_i)\}_{i=1}^{n}$ be the original task data and $D_{wm} = \{c_j\}_{j=1}^{m}$ be the WM carrier set data. Let h be the function of the original model and f be the function of the private model. Let θ_1 the parameters of h and θ_2 be the parameters of f. Let *signature* be the owner's signature and $PL = \{(p_k, l_k)\}_{k=1}^{z}$ be the set of predefined position–label pairs (e.g., position: top left, label: 1 and position: bottom right, label: 4) where z is the total number of positions at which the signature can be located on a WM carrier set sample. Let *sign* be the function that puts a *signature* on a carrier set sample c and returns the signed sample c^{p_k} and its corresponding label l_k as:

$$(c^{p_k}, l_k) = sign(signature, c, p_k).$$

Let D_{wm}^{signed} be the signed carrier set samples that contain all the (c^p, l) pairs. We use D_{org} and D_{wm}^{signed} to train both h and f to perform T_{org} and T_{wm}.
Typically, the function h tries to map each $x_i \in D_{org}$ to its corresponding y_i, that is, $h(x_i) = y_i$.
Let $f(h)$ be the composite function that aims at mapping each $c_j^{p_k}$ to its corresponding l_k, that is, $f(h(c^{p_k})) = l_k$.

- **Embedding phase.** We formulate the embedding phase as an MTL problem where we jointly learn two tasks that share some parameters in the early layers and then have task-specific parameters in the later layers. The shared parameters in our case are θ_1, while θ_2 are the WM task-specific parameters. We compute the weighted combined loss L as

$$L = \alpha Loss(h(x), y) + (1 - \alpha) Loss(f(h(c^p)), l),$$

where $h(x)$ represents the predictions on the original task samples, $f(h(c^p))$ represents the predictions on D_{wm}^{signed} samples, $Loss(h(x), y)$ is the loss function that penalizes the difference between the original model outputs $h(x)$ and the original data targets y, $Loss(f(h(c^p)), l)$ is the loss function that penalizes the difference between the composite model outputs $f(h(c^p))$ and the signed WM carrier set's target l, and α is the combined weighted loss parameter. Then, we seek θ_1 and θ_2 that make L small enough to get acceptable accuracy on both T_{org} and T_{wm}. Once this is done, the WM has been successfully embedded while preserving the accuracy of the original task T_{org}.

- **Verification phase.** The verification function V checks whether a claimer (also known as the *prover*), who has delivered her *signature* and WM carrier set D_{wm} to the authority (also known as the *verifier*), is the legitimate owner of a remote model h'. If the prover is the legitimate owner of h', he/she will be able to pass the verification process and thus prove her ownership of h'. That is, because he/she possesses the private model f, which was trained to decode h' predictions on her signed D_{wm}.

Here, r represents the number of the required rounds in the verification process and T denotes the threshold needed to prove the ownership of h'. Note that the authority also knows the signing function *sign* used to sign D_{wm} samples in order to obtain (c^{p_k}, l_k) pairs.

The function V can be expressed as $V(\{(f(h'(c^{p_k})), l_k, p_k)\}_{k=1}^{r}, T) = \{True, False\}$.

4.2. Watermark Carrier Set Signing and Labeling

The methodology we use for labeling the WM carrier set is key in our approach. In contrast to related works, which assign a unique label to each of the WM carrier set samples, our labeling method allows for a single sample to carry more than one label. More precisely, any sample $c \in D_{wm}$ can take one of z labels $\{l_k\}_{k=1}^{z}$, where z is the number of predefined positions $\{p_k\}_{k=1}^{z}$ at which the *signature* of the owner can be placed. Besides the z positions, if a sample is not signed by the legitimate owner, it uses label 0 by default. Moreover, if the sample is not in D_{wm}, it uses label 0 by default even if it is signed by the owner. Algorithm 1 formalizes the method used to sign and label the D_{wm} samples.

First and foremost, the owner's information and the metadata of her model are endorsed by the authority. This information is a string of arbitrary length. After that, Algorithm 1 returns the signed D_{wm}^{signed} WM carrier set consisting of pairs (signed D_{wm} sample, label), a signed D_{dif}^{signed} consisting of pairs (signed sample from a set D_{dif} of different distribution, 0), and the owner's signature *signature* used to sign the samples. The inputs to Algorithm 1 are:

1. The owner's information string $infStr$ that has been endorsed by the authority.
2. The size of the signature s to be placed on the WM carrier set samples.
3. The owner's WM carrier set D_{wm}.
4. The set of position–label pairs $PL = \{p_k, l_k\}_{k=1}^{z}$ that defines the signature positions and their corresponding labels.
5. A small set of samples D_{dif} from other distributions than D_{wm}.

Algorithm 1 starts its work by taking the hash value for $infStr$ and then converting it to a squared array of size s, as follows. In our implementation we use *SHA256*, which yields 256 bits that are converted to 64 characters by digesting them to hexadecimal. The last s (with $s \leq 64$) among the digested characters are converted to a decimal vector of length s. The decimal vector values are normalized between 0 and 1 by dividing them by the maximum value in the vector. The normalized vector is then reshaped into a squared array. The resulting array represents the owner's *signature*. Note that it is also possible to use any hashing function different from SHA256.

Algorithm 1 Signing a WM carrier Set

Input: Owner's information $infStr$, owner's signature size s, owner's WM carrier set D_{wm}, signature positions/labels set PL, other distributions' samples D_{dif}

Output: signed labeled WM samples D_{wm}^{signed}, signed samples from different distributions D_{dif}^{signed}, owner's signature $signature$

1: $signature \leftarrow hashAndReshape(infStr, s)$ //The owner signature.
2: $fakeStr \leftarrow modify(infStr)$ //Fake information string.
3: $signature_{fake} \leftarrow hashAndReshape(fakeStr, s), signature_{fake} \neq signature$ //A fake signature.
4: $D_{wm}^{signed}, D_{dif}^{signed} = [\,], [\,]$
5: **for** each sample c in D_{wm} **do**
6:     **for** each position, label (p_k, l_k) in PL **do**
7:         $c^{p_k} \leftarrow sign(signature, c, p_k)$
8:         $Add((c^{p_k}, l_k), D_{wm}^{signed})$
9:     **end for**
10:     $p_k \leftarrow selectRandomPosition()$
11:     $c^{p_k} \leftarrow sign(signature_{fake}, c, p_k)$
12:     $Add((c^{p_k}, 0), D_{wm}^{signed})$
13:     $Add((c, 0), D_{wm}^{signed})$
14:     $fakeStr \leftarrow modify(infStr)$ //New fake information string.
15:     $signature_{fake} \leftarrow hashAndReshape(fakeStr, s), signature_{fake} \neq signature$
16: **end for**
17: **for** each sample d in D_{dif} **do**
18:     **for** each position, label (p_k, l_k) in PL **do**
19:         $d^{p_k} \leftarrow sign(signature, d, p_k)$
20:         $Add((d^{p_k}, 0), D_{dif}^{signed})$
21:     **end for**
22: **end for**
return $D_{wm}^{signed}, D_{dif}^{signed}, signature$

Once we obtain $signature$, we start the labeling step of the WM carrier set D_{wm}. For each $c \in D_{wm}$, we replicate c for z times where z is the total number of possible positions $\{p_k\}_{k=1}^{z}$ of the signature. Then, we use the $sign$ function to place $signature$ in the position p_k to obtain the (c^{p_k}, l_k) pair.

We also leave one copy of each sample without signing and assign it the label 0. That is, if a carrier set sample c is not signed with $signature$, it will be represented by the $(c, 0)$ pair.

We then do two steps:

1. We generate a fake information string $fakeStr$ by making a slight modification to $infStr$. Then, we generate $signature_{fake}$ following steps similar to those above followed to generate the real owner's signature $signature$. After that, we sign the D_{wm} samples each with a different fake signature and a randomly chosen position p_k and, instead of assigning to the signed sample the corresponding label l_k, we assign it the label 0. To obtain a new fake signature, we again make a slight random modification in $infStr$ and generate the fake signature in the same way as above.

2. We take samples from other distributions D_{dif} and sign them with the real owner's signature as we did with the D_{wm} samples. We assign them the label 0. We use samples from different distributions to avoid triggering the WM just with the owner's real signature. In other words, we make the triggering of the WM from a marked model dependent on the carrier set distribution in addition to the pattern of the owner's signature.

The goal of the above two steps is to make the marked model h^* output the information that tells the position of a signature only if we pass to it a sample that *belongs to D_{wm} and is* *signed with the real signature*. Otherwise, h^* ignores the presence of any different signature from *signature* on D_{wm} samples. This also avoids h^* responding to samples from different distributions than the D_{wm} distribution.

Finally, Algorithm 1 returns the signed WM samples D_{wm}^{signed}, the signed samples from different distributions D_{dif}^{signed}, and the signature *signature* that will be used to trigger the marked model h^*. Note that this process is performed only once, before the WM is embedded.

4.3. Watermark Embedding

To successfully embed the WM in the original model h without compromising the accuracy of the original task, we jointly train both h and the private models f simultaneously. As a large amount of the carrier set samples have been signed, we first randomly select one-fifth of D_{wm}^{signed} for training. The random selection allows for the representation of all the possible states while reducing the carrier set size. The signed samples from other distributions D_{dif}^{signed} are combined with those randomly selected and assigned to D_2. In the end, we add D_2 to the original task data D_{org}. The resulting combined data set $D = D_{org} \cup D_2$ are used in the training step as specified next.

During joint training, a batch b is taken from D. Then, b is separated into two sub-batches: $\{x, y\} \in D_{org}, \{c, l\} \in D_2$. $\{x\}$ is passed to the original model h and the loss $L_f(h(x), y)$ is calculated. On the other hand, $\{c\}$ is first passed to h, and then the predictions of the original model $h(c)$ are passed to the private model f; the loss $L_f(f(h(c)), l)$ is afterwards calculated. As we deal with two classification tasks, the cross-entropy loss function is used to calculate the loss for both tasks.

We use the parameter α to balance the weight of $L_f(h(x), y)$ and $L_f(f(h(c)), l)$ before we add them up in the joint loss L. Parameter α allows us to choose the best combination of the weighted loss that preserves the accuracy of T_{org} while embedding WM successfully. Then, the parameters of h, f are optimized to minimize L.

Reducing $L_f(h(x), y)$ forces h to predict the correct class for x, while reducing the watermarking task loss $L_f(f(h(c)), l)$ forces the private model to distinguish the distribution of the WM carrier set D_{wm}, and predict the location of the owner's signature in its samples. The original model, in addition to performing the original task, also executes the first part of the watermarking task by outputting the features needed to find the position of the signature. By using these features as input, the private model performs the second part of the watermarking task, which consists in identifying the signature position.

Regarding the architecture of the private model f, the number of inputs corresponds to the size of h predictions, whereas the number of outputs corresponds to the number of classes of the WM task $z + 1$. We also add at least one hidden layer in between. The hidden layer enriches the information coming from the original model before passing it to the output layer of the private model.

Algorithm 2 summarizes the process of embedding the WM. It takes an unmarked model h that might be pretrained or be trained from scratch, the private model f, the original data set D_{org}, the signed WM carrier set D_{wm}^{signed}, signed samples from other distributions D_{dif}^{signed}, and the joint loss balancing parameter α. The output of the embedding phase is a marked model h^* along with its corresponding private model f.

Algorithm 2 Watermark Embedding

Input: Unmarked DL model h, private model f, original data set D_{org}, signed WM carrier set D_{wm}^{signed}, signed samples from other distributions D_{dif}^{signed}, batch size BS, weighted loss parameter α.

Output: Marked model h^*, corresponding private model f.

1: $s = size(D_{wm}^{signed})/5$
2: $D_2 \leftarrow randomSample(D_2, s)$
3: $D_2 \leftarrow D_2 \cup D_{dif}^{signed}$
4: $D \leftarrow D_{org} \cup D_2$
5: $L_f = crossEntropy()$ //Loss function
6: **for** each batch b of size BS in D **do**
7: $\{x,y\}, \{c,l\} \leftarrow split(b)$, with $\{x,y\} \in D_{org}$ and $\{c,l\} \in D_2$
8: $L \leftarrow \alpha L_f(h(x),y) + (1-\alpha)L_f(f(h(c)),l)$
9: $optimize(L)$
10: **end for**
return h^*, f

4.4. Watermark Extraction and Verification

The verification process of ownership involves a would-be owner in the role of prover and the authority in the role of verifier. The would-be owner claims that a remote model h' is part of his/her IP. The authority is given the WM carrier set D_{wm}, the would-be owner's *signature*, the signing function *sign*, and remote access to h'. The authority sets an accuracy threshold T and a number of required verification rounds r to decide whether h' is the IP of the would-be owner. In each round, the authority randomly selects a sample c from D_{wm}, signs it using *signature* in a random position p_k, and sends the signed sample c^{p_k} to the remote model h'. The predictions $h'(c^{p_k})$ (which contain the encoded WM information) are forwarded to the would-be owner. The latter passes them to her private model f to obtain $l_k = f(h'(c^{p_k})$. As the relationship between positions and labels is one-to-one, the would-be owner can use l_k to tell the authority the position p_k of her signature in c. After r rounds, the accuracy acc of the would-be owner at detecting the positions is the number of correct answers divided by r. If $acc \geq T$, then authority certifies that h' is owned by the would-be owner.

Note that the authority can also send the samples without signing them or sign them using fake signatures different from *signature*. In this case, the would-be owner should tell the authority that this sample does not contain her signature. That is possible because in these cases the private model gives them the label 0. Algorithm 3 formalizes the verification process.

Algorithm 3 Watermark Verification

Input: Remote access to h', threshold T, number of rounds r

Output: Boolean decision d (True or False) on h''s ownership.

1: $correct = 0$
2: $d = False$ //Decision on the ownership of h'.
3: **for** each round $i = 1, 2, \ldots r$ **do**
4:      $c \leftarrow randomSample(D_{wm})$
5:      $p_k \leftarrow \text{randomPosition}(), k \in 1, 2, \ldots z$
6:      $c^{p_k} \leftarrow sign(signature, c, p^k)$
7:      $predictions \leftarrow h'(c^{p_k})$
8:      $l_k \leftarrow f(predictions)$
9:      $answer \leftarrow$ Position corresponding to l_k
10:      **if** $answer = p_k$ **then**
11:          $correct \leftarrow correct + 1$
12:      **end if**
13: **end for**
14:
15: $acc = correct/r$
16: **if** $acc \geq T$ **then**
17:      $d \leftarrow True$
18: **end if**
     return d

5. Experimental Results

In this section, we evaluate the performance of *KeyNet* on two image classification data sets and with two different DL model architectures. First, we present the experimental setup. After that, we evaluate the proposed framework performance against the requirements stated in Table 1. We focus on robustness, authentication, scalability, capacity, integrity, and fidelity, but, as our framework partly fulfills the rest of requirements, we also assess its performance on each of them.

The code and the models used in this section are available at https://github.com/NajeebJebreel/KeyNet.

5.1. Experimental Setup

Original task data sets and DL models. We used two image classification data sets: CIFAR10 [38] and FMNIST5. CIFAR10 has 10 classes, while FMNIST5 is a subset of the public data set Fashion-MNIST [39]; FMNIST5 contains the samples that belong to the first five classes in Fashion-MNIST (classes from 0 to 4). Table 2 summarizes the original task data sets, the carrier set, and the DL models and their corresponding private models.

Table 2. Data sets and deep learning model architectures. $C(3, 32, 5, 1, 2)$ denotes a convolutional layer with 3 input channels, 32 output channels, a kernel of size 5×5, a stride of 1, and a padding of 2, $MP(2, 1)$ denotes a max-pooling layer with a kernel of size 2×2 and a stride of 1, and $FC(10, 20)$ indicates a fully connected layer with 10 inputs and 20 output neurons. We used *ReLU* as an activation function in the hidden layers. We used *LogSoftmax* as an activation function in the output layers for all DL models. The rightmost column contains the architecture of the corresponding private models.

Data Set	WM Carrier Set	DL Model	DL Model Architecture	Private Model Architecture
CIFAR10	STL10	ResNet18	See [40].	FC(10,20), FC(20,10), FC(10, 6)
		VGG16	See [41].	(496 learnable parameters)
FMNIST5	MNIST	CNN	C(3,32,5,1,2), MP(2,1), C(32,64,3,1,2), MP(2,1), FC(4096,4096), FC(4096,5)	FC(5, 10), FC(10,20), FC(20,6)
		LeNet	See [42].	(411 learnable parameters)

Watermark carrier sets. We employed three different data sets as WM carrier sets: STL10 [43], MNIST [44], and Fashion-MNIST (the latter was used only in attacks). We applied Algorithm 1 to label the carrier set's images. Then, we passed the carrier set, the owner's information, the signature size, a fake signature, some samples from different distributions, and a list containing the labeling order of the positions of the owner's signature in the carrier set. We used the following labeling order: 1: Top left, 2: Top right, 3: Bottom left, 4: Bottom right, and 5: Image center. Algorithm 1 assigns label 0 to an image if (i) the image belongs to the carrier set but does not carry any signature, (ii) the image belongs to the carrier set but carries a signature different from the owner's signature, or (iii) the image does not belong to the carrier set distribution (even if it is signed with the owner's real signature). For WM accuracy evaluation, we randomly sampled 15% of the WM carrier set. After that, we signed them in different random positions and assigned them the corresponding labels. Figure 2 shows some examples of signed carrier set images and their corresponding labels.

Figure 2. Examples of signed STL10 carrier set images employed with the CIFAR10 data set. Each image shows the signature position and its corresponding label.

Attacker configurations. We assumed the attacker has varying percentages of the training data, ranging from 1% to 30% of the original training data. The attacker's training data were randomly sampled from the original training data. We also assumed that the WM carrier set distribution is a secret between the owner and the authority, so we assigned the attacker different WM carrier sets from those of the owner. The attacker's private model was slightly different as well, because the owner's private model and its architecture are secret. The rest of the attacker's configurations and hyper-parameters were the same as the owner's. Table 3 summarizes the attacker's WM carrier sets and private model architectures.

Table 3. Attacker's WM carrier sets and private models. The attacker's WM carrier set and private model differ from the owner's.

Data Set	Owner's WM Carrier Set	Attacker's WM Carrier Set	Attacker's Private Model Architecture
CIFAR10	STL10	Fashion-MNIST	FC(10,20),FC(20,30), FC(30, 6) (980 learnable parameters)
FMNIST5	MNIST	STL10	FC(5, 20), FC(20,10), FC(10,6) (360 learnable parameters)

Performance metric. We used *accuracy* as performance metric to evaluate all the original and WM tasks. *Accuracy* is the number of correct predictions divided by the total number of predictions.

Training hyperparameters. We used the cross-entropy loss function and the stochastic gradient descent (SGD) optimizer with learning rate = 0.001, momentum = 0.9, weight decay = 0.0005, and batch size = 128. We trained all the original unmarked models for 250 epochs. To embed the WM from scratch, we trained the combined model for 250 epochs. To embed the WM in a pretrained model, we combined the private model and fine-tuned the combination for 30 epochs.

To jointly train the original and private models, we used parameter α to weight the original task loss and the WM task loss before optimization. For CIFAR10 we used $\alpha = 0.9$ when embedding the WM in a pretrained model, while we used $\alpha = 0.95$ when embedding the WM into a DL model from scratch. For FMNIST5 we used $\alpha = 0.85$ to embed the WM in a pretrained model, while we used $\alpha = 0.9$ to embed the WM from scratch. The experiments were implemented using Pytorch 1.6 and Python 3.6.

5.2. Experiments and Results

First, we made sure that an accurate private model could not be obtained (and therefore the ownership of a DL model could not be claimed) by using only the predictions of a black-box DL model. To do so, we queried different unmarked DL models with all the signed samples in the owner's WM carrier set, and we used the predictions as input features to train the private model. Table 4 shows the performance of the private models obtained in this way after 250 epochs.

Table 4. Accuracy of the private models at detecting the position of the owner's signature in the WM carrier set when trained for 250 epochs with the predictions of black-box models.

Data Set	Black-Box DL Model	Watermark Detection Accuracy %
CIFAR10	ResNet18	31.25
	VGG16	30.14
FMNIST5	CNN	34.42
	LeNet	33.26

It can be seen that the average accuracy of the private model at detecting the signature position inside the WM carrier set is as low as 32.27%. This accuracy was obtained by granting unconditional query access to the black-box model and by using its predictions as input to train the private model. Based on that, we decided to set threshold $T = 0.9$, which is nearly three times greater than the above average accuracy. Therefore, to prove her ownership of a black-box DL model, the owner's private model must detect the signature positions in the WM carrier set with an accuracy greater than or equal to 90%.

In the following, we report the results of *KeyNet* on several experiments that test its fulfillment of the requirements depicted in Table 1.

Table 5. Fidelity results. Column 3 shows the accuracy of the unmarked models in the original tasks (baseline accuracy) before embedding the WM. Columns 4 and 5 show the accuracy of the marked model in the original task after embedding WM by fine-tuning a pretrained model or by training the combined model from scratch. Columns 6 and 7 show the accuracy of the private model in detecting the WM using the predictions of the corresponding marked model. To embed the WM in a pretrained model, we fine-tuned it for 30 epochs while we trained models from scratch for 250 epochs.

Data Set	DL Model	Unmarked Model Accuracy %	Marked Model Accuracy %		Watermark Detection Accuracy %	
			By Fine-Tuning (30 Epochs)	From Scratch (250 Epochs)	By Fine-Tuning	From Scratch
CIFAR10	ResNet18	91.96	92.07	92.53	99.96	99.97
	VGG16	90.59	90.52	91.74	99.68	99.89
FMNIST5	CNN	92.08	92.42	92.32	99.98	99.90
	LeNet	90.68	89.94	89.94	99.55	99.79

Fidelity. Embedding the WM should not decrease the accuracy of the marked model on the original task. As shown in Table 5, the marked model's accuracy is very similar to that of the unmarked model. This is thanks to the joint training, which simultaneously minimizes the loss for the original task and the WM task. Furthermore, *KeyNet* did not only preserve the accuracy in the original task, but sometimes it even led to improved accuracy. That is not surprising, because the watermarking task added a small amount of noise to the marked model, and this helped reduce overfitting and thus generalize better.

KeyNet therefore fulfills the fidelity requirement by reconciling accuracy preservation for the original task and successfully embedding of the WM in the target models.

Reliability and robustness. *KeyNet* guarantees a robust DL watermarking and allows legitimate owners to prove their ownership with accuracy greater that the required threshold $T = 90\%$. Table 5 shows that WM detection accuracy was almost 100%, and thus our framework was able to reliably detect the WM.

We assess the **robustness** of our framework against three types of attacks: *fine-tuning* [45], *model compression* [46,47], and *WM overwriting* [13,48]:

- *Model fine-tuning.* Fine-tuning involves retraining a DL model with some amount of training data. It may remove or corrupt the WM information from a marked model because it causes the model to converge to another local minimum. In our experiments, we sampled 30% of the original data and used them to fine-tune the marked model by optimizing its parameters based only the loss of the original task. Table 6 outlines the impact of fine-tuning on the WM detection accuracy with all benchmarks. We can notice that *KeyNet* is robust against fine-tuning and was able to preserve a WM detection accuracy of about 97% after 200 epochs. The explanation for this strong persistence against fine-tuning is that *KeyNet* does not embed the WM information within the decision boundaries of the original task classes. Therefore, the effect of fine-tuning on the WM is very small.

- *Model compression.* We used the compression approach proposed in [47] to prune the weight parameters in the marked DL models. To prune a particular layer, we first sorted the weights in the specified layer by their magnitudes. Then, we masked to zero the smallest magnitude weights until the desired pruning level was reached. Figure 3 shows the impact of model compression on both WM detection accuracy and original task accuracy with different pruning rates. We see that *KeyNet* is robust against model compression, and the accuracy of the WM remains above the threshold $T = 90\%$ as long as the marked model is still useful for the original task. This is consistent because when the marked model becomes useless due to excessive compression, the owner will not be interested in claiming its ownership.

- *Watermark overwriting.* Assuming that the attacker is aware of the methodology used to embed the WM, he may embed a new WM that may damage the original one. In our experiments, we assumed that the attacker knows the methodology but knows neither the owner's carrier set nor the owner's private model architecture. We studied the effect on the WM of the attacker's knowing various fractions of the original training data, ranging from 1% to 30%. We chose the lower bound 1% based on the work in [49]; the authors of that paper demonstrate that an attacker with less than 1% of the original data is able to remove the watermark with a slight loss in the accuracy of the original task.

Table 6. Fine-tuning results. In the fine-tuning attack, the marked models were retrained based on the original task loss only.

Data Set	CIFAR10						FMNIST5					
DL model	ResNet18			VGG16			CNN			LeNet		
Number of epochs	50	100	200	50	100	200	50	100	200	50	100	200
Marked model Accuracy %	92.40	92.33	92.47	91.31	91.64	91.69	92.30	92.52	92.40	89.84	90.06	90.12
Watermark detection Accuracy %	98.19	98.05	99.12	97.20	94.72	96.67	97.35	97.02	96.92	98.23	97.42	96.4

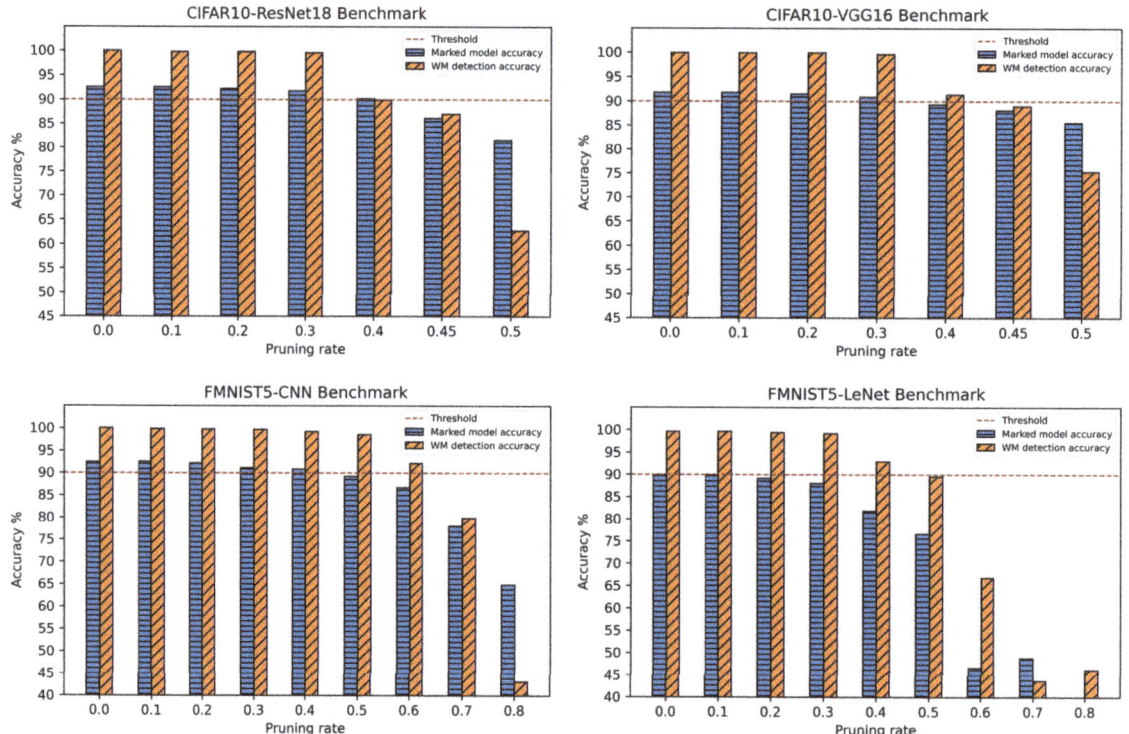

Figure 3. Robustness against model compression. The X-axis indicates the pruning levels we used for each marked model. The blue bars indicate the marked model accuracy in the original task, while the orange bars indicate the accuracy of WM detection. The horizontal dotted line indicates the threshold $T = 90\%$ used to verify the ownership of the model.

To overwrite the WM, the attacker selected his/her own carrier set and signed it using Algorithm 1 with his/her signature. Then, he/she trained her private model along with the marked model in the same way as in Algorithm 2. Tables 7 and 8 summarize the results of WM overwriting experiments. The attacker was able to successfully overwrite the original WM and successfully embed her new WM, but this was done at the cost of a substantial accuracy loss in the original task when using a fraction of the training data up to 10%. Thus, our watermark easily survives the attacks in the conditions described in [49]. For fractions above 10%, the accuracy of the marked model became competitive, but an attacker holding such a large amount of training data can easily train her own model and has no need to pirate the owner's model [18].

Table 7. Overwriting attack results with CIFAR10 marked models. The table shows the accuracy before and after overwriting each marked model and its corresponding private model depending on the fraction of training data known by the attacker (from 1% to 30%).

Dataset	CIFAR10											
DL Model	ResNet18						VGG16					
Data fraction %	1	3	6	10	20	30	1	3	6	10	20	30
Marked model Accuracy before %	92.53	92.53	92.53	92.53	92.53	92.53	91.74	91.74	91.74	91.74	91.74	91.74
Marked model Accuracy after %	39.05	63.75	83.31	86.35	89.91	90.9	34.61	71.86	81.2	83.9	88.07	89.67
Owner's WM detection Accuracy after %	24.53	20.35	22.27	28.3	37.33	41.15	32.32	30.88	28.61	32.48	30.32	44.4
Attacker's WM detection Accuracy %	99.97	99.89	99.95	99.9	99.94	99.97	99.69	99.68	99.89	99.87	99.9	99.96

Table 8. Overwriting attack results with FMNIST5 marked models. The table shows the accuracy before and after overwriting each marked model and its corresponding private model depending on the fraction of training data known by the attacker (from 1% to 30%).

Dataset	FMNIST5											
DL Model	CNN						LeNet					
Data fraction %	1	3	6	10	20	30	1	3	6	10	20	30
Marked model Accuracy before %	92.32	92.32	92.32	92.32	92.32	92.32	89.94	89.94	89.94	89.94	89.94	89.94
Marked model Accuracy after %	76.18	81.88	87.86	89.1	91.38	91.84	74.64	79.44	86.36	88.86	89.58	89.52
Owner's WM detection Accuracy after %	26.97	28.53	38.52	46.83	70	68.03	26.32	18.71	43.99	57.4	75.83	65.66
Attacker's WM detection Accuracy %	100	100	100	100	100	100	99.25	99.65	99.84	99.92	99.89	99.92

Integrity. *KeyNet* meets the integrity requirement by yielding low WM accuracy detection with unmarked models, and thus it does not falsely claim ownership of models owned by a third party. In our experiments, there were 6 classes for the watermarking task. Looking at Table 9, the accuracy of falsely claimed ownership of unmarked models is not far from guessing 1 out of 6 numbers randomly, which equals approximately 16.6%.

Authentication. *KeyNet* fulfills the authentication requirement by design. Using a cryptographic hash function such as *SHA256* to generate the owners' signatures establishes a strong link between owners and their WMs. Furthermore, the verification protocol of *KeyNet* provides strong evidence of ownership. When the authority uses a fake signature, the marked model does not respond. This dual authentication method provides unquestionable confidence in the identity of the legitimate owner.

Security. As *KeyNet* embeds the WM in the dynamic content of DL models through joint training, and as modern deep learning models contain a huge number of parameters, detecting the presence of the WM in such models is infeasible. In case the attacker knows that a model contains WM information and wants to destroy it, he/she will only be able to do so by also impairing the accuracy of the model in the original task. Regarding the security of the owner's signature, the use of a strong cryptographic hash function, such as SHA256, provides high security, as we next justify. On the one hand, if the signature size s is taken long enough, it is virtually impossible for two different parties to have the same signature: the probability of collision for s hexadecimal digits is $1/16^s$, so $s = 25$

should be more than enough. On the other hand, even if the owner's signature is known by an attacker, the cryptographic hash function makes it impossible to deduce the owner's information from her signature.

Unforgeability. To prove ownership of a DL model that is not his/hers, an attacker needs to pass the verification protocol (Algorithm 3). However, the private model allowing watermark extraction is kept secret by the legitimate owner. Without the private model, even if the attacker knows both the WM carrier set and the owner's signature, the attacker can only try a random strategy. Yet, the probability of randomly guessing the right position at least a proportion T of r rounds is at most $1/z^{\lfloor Tr \rfloor}$. This probability can be made negligibly small by increasing the number r of verification rounds.

Thus, *KeyNet* partially meets the unforgeability requirement: an attacker can embed additional WMs into a marked model, but cannot claim ownership of another party's WM.

Capacity. Capacity can be viewed from two perspectives: (i) the framework allows the inclusion of a large amount of WM information, and (ii) triggers available in the verification process are large enough. Given that hashes are one-way functions with fixed length, the information that can be embedded in them is virtually unlimited. In our experiments, we used a medium-sized signature of $s = 25$ characters. Nevertheless, *KeyNet* allows flexibility in specifying various signature sizes and in using hash functions other than SHA256. On the other hand, *KeyNet* can use a large number of samples in WM verification. In addition to using all samples belonging to a certain distribution (the WM carrier set), it allows using samples from other distributions due to the method of labeling and training used. The marked model gives the signature information if the signature is placed on top of a WM carrier set's sample, while samples from different distributions are given the label 0 (even if they are signed with the signature of the legitimate owner).

Uniqueness and scalability. *KeyNet* can be easily extended to produce unique copies of a DL model for each user, as well as scale to cover a large number of users in the system. Furthermore, it can link a remote copy of a DL model with its user with minimal effort and high reliability.

Table 9. Integrity results with unmarked models. Each private model was tested with two different unmarked models: one model has the same topology as its corresponding marked model, the other one has a different topology. The last four columns show the accuracy detection obtained with the unmarked models.

Dataset	DL Model	Watermark Detection Accuracy with Marked Models%	Watermark Detection Accuracy with Unmarked Models %			
			Same Topology	Accuracy	Different Topology	Accuracy
CIFAR10	ResNet18	99.97%	ResNet18	18.92%	VGG16	19.80%
CIFAR10	VGG16	99.89%	VGG16	7.92%	ResNet18	12.32%
FMNIST5	CNN	99.98%	CNN	12.96%	LeNet	10.97%
FMNIST5	LeNet	99.55%	LeNet	17.93%	CNN	17.75%

In our experiments, we distributed two unique copies of the FMNIST5-CNN model: one for *User1* and another for *User2*, each copy having its corresponding private model. We took a pretrained FMNIST5-CNN model and fine-tuned it for 30 epochs to embed the WM linked to a specific user. To do so, we signed two copies of the WM carrier set, where each copy was signed using different joint signatures. Once we got two unique carrier sets, we trained two unique marked models, each one with its corresponding private model using Algorithm 2. In the end, we got two unique marked copies of the model with their corresponding private models and users. We distributed each copy to its corresponding user.

We then assumed that *User 1*, respectively, *User 2*, leaked their model, and we tried to find the leaker as follows.

1. We took a small set (say 6 samples) of the WM carrier set.
2. We signed a copy of these samples in random places with *User1*'s joint signature; another copy was also signed in the same way for *User2*.
3. We queried h' (the allegedly leaked model) with the samples signed by *User1* to obtain their predictions. We did the same with *User2* samples.

4. We passed the predictions from samples signed with *User1*'s signature to her private model and calculated the accuracy at detecting the WM. We did the same with *User2*'s predictions and his private model.

Figure 4a shows the results of model owner detection if *User1* leaked her model. We see that we were able to determine that the model copy was most likely leaked by *User1*. Figure 4(a1) shows the normalized confusion matrix of *User1*'s private model in detecting the WM information using the predictions of *User1*'s remote model. It shows that the accuracy at detecting signature positions was almost 100% when we sent the samples signed by *User1*. Figure 4(a2) shows the normalized confusion matrix of *User2*'s private model in detecting the WM information by using the predictions of *User1*'s remote model when the samples were signed with *User2*' signature. As *User1*'s model was trained to distinguish only *User1*'s signature position, it output features that led *User2*'s private model to provide label 0 for samples signed by *User2*.

Figure 4b provides similar results when *User2* leaked his model. The same conclusions hold. Note that the private models were unable to distinguish the signature positions and output the label 0 when they were fed with predictions of non-corresponding marked models and non-corresponding signatures. This is an interesting feature of *KeyNet*, as all the remote models and their private models learned a common representation of label 0.

Regarding **scalability**, if we want to query a remote model in case we have u users and we decide to use m signed samples for verification, then the number of remote model queries will be $u \times m$, and thus linear in u.

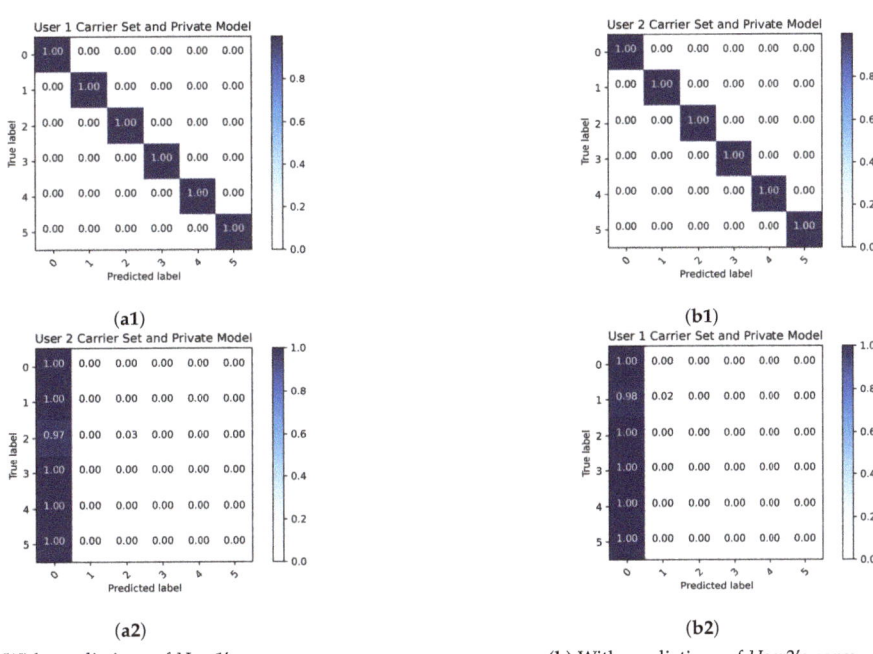

(a) With predictions of *User1*'s copy (b) With predictions of *User2*'s copy

Figure 4. Normalized confusion matrices of the accuracy in detecting the individual copies of the FMNIST5-CNN model distributed among two users. Subfigure (**a**) shows the detection accuracy of the predictions of *User1*' copy. Subfigure (**a1**) shows the confusion matrix of *User1*'s private model when *User1*'s copy was queried by samples signed by *User1*. Subfigure (**a2**) shows the confusion matrix of *User2*'s private model when *User1*'s copy was queried by samples signed by *User2*. Subfigure (**b**) shows the same results for *User2*'s model.

Efficiency and generality. The efficiency of *KeyNet* is related to the size of the output of the model to be marked. The smaller the number of output neurons, the fewer the parameters of the private model. On the other hand, our framework allows embedding the WM from scratch or by fine-tuning; the latter contributes to efficiency. Regarding **generality**, even though in our work we use image classification tasks that output softmax layer probabilities (confidence) for the input image with each class, *KeyNet* can be extended to cover a variety of ML tasks that take images as input and output multiple values such as multi-labeling tasks, semantic segmentation tasks, image transformation tasks, etc.

6. Conclusions and Future Work

We have presented *KeyNet*, a novel watermarking framework to protect the IP of DL models. We use the final output distribution of deep learning models to include a robust WM that does not fall in the same decision boundaries of original task classes. To make the most of this advantage, we design the watermarking task in an innovative way that makes it possible (i) to embed a large amount of WM information, (ii) to establish a strong link between the owner and her marked model, (iii) to thwart the attacker from overwriting the WM information without losing accuracy in the original task, and (iv) to uniquely fingerprint several copies of a pretrained model for a large number of users in the system.

The results we obtained empirically prove that *KeyNet* is effective and can be generalized to various data sets and DL model architectures. Besides, it is robust against a variety of attacks, it offers a very strong authentication linking the owners and their WMs, and it can be easily used to fingerprint different copies of a DL model for different users.

As a future work, we plan to extend the framework to cover computer vision tasks that take images as input and output images as well. We also intend to study ways to estimate the watermark capacity of a deep neural network depending on its topology, the complexity of the learning task, and the watermark to be embedded.

Author Contributions: Conceptualization: N.M.J. and J.D.-F.; methodology, N.M.J.; validation: N.M.J., D.S., and A.B.-J.; formal analysis, N.M.J. and J.D.-F.; investigation, N.M.J. and A.B.-J.; writing—original draft preparation: N.M.J.; writing—review and editing, J.D.-F. and D.S.; funding acquisition, J.D.-F. and D.S. All authors have read and agreed to the published version of the manuscript.

Funding: This research was funded by the European Commission (projects H2020-871042 "SoBig-Data++" and H2020-101006879 "MobiDataLab"), the Government of Catalonia (ICREA Acadèmia Prizes to J. Domingo-Ferrer and D. Sánchez, FI grant to N. Jebreel and grant 2017 SGR 705), and the Spanish Government (projects RTI2018-095094-B-C21 "Consent" and TIN2016-80250-R "Sec-MCloud").

Acknowledgments: Special thanks go to Mohammed Jebreel, for discussions on an earlier version of this work, and to Rami Haffar, for implementing some of the experiments. The authors are with the UNESCO Chair in Data Privacy, but the views in this paper are their own and are not necessarily shared by UNESCO.

Conflicts of Interest: The authors declare no conflict of interest.

Abbreviations

The following abbreviations are used in this manuscript:

DL	Deep learning
FMNIST5	The samples that belong to the classes [0–4] in Fashion-MNIST data set.
IP	Intellectual property
MDPI	Multidisciplinary Digital Publishing Institute
ML	Machine learning
MLaaS	Machine learning as a service
MSE	Mean square error
MTL	Multi-task learning
SHA	Secure Hash Standard algorithm
SN	Serial number
WM	Watermark

References

1. Deng, L.; Yu, D. Deep learning: Methods and applications. *Found. Trends Signal Process.* **2014**, *7*, 197–387. [CrossRef]
2. LeCun, Y.; Bengio, Y.; Hinton, G. Deep learning. *Nature* **2015**, *521*, 436–444. [CrossRef] [PubMed]
3. Dargan, S.; Kumar, M.; Ayyagari, M.R.; Kumar, G. A survey of deep learning and its applications: A new paradigm to machine learning. *Arch. Comput. Methods Eng.* **2019**, *27*, 1071–1092. [CrossRef]
4. Adiwardana, D.; Luong, M.T.; So, D.R.; Hall, J.; Fiedel, N.; Thoppilan, R.; Yang, Z.; Kulshreshtha, A.; Nemade, M.; Lu, Y.; et al. Towards a human-like open-domain chatbot. *arXiv* **2020**, arXiv:2001.09977.
5. Ribeiro, M.; Grolinger, K.; Capretz, M.A. Mlaas: Machine learning as a service. In Proceedings of the 2015 IEEE 14th International Conference on Machine Learning and Applications (ICMLA), Miami, FL, USA, 9–11 December 2015; pp. 896–902.
6. Yao, Y.; Xiao, Z.; Wang, B.; Viswanath, B.; Zheng, H.; Zhao, B.Y. Complexity vs. performance: Empirical analysis of machine learning as a service. In Proceedings of the 2017 Internet Measurement Conference, London, UK, 1–3 November 2017; pp. 384–397.
7. Tramèr, F.; Zhang, F.; Juels, A.; Reiter, M.K.; Ristenpart, T. Stealing machine learning models via prediction apis. In Proceedings of the 25th USENIX Security Symposium (USENIX Security 16), Austin, TX, USA, 10–12 August 2016; pp. 601–618.
8. Wang, B.; Gong, N.Z. Stealing hyperparameters in machine learning. In Proceedings of the 2018 IEEE Symposium on Security and Privacy (SP), San Francisco, CA, USA, 20–24 May 2018; pp. 36–52.
9. Hartung, F.; Kutter, M. Multimedia watermarking techniques. *Proc. IEEE* **1999**, *87*, 1079–1107. [CrossRef]
10. Sebé, F.; Domingo-Ferrer, J.; Herrera, J. Spatial-domain image watermarking robust against compression, filtering, cropping, and scaling. In *International Workshop on Information Security*; Springer: Berlin/Heidelberg, Germany, 2000; pp. 44–53.
11. Furht, B.; Kirovski, D. *Multimedia Security Handbook*; CRC Press: Boca Raton, FL, USA, 2004.
12. Lu, C.S. *Multimedia Security: Steganography and Digital Watermarking Techniques for Protection of Intellectual Property: Steganography and Digital Watermarking Techniques for Protection of Intellectual Property*; IGI Global: Hershey, PA, USA, 2004.
13. Uchida, Y.; Nagai, Y.; Sakazawa, S.; Satoh, S. Embedding watermarks into deep neural networks. In Proceedings of the 2017 ACM on International Conference on Multimedia Retrieval, Bucharest, Romania, 6–9 June 2017; pp. 269–277.
14. Zhang, J.; Gu, Z.; Jang, J.; Wu, H.; Stoecklin, M.P.; Huang, H.; Molloy, I. Protecting intellectual property of deep neural networks with watermarking. In Proceedings of the 2018 on Asia Conference on Computer and Communications Security, Incheon, Korea, 4–8 June 2018; pp. 159–172.
15. Adi, Y.; Baum, C.; Cisse, M.; Pinkas, B.; Keshet, J. Turning your weakness into a strength: Watermarking deep neural networks by backdooring. In Proceedings of the 27th USENIX Security Symposium (USENIX Security 18), Baltimore, MD, USA, 15–17 August 2018; pp. 1615–1631.
16. Chen, H.; Rouhani, B.D.; Fu, C.; Zhao, J.; Koushanfar, F. Deepmarks: A secure fingerprinting framework for digital rights management of deep learning models. In Proceedings of the 2019 International Conference on Multimedia Retrieval, Ottawa, ON, Canada, 10–13 June 2019; pp. 105–113.
17. Le Merrer, E.; Perez, P.; Trédan, G. Adversarial frontier stitching for remote neural network watermarking. *Neural Comput. Appl.* **2020**, *32*, 9233–9244. [CrossRef]
18. Li, H.; Wenger, E.; Zhao, B.Y.; Zheng, H. Piracy Resistant Watermarks for Deep Neural Networks. *arXiv* **2019**, arXiv:1910.01226.
19. Rouhani, B.D.; Chen, H.; Koushanfar, F. Deepsigns: A generic watermarking framework for ip protection of deep learning models. *arXiv* **2018**, arXiv:1804.00750.
20. Chen, H.; Rouhani, B.D.; Koushanfar, F. BlackMarks: Blackbox Multibit Watermarking for Deep Neural Networks. *arXiv* **2019**, arXiv:1904.00344.
21. Xu, X.; Li, Y.; Yuan, C. "Identity Bracelets" for Deep Neural Networks. *IEEE Access* **2020**, *8*, 102065–102074. [CrossRef]
22. Boenisch, F. A Survey on Model Watermarking Neural Networks. *arXiv* **2020**, arXiv:2009.12153.
23. Wang, J.; Wu, H.; Zhang, X.; Yao, Y. Watermarking in deep neural networks via error back-propagation. *Electron. Imaging* **2020**, *2020*, 22-1–22-9. [CrossRef]
24. Fan, L.; Ng, K.W.; Chan, C.S. Rethinking deep neural network ownership verification: Embedding passports to defeat ambiguity attacks. In Proceedings of the Advances in Neural Information Processing Systems, Vancouver, BC, Canada, 8–14 December 2019; pp. 4714–4723.
25. Wang, T.; Kerschbaum, F. Robust and Undetectable White-Box Watermarks for Deep Neural Networks. *arXiv* **2019**, arXiv:1910.14268.
26. Guo, J.; Potkonjak, M. Watermarking deep neural networks for embedded systems. In Proceedings of the 2018 IEEE/ACM International Conference on Computer-Aided Design (ICCAD), San Diego, CA, USA, 5–8 November 2018; pp. 1–8.
27. Hitaj, D.; Mancini, L.V. Have you stolen my model? evasion attacks against deep neural network watermarking techniques. *arXiv* **2018**, arXiv:1809.00615.
28. Li, Z.; Hu, C.; Zhang, Y.; Guo, S. How to prove your model belongs to you: A blind-watermark based framework to protect intellectual property of DNN. In Proceedings of the 35th Annual Computer Security Applications Conference, San Juan, Puerto Rico, 9–13 December 2019; pp. 126–137.
29. Cao, X.; Jia, J.; Gong, N.Z. IPGuard: Protecting the Intellectual Property of Deep Neural Networks via Fingerprinting the Classification Boundary. *arXiv* **2019**, arXiv:1910.12903.

30. Wu, H.; Liu, G.; Yao, Y.; Zhang, X. Watermarking Neural Networks with Watermarked Images. *IEEE Trans. Circuits Syst. Video Technol.* **2020**. [CrossRef]
31. Caruana, R. Multitask learning. *Mach. Learn.* **1997**, *28*, 41–75. [CrossRef]
32. Ruder, S. An overview of multi-task learning in deep neural networks. *arXiv* **2017**, arXiv:1706.05098.
33. Mrkšić, N.; Séaghdha, D.; Thomson, B.; Gašić, M.; Su, P.; Vandyke, D.; Wen, T.; Young, S. Multi-domain dialog state tracking using recurrent neural networks. In Proceedings of the ACL-IJCNLP 2015-53rd Annual Meeting of the Association for Computational Linguistics and the 7th International Joint Conference on Natural Language Processing of the Asian Federation of Natural Language Processing, Beijing, China, 26–31 July 2015; Volume 2, pp. 794–799.
34. Li, S.; Liu, Z.Q.; Chan, A.B. Heterogeneous multi-task learning for human pose estimation with deep convolutional neural network. In Proceedings of the IEEE Conference on Computer Vision and Pattern Recognition Workshops, Columbus, OH, USA, 23–28 June 2014; pp. 482–489.
35. Zhang, W.; Li, R.; Zeng, T.; Sun, Q.; Kumar, S.; Ye, J.; Ji, S. Deep model based transfer and multi-task learning for biological image analysis. *IEEE Trans. Big Data* **2016**, *6*, 322–333. [CrossRef]
36. Neelakantan, A.; Vilnis, L.; Le, Q.V.; Sutskever, I.; Kaiser, L.; Kurach, K.; Martens, J. Adding gradient noise improves learning for very deep networks. *arXiv* **2015**, arXiv:1511.06807.
37. Ndirango, A.; Lee, T. Generalization in multitask deep neural classifiers: A statistical physics approach. In Proceedings of the Advances in Neural Information Processing Systems, Vancouver, BC, Canada, 8–14 December 2019; pp. 15862–15871.
38. Krizhevsky, A. Learning Multiple Layers of Features from Tiny Images. 2009. Available online: https://www.cs.toronto.edu/~kriz/learning-features-2009-TR.pdf (accessed on 22 January 2021).
39. Xiao, H.; Rasul, K.; Vollgraf, R. Fashion-mnist: A novel image dataset for benchmarking machine learning algorithms. *arXiv* **2017**, arXiv:1708.07747.
40. He, K.; Zhang, X.; Ren, S.; Sun, J. Deep residual learning for image recognition. In Proceedings of the IEEE Conference on Computer Vision and Pattern Recognition, Las Vegas, NV, USA, 27–30 June 2016; pp. 770–778.
41. Simonyan, K.; Zisserman, A. Very deep convolutional networks for large-scale image recognition. *arXiv* **2014**, arXiv:1409.1556.
42. LeCun, Y. LeNet-5, Convolutional Neural Networks. Available online: http://yann.lecun.com/exdb/lenet (accessed on 22 January 2021).
43. Coates, A.; Ng, A.; Lee, H. An Analysis of Single Layer Networks in Unsupervised Feature Learning. In Proceedings of the AISTATS 2011, Fort Lauderdale, FL, USA, 11–13 April 2011; pp. 215–223.
44. LeCun, Y.; Cortes, C.; Burges, C.J.C. MNIST Handwritten Digit Database. 2010. Available online: http://yann.lecun.com/exdb/mnist/ (accessed on 22 January 2021).
45. Tajbakhsh, N.; Shin, J.Y.; Gurudu, S.R.; Hurst, R.T.; Kendall, C.B.; Gotway, M.B.; Liang, J. Convolutional neural networks for medical image analysis: Full training or fine tuning? *IEEE Trans. Med. Imaging* **2016**, *35*, 1299–1312. [CrossRef] [PubMed]
46. Han, S.; Mao, H.; Dally, W.J. Deep compression: Compressing deep neural networks with pruning, trained quantization and huffman coding. *arXiv* **2015**, arXiv:1510.00149.
47. Han, S.; Pool, J.; Tran, J.; Dally, W. Learning both weights and connections for efficient neural network. In Proceedings of the Advances in Neural Information Processing Systems, Montréal, QC, Canada, 7–11 December 2015; pp. 1135–1143.
48. Shafieinejad, M.; Wang, J.; Lukas, N.; Li, X.; Kerschbaum, F. On the robustness of the backdoor-based watermarking in deep neural networks. *arXiv* **2019**, arXiv:1906.07745.
49. Aiken, W.; Kim, H.; Woo, S. Neural Network Laundering: Removing Black-Box Backdoor Watermarks from Deep Neural Networks. *arXiv* **2020**, arXiv:2004.11368.

Article

Block-Based Steganography Method Using Optimal Selection to Reach High Efficiency and Capacity for Palette Images

Han-Yan Wu *, Ling-Hwei Chen and Yu-Tai Ching

Department of Computer Science, National Chiao Tung University, Hsinchu 300, Taiwan; lhchen@cc.nctu.edu.tw (L.-H.C.); ytc@cs.nctu.edu.tw (Y.-T.C.)
* Correspondence: hywu.cs02g@nctu.edu.tw

Received: 11 October 2020; Accepted: 2 November 2020; Published: 4 November 2020

Abstract: The primary goal of steganographic methods is to develop statically undetectable methods with high steganographic capacity. The embedding efficiency is one kind of measure for undetectability. Block-based steganography methods have been proposed for achieving higher embedding efficiency under limited embedding capacity. However, in these methods, some blocks with larger embedding distortions are skipped, and a location map is usually incorporated into these methods to record the embedding status of each block. This reduces the embedding capacity for secret messages. In this study, we proposed a block-based steganography method without a location map for palette images. In this method, multiple secret bits can be embedded in a block by modifying at most one pixel with minimal embedding distortion; this enables each block to be used for data embedding; thus, our method provides higher embedding capacity. Furthermore, under the same capacity, the estimated and experimental embedding efficiencies of the proposed method are compared with those of Imaizumi et al. and Aryal et al.'s methods; the comparisons indicate that the proposed method has higher embedding efficiency than Imaizumi et al. and Aryal et al.'s methods.

Keywords: block embedding; embedding capacity; embedding efficiency; optimal selection; parity assignment

1. Introduction

Steganography is a technique for secret communication, in which secret messages are embedded into common digital media such as images, audios, and videos. The original media is called "cover", and the embedded media is called "stego". Of these media, images are the most popular because they are widely transmitted over the Internet. Many image-based steganography methods [1–17] have been proposed and applied in raw [1–5], JPEG [6], VQ [7], and absolute moment block truncation coding (AMBTC) [8] images. However, the application in palette images [9–17] is limited. Palette images [18] have gained popularity. Graphics interchange format (GIF) is a type of palette image frequently used by young consumers to communicate and express themselves. GIF animations are widely used on social media platforms such as Tumblr, Twitter, Facebook, and Line [18,19].

A palette image includes a palette and an index table. The palette consists of a few (generally no more than 256) colors. Each pixel is represented by a color in the palette, and the index table records each pixel's corresponding color index. In general, the order of colors in the palette is random. Because only limited colors are used in palette images, modifying a pixel's color index considerably distorts the pixel color. Thus, embedding data into a palette image is more challenging than in other image formats.

Embedding methods are of two types. In pixel-based methods (PBMs) [9–14], a pixel is used as a unit to embed secret data. In block-based methods (BBMs) [15–17], a block is used as a unit to embed secret data.

Fridrich [11] proposed a method in which the colors of a palette are partitioned into two sets with different parities ($R + G + B$ mod 2) to represent one secret bit. The capacity of this method is 1 bit per pixel (bpp). Under the same embedding capacity, Fridrich and Du [12] proposed an optimal parity assignment algorithm to improve image quality. Tzeng et al. [13] proposed an adaptive data-hiding scheme for palette images based on local complexity. An embedding capacity of approximately 0.1 bpp is used for most images [20]. Tanaka et al. [14] proposed an algorithm to partition colors into 2^k sets. Each set represents one type of k-bit secret data. For each pixel, according to the secret data, the closest color in the corresponding set is determined to replace the pixel's color. The embedding capacity is increased to k bpp.

In [9–12,14], each pixel was used to embed secret data in PBMs. Therefore, the embedding distortion for a pixel may be large. In [13], an adaptive scheme was provided to skip pixels with large distortions. However, this reduced the capacity.

Imaizumi and Ozawa [15] proposed a BBM to embed k bits into each 3×3 block. In this method, first, all colors in a palette are reordered according to the color Euclidean distance. Next, for each block, the sum of all color indices is calculated and divided by 2^k to obtain a remainder. Then, some pixels in the block are selected, and their color indices are adjusted to obtain a remainder equal to the value of k embedding secret data bits with the least embedding distortion. The embedding capacity is k9 bpp. Imaizumi and Ozawa [16] adopted a block size of 2×2 to improve the embedding capacity of their previous method [15]. Subsequently, Aryal et al. [17] used a block size of $1 \times 2^{k-2} + 1$ to improve the embedding capacity of the aforementioned method [16] and used the L^*a^*b color space to replace the RGB color space to improve image quality. In all of these BBMs [15–17], the palette of an image is first reordered. Then, for each block, under the consideration of minimum embedding distortion, several pixels are selected, and their color indices are modified by $+1$ or -1. In the reordered palette, two colors with adjacent color indices may not be similar; some selected pixels may have large embedding distortion, which degrades image quality after data embedding. Furthermore, the color indices of some selected pixels may overflow or underflow after data embedding. To avoid using these blocks, an additional location map is required to record if a block is used to embed secret data. This reduces the embedding capacity for secret data because some blocks are skipped and some are used to embed the location map.

To address the aforementioned problem, a novel BBM for palette images was proposed in this study. First, Tanaka et al.'s k-bit parity assignment [14] was used to assign a k-bit parity to each color in the palette of an image. Then, for each block, at most one pixel was modified for data embedding, and no location map was required for data extraction. The proposed method provided higher capacity.

Note that the primary goal of steganographic methods [21] is to develop statically undetectable methods with high steganographic capacity. Steganographic capacity [21] is defined as the maximum number of bits that can be hidden in a given cover work, such that the probability of detection by an adversary is negligible. The embedding efficiency [21] is one kind of measure for undetectability, and it is defined as the number of embedded random message bits per embedding change. Crandall [22] mentioned that the most obvious method to reduce the possibility of detecting hidden information is to reduce the change density in the cover image. Since decreasing the change density raises the embedding efficiency, higher embedding efficiency will lower the detectability. Since BBMs reduce the change density, the detectability of these methods is lower.

To measure the undetectability of the proposed method, chi-square attack [23], RS steganalysis [24], and embedding efficiency are used. Estimation and experimental results demonstrated that the proposed method provided higher undetectability than the aforementioned BBMs [16,17].

The remainder of this paper is organized as follows. Related works are introduced in Section 2. The proposed method is presented in Section 3. The analysis of embedding capacities is given in Section 4. Experimental results are provided in Section 5. Finally, conclusions are presented in Section 6.

2. Related Works

In this section, the parity assignment method proposed by Tanaka et al. [14] and referenced in the proposed method is first described. Then, the method proposed by Aryal et al. [17] is described; it is used to make a comparison with the proposed method.

2.1. Parity Assignment Method Proposed by Tanaka et al.

Tanaka et al. proposed an algorithm to assign k parity bits to each color in the palette of an image. The algorithm contains two parts. In the first part, from the palette, 2^k closest colors ($c'_0, \ldots, c'_{2^k-1}$) are determined sequentially, c'_i is assigned a k-bit parity with value i. Next, 2^k sets ($S_0, \ldots, S_{2^k-1}$) are established, that is, $S_i = \{c'_i\}$. In the second part, from the unassigned colors, the color c with the minimal distance from the last assigned color is determined. Next, the minimal distance d_p of c from each set S_p is evaluated. Then, the maximal distance $d_{p'}$ among $\{d_p | p = 0, \ldots, 2^k - 1\}$ is determined and p' is assigned as the parity of color c. The procedure is repeated until all colors are assigned.

In the algorithm, the distance d_{c_i,c_j} between two colors $c_i = (r_i, g_i, b_i)$ and $c_j = (r_j, g_j, b_j)$ is defined using the following expression:

$$d_{i,j} = \sqrt{(r_i - r_j)^2 + (g_i - g_j)^2 + (b_i - b_j)^2}. \tag{1}$$

The details of the parity assignment are described as follows:

Step 1: Let A be the set of all colors in the palette. Let $S_q = \phi$, and assign parity q to S_q; $q = 0, \ldots, 2^k - 1$.
Step 2: Let $h = 0$. Find an initial color c'_h using the following expression:

$$c'_h = \underset{c_i \in A}{\mathrm{argmin}}(256^2 r_i + 256 g_i + b_i), \tag{2}$$

$S_h = S_h \cup \{c'_h\}$; $A = A \setminus \{c'_h\}$.

Step 3: Let $h = h + 1$. Find color c'_h in A with the minimum distance from c'_{h-1} using the following equation:

$$c'_h = \underset{c_i \in A}{\mathrm{argmin}} d_{c'_{h-1}, c_i}, \tag{3}$$

$S_h = S_h \cup \{c'_h\}$; $A = A \setminus \{c'_h\}$.

Step 4: Repeat Step 3 until $h = 2^k - 1$.
Step 5: Let $h = h + 1$. Find color c'_h in A with the minimum distance from c'_{h-1} using Equation (3).
Step 6: In each S_q, $q = 0, \ldots, 2^k - 1$, find the color in S_q with the minimum distance md_q from c'_h using the following expression:

$$md_q = \underset{c_i \in S_q}{\mathrm{min}} d_{c'_h, c_i}, \tag{4}$$

Step 7: Find the maximum distance $md_{q'}$ among all md_q using the following expression:

$$q' = \underset{q}{\mathrm{argmax}}\, md_q, \tag{5}$$

$S_{q'} = S_{q'} \cup \{c'_h\}$, $A = A \setminus \{c'_h\}$.

Step 8: Repeat Steps 5 to 7 until A is empty.

2.2. Aryal et al.'s Method

Aryal et al.'s method [17] improves the capacity and image quality of Imaizumi et al.'s method [16]. In the method, the color c of each pixel in the *RGB* color space is first converted to color (L*, a*, b*) in the *L*a*b* color space, and the CIEDE2000 formula [25] is used to calculate the color distance. The method includes three processes: Palette reordering, block embedding, and extraction. In the method, the *k*-bit messages are embedded into each $2^{k-2} + 1$ pixel matrix. For convenience, we assumed $k = 3$ in the following processes.

2.2.1. Palette Reordering Process

Step 1: Let the original palette P be $\{c_0, \ldots, c_{255}\}$, the new palette P' be $\{c'_0, \ldots, c'_{255}\}$, and $A = P$.
Step 2: Set $h = 0$. Find the first color c'_h in P' using the following expression:

$$c'_h = \underset{c_i \in A}{\operatorname{argmin}} L^*_i, \tag{6}$$

where L^*_i is the luminance component of color c_i in the *L*a*b* color space.

Step 3: Let $A = A \setminus \{c'_h\}$, $h = h + 1$. Find color c'_h in A with the minimum distance from c'_{h-1} using the following expression:

$$c'_h = \underset{c_i \in A}{\operatorname{argmin}} \Delta E_{c'_{h-1}, c_i}, \tag{7}$$

where $\Delta E_{c'_{h-1}, c_i}$ is the CIEDE2000 color distance [25] between c'_{h-1} and c_i.

Step 4: Repeat Step 3 until $h = 255$.

2.2.2. Embedding Process

Step 1: Divide the cover image into nonoverlapping blocks, each of which contains 1×3 pixels.
Step 2: Reorder palette P to obtain a new palette P' using the palette reordering process.
Step 3: Consider a block B with three pixels (B_0, B_1, B_2) and three secret data bits w.
Step 4: Let I_i be the color index of B_i in P', $i = 0, 1, 2$.
Step 5: Calculate T_0 and T_1 using the following equations.

$$T_0 = I_0 \bmod 2. \tag{8}$$

$$T_1 = (I_1 + I_2) \bmod 4. \tag{9}$$

Step 6: Obtain t_0 and t_1 based on Table 1 and secret data w.
Step 7: If $T_0 = t_0$ and $T_1 = t_1$, then go to Step 10.
Step 8: If $|T_0 - t_0| = 1$, then I_0 is changed by +1 or −1; this depends on whether $\Delta E_{c'_{I_0-1}, c'_{I_0}}$ or $\Delta E_{c'_{I_0+1}, c'_{I_0}}$ is smaller.
Step 9: If $|T_1 - t_1| \neq 0$, then three cases are possible:

Case 1: If $|T_1 - t_1| = 2$, then I_1 and I_2 are changed by +1 or −1; this depends on whether $\Delta E_{c'_{I_1+1}, c'_{I_1}} + \Delta E_{c'_{I_2+1}, c'_{I_2}}$ or $\Delta E_{c'_{I_1-1}, c'_{I_1}} + \Delta E_{c'_{I_2-1}, c'_{I_2}}$ is smaller.
Case 2: If $T_1 - t_1 = 1$ or $T_1 - t_1 = -3$, then either I_1 or I_2 is changed by −1; this depends on whether $\Delta E_{c'_{I_1-1}, c'_{I_1}}$ or $\Delta E_{c'_{I_2-1}, c'_{I_2}}$ is smaller.
Case 3: If $T_1 - t_1 = -1$ or $T_1 - t_1 = 3$, then either I_1 or I_2 is changed by +1; this depends on whether $\Delta E_{c'_{I_1+1}, c'_{I_1}}$ or $\Delta E_{c'_{I_2+1}, c'_{I_2}}$ is smaller.

Step 10: Go to Step 3 until all secret data are embedded.

If any $\Delta E > 5$ in the embedding process, the current block is skipped, and no secret data are embedded. An additional location map is required for recording if a block is used to embed secret data.

Table 1. Relation between secret data w and (t_0, t_1).

w (3 Bits)	t_0	t_1
7 (111)	0	3
6 (110)	0	2
5 (101)	0	1
4 (100)	0	0
3 (011)	1	0
2 (010)	1	1
1 (001)	1	2
0 (000)	1	3

2.2.3. Extraction Process

Step 1: Divide the stego image into nonoverlapping blocks, each of which contains 1×3 pixels.

Step 2: Reorder palette P to obtain a new palette P' through the palette reordering process used in the embedding process.

Step 3: According to the location map, consider an embedded block B with three pixels (B_0, B_1, B_2). Let I_i be the color index of B_i in P', $i = 0, 1, 2$.

Step 4: Calculate t_0 and t_1 using the following equations:

$$t_0 = I_0 \bmod 2. \quad (10)$$

$$t_1 = (I_1 + I_2) \bmod 4. \quad (11)$$

Step 5: Extract w according to Table 1, t_0 and t_1.

Step 6: Go to Step 3 until all embedded blocks are processed.

In Imaizumi et al. and Aryal et al.'s methods, for data extraction, the receiver requires the positions of embedded blocks. Thus, a location map with one bit for each block should be transmitted to the receiver; this will reduce the embedding capacity for secret data, and will be discussed in Section 4. To overcome this disadvantage, a novel BBM was proposed; it does not require a location map.

3. Proposed Method

To avoid using a location map and to obtain higher embedding efficiency and capacity, a novel BBM for palette images is proposed. The method includes three processes: Parity assignment, embedding, and extraction. In the parity assignment process, Tanaka et al.'s assignment [14] is used to assign a k-bit parity to each color in a palette. Through the assignment, a stego image with lower embedding distortion can be obtained, such that a location map is not required for secret data extraction. In the embedding process, an optimal scheme is provided to select the pixel in a block with the minimal embedding distortion; this makes each block used for data embedding. The embedding process is performed as follows:

3.1. Embedding Process

Step 1: Divide the cover image into nonoverlapping blocks, each of which contains $n \times m$ pixels.

Step 2: Use Tanaka et al.'s parity assignment to assign a k-bit parity to each color in palette P.

Step 3: Take one block B with pixels $(B_0, \ldots, B_{n \times m - 1})$ and k secret data bits w sequentially.

Step 4: Let c_{B_j} be the color of B_j, and q_j be the parity of c_{B_j}, $0 \le j \le n \times m - 1$.

Step 5: Calculate r using the following expression:

$$r = \sum_{j=0}^{n \times m - 1} q_j \bmod 2^k. \tag{12}$$

Step 6: If $r = w$, then go to Step 10.

Step 7: For each pixel B_j, parity q'_j is calculated using the following equation:

$$q'_j = \left(q_j + w - r + 2^k\right) \bmod 2^k, j = 0, \ldots, n \times m - 1. \tag{13}$$

Step 8: For each pixel B_j, find a new color $c^*_{B_j}$ with parity q'_j according to the following equation:

$$c^*_{B_j} = \operatorname*{argmin}_{c_i \in S_{q'_j}} d_{c_{B_j}, c_i}, \tag{14}$$

where $S_{q'_j}$ is the set of all colors with parity q'_j.

Step 9: Consider pixel B_α satisfying the following expression, and set the color of B_α to be $c^*_{B_\alpha}$.

$$\alpha = \operatorname*{argmin}_{j \in \{0, \ldots, n \times m - 1\}} d_{c_{B_j}, c^*_{B_j}}, \tag{15}$$

Step 10: Repeat Steps 3 to 9 until all blocks are processed.

In Step 2, Tanaka et al.'s parity assignment is used; it makes each color be able to find a closer color in each set with a different parity. In Step 8, for each pixel, we always select the color with the required parity and the minimal embedding distortion to replace the original color. In Step 9, at most one pixel is modified with the minimal embedding distortion. Through these three steps, each block is used to embed secret data, and the embedding quality is also improved.

3.2. Extraction Process

In the extraction process, the receiver uses the same parity assignment as that used in the embedding process to assign a k-bit parity to each color. The extraction process is as follows:

Step 1: Divide the stego image into nonoverlapping blocks, each of which contains $n \times m$ pixels.
Step 2: Use Tanaka et al.'s parity assignment to assign a k-bit parity to each color in palette P.
Step 3: Take a block B with pixels $(B_0, \ldots, B_{n \times m - 1})$ sequentially.
Step 4: Use Equation (12) to obtain r.
Step 5: Set r to be the k secret data bits w.
Step 6: Repeat Steps 3 to 5 until all blocks are processed.

Because each block is used to embed secret data, the receiver does not require a location map in data extraction.

4. The Analysis for Embedding Capacities

As mentioned previously, both Imaizumi et al. [16] and Aryal et al.'s [17] methods need a location map in the extraction process; thus, the location map should be transmitted through another channel or be embedded in the stego image. However, it is unreasonable to transmit the location map through another channel. Thus, in the following, we only consider the location map embedded in the stego image. Let an image size be $N \times M$, block size be $n \times m$, the embedding bits for each block be k, then the total block number $T = \lfloor N \times M / (n \times m) \rfloor$. Assume that in the location map, each block is represented by one bit, 1 stand for the corresponding block used for embedding; 0 for skipping. Let X be the size of the location map, assume that the location map is embedded in the first $\lceil X/k \rceil$ blocks, then the number of available blocks for secret data embedding is $T - \lceil X/k \rceil$. Thus, X should satisfy the following equation:

$$X = T - \lceil X/k \rceil. \tag{16}$$

Note that the embedding capacity (bits) is kX. Let an image size be 256×256 and block size be 2×2, then $T = 16384$. Let $k = 3$; through Equation (16), we can obtain $X = 12,288$, that is, the number of available blocks for secret data embedding is 12,288, and the block number needed for recording the location map is 4096. Table 2 shows embedding capacities for Imaizumi et al.'s, Aryal et al.'s, and the proposed methods. In the table, we can see that the proposed method is superior to Imaizumi et al. and Aryal et al.'s methods in embedding capacity.

Table 2. The comparisons of embedding capacities among Imaizumi et al.'s [16], Aryal et al.'s [17], and the proposed methods for image size 256×256 and $k = 3$.

Block Size	2 × 2		1 × 3	
Embedding Method	[16]	Proposed Method	[17]	Proposed Method
Total Block number (T)		16,384		21,845
Location map size (X bits)	12,288	0	16,383	0
Block number needed for record location map ($\lceil X/k \rceil$)	4096	0	5461	0
Number of available blocks for secret data embedding ($T - \lceil X/k \rceil$)	12,288	16,384	16,384	21,845
Maximum embedding capacity (bits)	36,864	49,152	49,152	65,535

5. Experimental Results

In the experiments, 25 images of 256×256 in Figure 1 were used. These images were obtained from the Standard Image Database [26] or CBIR Image Database [27] and in the TIFF or JPG format. Photopea [18] was first used to resize and crop each image to 256×256, then Cloudconvert [18] was applied to convert TIFF (JPG) format into the GIF format. The embedded secret data were generated using a pseudorandom number generator. Image quality was measured using the peak signal-to-noise ratios (PSNRs). Chi-square attack, RS steganalysis, and embedding efficiency were used to measure the undetectability of a steganography method.

5.1. PSNR Comparisons

To demonstrate the effectiveness of our method, we conducted three experiments for comparing the image qualities of the proposed method with those of Imaizumi et al. [16] and Aryal et al. [17] under the same embedding capacity. The first two experiments assume that the location map needed by Imaizumi et al. and Aryal et al.'s methods is not embedded in the stego image, and it is sent through another channel. The third experiment assumes that the location map needed by Imaizumi et al. and Aryal et al.'s methods is embedded in the stego image; thus, the embedding capacity is reduced.

Figure 1. Twenty-five test images.

In the first experiment, Imaizumi et al.'s and the proposed methods with capacities of 15,000 and 30,000 bits were conducted. First, each image was divided into 128×128 blocks, each of which has size 2×2. Then, each block was embedded k bits, $k = 1, 2$. Part of results is depicted in Tables 3 and 4. These tables reveal that the image qualities of the proposed method were the best. This means that the proposed method actually has lower embedding distortion for each block such that each block can be used for data embedding. In the following, more details of explanation are described.

Table 3. Peak signal-to-noise ratios (PSNRs) of Imaizumi et al.'s [16] and the proposed methods.

Capacity (Bits)	15,000, $k = 1$		30,000, $k = 2$	
	[16]	Proposed Method	[16]	Proposed Method
Aerial	38.78	41.99	36.71	39.31
Airplane	46.29	47.18	42.95	44.09
Balloon	45.10	48.04	42.14	44.14
Earth	43.70	50.61	42.45	47.22
Girl	42.57	43.33	39.40	40.12
Lena	41.51	45.21	39.17	41.89
Parrots	40.22	42.22	37.05	38.54
Pepper	41.42	42.53	38.02	39.17
Mandrill	38.82	40.34	35.81	37.30
Couple	41.44	46.16	39.77	43.18
Sailboat	40.62	43.96	38.24	40.76
Milkdrop	45.61	47.47	42.09	43.35

Table 4. PSNRs of Imaizumi et al.'s [16], Aryal et al.'s [17], and the proposed methods with a capacity 45,000 bits and $k = 3$.

Block Size	2 × 2		1 × 3	
	[16]	Proposed Method	[17]	Proposed Method
Bell	34.39	41.45	37.51	41.13
Bricks	36.00	35.44	34.97	36.95
Church	36.21	42.07	38.06	41.29
Cliffs	33.28	39.51	36.05	39.50
Kangaroo	36.53	40.31	32.63	39.99
Kinkaku-ji Temple	34.60	38.61	34.66	38.54
Monkeys	36.08	39.53	34.87	39.99
Mosque	37.42	40.38	38.70	40.03
Painting	35.94	41.79	37.58	41.47
Rice paddies	36.18	41.18	36.46	40.93
Statue	30.79	39.28	35.25	38.77
Sydney Opera House	40.18	43.87	39.07	43.80
Temple	40.22	40.38	36.39	40.51

In Imaizumi et al.'s method, the palette is reordered; this increases the distance between two neighboring colors (i.e., two colors with index difference 1) when their indices are large. In data embedding, if one pixel's color c with index i is replaced by color c', then the index of c' is $i - 1$ or $i + 1$. However, when i is large, these two colors with the index difference of 1 may not be close; this increases the embedding distortion.

To provide more explanation, the image Lena was used with setting $k = 1$. Figure 2 illustrates the result of Tanaka et al.'s parity assignment. Figure 2a depicts all colors with parity 0, and Figure 2c illustrates all colors with parity 1. Figure 2b depicts the corresponding closest color with parity 1 of each color in Figure 2a. Figure 2d depicts the corresponding closest color with parity 0 of each color in Figure 2c. From these figures, we can determine that for each color with parity 0 (1), a similar color with parity 1 (0) can always be found.

Figure 3 illustrates the result of Imaizumi et al.'s palette reordering. Figure 3a displays the reordered color palette. Figure 3b denotes the best replacing one of each color in Figure 3a when embedding data. Figure 3c illustrates the enlarged part of the rectangle marked by red color in Figure 3a. Figure 3d depicts the enlarged part of the rectangle marked by red color in Figure 3b. These figures indicate that some colors may be replaced by an unsimilar color during data embedding.

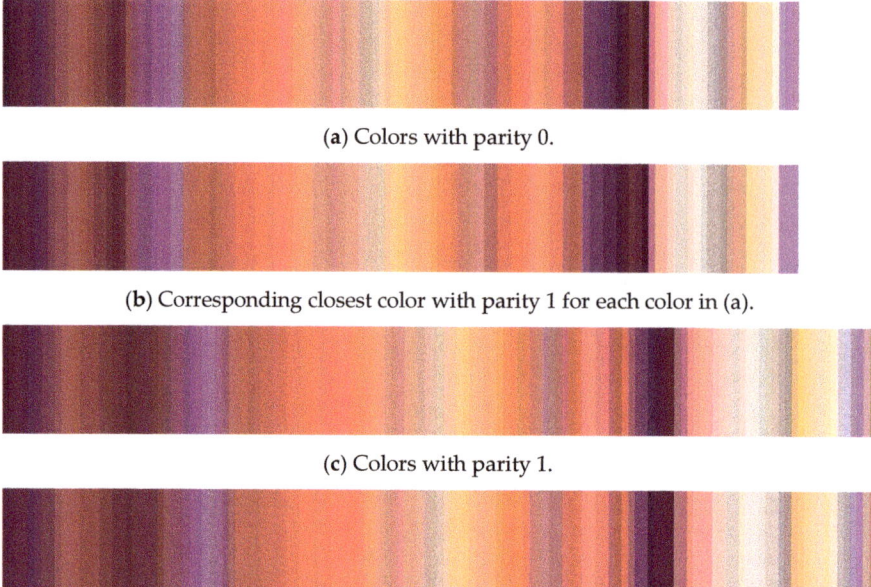

(a) Colors with parity 0.

(b) Corresponding closest color with parity 1 for each color in (a).

(c) Colors with parity 1.

(d) Corresponding closest color with parity 0 for each color in (c).

Figure 2. Results of Tanaka et al.'s parity assignment with $k = 1$ for Lena.

(a) The reordering palette using Imaizumi et al.'s method.

(b) The corresponding replacing color for each color in (a).

(c) Enlarged part of the rectangle marked by red color in (a).

(d) Enlarged part of the rectangle marked by red color in (b).

Figure 3. Results of Imaizumi et al.'s palette reordering for Lena.

In the second experiment, we compared the proposed method with the methods proposed by Imaizumi et al. [16] and Aryal et al. [17] with a capacity of 45,000 bits and $k = 3$. Note that for the image Couple, only 43,845 bits can be embedded using Aryal et al.'s method. Part of results is listed in Table 4, which reveals that the proposed method provides the best image quality under the same capacity. The reason is the same as that in experiment 1. Furthermore, our method modifies at most one pixel during data embedding; other methods [16,17] may modify more than one pixel during data embedding.

As mentioned previously, Imaizumi et al. and Aryal et al.'s methods need an extra location map to record which blocks are used for embedding, in experiment 3, the location map is embedded into a stego image. According to Table 2, the maximum valid embedding capacity of Imaizumi et al. and Aryal et al.'s methods are $12,288 \times k$ and $16384 \times k$, respectively. Table 5 shows part of image qualities of Imaizumi et al.'s, Aryal et al.'s, and our methods under the same embedding capacity. Note that to enforce embedding the location map in the first 4096 (5467) blocks for Imaizumi et al.'s (Aryal et al.'s) method, all indices 0 (255) of pixels in these blocks are changed to 1 (254) before embedding; this will avoid overflow/underflow after embedding. From these tables, we can see that image qualities of the proposed method are always superior to those of Imaizumi et al. and Aryal et al.'s methods under the same embedding capacity. The main reason is that embedding the location map will occupy several blocks and reduce the embedding capacity. Thus, under the same embedding capacity, those blocks used for embedding the location map in Imaizumi et al. and Aryal et al.'s methods will be skipped for data embedding in the proposed method. This will make the proposed method have higher image quality.

Table 5. PSNRs of Imaizumi et al.'s [16], Aryal et al.'s [17], and the proposed methods with $k = 3$.

Block Size	2 × 2		1 × 3	
Capacity	$12,288 \times k$		$16,384 \times k$	
	[16]	Proposed Method	[17]	Proposed Method
Aerial	33.07	38.35	29.22	36.91
Airplane	37.05	42.62	34.96	40.66
Balloon	35.82	42.13	33.78	40.52
Earth	38.94	45.60	39.14	43.99
Girl	33.53	38.89	30.55	37.33
Lena	34.34	40.30	32.52	38.61
Parrots	31.60	36.52	29.86	34.97
Pepper	32.72	37.58	30.72	36.05
Mandrill	30.81	35.91	27.00	34.25
Couple	35.48	41.76	32.75	40.16
Sailboat	33.92	39.52	31.18	37.99
Milkdrop	35.58	40.99	33.50	39.20

5.2. Chi-Square Attack and RS Steganalysis

In steganography, the main goal for a stego image is statistically undetectable [21] (p. 52). To test whether the embedded images are detectable, chi-square attack [23], RS steganalysis [24], and embedding efficiency [21] were conducted. Chi-square attack and RS steganalysis are discussed in this section, and embedding efficiency in Section 5.3.

Each of chi-square attack and RS steganalysis has two experiments, one embedded $15,000 \times k$ bits ($k = 1, 2, 3$) for Imaizumi et al.'s and the proposed methods. The other embedded $15,000 \times k$ bits ($k = 3$) for Aryal et al.'s and the proposed methods.

Chi-square attack employs Pearson's chi-square test to determine whether there is a statistically significant difference between the expected frequencies and the observed frequencies in one or more categories of an image, and it can detect whether a palette image is embedded by messages. The details of applying the chi-square attack to steganography methods are described as follows:

Step 1: Let the palette indices of a palette image be divided into K categories, each category contains a pair of indices $(2i, 2i + 1)$, $i = 0, \ldots, K - 1$. Let E_i and O_i be the theoretically expected and observed frequencies of pixels with index $2i$ after embedding messages, respectively. Then

$$E_i = \frac{\text{The number of pixels with color index } 2i \text{ or } 2i + 1}{2}, \tag{17}$$

$$O_i = \text{The number of pixels with color index } 2i. \tag{18}$$

Step 2: The χ^2 statistic is given as

$$\chi^2_{K-1} = \sum_{i=0}^{K-1} \frac{(O_i - E_i)^2}{E_i} \text{ with } K - 1 \text{ degrees of freedom.} \tag{19}$$

Step 3: Let p_v represent the embedding probability, p_v can be calculated by the following equation:

$$p_v = 1 - \frac{1}{2^{\frac{K-1}{2}} \Gamma\left(\frac{K-1}{2}\right)} \int_0^{\chi^2_{K-1}} e^{-\frac{x}{2}} x^{\frac{K-1}{2}-1} dx. \tag{20}$$

In chi-square attack, the results for three methods are $p_v = 0$; this means that the three methods can resist chi-square attack. There are two reasons: (1) These three methods are block-based; the embedding capacities are limited and lower than 1 bpp; this will make chi-square attack fail [21]; (2) chi-square attack is used to detect LSB-based methods, but these three methods are not LSB-based methods.

Chi-square attack just uses sample counts and neglects spatial correlations among pixels in the stego image. Fridrich et al. [24] introduced RS steganalysis for detection of LSB embedding that utilizes sensitive dual statistics derived from spatial correlations in image.

In RS steganalysis, for a given image I, through a given local mask, two flipping functions, and a discrimination function, all pixels of the image can be classified into three groups: Regular, singular, and unchanged. Given a non-negative mask m, we can obtain the relative frequency of the regular group denoted as R_+ and the relative frequency of the singular group denoted as S_+. Then through the mask $-m$, we can obtain the relative frequency of the regular group denoted as R_- and the relative frequency of the singular group denoted as S_-. Let p_e be the embedding rate in f, RS steganalysis can estimate p_e by solving the following equation:

$$2(d_1 + d_0)z^2 + (d_{-0} - d_{-1} - d_1 - 3d_0)z + d_0 - d_{-0} = 0, \tag{21}$$

where

$$\begin{aligned} d_0 &= R_+(p_e/2) - S_+(p_e/2), \ d_1 = R_+(1 - p_e/2) - S_+(1 - p_e/2), \\ d_{-0} &= R_-(p_e/2) - S_-(p_e/2), \ d_{-1} = R_-(1 - p_e/2) - S_-(1 - p_e/2), \end{aligned} \tag{22}$$

and $R_+(p/2)$ represents R_+ of a stego image with p pixels embedded (i.e., the LSBs of $p/2$ pixels flipped from a cover image). Thus, we can obtain $R_+(p_e/2)$ easily through f; furthermore, by flipping the LSB of each pixel in I to get I', we can also obtain $R_+(1 - p_e/2)$ through I'. S_+, S_-, and R_- can be obtained by the similar way. Then, p_e is calculated from the root z of Equation (20), whose absolute value is smaller, by the following equation:

$$p_e = \frac{z}{z - \frac{1}{2}}. \tag{23}$$

Two experiments are conducted, one for Imaizumi et al.'s [16] and the proposed methods uses block size 2×2 and three capacities (23%, 46%, and 69%); the other for Aryal et al.'s [17] and the proposed methods uses block size 1×3 and the same three capacities. In the experiments, the mask m is defined as [0 1 1 0]. Tables 6 and 7 show part of the p_es of Imaizumi et al.'s, Aryal et al.'s, and the proposed methods. Note that both Imaizumi et al. and Aryal et al.'s methods embedded message by reordering the original palette, so there are two results for their methods by analyzing the original and the reordering palettes. From these tables, we can see that RS steganalysis cannot estimate p_e accurately. The reason is that these three methods are not LSB-based methods. We can conclude that the three methods can resist RS steganalysis and are undetectable.

Table 6. The results of RS steganalysis for Imaizumi et al.'s [16] and the proposed methods with block size 2 × 2.

Method	Proposed Method				Imaizumi et al.				Imaizumi et al.			
Palette	Original				Original				Reordering			
k	0	1	2	3	0	1	2	3	0	1	2	3
	Actual embedding rate (%)											
	0	23	46	69	0	23	46	69	0	23	46	69
	Estimated embedding rate (%)											
Aerial	0	−3	−5	1	0	10	10	16	−20	10	18	32
Airplane	−16	−1	2	8	−16	−37	−56	−80	−9	−12	−5	−9
Balloon	−11	−19	−17	−20	−11	−14	−12	−21	7	6	0	3
Earth	−18	−12	−12	−16	−18	−23	−28	−26	21	14	14	−15
Girl	12	−23	−18	−30	12	10	−4	−7	−16	−8	−18	−19
Lena	0	12	11	12	0	2	−9	−4	4	6	10	8
Parrots	11	−1	1	2	11	12	11	15	−9	−6	−7	−6
Pepper	−1	11	11	11	−1	−1	−3	−2	4	2	6	−4
Mandrill	0	0	0	−1	0	3	8	−11	5	10	9	7
Couple	−11	−2	−11	−7	−11	5	−12	−4	−16	20	18	22
Sailboat	11	−15	−25	−24	11	12	10	5	−12	−12	−9	−12
Milkdrop	15	10	10	13	15	14	18	14	−1	2	0	−1

5.3. Embedding Efficiency

Another measurement for undetectability is embedding efficiency [21]. The embedding efficiency is defined as the number of embedded random message bits per embedding change [21]. According to this definition, embedding efficiency (EF) can be expressed as follows:

$$EF = \frac{\text{number of embedding bits}}{\text{number of embedding pixel changes}}. \quad (24)$$

Methods with higher embedding efficiency are more undetectable, because under the same capacity, higher embedding efficiency methods will change less pixels than lower embedding efficiency methods. For $k = 3$, according to Equation (24), the estimated embedding efficiency of the proposed method (EF_p) can be calculated by Equation (25).

$$EF_p = \frac{3}{0 \times p_0 + 1 \times p_1}, \quad (25)$$

where p_i stands for the probability of i pixel changed in a block, here $p_0 = 1/8$ and $p_1 = 7/8$.

The estimated embedding efficiency of Imaizumi et al.'s method (EF_i) can be calculated by Equation (26).

$$EF_i = \frac{3}{0 \times p_0 + 1 \times p_1 + 2 \times p_2 + 3 \times p_3 + 4 \times p_4}, \quad (26)$$

where p_i stands for the probability of i pixel changed in a block, here $p_0 = 1/15$, $p_1 = p_2 = p_3 = 4/15$, and $p_4 = 2/15$.

The estimated embedding efficiency of Aryal et al.'s method (EF_a) can be calculated by Equation (27).

$$EF_a = \frac{3}{(p_0) \times (1 \times p_1 + 2 \times p_2) + (1 - p_0) \times ((1+1) \times p_1 + (1+2) \times p_2)}. \tag{27}$$

where p_0 stands for the probability of B_0 unchanged, p_i stands for the probability of i pixels from $\{B_1, B_2\}$ changed, here $p_0 = 1/2$, $p_1 = 4/7$, and $p_2 = 2/7$.

Table 8 shows the estimated embedding efficiencies of the proposed, Imaizumi et al.'s [16], and Aryal et al.'s [17] methods obtained by using Equations (25)–(27). Table 9 shows part of experimental embedding efficiency calculated by applying Equation (24) to each stego image, which is obtained by one of Imaizumi et al.'s, Aryal et al.'s and the proposed methods. From these tables, we can see that either estimated embedding efficiency or experimental one, the proposed method has higher embedding efficiency than those of Imaizumi et al. and Aryal et al.'s methods. This means that the proposed method is less detectable than Imaizumi et al. and Aryal et al.'s methods.

Table 7. The results of RS steganalysis for Aryal et al.'s [17] and the proposed methods with block size 1×3.

Method	Proposed Method				Aryal et al.				Aryal et al.			
Palette	Original				Original				Reordering			
k	0	3	3	3	0	3	3	3	0	3	3	3
	Actual embedding rate (%)											
	0	23	46	69	0	23	46	69	0	23	46	69
	Estimated embedding rate (%)											
Bell	−11	−11	−11	−13	−11	−16	−15	−19	−12	−17	−16	−10
Bricks	−27	−39	−55	−39	−27	−28	−31	−46	5	0	1	−9
Church	11	11	15	17	11	11	14	16	4	4	4	−2
Cliffs	−9	−12	−19	−20	−9	−7	−6	−4	2	1	0	2
Kangaroo	−40	−46	−40	−43	−40	−52	−60	−75	−39	−44	−47	−43
Kinkaku-ji Temple	−15	−16	−24	−31	−15	−19	−25	−30	4	2	−1	−4
Monkeys	4	5	5	8	4	0	−6	−9	−2	−2	2	3
Mosque	−15	−11	−10	−8	−15	−14	−17	−19	−2	−2	0	8
Painting	−11	−13	−19	−22	−11	−12	−22	−35	−5	−9	−13	−17
Rice paddies	−148	−143	−144	−158	−148	−151	−138	−131	−54	−40	−39	−38
Statue	18	16	17	18	18	23	25	29	−9	−8	−11	−4
Sydney Opera House	1	−2	−6	−7	1	−2	1	−2	8	14	15	17
Temple	−18	−16	−14	−17	−18	−48	−50	−45	6	11	15	13

Table 8. Estimated embedding efficiencies of Imaizumi et al.'s [16], Aryal et al.'s [17], and the proposed methods with $k = 3$.

Block Size	2×2		1×3	
Methods	[16]	Proposed Method	[17]	Proposed Method
	1.406	3.428	1.909	3.428

Table 9. Experimental embedding efficiencies of Imaizumi et al.'s [16], Aryal et al.'s [17], and the proposed methods with $k = 3$.

Block Size	2×2		1×3	
Capacity (Bits)	49,152		65,535	
Methods / Images	[16]	Proposed Method	[17]	Proposed Method
Aerial	1.492	3.417	2.006	3.442
Airplane	1.499	3.415	1.994	3.431
Balloon	1.497	3.430	1.999	3.423
Earth	1.500	3.415	1.994	3.425
Girl	1.490	3.454	2.007	3.450
Lena	1.491	3.412	1.996	3.431
Parrots	1.496	3.445	1.988	3.424
Pepper	1.482	3.401	2.011	3.427
Mandrill	1.507	3.434	2.015	3.442
Couple	1.482	3.432	2.012	3.440
Sailboat	1.505	3.425	1.996	3.427
Milkdrop	1.500	3.411	1.993	3.442

6. Conclusions

As mentioned previously, some BBMs produce large embedding distortions in some blocks; a location map is incorporated into these methods to record which blocks are used for data embedding. This will reduce the embedding capacity for secret data. To avoid this disadvantage, in this paper, we have proposed a BBM for palette images. The method modifies at most one pixel in a block. If modification is required, one optimal pixel with minimal embedding distortion is selected; this makes each block be used to embed secret data; that is, the embedding capacity of the proposed method is larger than that of the state-of-the-art BBMs. As to the undetectability, chi-square attack, RS steganalysis, and the embedding efficiency are used. Imaizumi et al.'s, Aryal et al.'s, and the proposed methods can resist chi-square attack and RS steganalysis. However, through the measure of embedding efficiency, both estimated and experimental efficiencies revealed that our method provided higher undetectability.

Author Contributions: Conceptualization, H.-Y.W. and L.-H.C.; methodology, H.-Y.W. and L.-H.C.; software, H.-Y.W.; validation, H.-Y.W. and L.-H.C.; writing—Original draft preparation, H.-Y.W.; writing—Review and editing, H.-Y.W. and L.-H.C.; visualization, H.-Y.W. and L.-H.C.; supervision, L.-H.C. and Y.-T.C. All authors have read and agreed to the published version of the manuscript.

Funding: This research received no external funding.

Conflicts of Interest: The authors declare no conflict of interest.

References

1. Zhang, X.; Sun, Z.; Tang, Z.; Yu, C.; Wang, X. High capacity data hiding based on interpolated image. *Multimed. Tools Appl.* **2016**, *76*, 9195–9218. [CrossRef]
2. Hussain, M.; Wahid, A.; Ho, A.T.; Javed, N.; Jung, K.-H. A data hiding scheme using parity-bit pixel value differencing and improved rightmost digit replacement. *Signal. Process. Image Commun.* **2017**, *50*, 44–57. [CrossRef]
3. Zhang, W.; Wang, S.; Zhang, X. Improving Embedding Efficiency of Covering Codes for Applications in Steganography. *IEEE Commun. Lett.* **2007**, *11*, 680–682. [CrossRef]
4. Chang, C.; Chou, Y. Using nearest covering codes to embed secret information in gray scale images. In Proceedings of the 2nd International Conference on Ubiquitous Information Management and Communication, Suwon, Korea, 31 January–1 February 2008; Associaion for Computing Machinery (ACM): New York, NY, USA.
5. Cao, Z.; Yin, Z.; Hu, H.; Gao, X.; Wang, L. High capacity data hiding scheme based on (7, 4) Hamming code. *SpringerPlus* **2016**, *5*, 175. [CrossRef] [PubMed]
6. Guo, Y.; Cao, X.; Wang, R.; Jin, C. A new data embedding method with a new data embedding domain for JPEG images. In Proceedings of the 2018 IEEE Fourth International Conference on Multimedia Big Data

(BigMM), Laguna Hills, CA, USA, 13–16 September 2018; Institute of Electrical and Electronics Engineers (IEEE): New York, NY, USA, 2018; pp. 1–5.
7. Hong, W.; Zhou, X.; Lou, D.-C.; Chen, T.S.; Li, Y. Joint image coding and lossless data hiding in VQ indices using adaptive coding techniques. *Inf. Sci.* **2018**, *245*, 245–260. [CrossRef]
8. Hong, W.; Chen, T.S.; Yin, Z.; Luo, B.; Ma, Y. Data hiding in AMBTC images using quantization level modification and perturbation technique. *Multimed. Tools Appl.* **2016**, *76*, 3761–3782. [CrossRef]
9. S-Tools. Available online: https://www.cs.vu.nl/~{}ast/books/mos2/zebras.html (accessed on 3 November 2020).
10. Ez Stego. Available online: http://www.informatik.htw-dresden.de/~{}fritzsch/VWA/Source/EzStego.java (accessed on 3 November 2020).
11. Fridrich, J. A new steganographic method for palette-based image. In Proceedings of the IS&T PICS Conference, Savannah, GA, USA, 25–28 April 1999.
12. Fridrich, J.; Du, R. Secure steganographic methods for palette images. *Comput. Vis.* **2000**, *1768*, 47–60. [CrossRef]
13. Tzeng, C.-H.; Yang, Z.-F.; Tsai, W.-H. Adaptive data hiding in palette images by color ordering and mapping with security protection. *IEEE Trans. Commun.* **2004**, *52*, 791–800. [CrossRef]
14. Tanaka, G.; Suetake, N.; Uchino, E. A steganographic method realizing high capacity data embedding for palette-based images. In Proceedings of the International Workshop on Smart Info-Media Systems in Asia, Osaka, Japan, 22–23 October 2009.
15. Imaizumi, S.; Ozawa, K. Multibit embedding algorithm for steganography of palette-based images. *Lect. Notes Comp. Sci.* **2014**, *8333*, 99–110. [CrossRef]
16. Imaizumi, S.; Ozawa, K. Palette-based image steganography for high-capacity embedding. *Bull. Soc. Photogr. Imag. Jpn.* **2015**, *25*, 7–11.
17. Aryal, A.; Motegi, K.; Imaizumi, S.; Aoki, N. Improvement of Multi-bit Information Embedding Algorithm for Palette-Based Images. Lecture Notes in Computer Science; Springer Science and Business Media LLC: Cham, Switzerland, 2015; Volume 9290, pp. 511–523.
18. EVONIK. Available online: https://www.corporate.evonik.com/ (accessed on 3 November 2020).
19. Miltner, K.M.; Highfield, T. Never gonna GIF you up: Analyzing the cultural significance of the animated GIF. *Soc. Media + Soc.* **2017**, *3*, 1–11. [CrossRef]
20. Zhao, H.; Wang, H.; Khan, M.K. Steganalysis for palette-based images using generalized difference image and color correlogram. *Signal. Process.* **2011**, *91*, 2595–2605. [CrossRef]
21. Cox, I.J.; Miller, M.L.; Bloom, J.A.; Fridrich, J.; Kalker, T. Applications and Properties. In *Digital Watermarking and Steganography*, 2nd ed.; Morgan Kaufmann: San Francisco, CA, USA, 2007; pp. 49–56.
22. Crandall, R. Some Notes on Steganography. Posted on Steganography Mailing List. 1998. Available online: http://dde.binghamton.edu/download/Crandall_matrix.pdf (accessed on 29 May 2018).
23. Westfeld, A.; Pfitzmann, A. Attacks on steganographic systems breaking the steganographic utilities EzStego, Jsteg, Steganos, and S-Tools. *Lec. Notes. Comput. Sci.* **2000**, *1768*, 61–75.
24. Fridrich, J.; Goljan, M. Practical steganalysis of digital images: State of the art. *Electron. Imaging 2002* **2002**, *4675*, 1–13. [CrossRef]
25. ISO/CIE 11664-6:2014 (Formerly CIE S 0146/E:2013). *Colorimetry—Part 6: CIEDE2000 Colour-Difference Formula*; CIE Central Bureau: Vienna, Austria, 2014.
26. Standard Image Database (SIDBA). Available online: http://www.ess.ic.kanagawa-it.ac.jp/app_images_j (accessed on 7 October 2018).
27. CBIR Image Database. Available online: http://imagedatabase.cs.washington.edu/groundtruth/ (accessed on 3 October 2020).

Publisher's Note: MDPI stays neutral with regard to jurisdictional claims in published maps and institutional affiliations.

© 2020 by the authors. Licensee MDPI, Basel, Switzerland. This article is an open access article distributed under the terms and conditions of the Creative Commons Attribution (CC BY) license (http://creativecommons.org/licenses/by/4.0/).

Article

A False Negative Study of the Steganalysis Tool Stegdetect

Benjamin Aziz [1], Jeyong Jung [2,*], Julak Lee [3] and Yong-Tae Chun [4]

1. School of Computing, University of Portsmouth, Portsmouth PO1 3HE, UK; benjamin.aziz@port.ac.uk
2. Department of Police Science, College of Social Sciences, University of Ulsan, Ulsan 44610, Korea
3. Department of Industrial Security, Chung-Ang University, Seoul 06974, Korea; julaklee71@cau.ac.kr
4. Department of Security Management, Kyonggi University, Suwon 16227, Korea; chunyongtae@kyonggi.ac.kr
* Correspondence: pancon@ulsan.ac.kr

Received: 7 October 2020; Accepted: 14 November 2020; Published: 19 November 2020

Abstract: In this study, we evaluated one of the modern automated steganalysis tools, Stegdetect, to study its false negative rates when analysing a bulk of images. In so doing, we used JPHide method to embed a randomly generated messages into 2000 JPEG images. The aim of this study is to help digital forensics analysts during their investigations by means of providing an idea of the false negative rates of Stegdetect. This study found that (1) the false negative rates depended largely on the tool's sensitivity values, (2) the tool had a high false negative rate between the sensitivity values from 0.1 to 3.4 and (3) the best sensitivity value for detection of JPHide method was 6.2. It is therefore recommended that when analysing a huge bulk of images forensic analysts need to take into consideration sensitivity values to reduce the false negative rates of Stegdetect.

Keywords: steganograph; steganalysis; stegdetect; digital forensics

1. Introduction

In recent times, the rapid growth in computer technology has become core in our lives. The technological advancement such as Cloud computing, Internet of Things, and social media platforms has brought about efficiency, effectiveness, and convenience to both individual and organisational users. However, there is a downside to all this. There are more and more tools on the market today, and the tools created by advanced technology will become more and more difficult to control. Enterprises must increase investment and introduce new defense solutions to deal with them. This all has provided a new type of risk and threats. Due to an increasing reliance upon devices those users are exposed to various Cyber security risks [1]. In particular, individuals as well as organisations which essentially value information secrecy and privacy were greatly concerned about how to secure their data. Information hiding has become a pivotal characteristic of digital society. Against this backdrop, several methods such as steganography and cryptography with complex algorithms have been developed to secure information privacy [2]. Cryptography is intended to conceal the content of messages via data encryption or scrambling, but it cannot hide their existence [3]. In contrast, steganography hides the very existence of secret information while being communicated in cover media files [2–5]. If successful, it attracts no suspicion at all of the presence of such secret information from the point of view of an external observer. This is the main reason why steganography in recent times has received much attention amongst security research. In addtion, steganography has found other uses, such as copyright and e-document forging prevention [6], secret image transfers over Clouds [7] and protection of private health records [8], amongst others.

The problem of detecting hidden content was first formulated in a clear manner by Simmons [9], who modelled the problem as two prisoners attempting to communicated in a covert manner secret messages related to the plan of escape from the prison, whilst the warden would inspect every message communicated. If suspecting that hidden content was included in a message, the warden would then destroy the message and send the two prisoners into solitary confinement. This is known as the prisoners problem. In fact, there are a lot of real life applications of steganography in politics, diplomacy, and the military [3].

In hiding information using a steganographic procedure, one needs both an embedding algorithm, which takes as input a cover media file in which the secret data message will be embedded resulting in a stego-file. On the other end, one needs a detection algorithm that identifies the stego-file with an affirmation of the existence of the secret message and an extraction algorithm to extract the secret message from the stego-file. This method used in extracting and detecting steganographic activities in any stego-file is called steganalysis. However, similar to any other numerical analysis, steganalysis can have false results, which can be divided into false positive, where an image is clean but it is flagged by the analysis tool as being loaded with a secret message, and false negative, where an image is loaded with a secret message but it is flagged by the analysis tool as being clean.

Previously, in [10], we presented a false positive rate study of the well-known image analysis tool, StegDetect [11]. In this paper, we continue the false rates study of StegDetect by investigating the rate of false negative cases that the tool exhibits. Understanding the rate of false negatives is equally as important as it demonstrates the rate at which the tool fails in detecting hidden content, something that has implications for security and privacy.

The rest of the paper is organised as follows. In Section 2, we discuss related work in current literature. In Section 3, we give an overview of the methodology we used to conduct our research, and describe the datasets used for the analysis. In Section 4, we present the results of the analysis. Finally, in Section 5, we discuss some of the limitations of our experiments and in Section 6, we conclude the paper giving directions for future work.

2. Related Work

In terms of information hiding, steganography and watermarking are interconnected [12]. Although they share some technical traits, the largest difference is their purpose of use. The former is aimed at engaging in secret communication while the latter is for verifying the identity and authenticity of the owner. Ref. [12,13] argue that imperceptibility, robustness, and payload capacity are parameters of steganography. Compared to this, watermarking concerns the most whether it is robust in order to avoid watermarks being removed or replaced. These parameters can be referred to distinguish it from watermarking and cryptography as well as to compare various types of steganograpy techniques.

There are two groups of people who use steganographic techniques. A steganographer uses analysis tools to reassure whether a steganographic process has been successful, and thus the message is undetectable or unreadable [14]. On the opposite side, a stegoanalyst attempts to detect and read stego-messages. In either way, steganalysis involves two stages: (1) identifying the existence of steganographic messages and (2) reading the embedded message [15].

Various digital steganography methods have been developed in recent years. One commonality is that all methods is based on the fundamental concept that secret messages are embedded in a cover medium to create an output, a stego-file. There are a wide range of steganograpy techniques depending on a type of a cover medium (e.g., text, image, video and audio).

It has been an ongoing debate whether steganography is used by terrorists or criminals [16]. scanned a couple of million images and identified 20,000 suspicious images using 'Stegdetect' [11]. Although no hidden messages were identified in the research, we cannot categorically conclude that stegnography was not misused by malicious actors. Before making the conclusion, available tools should be examined whether they are reliable or not. Therefore it is of importance to check their reliability. However, there have been few research on this.

Detection of steganographic messages does not necessarily have to reveal the hidden content, but merely detecting their presence can carry significant implications in that this can draw unwanted attention from opposite parties. As such, the precision of the detection algorithm is one of its important attributes. This presents a crucial implication to digital forensic analysts. Ref. [17] defined digital forensic as the approved method used to preserve, collect, validate, identify, analyse, interpret evidence obtained for a digital investigation. In the digital communication era, any sort of criminal investigations are bound to involve digital devices. To establish facts in a court, digital data stored on devices such as computers and smartphones have to be investigated by a forensics analyst.

As malicious actors are equipped with state-of-the-art technologies, forensic analysts have tried to keep pace with them. According to [18], in digital crime there are different methods used by an analyst during their investigation. These methods throughout the investigation must be done in a forensically sound manner. Ref. [19] noted that an investigation is successful and acceptable if the evidence obtained from the original source is not altered in any way. Morever, to raise criminal arrests and convictions, forensic analysts need to ponder over how to reduce the false negative ratio of a tool. If the false negative ratio is high, this indicates that there is a high possibility that a stego-file is not detected, failing to weed out criminals. In this respect, this study aims to investigate the false negative rates of a steganalysis tool, Stegdetect, in order to examine whether this is a reliable tool for digital forensic analysts. This paper complements an earlier study on the false positive rates for Stegdetect carried out in [10].

There are many tools currently in the market for exposing hidden content in images. StegExpose [20,21] is an open-source Java-based steganalysis tool. The tool was designed primarily as a bulk analyser for lossless images, it works by classifying images as clean or stego images based on whether or not a pre-defined analysis threshold has been exceeded. In its standard operation, StegExpose is aimed at detecting different methods (nonlinear adaptive encoding, equidistribution and pseudorandom distribution) Least Significant Bit (LSB) originating from many tools including SilentEye [22], OpenPuff [23] and OpenStego [24]. StegSecret [25], like StegExpose, is also an open-source Java-based tool. It features a very simple graphical user interface, and is aimed at high performance bulk analysis, however this comes at the cost of lack of customisation; the tool is less configurable compared to StegExpose.

Other approaches have been combined in recent times to enhance steganalysis techniques. For example, the authors in [26] used convolutional neural networks to identify noise in different regions in an image and the relationship between noise in different sub-regions, and then classify images according to whether features of the image indicate the presence of hidden content or not. In [27], the authors use ensemble learning methods to construct effective steganalysis of images, which searches for colour correlativity between pixels and colour channels. Convolutional neural networks are used again in [28] as a method to embed hidden content in cover images. Most of these machine learning approaches suffer from lack of transparency as to how general the method can effectively either embed or analyse hidden content.

3. Methodology

The study has selected one of the automated steganalysis tools, Stegdetect [11] developed by Niels Provos. The purpose of the tool is to identify steganographic content by analysing JPEG images. It is able to detect several steganographic methods (F5 (header analysis), JPHide, invsible secret, outguest and camouflage) [29]. In analysing JPEG images it expresses the level of detection accuracy by appending stars (*, **, ***) to whichever steganographic method is detected. One star means the level of confidence in the detection of the specific steganographic method is low, two star means the level of confidence in the identification of steganographic method is quite good, and three star shows a high level of confidence in it. In this paper, we have used Stegdetect Windows version 0.4 which has an easy to use graphical interface. The tool's detection rate was based on the sensitivity value which is between 0.1 and 10.0. However, we have considered sensitivities of (0.1, 0.3, 0.5, 0.7, 10.0). Ref. [10] indicated that the sensitivity values affect the tool's false-negative ratio.

To achieve the purpose of the paper, we looked for a popular steganographic method that embeds data in JPEG image which is detectable by Stegdetect. JPHide [30] has both Windows and Linux version developed by A. Latham in 1999. In this paper we have chosen the Window version 0.5 with a user-friendly interface. Jphide uses least significant bit of the discrete cosine transform coefficient to hide data into any image with JPEG format. Meanwhile, according to [30], 5% insertion rate of data into an image will be very difficult to identify in the absence of the original image. Detection of the Jphide method is independent of the size of the message embedded into the image. This below shows the process we used in generating stego images.

The Image Dataset

To help us study the false negative using Stegdetect to analyse steganography content automatically, the tool require images that contain embedded data. This research is based upon hiding bits of messages into 2000 JPEG images files using the embedding tool, JPHide. We searched and selected images from Sam Houston State University, University of Washington and Google image databases. Unfortunately, with our initial google images, there was a problem with the size of the images which affected the stego-object, which made statically modified after embedding obvious. To resolve the issue the following parameters were set for the downloading from google.

- Size of image: 2 MP (1600 × 1200);
- Colour of image: Any;
- Type of image: Any;
- Time: Any;
- Image file type: JPG files;
- Usage rights—not filtered by license.

However, we also activated both the search ON/OFF for the downloading of 300 images from Google to get the effect of this parameter on the outcome of the analysis. In addition to this, we also downloaded 700 clean JPEG images from University of Washington (Department of Computer science and Engineering) and 1000 images from Sam Houston State University image, 500 untouched and 500 manipulated with 75 bot quality.

Figure 1 shows samples of images hidden with messages using jphide. An automated utility, Stegdetect, which analyses bulk images with a hidden message with JPHide has been chosen to study its false negatives. For this purpose, we obtained JPHide version 0.5 as well as the Windows version of Stegdetect. We regulated the sensitivity value of Stegdetect against 2000 stego-object (obtained from different image databases such as google, Sam Houston State University and University of Washington). It was installed on a Windows 7 enterprise core i5 with 8 GB RAM.

Figure 1. Sample results of the jphide method.

4. Results

All the results were analysed and interpreted in different phases deepening on the image dataset. Phase one analysed a total of 500 images manipulated by seam-carve from SAM Houston university image database, both at 75 quality before embedding using jphide with randomly generated bits. The table below gives a summary of the overall detection during the analysis.

We noted that detection of jphide method in the images was based on the changes in the sensitivity values. However, other algorithms detected by the tool are the circumstances in which stegdetect during the analysis identified other steganographic methods which during the embedding process we did not use. Table 1 shows that the highest ratio of detection with sensitivity results is 67.13% of the manipulated images by seam-carve which considering the level of the ratio is very high. Meanwhile, detection results for jphide were very low.

Table 1. Rate of sensitivity results from 500 images manipulated by seam-carve.

Sensitivity Value	False Negative	Likely False Positive (Skipped)	jphide(*)	jphide(**)	jphide(***)	OTHER_ALG
0.1–10.0	67.13%	2.00%	11.80%	14.71%	4.07%	0.29%

All results for false negative, jphide and other algorithm keep changing with change in sensitivity as shown in Table 2. The beginning of the analysis with low sensitivity value (0.1) the false negative ratio was very high (98%). However, a systematic drop was realised in the false negative ratio between sensitivity values 0.1 and 0.7, furthermore, the false negative ratio with sensitivity values 5.2–10.0 had a drastic drop as shown in Table 2 below. Here it becomes clear that the tool became more effective in detecting steganographic method used in embedding the secret messages.

Table 2. Results from manipulated images by seam-carve based on sensitivity values.

Sensitivity Value	False Negative	Likely False Positive (Skipped)	jphide(*)	jphide(**)	jphide(***)	OTHER_ALG
0.1	98.00%	2.00%	0.00%	0.00%	0.00%	0.00%
0.3	97.80%	2.00%	0.00%	0.00%	0.00%	0.20%
0.5	97.80%	2.00%	0.00%	0.00%	0.00%	0.20%
0.7	96.40%	2.00%	1.40%	0.00%	0.00%	0.20%
1.5	89.40%	2.00%	6.20%	2.00%	0.00%	0.40%
3.4	87.20%	2.00%	2.20%	0.00%	8.20%	0.40%
5.2	17.60%	2.00%	69.60%	2.20%	8.20%	0.40%
7.3	11.40%	2.00%	17.40%	59.00%	9.30%	0.40%
10.0	8.60%	2.00%	9.40%	69.20%	10.40%	0.40%

As shown in Figure 2 above, between sensitivity values 0.1 and 0.5 there were no changes in the results for jphide. Meanwhile, detection of jphide increased substantially between 0.7 and 10.0 with their related confidence levels (*, **, ***). Between 0.1 and 0.5 jphide (*) was stable until it got to the range 0.7–3.4 when there was fluctuation in the detection ratio, it then had a sharp increased with 5.2 sensitivity, after which it experienced another sharp decrease between (7.3 and 10.0). For jphide (**) between 1.5 and 10.0 there was a constant increase except with sensitivity of 3.4 which experience some drop. However, jphide (***) maintained the increasing of its ratio.

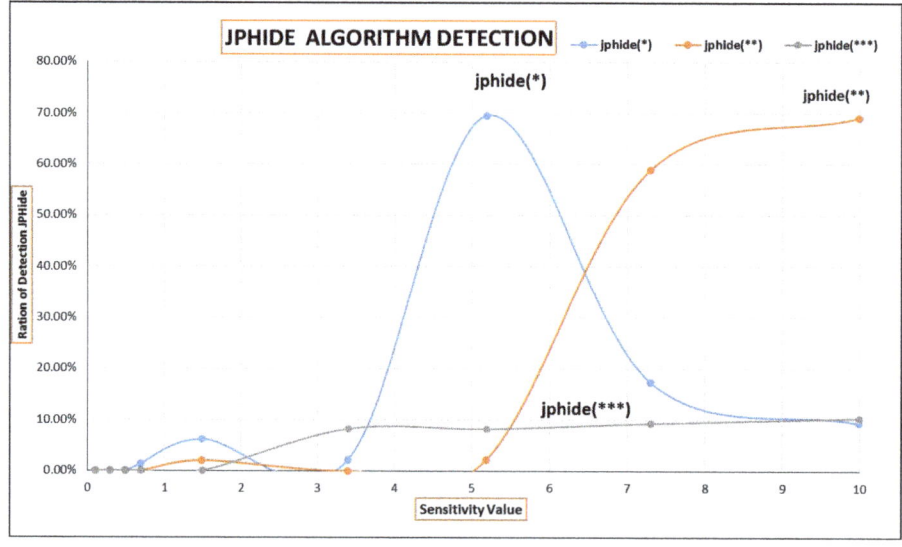

Figure 2. Changes in the jphide rate with different sensitivities for seam carve manipulated images.

As per the analysis above, the level of confidence in detection by stegdetect is directly proportional to the sensitivity values. Meaning, the higher the sensitivity value the higher the confidence in detecting jphide. Furthermore, the high increase of confidence in detecting jphide was between (3.4 and 10.0). During the analysis, stegdetect detect other steganographic methods in the images other than jphide which we used. Figure 3 below shows that 0.2% of the detection was for other algorithms between 0.3 and 0.7 sensitivity which stegdetect claims was used in embedding secret messages in those images. Meanwhile, the percentage of other algorithm detected increased to 0.4% between (1.5 and 10.0). Finally, the images from the database were already manipulated before jphide method was used to embed the messages. It is therefore possible that the images were manipulated using any of the algorithms detected during the analysis.

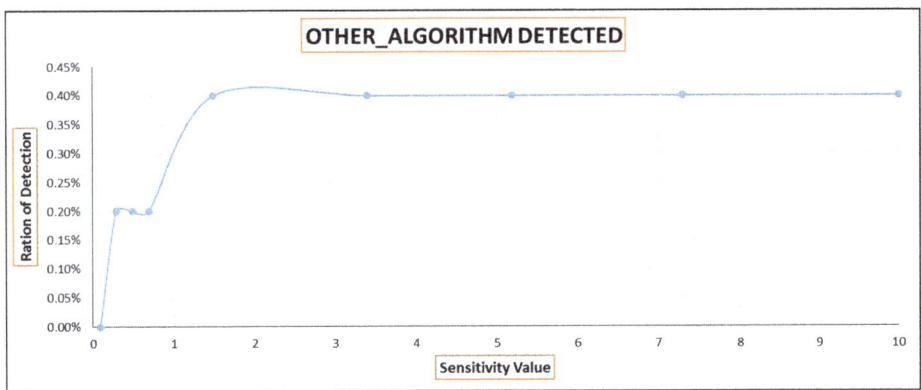

Figure 3. Changes in other algorithms detected with different sensitivities.

Phase two of the analysis was focused on 500 Seam-carve untouched (clean) images from SAM Houston university image database which were embedded with a secret message using jphide. Compared to the detection results of the manipoulated images, there was slight incease in the detection for the false negative ratio, skipped (false positive likely) and jphide (*) while other algorithms and jphide (**, ***) experience a slight decreased with different sensitivity as shown in Table 3 below.

Table 3. Rate of sensitivity results from 500 seam-carve untouched images.

Sensitivity Value	False Negative	Likely False Positive (Skipped)	jphide(*)	jphide(**)	jphide(***)	OTHER _ALG
0.1–10.0	67.78%	2.40%	11.91%	14.09%	3.62%	0.20%

As show in Table 3 above, 67.78% of the overall detection was false negative which is very high. However, with an increase in sensitivity, the detection ratio for false negative, jphide and other algorithm all changed. Furthermore, as shown in Table 4 below, there was a significant increase in the confidence detection of steganographic method jphide with changes in sensitivity values. We observe slight changes in the detection between the manipulated and the untouched Seam-carving images. Detection of jphide in the untouched images embedded with bits of messages started with 0.5 sensitivity while detection for jphide in the manipulated images started with 0.7 sensitivity, after which there was a continuous increase in the confidence in detection of jphide method.

Table 4. Results of 500 images from seam carve untouched images with different sensitivity values.

Sensitivity Value	False Negative	Likely False Positive (Skipped)	jphide(*)	jphide(**)	jphide(***)	OTHER_ALG
0.1	97.60%	2.40%	0.00%	0.00%	0.00%	0.00%
0.3	97.60%	2.40%	0.00%	0.00%	0.00%	0.00%
0.5	97.40%	2.40%	0.20%	0.00%	0.00%	0.00%
0.7	96.20%	2.40%	1.40%	0.00%	0.00%	0.00%
1.5	90.80%	2.40%	4.40%	2.00%	0.20%	0.20%
3.4	87.20%	2.40%	3.40%	0.20%	6.40%	0.40%
5.2	20.60%	2.40%	66.60%	3.40%	6.60%	0.40%
7.3	12.60%	2.40%	20.20%	55.00%	9.40%	0.40%
10.0	10.00%	2.40%	11.00%	66.20%	10.00%	0.40%

The false negative results for untouched seam-carving images at the beginning were high 97.60% as shown in Figure 4 with 0.1 sensitivity value, this result is not different from the manipulated images, however there was slight decrease between 0.1 and 3.4, then there was massive fall in the false negative between 5.2 and 10.0 with increase in sensitivity value.

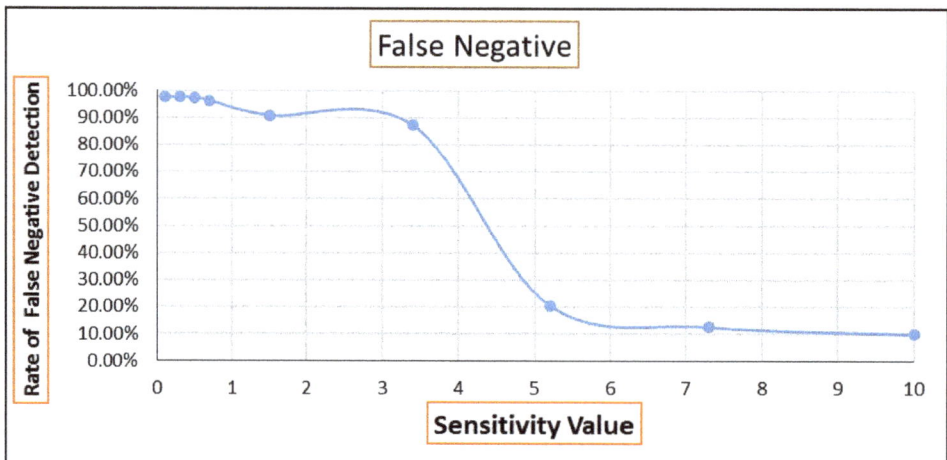

Figure 4. Overall false negative rate seam-carving untouched images with different sensitivity values.

The detection results for jphide (*, **, ***) between 0.5 and 3.4 was very marginal until the sensitivity was increased to 5.2 when jphide (*) had sharp increase meanwhile, with continuous increase in the sensitivity value between 7.3 and 10.0 the detection of jphide (*) experience a continuous decline, at the same time between 5.2 and 10.0 the level of confidence in detecting jphide (**) had a continuous increase while jphide (***) maintained its steady increase as shown in Figure 5 below.

Figure 6 shows that there was no effect of the sensitivity between 0.1 and 0.7 on the results for other algorithm detected, then between 1.5 and 10.0 there was a minor increase in the detection of other algorithms by the tool. However, between 3.4 and 10.0 the tool (stegdetect) maintain a constant detection ratio for other algorithms.

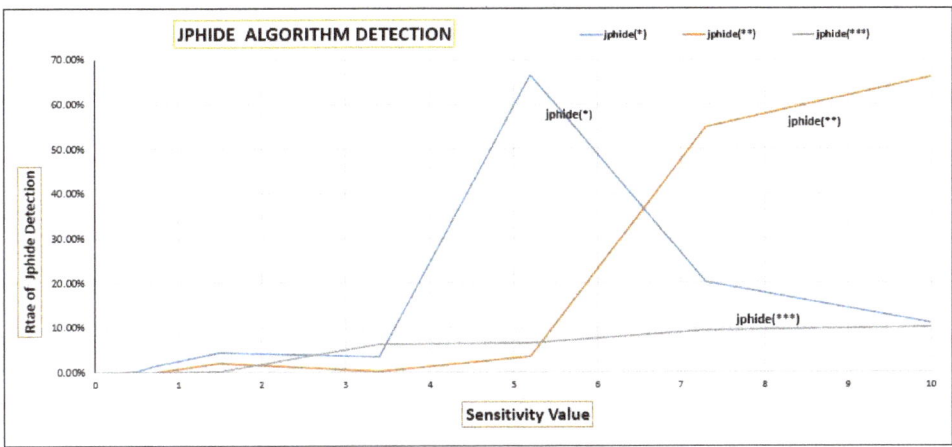

Figure 5. Changes in the jphide rate with different sensitivities for seam carve untouched images.

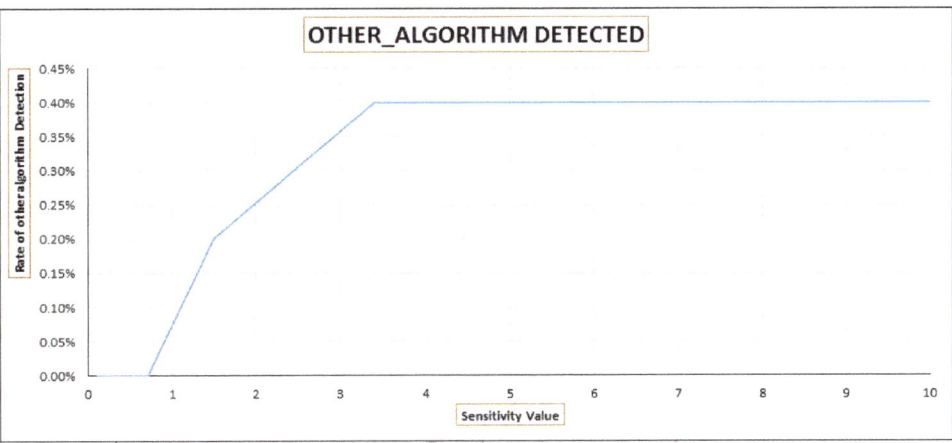

Figure 6. Changes in other algorithms detected with different sensitivities.

Phase three of the experiment analysis 700 images from the Department of Computer and Engineering, university of Washington image database. Each image was embedded with a different generated bits of a message using jphide. During the analysis of the 700 stego-images, 3.71% resulted in error between 0.1 and 10.0 sensitivity which compared to the volume of the images involved is quite small. In the case of the error images, stegdetect could not analysis because of the following stated reason. 1. Bogus DQT index 6, 2. Invalid JPEG file structure: SOS before SOF, and the last 3. Quantization Table 0×00 and 0×01 was not defined. The error rate can be seen in Table 5 below. It wealth noting that all the images analysed were subject to frequency counts. In other words, the analysis of any detection (false negative or jphide) was added to find the highest detection ratio (i.e., a number of times a specific detection occur). After which they were quantified as shown in Table 5 below.

Table 5. Results of 700 images from Washington University image database with different sensitivity values.

Sensitivity Value	False Negative	Likely False Positive (Skipped)	jphide(*)	jphide(**)	jphide(***)	OTHER_ALG
0.1	78.29%	18.00%	0.00%	0.00%	0.00%	3.71%
0.3	77.14%	18.00%	1.00%	0.14%	0.00%	3.71%
0.5	77.00%	18.00%	0.57%	0.57%	0.14%	3.71%
0.7	75.86%	18.00%	1.29%	0.43%	0.71%	3.71%
1.5	71.43%	18.00%	4.14%	1.43%	1.29%	3.71%
3.4	43.43%	18.00%	27.86%	3.00%	4.00%	3.71%
5.2	20.71%	18.00%	23.43%	27.14%	7.00%	3.71%
7.3	18.00%	18.00%	8.43%	24.43%	27.43%	3.71%
10.0	17.71%	17.57%	3.29%	22.86%	34.86%	3.71%

The false negative result between 0.1 and 1.5 sensitivity was 78.29% which is a bit high, then when the sensitivity was change between 3.4 and 10.0 there was a sharp drop and a continuous decline until it reaches 17.71%. Moreover, comparing the false negative results of the previous seam-carving images (both manipulated and untouched images) we realised that with the previous experiment between 0.1 and 3.4 they had a significantly higher false negative ratio which was 80% to 98% before it had a sharp decline. Though the images from Washington University seem to have had a low false negative ratio compared to the seam-carving images, they all seem to have had a sharp decrease at some point, then when the sensitivity was set to 5.2 it maintained a slow but steady decrease as shown in Figure 7 below.

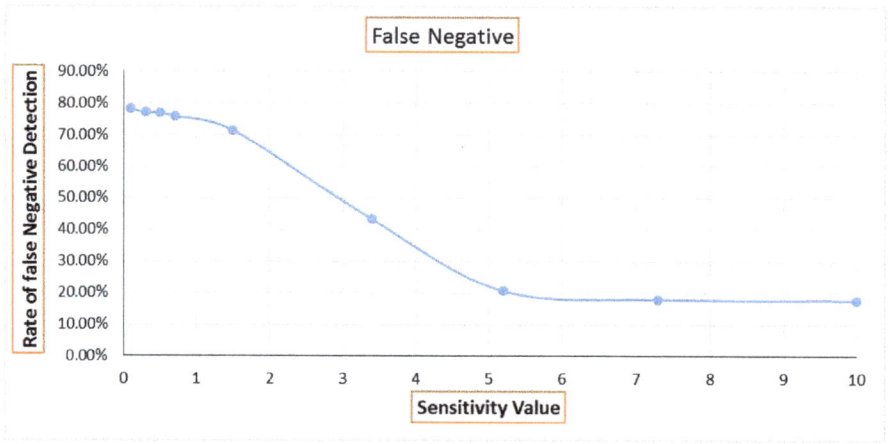

Figure 7. Overall false negative rate of Washington university image database with different sensitivity values.

The detection results of jphide (*, **, ***) started between sensitivity values (0.3 and 1.5), then there was a significant increase in the detection between (3.4 and 10.0). The detection for jphide (*) was consistently increasing until 3.4–5.4 sensitivity when there was a height jump, meanwhile, between 7.3 and 10.0 sensitivity the detection for jphide (*) started to decrease and jphide (**) also had similar result like in the case of jphide (*) where it experience a stable increase then a slight decrease with 0.7 sensitivity before it started to increase in detection again between 1.5 and 10.0 sensitivity. Finally, jphide (***) maintain a continuous steady increase in detection between 0.5 and 5.2 then a height jump in the detection between 7.3 and 10.0 as shown in Figure 8 graph below.

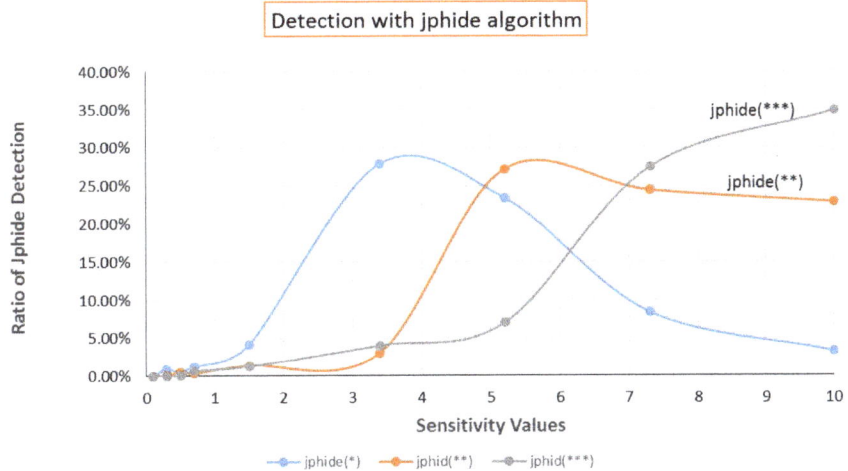

Figure 8. Changes in the jphide rate with different sensitivities for Washington university image database.

Phase four analysis 300 image from google (SAFE ON/OFF), the results for skipped false negative likely, and errors were changed with different sensitivity, other algorithms detection was constant between 0.7 and 10.0. The detection results for false negative was still between (0.1 and 3.4). However, with (5.2–10.0) sensitivity just like the previous experiment, there was a significant fall in the false negative ratio as shown in Figure 9 graph below.

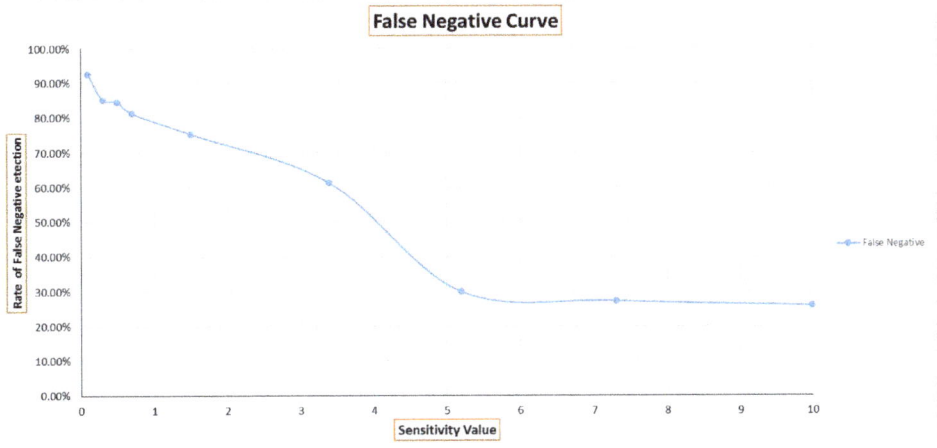

Figure 9. Overall false negative rate of google image database (SAFE ON) with different sensitivity values.

Again comparing the results with the other experiments conducted earlier the confidence level in jphide detection ratio keep change with changes in the sensitivity value as shown in Figure 10 below. For this set of images jphide (*) had similar results we acquired from the images from seam carve and Washington university image databases, respectively. For all those experiment there was sharp increase in detection ratio and then another sharp decline in detection for jphide (*) with different sensitivity values. However, jphide (** and ***) had a different results from all the other experiments performed, for this experiment we realised a continuous increment in the detection ratio for both jphide (** and ***) with increasing sensitivity value as shown in Figure 10 below.

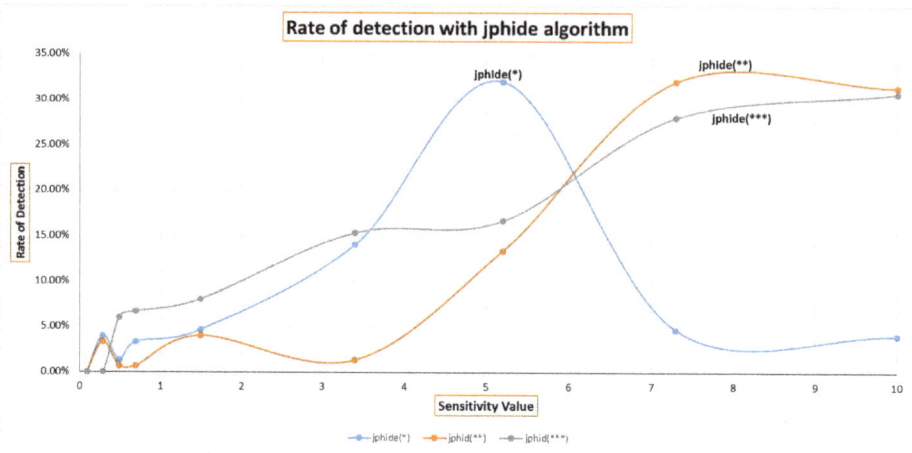

Figure 10. Changes in the jphide rate with different sensitivities for google image database (SAFE ON).

We realised that there were different results especially for the jphide and false negative from all previous experiments. For instance, between (0.5 and 10.0) sensitivity there was continuous and significantly higher confidence in detecting jphide (***) from the previous experiments. However, Google safe (OFF) as shown in Table 6 below gives slightly different results considering the confidence in detecting jphide (***).

Table 6. Results of 150 images from google image database (SAFE OFF) with different sensitivity values.

Sensitivity Value	False Negative	Likely False Positive (Skipped)	jphide(*)	jphide(**)	jphide(***)	OTHER_ALG
0.1	90.67%	4.67%	0.00%	0.00%	0.00%	0.67%
0.3	90.67%	4.67%	0.00%	0.00%	0.00%	0.67%
0.5	89.33%	4.67%	1.33%	0.00%	0.00%	0.67%
0.7	87.33%	4.67%	3.33%	0.00%	0.00%	0.67%
1.5	84.67%	4.67%	2.67%	2.00%	1.33%	0.67%
3.4	74.67%	4.67%	9.33%	1.33%	5.33%	0.67%
5.2	33.33%	4.67%	41.33%	9.33%	6.67%	0.67%
7.3	30.00%	4.67%	7.33%	40.00%	13.33%	0.67%
10.0	29.33%	4.67%	4.00%	41.33%	16.00%	0.67%

The highest was again at the beginning of the experiment was the false negative ratio 90.67%, which is much different from the previous experiment, and had a further drop with increasing sensitivity. Figure 11 shows that the curve is not different from the previous experiment.

The detection results for jphide (***) from google safe (OFF) is different from the results from the safe (NO) results. With the safe (off) detection of jphide (***) started and continuous to increase between (1.5 and 10), but detection for jphide (***) in safe (ON) started between (0.5 and 10.0), and jphide (*) continuous to increase in detection between 0.5 and 5.2 before the detection started to fall has sensitivity increase between 7.3 and 10.0. Finally, jphide (**) results at 1.5–5.2 sensitivity there was a steady increase before a quick and continues increase between 7.3 and 10.0. The two image groups were compared to show how the properties of images can affect the detection of Jphide method in images. Figure 12 gives a graphical representation of the jphide results.

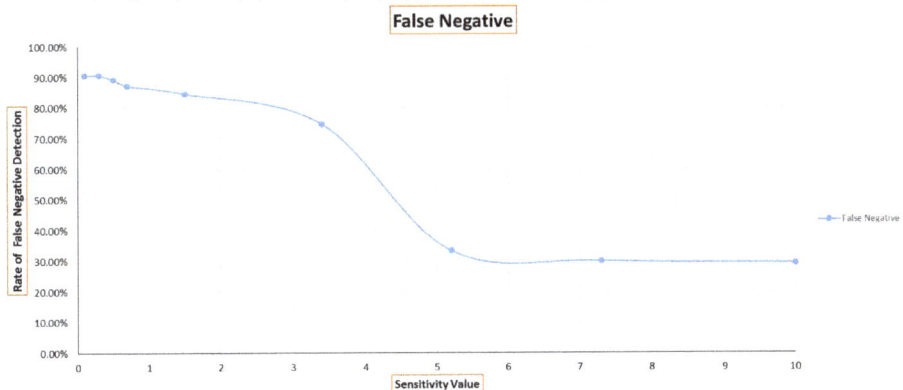

Figure 11. Overall false negative rate of google image database (SAFE OFF) with different sensitivity values.

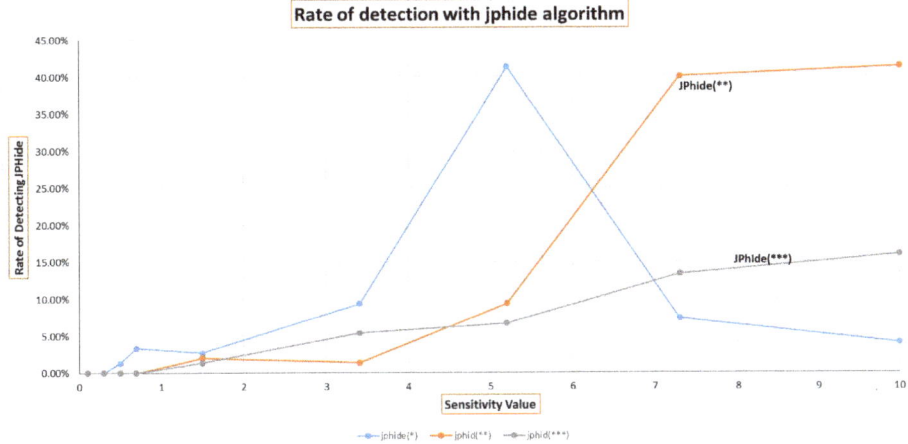

Figure 12. Changes in the jphide rate with different sensitivities for google image database (SAFE OFF).

The final phase, analysis the overall false negative ratio of the tool, this is to help forensic analyst during an investigation by providing accurate statistics of stegdetect false negative ratio, because in the court of law the forensic analyst must prove beyond every reasonable doubt that the results of the tool can be relied upon as evidence. This analysis was done using the results from all the different image databases, note that all the images had different properties, because there were some that had been manipulated with dotted at a quality of 75 and there were those that were untouched. The overall false negative results for all the different images it is very high between (0.1 and 3.4) but had a quick fall between (5.2 and 10.0), and as the false negative results drop the confidence in detecting jphide (*, **, ***) increases, this is an important information for the analyst investigating images from different sources. Especially noting that false negative ratio of the tool and how the higher the sensitivity between (5.2 and 10.0) influences the results of bulk images under investigation. Table 7 shows all the false negative values for the different datasets used.

Figure 13 below present the overall false negative ratio which was very high, but there is very important information about the graph the forensic analyst need to know. We set our acceptable false negative ratio to be 21%, which intersect with the mean of all the false negative at some point on the sensitivity. All the different image at 5.2 sensitivity had a quick fall in the false negative ratio but with a continuous increase in the sensitivity gave a stable and slow decline in the false negative ratio.

Note, with our acceptable 21% false negative its correspondent sensitivity is 6.2. This will inform the analyst on the kind of sensitivity they can use depending on their acceptable false negative ratio during an investigation. During the analysis, the following observations were noted,

I. Between (0.1 and 5.0) the tool seem not to be very sensitivity in detecting steganographic method in images.
II. Between (6.2 and 10.0) the analyst is likely to get a more accurate and a more reliable, which give a low false negative result. In this case, there is a likelihood that the tool runs slow because its become very sensitive in detecting steganographic methods in JPEG images.

Table 7. Overall false negative rates of ALL the different image databases with different sensitivity values.

Sensitivity Value	Seam-carve False Negative	Untouched Images False Negative	WU Images False Negative	Google (SAFE ON) False Negative	Google (SAFE OFF) False Negative
0.1	98.00%	97.60%	78.29%	92.67%	90.67%
0.3	97.80%	97.60%	77.14%	85.33%	90.67%
0.5	97.80%	97.40%	77.00%	84.67%	89.33%
0.7	96.40%	96.20%	75.86%	81.33%	87.33%
1.5	89.40%	90.80%	71.43%	75.33%	84.67%
3.4	87.20%	87.20%	43.43%	61.33%	74.67%
5.2	17.60%	20.60%	20.71%	30.00%	33.33%
7.3	11.40%	12.60%	18.00%	27.33%	30.00%
10.0	8.60%	10.00%	17.71%	26.00%	29.33%

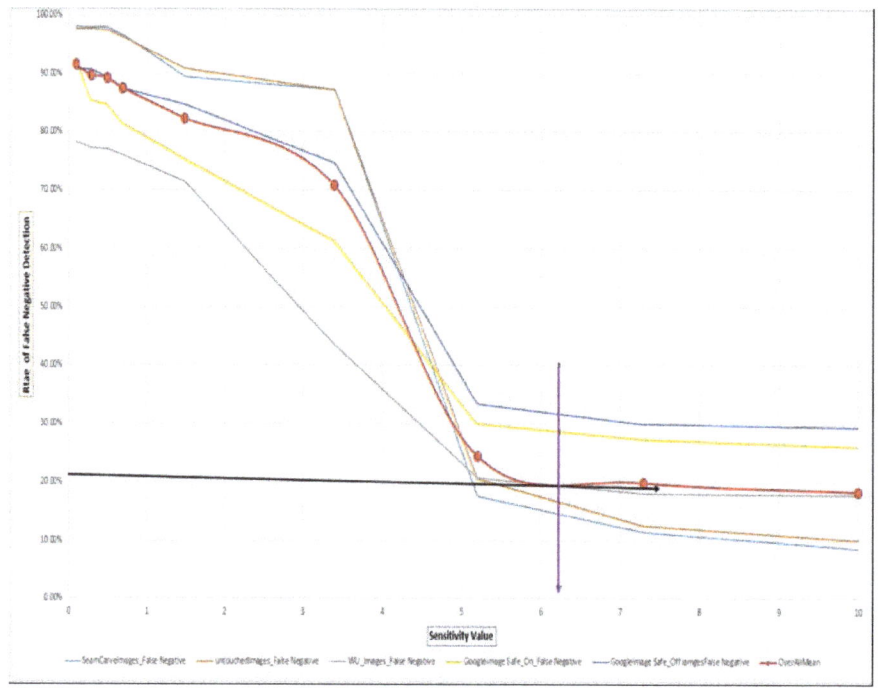

Figure 13. Overall false negative ratio from all different image databases.

5. Limitations of the Experiment

The research we conducted in this paper was constrained by a number of limitations. We attempt below to summarise these:

- In terms of the algorithms behind StegDetect, these are not known as they are not published by the developers of the tool, therefore, our understanding of the behaviour of the tool remains at the level of black box testing. We consider this to a certain extent sufficient from the perspective of the end users community. If such algorithms were made public, we would be able to use the results of this work as well as the previous work [10] to make recommendations on how to improve the algorithms.
- The initial plan was to collect a large sample size of images, but the research started to run into problems when collecting images from google images database. In steganography process, to get a good quality stego cover, there are some qualities that the cover medium needs to meet. First is capacity, which refers to the amount of hidden data it can contain. Secondly is security, which makes it unable for any intruder access. Lastly is its robustness, the ability or the amount of distortion its can withstand. However, the initial images from google after embedding the secret message had a notable modification of the stego cover.
- Furthermore, we wanted to compare the detection ratio of the different methods stegdetect claims to detect, so we used jsteg and F5, but could not give any informative results to analysis as shown in the graph below. Reddy (2007) noted that is difficult for stegdetect to detect F5 method.

6. Conclusions

The main purpose of steganography is to hide secret data during communication to avoid intruders from discovering the hidden message within the stego image without the right permission. Meanwhile, [29] stated that steganalysis is not as straight forward as steganography, this is a disadvantage to the forensic analyst who will be trying to detect hidden data in stego images. However, in steganalysis, only a few can automatically analyse a bulk of stego images at the same. To check the accuracy of a steganalysis tool which will help forensic analyst, our research exam the false negative rate of Stegdetect one of the popular steganalysis tools in the market. In our experimental results, we observed that when the sensitivity values were sets between (0.3 and 0.7) for all the various image databases jphide started to be detected. It could be concluded that the different sensitivity value range affects the detection rate for this method (jphide). The main purpose of the study was about the false negative rate of the tool, we concluded that the tool has a high false negative rate, especially between (0.1 and 3.4) sensitivity. We recommend that the best sensitivity value for detection of jphide method should be 6.2. This detection sensitivity value is very important for the forensic analyst. Because the false negative ratio had a deep sharp fall from this point onwards. However, we recommended that forensic analyst using stegdetect need to take into consideration the sensitivity values with the high false negative value when analysing a huge bulk of images. Moreover, based on our analysis of the tool, we observed and proposed a reference point of the sensitivity value with its related quantified false negative rate based on the mean of all the various image databases. Overall, the mean proposed can act as a baseline which will help the forensic analyst in making a much better decision during their investigation proceedings. However, based on the mean of all the false negatives of the tool, it is also argued that it has a high probability of false negative ratio between 0 and 10% even if the sensitive value is set beyond our recommended.

In conclusion, the fight between steganalysis methods and steganographic methods will ever continue. As more sophisticated steganographic algorithms are developed every day, a more powerful and sophisticated universals algorithms will also be required in detecting these steganography methods. This will be a more challenging but exciting research area in the near future. Currently, most steganalysis tools are very good in detecting specific steganographic methods. Example, Stegdetect which is an automated steganalysis tool is very good and effective in detecting content hidden in JPEG image formats than any other image format like Tiff, PNG and Gif. However, it is also more effective in detecting specific steganographic methods such as jphide, F5, invisible secret, jsteg and outguess than any other steganographic method. In this view, a future research should be conducted to consider a universal steganalysis tool. With current advancement in technologies for secure communication and its issues of privacy for individual users, a further research need to be considered to find the effect steganalysis tools will have on security protocols.

Additionally, we also plan to conduct a more complete comparative study of the available steganalysis tools, in order to obtain a more general understanding of what can be achieved and the degree of accuracy.

Author Contributions: B.A. contributed through the outlining of the idea underlying the paper and the implementation of the analysis of the tool. J.J. contributed through applying the methodology and writing—the original draft. J.L. made a contribution through writing—reviewing and editing and supervising. Y.-T.C. contributed through administrating the project and supporting resources. All authors have read and agreed to the published version of the manuscript.

Funding: This work was supported by the 2020 Research Fund of University of Ulsan.

Acknowledgments: The authors acknowledge the comments and feedback they received from the anonymous reviewers, all of which helped to improve the presentation of the paper.

Conflicts of Interest: The authors declare no conflict of interest.

References

1. Moradoff, N. Biometrics: Proliferation and constraints to emerging and new technologies. *Secur. J.* **2010**, *23*, 276–298. [CrossRef]
2. Li, Y.; Xiong, C.; Han, X.; Xiang, R.; He, F.; Du, H. Image steganography using cosine transform with large-scale multimedia applications. *Multimed. Tools Appl.* **2018**, *81*, 161.
3. Anderson, R.J.; Petitcolas, F.A.P. On the Limits of Steganography. *IEEE J. Sel. Areas Commun.* **1998**, *16*, 474–481. [CrossRef]
4. Ghebleh, M.; Kanso, A. A robust chaotic algorithm for digital image steganography. *Commun. Nonlinear Sci. Numer. Simul.* **2014**, *19*, 1898–1907. [CrossRef]
5. Chaeikar, S.S.; Zamani, M.; Manaf, A.B.A.; Zeki, A.M. PSW statistical LSB image steganalysis. *Multimed. Tools Appl.* **2018**, *77*, 805–835. [CrossRef]
6. Channalli, S.; Jadhav, A. Steganography an art of hiding data. *arXiv* **2009**, arXiv:0912.2319.
7. Abd El-Latif, A.A.; Abd-El-Atty, B.; Elseuofi, S.; Khalifa, H.S.; Alghamdi, A.S.; Polat, K.; Amin, M. Secret images transfer in cloud system based on investigating quantum walks in steganography approaches. *Phys. A Stat. Mech. Appl.* **2020**, *541*, 123687. [CrossRef]
8. Hashim, M.M.; Rhaif, S.H.; Abdulrazzaq, A.A.; Ali, A.H.; Taha, M.S. Based on IoT Healthcare Application for Medical Data Authentication: Towards A New Secure Framework Using Steganography. In Proceedings of the IOP Conference Series: Materials Science and Engineering, 3rd International Conference on Sustainable Engineering Techniques (ICSET 2020), Baghdad, Iraq, 15 April 2020; Volume 881, p. 012120.
9. Simmons, G.J. The prisoners' problem and the subliminal channel. In *Advances in Cryptology*; Springer: Berlin/Heidelberg, Germany, 1984; pp. 51–67.
10. Khalind, O.S.; Hernandez-Castro, J.C.; Aziz, B. A study on the false positive rate of Stegdetect. *Digit. Investig.* **2013**, *9*, 235–245. [CrossRef]
11. Provos, N. StegDetect. 2020. Available online: https://github.com/abeluck/stegdetect (accessed on 17 November 2020).
12. Cheddad, A.; Condell, J.; Curran, K.; Mc Kevitt, P. Digital image steganography: Survey and analysis of current methods. *Signal Process.* **2010**, *90*, 727–752. [CrossRef]
13. Zhang, L.; Gao, Y.; Xia, Y.; Dai, Q.; Li, X. A fine-grained image categorization system by cellet-encoded spatial pyramid modeling. *Multimed. Tools Appl.* **2015**, *62*, 564–571. [CrossRef]
14. Bailey, K.; Curran, K. An evaluation of image based steganography methods. *Multimed. Tools Appl.* **2006**, *30*, 55–88. [CrossRef]
15. Zöllner, J.; Federrath, H.; Klimant, H.; Pfitzmann, A.; Piotraschke, R.; Westfeld, A.; Wicke, G.; Wolf, G. Modeling the Security of Steganographic Systems. In *International Workshop on Information Hiding*; Springer: Berlin/Heidelberg, Germany, 1998; pp. 344–354.
16. Provos, N. Scanning USENET for Steganography. 2001. Available online: http://niels.xtdnet.nl/stego/usenet.php (accessed on 17 November 2020).

17. Agarwal, A.; Gupta, M.; Gupta, S.; Gupta, S. Systematic digital forensic investigation model. *Int. J. Comput. Sci. Secur.* **2011**, *5*, 118–131.
18. Dezfoli, F.N.; Dehghantanha, A.; Mahmoud, R.; Sani, N.F.B.M.; Daryabar, F. Digital forensic trends and future. *Int. J. Cyber Secur. Digit. Forensics* **2013**, *2*, 48–76.
19. Casey, E. *Digital Evidence and Computer Crime: Forensic Science, Computers, and the Internet*; Academic Press: Cambridge, MA, USA, 2011.
20. Boehm, B. Stegexpose-A tool for detecting LSB steganography. *arXiv* **2014**, arXiv:1410.6656.
21. Boehm, B. StegExpose. 2020. Available online: https://github.com/b3dk7/StegExpose (accessed on 17 November 2020).
22. SilentEye. SilentEye. 2020. Available online: https://achorein.github.io/silenteye/ (accessed on 17 November 2020).
23. OpenPuff. OpenPuff. 2018. Available online: https://embeddedsw.net/doc/OpenPuff_Help_EN.pdf (accessed on 17 November 2020).
24. OpenStego. OpenStego. 2020. Available online: https://www.openstego.com/ (accessed on 17 November 2020).
25. StegSecret. StegSecret. 2020. Available online: http://stegsecret.sourceforge.net/ (accessed on 17 November 2020).
26. You, W.; Zhang, H.; Zhao, X. A Siamese CNN for Image Steganalysis. *IEEE Trans. Inf. Forensics Secur.* **2020**, *16*, 291–306. [CrossRef]
27. Shojae Chaeikar, S.; Ahmadi, A. Ensemble SW image steganalysis: A low dimension method for LSBR detection. *Signal Process. Image Commun.* **2019**, *70*, 233–245, [CrossRef]
28. Kim, J.; Park, H.; Park, J. CNN-based image steganalysis using additional data embedding. *Multimed. Tools Appl.* **2020**, *79*, 1355–1372. [CrossRef]
29. Ibrahim, A. Steganalysis in Computer Forensics. In Proceedings of the 5th Australian Digital Forensics Conference, Perth, Australia, 3–4 December 2007; p. 10.
30. Latham, A. Steganography: JPHIDE and JPSEEK. 1999. Available online: https://github.com/h3xx/jphs (accessed on 17 November 2020).

Publisher's Note: MDPI stays neutral with regard to jurisdictional claims in published maps and institutional affiliations.

© 2020 by the authors. Licensee MDPI, Basel, Switzerland. This article is an open access article distributed under the terms and conditions of the Creative Commons Attribution (CC BY) license (http://creativecommons.org/licenses/by/4.0/).

Article

Velody 2—Resilient High-Capacity MIDI Steganography for Organ and Harpsichord Music

Eric Järpe [1,*] and Mattias Wecksén [2]

1 Department of Intelligent Systems and Digital Design, Halmstad University, 301 18 Halmstad, Sweden
2 Department of CERES, Halmstad University, 301 18 Halmstad, Sweden; mattias.wecksten@hh.se
* Correspondence: eric.jarpe@hh.se; Tel.: +46-729-773-626

Abstract: A new method for musical steganography for the MIDI format is presented. The MIDI standard is a user-friendly music technology protocol that is frequently deployed by composers of different levels of ambition. There is to the author's knowledge no fully implemented and rigorously specified, publicly available method for MIDI steganography. The goal of this study, however, is to investigate how a novel MIDI steganography algorithm can be implemented by manipulation of the velocity attribute subject to restrictions of capacity and security. Many of today's MIDI steganography methods—less rigorously described in the literature—fail to be resilient to steganalysis. Traces (such as artefacts in the MIDI code which would not occur by the mere generation of MIDI music: MIDI file size inflation, radical changes in mean absolute error or peak signal-to-noise ratio of certain kinds of MIDI events or even audible effects in the stego MIDI file) that could catch the eye of a scrutinizing steganalyst are side-effects of many current methods described in the literature. This steganalysis resilience is an imperative property of the steganography method. However, by restricting the carrier MIDI files to classical organ and harpsichord pieces, the problem of velocities following the mood of the music can be avoided. The proposed method, called Velody 2, is found to be on par with or better than the cutting edge alternative methods regarding capacity and inflation while still possessing a better resilience against steganalysis. An audibility test was conducted to check that there are no signs of audible traces in the stego MIDI files.

Keywords: MIDI; velocity values; carrier file; stego file; capacity; steganalysis resilience; audibility; file-size change-rate; mean absolute error; peak signal-to-noise ratio

Citation: Järpe, E.; Wecksén, M. Velody 2—Resilient High-Capacity MIDI Steganography for Organ and Harpsichord Music. *Appl. Sci.* **2021**, *11*, 39. https://dx.doi.org/10.3390/app11010039

Received: 26 November 2020
Accepted: 19 December 2020
Published: 23 December 2020

Publisher's Note: MDPI stays neutral with regard to jurisdictional claims in published maps and institutional affiliations.

Copyright: © 2020 by the author. Licensee MDPI, Basel, Switzerland. This article is an open access article distributed under the terms and conditions of the Creative Commons Attribution (CC BY) license (https://creativecommons.org/licenses/by/4.0/).

1. Introduction

Steganography provides means for hiding information, not just making it intelligible by encrypting it. The concealment of a message at all can be the difference between life and death in cases when the very sending of a message (encrypted or not) is considered a crime and a threat to the authorities. The techniques of steganography have sometimes been criticized for serving criminals seeking to operate outside the law, but the use of it for whistleblowers and for freedom fighters (e.g., [1]) who are in countries with authoritarian regimes is well documented.

The technique of steganography does not by itself change a message, but merely hides its existence in other information. This is what distinguishes steganography from cryptography. Nevertheless, steganography is very often used in combination with cryptography, by first encrypting a message and then hiding it. This combination makes a very strong protection against revealing a secret message since upon looking for hidden messages it may be impossible to perform cryptanalysis on all possibly hidden data found in any of a great number of files. Thus, in effect, adding an encryption step can greatly improve security aspects of the message exchange—the content of the communication is not only secret but even the very existence that any kind of communication took place is unknown. This is an additional property that can be crucial in some circumstances where the occurrence of encrypted messages can draw attention from the authorities. Since the percentage of users of steganography is unknown to a much larger extent than is the case for e.g., cryptography, it is harder to motivate its relevance [2]. This is the reason why there are few reports on the numbers of use of such methods. However, this does not mean that methods of steganography are not used.

Steganography may be deployed in many respects, but in modern times it usually means involving computer files. This study focuses on musical steganography through the MIDI format. The MIDI format is a standard music protocol used worldwide to create music and to facilitate its accessibility.

1.1. Related Literature

Ever since 2000, the MIDI format has been subject to methods of steganography. Worth noting are e.g., pioneer works of Inoue and Matsumoto [3] and Adli and Nakao [4]. In the former, which was preceded by several conference papers by the same authors, three requirements for steganography of MIDI files are established. These requirements are (1) that MIDI music sounds the same after steganography as it did before, (2) that the stego MIDI file should satisfy the requirements of the MIDI format, and (3) that extraction of the hidden message from the stego MIDI file should be very difficult without the proper stego key. The authors continue to outline a method for encoding data in MIDI files using permutations of note events. In the latter, three methods of steganography are briefly specified. 2009 Yamamoto and Iwakiri [5] made a short but dense paper where they present a cunning method to implement the hidden message by LSB modifications of durations of notes. This gives a high capacity, relatively speaking, for hiding messages compared to the size of the carrier file. It is claimed that little performance quality is lost which is demonstrated with a χ^2-test. An ambitious study was made in Wu and Chen [6] and just recently pursued by Liu and Wu [7] about a method which modifies the way delta-times (i.e., the time elapsed between MIDI events) may be represented in the MIDI format. This renders them high capacity methods which, in the latter paper, is also claimed to be performance preserving, which means that no distortion of any kind is added to the MIDI file upon steganography with that method. Nevertheless, it inflates the MIDI file substantially and is thus not property preserving. Another recent contribution to the field is Wu, Hsiang and Chen [8] where an extremely cautious variant of velocity modification is defined by preserving the common increasing or decreasing trends in velocity among sequences of notes with increasing and decreasing pitch. There are also many methods that deal with steganography of files of the MP3 format, e.g., [9–12]. These methods may be interesting to compare to from a property perspective. For instance capacity and audibility may be considered for any music format regardless of which technique is used. Still, many comparisons are difficult because of different formats.

Aspects of capacity, robustness and transparency are mentioned in Lang et al [13]. This is an extensive inventory of the techniques for steganography in general and it even touches upon steganalysis. A more recent survey study is given by Sumathi, Santanam and Umamaaheswari [14] which also considers various steganography methods, not just audio.

1.2. Aspects of Steganalysis Resilience

Picture the steganalyst trying to make out whether or not a particular MIDI file is a case of steganography or not. Then, many properties would be more revealing while others are entirely plausible in a stego MIDI file. A few examples of this are:

A. Inflation of a MIDI file making the size grow upon steganography is an obvious problem. Hiding the secret message in non-audio related parts of the MIDI file does not leave any audible traces but is still among the simplest kinds of music steganography to detect. Examples of this are Adli and Nakao [4], Wu and Chen [6] and Liu and Wu [7].

B. In Vaske, Wecksten and Järpe [15] there are two values of the velocity throughout the stego MIDI file. This is quite unnatural to appear in any MIDI file since the MIDI music is mainly entered in one of two ways: either by automatically scanning notes which are translated to MIDI code by some software which would make only one value of velocity (i.e., all velocity values would be identical), or the music would be played on some MIDI keyboard and entered by some MIDI sequencer program thus resulting in many different velocity values.

C. A few methods leave audible traces (such as clicks or chirps) in the stego file. This is less common in steganography of MIDI files but does occur in music steganography of other formats, such as in Szczypiorski and Zydecki [12] and Adli and Nakao [4].

The method proposed by Liu and Wu [7] is based on the technique of altering the coding of delta times and use this encoding for permutation-based data encoding. While the method has no performance effect it does severely inflate the file size and introduce redundant data that does not contribute to the performance, which would most likely trigger a steganalyst.

By Wu, Hsiang and Chen [8] a method based on the technique of adjusting the velocities of some of the note-on events was proposed. While the goal of this strategy is to make the adjustments in such a way that the performance effect is minimized, it still changes the velocity values and is therefore classified as having a performance effect, even if not registered by mere listening to the music.

In Vaske, Wecksten and Järpe [15] a method based on a simple technique of adjusting the velocities of note-on events up or down one bit was introduced. While impossible to register such a minuscule change for a listener it is considered to have a performance effect and will also leave a telltale pattern of suspect artefacts.

The method proposed by Wu and Chen [6] manipulates the coding of the delta-time events and code data directly into these events. This strategy inflates the file size according to the authors and introduces a minuscule performance effect within a set tolerance.

In Yamamoto and Iwakiri [5] a method which manipulates the duration between events to encode data was proposed. The authors show experimental evidence of naturally occurring fluctuations which would allow the embedding to take place without being noted as suspicious. However, the suggested strategy does introduce a minuscule performance effect.

The LSB method suggested by Adli and Nakao [4] simply encodes the clear text message in the LSB of the velocity of the note-on event. This strategy does introduce a minuscule change in the performance effect, but also since no intermediate step of processing the data exists there will be non-random patterns in the LSB of the velocity values which could be detected.

The repeated command method proposed by Adli and Nakao [4] encodes data using repeating commands configured in such a way that only the last command of a series will affect the output from the interpreted MIDI file. This will inflate the file size and show up as suspect artefacts.

In Adli and Nakao [4] a SysEx method that encodes data in non-standard commands that would normally not contribute to the interpreted MIDI file output was proposed. This strategy inflates the file and shows up as suspect artefacts. The authors also claim that although output is normally not affected, in some cases there is a notable performance effect. Since this strategy does not adhere to the MIDI file standard it would also violate the second rule of SMF steganography, requiring that "The stego SMF flawlessly satisfies the specification of the standard MIDI files" as described in [3].

The method proposed by Inoue, Suzuki and Matsumoto [3] encodes data by the permutation of the order of notes in simulnotes. This strategy does not inflate the file size nor does it have any performance effect, and the two suggested strategies of permutation tries to mimic two common standards of event arrangement in the simulnotes to avoid steganalysis.

The method purposed in this paper is to develop a balanced picture of what aspects are more important in MIDI steganography and put the suggested method for MIDI steganography, Velody 2, into its scientific context among alternative methods.

2. The Proposed Method

The suggested method Velody 2 consists of encoding encrypted data at high capacity into the velocities of the note-on events, while mimicking humanization available in tools with MIDI support such as Ableton Live [16]. The source code of the proposed method is publicly available at http://github.com/wecksten/Velody-2.0 as referred to in Appendix A. It achieves the properties of being blind, high capacity and provides steganalysis resilience of data embedding.

The effect from using this method is that it sets the velocities to values within a narrow interval to be specified, thus removing potential mood swings in the velocity parameter of the music. This effect is minimized by restricting the use of it for organ and harpsichord music (which naturally is performed with close to constant velocities). Therefore, suspicion from steganalysts is avoided regarding the audible change of velocities. Nevertheless, the method can be used with little artificial effect on a wider range of music, as indicated by including the piano piece Für Elise by Ludwig van Beethoven in the set of MIDI songs in the experiment to test for audibility effects of the method. Of course, it is not restricted to single-instrument music, but restricting it to organ and harpsichord merely means requiring that the steganography is performed only on the velocities of these instruments though they could be a part of a larger ensemble. An example of music for an ensemble with multiple instruments is Cantata Cantata Gott der Herr ist Sonn und Schild by J.S. Bach which was part of this study.

Regarding the property of performance preservation, using Velody 2 for steganography of organ and harpsichord music should not change performance to any extent that leads to suspicions from steganalysis. As for the property of reversibility, if the point with this is to be able to show a MIDI file which does not contain any hidden message once having extracted it, this can be achieved in other ways. Therefore, this property is regarded as less important compared to the properties of steganalysis resilience and capacity for instance.

To embed a plaintext message in a carrier MIDI file the process can be split up into three steps: (1) data preparation, (2) data encryption, and (3) data encoding. The extraction process of a plaintext message from a stego MIDI file is performed in a very similar manner by reversing the order of the steps (4) data decoding, (5) data decryption, and (6) data unboxing.

2.1. Preparation

To be able to extract just the embedded message and nothing more, the message length needs to be known. This can be done in many ways, but assuming that most messages will be less than 256 bytes of length one approach is to add an eight-bit message header to indicate the message length. This approach allows for longer messages if that would be required by stacking several blocks after one another. Assuming most messages are less than two blocks in length this approach will have the same or less overhead than an approach where 16 bits would be used to indicate the message length. To prepare the data for encryption the clear text message M of length w bytes where $w = |M|$, M is divided into n blocks $B_1, B_2, \ldots, B_n$, where $n = \lceil \frac{w}{256} \rceil$. An eight-bit header H_i is introduced for each block B_i, where $H_i = |B_i|$ and where $|B_i|$ is the block size in bytes. As can be seen in the Figure 1, the prepared message P is equal to the assembly $P = (S, H_1, B_1, H_2, B_2, \ldots, H_n, B_n)$.

2.2. Encryption

The prepared message P is encrypted using a standard synchronous stream cypher and a shared key generating the encrypted message $E = F(P)$ which is very similar to random data in distribution.

2.3. Encoding

The carrier MIDI file is unpacked into a stream of MIDI messages S_1, S_2, S_m where each message of the type "note-on" is evaluated for data embedding. If the velocity for the "note-on" event S_i is less than 2^{N_e} the velocity $v_i = velocity(S_i)$ is replaced with a random number between a lower bound l and an upper bound $u = 2^{\lfloor \log v_i \rfloor + 1} - 1$. If the velocity for the "note-on" event S_i is greater than or equal to 2^{N_e} the velocity is LSB encoded with the next N_e bits from the encrypted message stream. LSB encoding is performed by clearing the N_e least significant bits of the velocity value and then adding the N_e bit long value from the encrypted message stream.

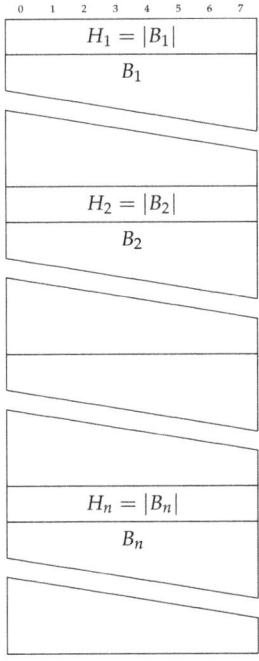

Figure 1. Data after preparation step. Each block of the message has been assigned a header that is equal to the following block size in bytes.

2.4. Decoding

The stego MIDI file is unpacked into a stream of MIDI messages S_1, S_2, S_m where each message of the type "note-on" is evaluated for data decoding. If the velocity for the "note-on" event S_i is greater than or equal to 2^{N_e} the velocity is LSB decoded using the N_e least significant bits. The LSB decoding is performed by pushing the N_e least significant bits of the velocity to the decoded data stream.

2.5. Decryption

The decoded message D is decrypted using a standard synchronous stream cypher and a shared key generating the prepared message $P = F(E)$.

2.6. Unboxing

The prepared message $P = (P_1, P_2, \ldots, P_n)$ is unboxed by reconstruction of the header value $H_i = P_j$ and then copying H_i bytes of data from the prepared message P to the clear text message M by adding the extracted data to the end of the clear text message $M = M + (P_{j+1}, P_{j+2}, \ldots, P_{j+H_i})$. This process is repeated until the prepared message P is out of data or the header value read from the prepared message is equal to 0. The full clear text message is now available in M.

2.7. Aspects of Authenticity

In [8], the authenticity of MIDI files is paid a lot of the focus. There, the increasing or decreasing velocities due to increasing or decreasing pitch of tones played is preserved. That approach renders the method a top score with regards to authenticity.

It is assumed that the MIDI music is sequenced either by some kind of automatic procedure, where all notes are given a constant velocity throughout the whole piece or by being played by somebody, possibly at half-speed, which then results in all notes having velocities in a broad interval and relatively few velocity values being exactly the same. Therefore, the predecessor to the proposed method, Velody [15] suffers a great deal in terms of authenticity upon inspection of the actual velocity values, since these velocities are to equal proportions either of two velocity values. Thus, close inspection of the velocities by a meticulous steganalyst would reveal clear deviance from both the stereotype patterns (either all one velocity value throughout the piece or a variety of velocities).

2.8. Hypothesis Test of Audibility

A drawback of a steganography method is if the method leaves audible marks in the music. To this end, a hypothesis test was carried out. In this test, people listened to 10 pairs of musical pieces selected from a database of classical MIDI music (please, refer to Appendix A for a description of the database). The songs selected were

1. bach1.mid: Cantata Cantata Gott der Herr ist Sonn und Schild, part 5, BWV 79e by J.S. Bach
2. bach2.mid: Trio Sonata no 1 for organ, part 1, BWV 525a by J.S. Bach
3. bach3.mid: Trio Sonata no 1 for organ, part 2, BWV 525b by J.S. Bach
4. bach4.mid: Toccata and Fugue in D minor for organ, BWV 565 by J.S. Bach
5. bach5.mid: Prelude and Fugue in E major and C major for organ, BWV 566 by J.S. Bach
6. bach6.mid: Prelude in D major for organ, BWV 568 by J.S. Bach
7. scarlatti1.mid: Sonata Allegrissimo in C major for harpsichord, K 100 by D. Scarlatti
8. scarlatti2.mid: Sonata Allegro in A major for harpsichord, K 101 by D. Scarlatti
9. scarlatti3.mid: Sonata Allegro in G major for harpsichord, K 102 by D. Scarlatti
10. beethoven.mid: Bagatelle no 25 in A minor, "Für Elise" for piano by L. van Beethoven

The experiment was presented at a web page (see Figure 2) where all 10 pairs of musical pieces were playable via buttons embedded into the page. For each pair of songs, there was one called File 1 and another called File 2. One of these was the original song and the other was the same song but modified through Velody 2 with a message hidden inside. For each pair, the listener was instructed to guess which of the files that were steganography by indicating this using radio buttons. Each pair consisted of two MIDI songs converted to flac-format to be playable more independently on different computers. Thus, the test was solely devoted to finding out audible differences between the original song and the corresponding stego song. It did not involve the inspection of eventlists or any other kind of analysis. The number of respondents who contributed to this experiment was 30. At the top of the page, apart from declaring their name, each participant should write a 7 character code which ensured that they had been given instructions about what to do and which also served to reduce the risk of the same person taking the test multiple times and being able to differentiate between groups of respondents in retrospect.

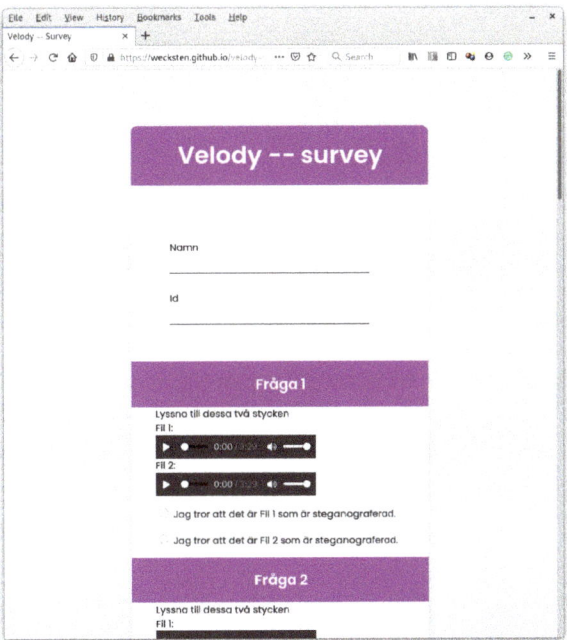

Figure 2. The experiment was carried out by encouraging people to listen to pairs of MIDI songs played by pressing buttons in a web form and indicating utilizing radio buttons which of the two alternatives included steganography.

2.9. Relevance of Power of a Hypothesis Test

If there was a detectable difference in the songs after steganography had been performed, this would be indicated by increasing the probability π of correctly guessing which song included steganography, i.e., making this probability $> \frac{1}{2}$. If, on the other hand, there were no signs of steganography manipulation at all, that probability π would be equal to $\frac{1}{2}$. Now, a hypothesis test could only prove the alternative, which in this case would be that $\pi > \frac{1}{2}$ as opposed to the null hypothesis $\pi = \frac{1}{2}$. The claim that there is no audible effect of Velody can never be proved by a hypothesis test. If the null is accepted this just means that effect could not be proved.

However, one might hypothesize, if there were audible effects due to the steganography method these effects would have to be so large that they resulted in a rejection of the null hypothesis. With a larger number of respondents this ability to prove an effect also if π was just a little larger than $\frac{1}{2}$, i.e., a large number of respondents would increase the power of the test.

2.10. Robustness

Another aspect of importance is robustness as considered by e.g., Lang et al [13]. Currently, the proposed method, Velody 2, is not implemented with any support for improving the robustness of the method. Including the hidden message with redundancy in the carrier would not contribute to robustness since MIDI file would not play and there would not even be an eventlist in the case of as much as one bit failing. However, one could just send the stego MIDI file with redundancy, i.e., sending the same stego MIDI file multiple times. In addition, the receiver could be assumed to have many alternative addresses so the transmission could still be made to many different addresses. This way of increasing robustness is claimed to lead to minimal suspicion. Still, this is rather recommended behaviour than a part of the Velody 2 method.

3. Results

The results are divided into those regarding security aspects, mainly steganalysis resilience aspects such as whether there are no audible revealing footprints of the steganography and other changes which may catch the attention of an alert steganalyst, and capacity aspects, such as embedding capacity, the number of bits per event and file-size change rate, following the definitions by Liu and Wu [7].

3.1. Steganalysis Resilience

The Velody 2 method proposed in this paper is based on a slight extension of a velocity LSB embedding algorithm, but where the strategy to embed the data tries to mimic the output of "Humanization" available in midi tools such as Abelton. The strategy does not inflate the file size and has a minuscule performance effect. However, it has been shown in a statistical experiment that the performance effect introduced is most likely not possible to detect for a human listener. A summary of these methods and their resilience in these respects is summarized in the Table 1.

Table 1. Summary of properties regarding resilience to steganalysis and to what extent these are satisfied by the different methods considered.

Method	Inflation	Performance Effect	Other Suspect Artifacts
Liu and Wu [7]	x	-	x
Wu, Hsiang and Chen [8]	-	x	-
Vaske, Wecksténs and Järpe [15]	-	x	x
Wu and Chen [6]	x	x	-
Yamamoto and Iwakiri [5]	-	x	-
Adli and Nakao:LSB [4]	-	x	x
Adli and Nakao:Repeated command [4]	x	-	x
Adli and Nakao:SysEx [4]	x	x	x
Inoue, Suzuki and Matsumoto [3]	-	-	-
Velody 2 (the proposed method)	-	x	-

From this table, the method in Inoue, Suzuki and Matsumoto [3] comes out best since it has no performance effect at all, it leaves a minimal amount of artificial traces while still not contributing to inflation. Other good methods are Liu and Wu [7], Wu, Hsiang and Chen [8], Yamamoto and Iwakiri [5] and Velody 2, the proposed method which are considered to suffer from only one of the shortcomings. Depending on which of these properties are more important these methods could be differently preferable.

In attempting to make a steganography method resilient it is important to leave as few traces of manipulation of the carrier upon performing the data hiding according to the method.

For instance drastically changing properties such as Mean Absolute Error (MAE), Peak Signal-to-Noise Ratio (PSNR) or file-size change-rate (F_r) in the information hiding process are shortcomings in that method in respect of steganalysis resilience. In Table 2 some values of these entities for a few methods are given. Here, it turns out that Velody 2 (the proposed method) and the method in Inoue, Suzuki and Matsumoto [3] are preferable with respect to file-size change-rate. Values of MAE and PSNR could not be compared since no such values were found for the other methods in the literature.

Table 2. Table of Mean Absolute Error (MAE), Peak Signal-to-Noise Ratio (PSNR) and file-size change-rates (F_r) for the methods considered. The file-size change-rates are as defined by Liu and Wu [7] and briefly explained in the text. Values within parentheses are standard errors.

Method	MAE	PSNR	F_r
Velody 2, 4 bits	6.27 (0.36)	24.64 (0.43)	0.00% (0.00%)
Velody 2, 5 bits	12.52 (0.81)	18.71 (0.50)	0.00% (0.00%)
Velody 2, 6 bits	25.37 (1.88)	12.62 (0.55)	0.00% (0.00%)
Wu, Hsiang and Chen [8]	unknown	24.99 [2] (0.60)	small
Liu and Wu [7]	unknown	unknown	40.47% [1]
Inoue, Suzuki and Matsumoto [3]	unknown	unknown	0.00% (0.00%)

[1] According to Liu and Wu [7]. [2] This is WSNR which is different to PSNR but still a variant of a Signal-to-Noise Ratio.

3.2. Audibility

There were 30 respondents to the audibility form which consisted of telling which of two alternatives of the same song was steganography for 10 different MIDI songs. The 10 songs were as listed in Section 2.8 and the results of this experiment are illustrated in the bar charts in Figure 3.

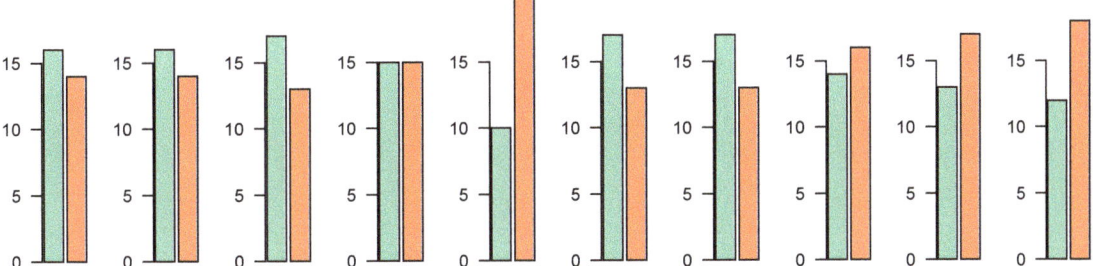

Figure 3. Barplots of the distribution of guesses divided into the 10 songs in the audibility experiment. A total of 30 respondents guessed each and every of the 10 pairs of songs about which one was steganography. The bars show the number of incorrect guesses in turquoise and the number correct guesses in orange for each pair of songs.

We tested the hypothesis that the suggested method left audible traces a test of whether the probability $\pi = P$ (a respondent cannot tell apart the stego MIDI file from the carrier MIDI file) exceeds 0.5 against the null hypothesis that the probability $\pi = 0.5$ (corresponding to the respondent choosing one of the alternatives entirely at random).

Letting each guess be coded as 0 if it is wrong and 1 if it is right, a binomial test is an obvious possibility since the sum S of correct guesses over all pairs of MIDI songs and all respondents is a sum of 0-1-variables which, assuming independence between songs and respondents and that all guesses are correct with equal probability π, is binomially distributed with parameters N and π. 30 respondents were signing up for the experiment and 10 pairs of songs making $n = 300$. In total, 153 correct guesses made the p-value of the binomial test

$$P(S > 153 \mid H_0) = \sum_{k=154}^{N} \binom{N}{k} \pi^k (1-\pi)^{N-k} \bigg|_{\substack{N=300 \\ \pi=0.5}} = 0.3431$$

which is well and truly above than any reasonable level of significance, i.e., there are no indications of standing a better chance of guessing which of the songs is steganography after listening to both MIDI carrier and stego MIDI file.

The more common test for this kind of question is a χ^2-test. Letting each song constitute a class, the number of correct guesses for each class was calculated. Under the assumption of independence between guesses and that each song was guessed to be steganography correctly with probability π the total number X of correct guesses for one respondent could be subjected to a χ^2-test of whether X is binomially distributed with parameters $n = 10$ and $\pi = 0.5$ or not. After merging classes so that the expected number of observations in each class exceeded 2, there were 5 classes and the test statistic turned out 5.8252 rendering a high p-value of 0.8171.

So, what does it mean that the null hypothesis $X \in Bin(10, 0.5)$ can not be rejected? Certainly, it does not prove that $X \in Bin(10, 0.5)$ and that $\pi = 0.5$ which corresponds to that respondents can not tell the stego MIDI file apart from the carrier file, only that no deviance in the distribution of X from $Bin(10, 0.5)$ can be found. How large would that deviance have had to be for the hypothesis test to prove it? That question is answered by looking at the power of the test as illustrated in Figure 4. From these curves, it is clear that for deviances of π about 0.08 from the null hypothesis value 0.5 the power is clearly greater than 0.95 meaning that the test most likely would have shown a significant difference in this case. For telling even smaller deviances from 0.5 with that great power a larger sample size is needed.

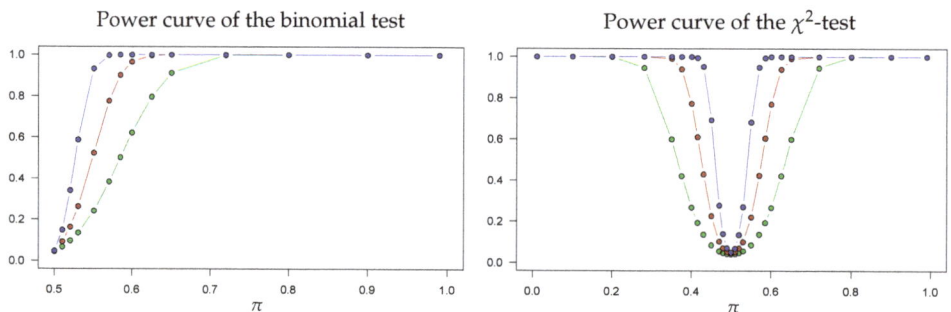

Figure 4. To the left: Power curve of the binomial test of deviance from the value 0.5 of the parameter $\pi = P$ (a respondent cannot tell apart the stego MIDI file from the carrier MIDI file.). To the right: Power curve of the χ^2-test of deviance from the binomial distribution with parameters $n = 10$ (since there are 10 questions in the experiment) and π. For both tests, the power depends on the sample size, i.e., the number of respondents in this case. Here, the sample size was 30 as indicated by the red curves, but had it been 10 the curves would have been as indicated in green and had it been 100 the curves would have been as indicated in blue.

3.3. Capacity

For evaluation of steganography methods, Liu and Wu [7] define several variables related to capacity, i.e., the number of bits that can be encoded into the carrier MIDI file referred to as embedding capacity N_c, the total number of embedded bits divided by the size of the carrier MIDI file before encoding referred to as the embedding rate E_r, the total number of embedded bits divided by the total number of events in the carrier MIDI file referred to as the number of bits/event N_e, and the absolute change of the carrier MIDI file before and after encoding divided by the size before encoding referred to as the file-size change rate F_t. Following their initiative, the suggested method is evaluated according to these key performance indicators and parameters and compared to the corresponding values of other methods. It is assumed that the full embedding capacity is used for encoding. See Table 3 for a comparison of a selection of steganography methods. As Table 3 shows, the Velody 2 strategy does not limit the number of available events until the N_e approaches 6 bits/event, and even then the reduction is small.

Table 3. Table of averages of capacity properties: the number of embedded secret bits N_b, number of bits per event N_e and embedding rate E_r as defined by Liu and Wu [7] and briefly explained in the text. Values within parentheses are standard errors.

Method	Notes	Available	N_b	N_e	E_r
Velody 2, 4 bits	2267 (474)	2267 (474)	9067 (1896)	4.00 (0.00)	6.43% (0.30%)
Velody 2, 5 bits	2267 (474)	2267 (474)	11,333 (2370)	5.00 (0.00)	8.03% (0.37%)
Velody 2, 6 bits	2267 (474)	2227 (467)	13,364 (2804)	5.91 (0.05)	9.48% (0.40%)
Wu, Hsiang and Chen [8]	4536 (1999)	753 (371)	919 (387)	0.55 (0.12)	1.11% (0.22%)
Liu and Wu [7]	unknown	unknown	492	1.95 (0.01)	7.29% [1]
Inoue, Suzuki and Matsumoto [3]	unknown	unknown	3120 (274)	unknown	4.01% [2]

[1] According to Liu and Wu [7]. [2] According to Inoue, Suzuki and Matsumoto [3].

It can also be seen that the E_r is high compared to other techniques. While the Velody 2 strategy most likely does not outperform the work of Wu, Hsiang and Chen [8] when it comes to the deviation in average velocity, this is of little practical effect since it according to the statistical experiment seems hard to detect this when listening and that there exist tools that creates exactly this type of deviation as a part of the music production process. The suggested strategy from Liu and Wu [7] achieves a fairly good N_e, but this comes at the cost of a low E_r value due to the file size expansion introduced by the strategy. The method proposed by Inoue, Suzuki and Matsumoto [3] achieves a good E_r value with no inflation, performance effects, or obvious artefacts. However, the optimal performance of this elegant strategy is still outperformed by the averaged performance of the Velody 2 method.

4. Discussion and Conclusions

A novel MIDI steganography method, called Velody 2, is presented. Its capacity turns out to be on par with the highest capacity methods available in the literature while still leaving few traces of manipulation, such as small values of Mean Absolute Error (MAE) and Peak Signal-to-Noise Ratio (PSNR). It also has no inflation and an experiment was carried out verifying that there are no signs of audible traces.

Regarding many methods suggested in the literature, the MIDI code shows artificial patterns that would not be likely, or even possible, to produce by generating the MIDI file merely by automatic sequencing from sheet music or input of a MIDI song by playing on a keyboard and possibly modifying it slightly afterwards. Examples of such artefacts are extra data not occurring normally in a MIDI song (as is the case with the padding in Liu and Wu [7]), simultaneous note events (so-called simulnotes) that may occur in any order without sounding different and neither causing inflation but where the sequencer always put these events in a certain order and deviance from that pattern should arouse suspicion (in Inoue, Suzuki and Matsumoto [3]), and only two values of velocities (as in Vaske, Weckstén and Järpe [15]). Such artificial giveaways are perfect signals to a steganalyst searching for indications of suspect MIDI steganography.

In the suggested method, velocities are scattered randomly within a narrow interval to be specified. This would have been the result of having played a piece on a keyboard or humanized using a midi software that supports randomization of the velocities. Of course, the mean level is constant and not drifting as is the case in a majority of MIDI music. Still, for harpsichord and organ music this poses no problem at all, and even if this is a strong restriction MIDI music is abundant within this subgroup. An audibility hypothesis test was carried out to see if there were audible traces in the stego MIDI files compared to the carrier files. However, the p-values here were 0.3431 (binomial test) and 0.8171 (chi-square test) meaning that no signs of steganography could be detected. If the music is entered by playing the piece on a keyboard this is also likely to cause starting time and duration of notes to be slightly fluctuating. Thus, if the velocities are scattered while starting times and duration are not this might be considered as an unrealistic artefact of the method. However, this is not at all unrealistic taking into account that the composer could well have quantized the notes after having made the keyboard recording, a very common kind of facility in many MIDI sequencer programs. Thus, the notes would be perfectly according to the measures and bars but velocity differences would remain.

Another aspect of footprint is the file-size change-rate (F_r). For Velody 2 this is 0, i.e., there is no change of the file-size at all. This makes it optimal in this respect together with the methods of Inoue, Suzuki and Matsumoto [3] and slightly better than Wu, Hsian and Chen [8]. In addition statistical estimators such as the Mean Absolute Error (MAE) and the Peak Signal-to-Noise Ratio (PSNR) of the various kinds of MIDI events in the music may be interesting from a steganalysis perspective. When having to check a vast material of MIDI music for suspect features, a steganalyst is unlikely to be able to go through each MIDI song's event list to check for revealing footprints such as those mentioned above, unless it is possible to fully automate. Instead, the search is likely to build on summarizing characteristics such as the MAE and PSNR of different MIDI events, and these could systematically be retrieved in an automatized process. Thus, steganography methods which stand out in such a listing are likely to be scrutinized for further indications of steganography. In the proposed method, averages of MAE, ranging from 6.27 to 25.37, and PSNR, ranging from 12.62 to 24.64, were calculated. Corresponding values for other methods have to be calculated to compare methods. This, however, remains as a task for future studies.

It could be argued that most likely a steganography method that creates output that has the reversibility property, thus where the carrier MIDI file can be restored from the stego MIDI file, is by definition not providing plausible deniability. The reason for this is that since the carrier MIDI file can be recreated from the stego MIDI file there has to be extra information available in the file that can be removed.

Veoldy 2 was not developed with robustness in mind. Therefore it does not include any steps to increase its properties in the aspects of robustness. Such development remains as a possibility for future studies.

To further investigate resilience to steganalysis the steganography methods could be submitted to the most common steganalysis tools. This has been done for audio steganography [17] and possibly other kinds of steganography [18] and investigating how successful the procedures are in these papers is an important step to properly finding out the ability of steganography methods to withstand the attempts made by steganalysts. Suggestions for improvements for future experiments include increasing the number of respondents as well as increasing the share of respondents that have training in playing and listening to music. The experiment itself could be improved by generating a large pool of carrier MIDI files and related stego MIDI files from which each experiment randomly generates a unique set of questions. This would reduce the opportunity of collusion leading to test bias.

Author Contributions: Formal analysis, M.W.; Investigation, E.J. and M.W.; Methodology, E.J.; Software, E.J. and M.W. All authors have read and agreed to the published version of the manuscript.

Funding: The research leading to the results reported in this work received funding from the Knowledge Foundation in the framework of SafeSmart Safety of Connected Intelligent Vehicles in Smart Cities Synergy project (2019–2023), grant number F2019/151.

Acknowledgments: The authors which to extend their sincere gratitude to all respondents in the experiment which provided data for the audibility test, see their name in the Appendix A below.

Conflicts of Interest: The authors declare no conflict of interest.

Appendix A

Data and source code is available at https://github.com/wecksten/Velody-2.

The respondents in the audibility experiment were: E. Spennare, T. Holtzberg, P. Wärnestål, M. Dougherty, A. Galozy, A. Olsson, M.R. Bouguelia, J. Johansson, O. Andersson, M.A. Rasool, O. Engelbrektsson, F. Johansson, S. Nilsson, M. Blom, T. Svane, J. Elmlund, A.

Alabdallah, S. Lindberg, M. Cooney, A. Stefanescu, L. Wandel, K. Eldemark, M. Menezes, E. Gustafsson, N. Benamer, K. Raats and V. Prgomet. Thank you all! Without you the experiment could not have been carried out.

References

1. CBC News. Blogger Sentenced in Iran to 19 Years. 2010. Available online: https://www.cbc.ca/news/world/blogger-sentenced-in-iran-to-19-years-1.885245 (accessed on 22 December 2020).
2. Biradar, R.; Umashetty, A. A Survey Paper on Steganography Techniques. *Int. J. Innov. Res. Comput. Commun. Eng.* **2016**, *4*, 721–730. [CrossRef]
3. Inoue, D.; Suzuki, M.; Matsumoto, T. Reviving Standard MIDI Files Steganography. In Proceedings of the Pacific Rim Workshop on Digital Steganography 2002 (STEG'02), Kitakyushu, Japan, 11–13 July 2002.
4. Adli, A.; Nakao, Z. Three Steganography Algorithms for MIDI Files. In Proceedings of the Fourth International Conference on Machine Learning and Cybernetics, Guangzhou, China, 18–21 August 2005; pp. 2401–2404. [CrossRef]
5. Yamamoto, K.; Iwakiri, M. A Standard MIDI File Steganography Based on Fluctuation of Duration. In Proceedings of the 2009 International Conference on Availability, Reliability and Security, Fukuoka, Japan, 16–19 March 2009; pp. 774–779. [CrossRef]
6. Wu, D.; Chen, M. Reversible data hiding in Standard MIDI Files by Adjusting Delta Time Values. *Multimed. Tools Appl.* **2015**, *74*, 9827–9844. [CrossRef]
7. Liu, Y.; Wu, D. A high-capacity performance-preserving blind technique for reversible information hiding via MIDI files using delta times. *Multimed. Tools Appl.* **2020**, *79*, 17281–17302. [CrossRef]
8. Wu, D.; Hsiang, C.; Chen, M. Steganography via MIDI Files by Adjusting Velocities of Musical Note Sequences with Monotonically Non-Increasing or Non-Decreasing Pitches. *IEEE Access* **2019**, *7*, 154056–154075. [CrossRef]
9. Yi, X.; Yang, K.; Zhao, X.; Wang, Y.; Yu, H. AHCM: Adaptive Huffman Code Mapping for Audio Steganography Based on Pyschoacoustic Model. *IEEE Trans. Inf. Forensics Secur.* **2019**, *14*, 2217–2231. [CrossRef]
10. Indrayani, R.; Nugroho, H.; Hidayat, R.; Pratama, I. Increasing the Security of MP3 Steganography Using AES Encryption and MD5 Hash Function. In Proceedings of the 2016 2nd International Conference on Science and Technology-Computer (ICST), Yogyakarta, Indonesia, 27–28 October 2016. [CrossRef]
11. Indrayani, R.; Nugroho, H.; Hidayat, R. An evaluation of MP3 Steganography Based on Modified LSB Method. In Proceedings of the 2017 International Conference on Information Technology Systems and Innovation (ICITSI), Bandung, Indonesia, 23–24 October 2017; pp. 257–260. [CrossRef]
12. Szczypiorski, K. StegIbiza: New Method for Information Hiding in Club Music. In Proceedings of the 2nd International Conference on Frontiers of Signal Processing (ICFSP), Warsaw, Poland, 15–17 October 2016; pp. 20–24. [CrossRef]
13. Lang, A.; Kraetzer, C.; Trofimova, N.; Ullerich, C.; Westfeld, A.; Bas, P.; Joacomarti, J.H.; Jiménez, D.M. *D.WVL.10 Audio Benchmarking Tools and Steganalysis*; Dittmann, J., Kraetzer, C., Eds.; Technical Report IST-2002-507932; Katholieke Universiteit Leuven: Leuven, Belgium, 2006.
14. Sumathi, C.P.; Santanam, T.; Umamaheswari, G. A Study of Various Steganographic Techniques Used for Information Hiding. *Int. J. Comput. Sci. Eng. Surv.* **2014**, *4*. [CrossRef]
15. Vaske, C.; Weckstén, M.; Järpe, E. Velody—A novel method for music steganography. In Proceedings of the 2017 3rd International Conference on Frontiers of Signal Processing (ICFSP), Paris, France, 6–8 September 2017; pp. 15–19. [CrossRef]
16. Ableton Live. Music Production with Live and Push. 2020. Available online: https://www.ableton.com (accessed on 22 December 2020).
17. Kraetzer, C.; Dittmann, J. Pros and Cons of Mel-cepstrum Based Audio Steganalysis Using SVM Classification. In *Lecture Notes in Computer Science, Proceedings of the Information Hiding, 9th International Workshop, IH 2007, Saint Malo, France, 11–13 June 2007; Revised Selected Papers*; Springer: Berlin/Heidelberg, Germany, 2007. [CrossRef]
18. Inoue, D.; Suzuki, M.; Okaniwa, T.; Matsumoto, T. Steganalysis of SMS Steganography. In Proceedings of the 2002 Symposium on Cryptography and Information Security, Shirahama, Japan, 29 January–1 February 2002; Volume I, pp. 313–318.

Article

Reversible and Plausibly Deniable Covert Channels in One-Time Passwords Based on Hash Chains [†]

Jörg Keller [1] and Steffen Wendzel [2,*]

[1] Faculty of Mathematics and Computer Science, FernUniversität in Hagen, 58084 Hagen, Germany; joerg.keller@FernUni-Hagen.de
[2] Department of Computer Science, Worms University of Applied Sciences, 67549 Worms, Germany
* Correspondence: wendzel@hs-worms.de
[†] This paper is an extended version of our paper published in European Interdisciplinary Cybersecurity Conference 2020, cf. https://doi.org/10.1145/3424954.3424966.

Abstract: Covert channels enable stealthy communications over innocent appearing carriers. They are increasingly applied in the network context. However, little work is available that exploits cryptographic primitives in the networking context to establish such covert communications. We present a covert channel between two devices where one device authenticates itself with Lamport's one-time passwords based on a cryptographic hash function. Our channel enables plausible deniability jointly with reversibility and is applicable in different contexts, such as traditional TCP/IP networks, CPS/IoT communication, blockchain-driven systems and local inter-process communications that apply hash chains. We also present countermeasures to detect the presence of such a covert channel, which are non-trivial because hash values are random-looking binary strings, so that deviations are not likely to be detected. We report on experimental results with MD5 and SHA-3 hash functions for two covert channel variants running in a localhost setup. In particular, we evaluate the channels' time performance, conduct statistical tests using the NIST suite and run a test for matching hash values between legitimate and covert environments to determine our channels' stealthiness.

Keywords: cryptographic hash function; hash chain; plausible deniability; steganography; covert channel

Citation: Keller, J.; Wendzel, S. Reversible and Plausibly Deniable Covert Channels in One-Time Passwords Based on Hash Chains [†]. *Appl. Sci.* **2021**, *11*, 731. http://doi.org/10.3390/app11020731

Received: 10 December 2020
Accepted: 11 January 2021
Published: 13 January 2021

Publisher's Note: MDPI stays neutral with regard to jurisdictional claims in published maps and institutional affiliations.

Copyright: © 2021 by the authors. Licensee MDPI, Basel, Switzerland. This article is an open access article distributed under the terms and conditions of the Creative Commons Attribution (CC BY) license (https://creativecommons.org/licenses/by/4.0/).

1. Introduction

A covert channel (CC) is an unforeseen communication channel in a system design. While the first covert channels for local computers were described in the 1970s (cf. [1]), the research of recent decades has discovered a plethora of new and sophisticated covert channels that aid the secret exchange of information between hosts, databases, network hosts and IoT devices. Due to their stealthy and policy-breaking nature, covert channels enable several actions related to cybercrime, such as the secret extraction of confidential information, barely detectable botnet command and control channels, and unobservable communication for cybercriminals. While legitimate use cases are imaginable as well, e.g., journalists using covert channels for secure exchange of dissident-related information, criminal use seems foremost, so that presentation of new covert channels also serves presentation of countermeasures.

We present the first CC that exploits cryptographic hash chains, which have become popular because some form (blockchain) is used in cryptocurrencies, although they had been used much earlier, e.g., by Lamport [2]. Hash chains are widely used, which renders them an attractive carrier for covert information that can be applied in various cybersecurity contexts, such as authentication systems, cryptocurrencies and blockchain-driven systems of all kinds. Thus, our proposed covert channels can be applied in several domains and contexts, which is an advantage in comparison to covert channels designed for legitimate communication systems (such as covert channels for specific smart building communication protocols).

Our covert channels can be considered an example of plausible deniability: Alice communicates with Bob over the covert channel. Both can state that every possible hash value is equally likely to occur. By modifying (alternating) bits of hash values, Alice and Bob can thus plausibly deny the existence of the covert channel. Moreover, we show that our channel allows Bob to restore the original message before forwarding it to the overt receiver, making our covert channel reversible. Alice and Bob, the covert sender and receiver, can be located directly with sender and receiver of the overt channel, but they can also be located on the communication path, realizing a man-in-the-middle (MitM) scenario.

Moreover, we present the CC in a parameterized manner so that our proposal really comprises a large number of possible CC instances that differ in steganographic bandwidth, robustness and stealthiness.

We sketch possible countermeasures against this CC, which are non-trivial because hash values are random-looking bit strings. To this end, we also perform experiments with MD5 and SHA-3 as cryptographic hash functions in Lamport's application of hash chains as one-time passwords, and give experimental results on the performance and detectability of CC use.

2. Fundamentals and Related Work

We will first introduce related fundamental concepts, followed by coverage of more sophisticated related work.

2.1. Fundamentals

A hash function is a function $h : U \to R$ that maps a possibly infinite universe, e.g., $U = \{0,1\}^*$, onto a finite set of hash values, e.g., $R = \{0,1\}^m$ [3]. A cryptographic hash function should have pre-image resistance, i.e., from a hash value $y \in R$ it is not possible (with reasonable effort) to compute a string $x \in U$ such that $h(x) = y$, 2nd pre-image resistance, i.e., from a given x with $h(x) = y$ it is not possible to compute $x' \in U, x' \neq x$ such that $h(x') = y$, and collision resistance, i.e., it is not possible to compute two strings $x, x' \in U, x' \neq x$ such that $h(x) = h(x')$. Examples of cryptographic hash functions are MD5 (message digest 5) [4], now outdated, and SHA-3 (secure hash algorithm 3) [5], the current standard for cryptographic hashing, based on the KECCAK hash function [6]. As $R \subset U$, a hash function can be applied repeatedly, i.e., for a seed $x_0 = s$, we can compute $x_{i+1} = h(x_i)$ for $i = 0, 1, 2, \ldots, n-1$. This sequence is called a hash chain. While it is easy to compute a hash chain in a forward direction, it cannot be computed in a backward direction, starting from x_n, because of the pre-image resistance property.

A one-time password (OTP) is a password only used once to authenticate an entity. As such, it is secure as long as it is secret and cannot be guessed prior to its use. Lamport [2] presented a scheme to generate OTPs from a hash function with pre-image resistance. Entity A uses a random and secret seed s to compute a hash chain $x_0, \ldots, x_n$, and transfers x_n to entity B via a secure channel. To authenticate, A sends $z = x_{n-1}$ over an insecure channel to B. B checks if $h(z) = x_n$. If yes, the authentication is approved, and B replaces x_n by $z = x_{n-1}$. If not, authentication has failed. For the next authentication, A sends $z = x_{n-2}$, and so on. Each password is only used once, and by the pre-image resistance, the next password cannot be guessed from the previous password. In addition, B need not keep x_n secret, as nothing can be inferred from this value. Haller's S/Key [7] and the TESLA protocol [8] use similar ideas.

A covert channel, as one form of steganography, defines a parasitic communication channel nested inside a computing environment that allows at least two different legitimate processes (or nodes) to access a shared resource. The covert channel exploits the legitimate processes in a way that allows the signaling of hidden information via the shared resource. The sender and receiver of a covert channel are called covert sender (CS) and covert receiver (CR), respectively. CS and CR are not necessarily identical with the overt sender and overt receiver (OS and OR) as CS and CR might act in an indirect manner or as a man-in-the-middle. Covert channels inside computer networks follow a set of known hiding patterns [9] to transfer information, e.g., by placing secret data inside unused or reserved header bits of network packets, by modifying header fields with random values, or by modulating the timings between succeeding network packets.

Reversible steganography allows the reconstruction of the original carrier message to the state *before* the steganographic data was embedded. For instance, it would allow *an original image to be completely restored after the extraction of hidden data embedded in a cover image* [10]. In man-in-the-middle scenarios, reversibility enables covert receivers to forward non-modified, i.e., innocent, original data to the covert receiver. As shown by Mazurczyk et al., reversibility is feasible for network covert channels: *full* reversibility refers to covert channels where the original carrier data can be restored completely, while *quasi*-reversibility refers to those covert channels that allow only the partial reconstruction of the original data [11]. Different categories of reversible data hiding are feasible. In our case, *intrinsic* data-hiding is applied, in which the covert receiver is able to achieve full reversibility without guessing (*implicit* reversibility techniques) or embedding of additional information that describe the original message (*explicit* reversibility techniques) [11].

Plausible deniability for a synthetic record is achieved when *there exists a set of real data records that could have generated the same synthetic data with (more or less) the same probability by which it was generated from its own seed* [12]. Plausible deniability is usually achieved by replacing pseudo-random data with encrypted covert data that also appear pseudo-random. Sometimes, it is also achieved by nesting secret information inside multiple layers of hidden information, where the surrounding layer is revealed to an observer in order to show cooperation. For instance, a steganographic filesystem might contain multiple layers of steganographic filesystems nested inside each other. Only outer layers are revealed to a warden while inner layers remain hidden.

2.2. Related Work

Covert channels have been proposed for several domains. For instance, Carrara and Adams surveyed out-of-band covert channels over physical media, such as light, sound and air [13] while other authors analyzed details of such channels, e.g., Hanspach and Goetz [14], Cronin et al. [15] and Matyunin et al. [16]. Network covert channel techniques have been summarized by Mazurczyk et al. [17], Wendzel et al. [9] and Zander et al. [18]. Detailed studies of specific network covert channels and their countermeasures were performed by Cabuk et al. [19], Xing et al. [20], Saenger et al. [21], Zander et al. [22] and Zhang et al. [23], just to mention a few. Further, several local covert channels have been studied, e.g., on smartphones by Mazurczyk et al. [24] and Urbanski et al. [25], in the architecture of processors by Wang and Lee [26], as well as in real-time schedulers by Chen et al. [27]. Most recently, covert channels in the Internet of Things has gained increasing attention, cf. works by Mileva et al. [28], Wendzel et al. [29] and Hildebrandt et al. [30].

Calhoun et al. [31] described a covert channel in which OTPs are used as an element for generating random data for a covert channel that exploits rate switching in 802.11 b WiFi networks. In comparison, our approach allows an Internet-wide application that is not limited to wireless environments. Moreover, our approach represents an indirect covert channel based on hash chain exploitation. To the best of our knowledge, no other covert channel has been published that exploits cryptographic hash chains.

Plausible deniability for steganography has been proposed by several authors, especially for filesystems (e.g., [32]). In the context of video streams, PRNG-output was utilized [33]. Rutkowska published a covert channel that embeds DES-encrypted data into third-party TCP initial sequence numbers (ISN) [34]. However, Murdoch and Lewies have shown that the channel by Rutkowska is detectable, since the distribution of ISN values does not match the distribution of DES-encrypted covert data [35]. Abad [36] presents a covert channel in the check sum of IP packets, which, however, does not use a cryptographic hash function.

Several methods for reversibility analysis of network covert channels have been studied by Mazurczyk et al. [11], while earlier works studied reversibility in digital media steganography, e.g., Chang and Lin in [10,37].

The remainder of this paper is structured as follows. Our two covert channels based on hash chains are introduced in Section 3. We discuss countermeasures for our covert channels in Section 4 and evaluate the performance and stealthiness characteristics of our channels in Section 5. Section 6 concludes and provides an outlook on future work.

3. Covert Channels in Hash Chains

We present multiple variants of a covert channel that can be used in OTPs based on hash chains. We assume that each hash value is transmitted as part of network packets between A and B, so that a modification of the hash value by CS can be hidden by re-computing the packet's check sum. The information flow would be $A \to CS \to CR \to B$. In such a case, our channel assumes a man-in-the-middle scenario. Alternatively, A and CS can be the same entity while B and CR can also be the same entity. However, our covert channel would also function if A and B are local processes inside an operating system, while CS and CR are part of an inter-process communication between A and B, or when A and B are CPS or IoT devices.

3.1. Channel Characteristics

Our channel has certain features that are traditionally used to categorize and describe covert channels:

1. Our channel variants allow *plausible deniability* as they replace selected bits of hash values in a pseudo-random manner so that the probability distribution of original and modified hash values are similar.
2. If CR is not just a passive observer but a hop on the path to B, CR is able to reconstruct the original hash value and can thus forward the illicit original message to B, rendering our approach *reversible*. This is feasible if, for example, B is a routing hop on a program in an IPC-chain between A and B. Due to the fact that we achieve full reversibility and do not exploit implicit or explicit reversibility methods, our technique is an *intrinsic* reversibility method.
3. Finally, our channel does not rely on indirect signaling methods, which makes it a *direct* covert channel. However, if CS applied a method to indirectly influence the transferred hash value, our channel would be a semi-passive one, while it would also be passive (indirect) if CR indirectly obtained the sent hash value (e.g., using a side channel) [38].
4. It does not matter for our covert channel whether the hash value is transmitted over a network or between local processes. The hash value can also be stored in a file at some point in time and then read later by another process, i.e., sender and receiver processes must not necessarily be active at the same time. However, in practice, most authentication scenarios would require A and B to be active simultaneously.

3.2. Covert Channel Variants

The secret message that CS wants to send is broken into t symbols from an alphabet $V = \{0, 1, \ldots, v-1\}$, i.e., the message comprises at most $l = \lfloor t \log_2 v \rfloor$ bits.

To embed a symbol $s_j \in V$ into a password x_i that is going to be transmitted, CS modifies the password by applying a transformation $T : R \times V \to R$, i.e., replaces x_i by a different password $x'_i = T(x_i, s_j)$. In the following, we will mostly use the notation $T_{s_j}(x_i)$ instead.

This password is intercepted by CR, who knows the previous password x_{i+1}. CR first tests if $h(x'_i) = x_{i+1}$. In that case, no symbol has been embedded and $x_i = x'_i$. Otherwise, for each possible symbol s, CR applies T_s^{-1} to x'_i and checks if hashing produces x_{i+1}. CR stops with the first hit, extracts symbol s_j of the secret message, and forwards the original password $x_i = T_{s_j}^{-1}(x'_i)$ to B.

Embedding is repeated until the complete message is transmitted. This requires that the number of symbols in the message is $t < n$, as we do not embed a symbol in the first password x_{n-1} to enable reversibility (see below).

The extracting procedure requires that T is injective in each argument, and that $T_s(x) \neq x$.

To implement T, we identify V with a subset of size v of $R = \{0,1\}^m$, and define $T_{s_j}(x) = x \oplus s_j$, where $\oplus$ denotes the bitwise exclusive OR operation. Then T is self-inverse, i.e., $T_s^{-1} = T_s$. An upper bound for $v = |V|$ is $2^m - 1 = |R \setminus \{00\cdots 0\}|$, so that the message might comprise up to $l = \lfloor (n-1) \log_2 (2^m - 1) \rfloor$ bits, i.e., almost $n \cdot m$ bits can be transmitted.

A first variant is found by defining set V of size $v = m$ comprising all m-bit strings with exactly one bit set to 1, i.e., embedding symbol s_j means to flip bit j of the password to be transmitted. We illustrate this variant in Figure 1.

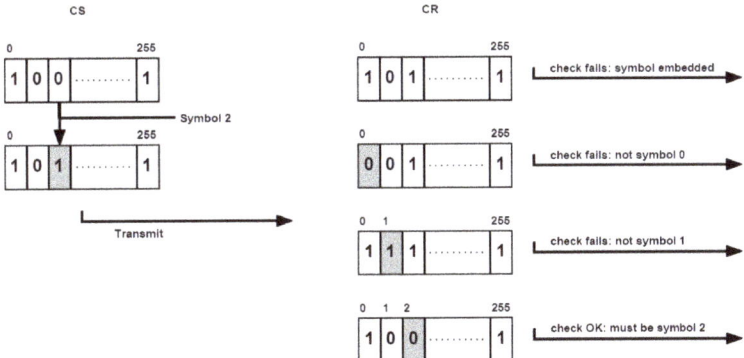

Figure 1. Example of variant 1. Covert sender (CS) embeds symbol 2 by flipping bit 2 of a password. Covert receiver (CR) first tries out which bit of the transmitted password must be flipped so that the check is successful, i.e., that its hash corresponds to the password stored at CR. Thus CR extracts symbol 2.

A much more restrictive variant could embed only one bit per password, e.g., by using $V = \{100\cdot 0, 010\cdot 0\}$. Please note that when a symbol is embedded in each password (except x_{n-1}), then we might even use $V = \{000\cdot 0, 100\cdot 0\}$, i.e., flipping bit 0 of the password only when a 1 is embedded, and leaving the password unmodified for embedding 0.

More liberal variants are also possible, e.g., defining V as the set of strings with one or two bits set to 1, resulting in $v = \binom{m}{1} + \binom{m}{2} = m(m+1)/2$, or taking all strings with at least $m/2$ bits set to 1, so that

$$v = |V| = \sum_{k=m/2}^{m} \binom{m}{k} = 2^{m-1},$$

by applying the binomial theorem with $a = b = 1$ and taking the symmetry of binomials into account [39]. Those variants might be useful for cases where m is small, e.g., when hash chains of a small width are used in WSN networks [40].

In order to decouple the embedded symbols from the particular message, i.e., to get random-looking symbols, the message might be encrypted before embedding, using a stream cipher or a block cipher with a chaining method such as cipher block chaining (CBC), to avoid the case when two identical symbols result in two identical encrypted symbols [3]. While this may increase stealthiness during communication, the computational effort on the receiver side, which may also threaten stealthiness (see below), can alternatively be optimized by using an encoding based on the frequency of symbols: the symbol with the highest frequency gets a code symbol that is checked first by CR, and so on. When using the frequencies of letters a to z in English texts from [41] and applying such coding, we get 7.5 evaluations on average, compared to 13 if symbols are encrypted and considered equi-probable.

Furthermore, if $t < n - 1$ symbols are embedded, we have the freedom to choose which of the $n - 1$ passwords are used for embedding, resulting in $\binom{n-1}{t}$ possibilities, and increasing stealthiness if not all passwords can be controlled by a warden.

Finally, the transformation function T might depend on i and/or on the index of the symbol to be embedded. For example, if we only embed one bit per password, we might modify bits $i \bmod m$ or $(i+1) \bmod m$ of x_i to embed symbols 0 and 1, respectively, instead of always using the same bit positions.

3.3. Hiding Pattern-Based Categorization

All variants perform a manipulation of (pseudo-)random packet fields as described by the *random value* pattern [9]. The random value pattern covers all hiding techniques that replace a legitimate (pseudo-)random bit string with a covert bit string that also follows a random distribution. Random value techniques have been implemented by several authors, rendering our proposed covert channel variants applicable in realistic environments. Moreover, such random values can be found in many network protocols, such as the IPID field in IPv4 or the ISN field in TCP.

On the sender side, the variants have very low effort and are thus hardly detectable. During transmission, an isolated packet will look innocent, as the one-time passwords look like random bitstrings, so that a possible bit flip is not likely to leave any trace or signature. Hence, detection during transmission seems non-trivial.

4. Countermeasures

Before experimentally evaluating our proposed channel, we first consider a broader set of potential countermeasures.

Note that in all variants, CR needs no knowledge of x_n stored by B. In the first transmitted password x_{n-1}, no symbol is transmitted. Then CR knows x_{n-1} when intercepting and forwarding that password, and can refer to it later on, duplicating B's work.

Variants that embed more symbols per password might be detectable more easily on the receiver side, as they encompass more evaluations of h. For example, the variant that embeds one of $v = m$ symbols by flipping one bit needs $m/2$ evaluations on average if symbols are equidistributed, which is the case if they are encrypted. This is a notable amount of computation if we consider that m might be 128 (MD5) or 512 (SHA-3). Yet those variants also have higher steganographic bandwidth.

Possible countermeasures on the receiver side, i.e., checking for unusual timing or energy due to repeated evaluation of the hash function, have been described in the previous section. However, they apply mostly if CR resides with the overt receiver (a similar scenario for energy-consumption-based covert channel detection has been proven to be feasible by Caviglione et al. [42]). If we have a man-in-the-middle scenario, only a jitter in transmission time from overt sender to overt receiver might be detectable.

Countermeasures during transmission are possible if a warden has knowledge of two successive packets with passwords x'_i and x'_{i-1}, i.e., has some knowledge of the application logic behind the packets. In this case, the warden can check if $h(x'_{i-1}) = x'_i$. If either password has been modified by CS, this equality will most likely not hold because of the hash function's collision resistance properties.

If the warden has only superficial knowledge of the application, i.e., knows only that the transmitted password must be a random bitstring, the warden can collect some passwords and submit them to a random number test suite such as Diehard [43] or NIST's suite [44]. If embedding of symbols creates artefacts, then the randomness should decrease if a CC is active. However, the test suites require a notable amount of bits to run, which might not be available, or take very long to collect. Thus, this might be an ex post analysis. Furthermore, if the set of code words V is a randomly chosen subset of R, and/or the symbols to be embedded are chosen in a quasi-random manner, e.g., by using encryption first, then the bitwise exclusive OR of two random bit strings might not be distinguishable.

Another possible countermeasure would be that A and B modify the passwords themselves, in a way that is not foreseeable by CS or CR. When A is about to send x_i, it already has knowledge about the following password x_{i-1}. Let us assume that both A and B have knowledge of a hash function $g : \{0,1\}^m \rightarrow \{0,1\}$. If $g(x_{i-1}) = 0$, then A sends x_i. If $g(x_{i-1}) = 1$, then A sends $\overline{x_i}$, i.e., x_i with all bits inverted. If g is a good hash function, then the second possibility will occur half of the time. If B receives a password x'_i, then it checks if either $h(x'_i)$ or $h(\overline{x'_i})$ equals x_{i+1}. In the latter case, B stores $\overline{x'_i}$.

As only two instead of one password value will be accepted, this scheme is still secure. But life is now more complicated for CR. It must now compare the four possible combinations of inverted and non-inverted passwords, i.e., its effort is notably increased, and stealthiness thus reduced. More complicated schemes are possible. Even if they are not preventing this covert channel, they can restrict bandwidth and/or can reduce stealthiness by forcing CR to perform more computation.

5. Experiments

We have implemented one variant of our covert channel in a hypothetical system that uses one-time passwords based on hash chains with cryptographic hash functions MD5 ($m = 128$) and SHA-3 ($m = 256$). The implementation was done in C, and we used existing open-source implementations for the cryptographic hash functions. For MD5, we used Peter Deutsch's 1999 free implementation that is based on the RFC 1321 specification [4] but does not use the reference implementation given there. For SHA-3 we used Andrey Jivsov's 2015 code from brainhub.org. As the system is not doing any real application, we implemented client and server, i.e., overt sender and receiver, together with CS and CR in one thread on the same computer, so that they transfer passwords through memory instead of an insecure network. In addition, client and server do no work besides computation of passwords. Hence, this implementation can be considered an extreme test with respect to stealthiness. The covert sender and receiver are placed directly with the client (sender) and server (receiver).

The covert channel transfers a null-terminated character string. We use $v = 64$ symbols with the following coding. Lower case letters are converted into upper case letters. ASCII characters 1 to 31 and from 95 onward are converted to blanks (ASCII character 32). ASCII characters 32 to 94, comprising upper case letters, digits and some punctuation marks, are converted to symbols 0 to 62, and ASCII character 0 (termination symbol) is converted to symbol 63. Please note that for the purpose of embedding into the binary hash value, we denote by symbol i a bit string of length m where only bit i is set to 1.

If encryption is used, then we employ a stream cipher that produces key stream symbols in the range 0 to 62, and encrypt by adding symbol and key symbol modulo 63, while termination symbol 63 remains unaltered. As the stream cipher, we employ the same cryptographic hash function as used in the OTP application. The seed is the cryptographic key, and we repeatedly hash. The bytes from the produced hash values are taken as modulo 63 and used as key stream symbols.

All experiments were performed on a Dell Latitude 5500 notebook with an Intel Core i5-8265U CPU at 1.6 GHz and 8 Gibibytes of main memory, running a Windows 10 operating system. We used gcc version 9.2.0 as the compiler, without activating optimizations.

5.1. Performance

To measure the performance impact of the covert channel, especially on the receiver, we use a hash chain of length $n = 16{,}384$ and a string of length $t = 16{,}382$ (plus termination symbol), i.e., we embed a symbol in each password except the first. As seed s, we use the string *Wonderful seed for Hash Chain*. As the secret message, we use a string solely comprising the repeated letter '?' (symbol 31). As the cryptographic key, we use the same string as for the seed.

The secret message is chosen such that, no matter if we use encryption or not, the number of hash function evaluations by CR is 32 (on average if encryption is used, with standard deviation 18), as we use only 63 of the 64 possible symbols during the message, and can ignore the influence for recognizing the last symbol because of the message length.

The results can be seen in Table 1. If a CC is used, the runtime is notably higher than without, while the runtimes for CC with encryption only marginally deviate from runtimes for CC without encryption. The difference between runtimes with and without CC, divided by $32 \cdot n$, amounts to 0.63 µs and 12.1 µs per evaluation of MD5 and SHA-3, respectively, which, multiplied by n, amounts to about half the runtime without CC.

Table 1. Runtime results of performance test.

OTP Hash Function	Without CC	With CC	With CC and Encrypt.
MD5	0.019 s	0.350 s	0.349 s
SHA-3	0.386 s	6.737 s	6.803 s

5.2. Randomness

To test if the covert channel can be detected by using a random number test suite, the exchanged passwords (with or without CC) were collected into a file of 256 kibibytes (MD5) or 512 kibibytes (SHA-3), respectively. Then we submitted the files to the NIST [44] suite. The results from test 1 of the NIST suite (frequency of zeroes and ones should be close to 0.5 for each), given as p-values, can be seen in Table 2. As the p-values are close to 1, all sequences seem random.

Table 2. p-values from NIST frequency test.

OTP Hash Function	Without CC	With CC	With CC and Encrypt.
MD5	0.968052	0.973558	0.986777
SHA-3	0.864040	0.905754	0.864040

Yet already the results from test 2 (cumulative sums) differ for the sequences, cf. Table 3. Thus we conclude that at least the CC without encryption might be detectable. This hope is fostered because in total 15 tests are available in the NIST suite, so there are more chances to detect CCs than we have explored. However, there is also a downside. Some of the tests need much more data than we provided, and already these data might need a long time to be collected. If we imagine that each minute an authentication takes place, then 11.3 days are needed to collect the data. Indeed, this assumption is only valid if authentications take place during night and day without any interruption or reduction of frequency. If limited to eight-hour working days Monday to Friday, it would take almost 7 weeks instead. Thus we have a tradeoff between chance of detection and time to detection.

Table 3. p-values from NIST cumulative sums test, averaged between forward and reverse tests.

OTP Hash Function	Without CC	With CC	With CC and Encrypt.
MD5	0.8212000	0.7555420	0.8038680
SHA-3	0.6928455	0.6198775	0.6928455

5.3. Detectability

If a warden would be capable of observing the originally generated as well as the transmitted hash values, it could compare both values. We assume that such a scenario is rather unlikely but it is of theoretical interest in order to determine the detectability of our channels.

We used the same covert channel as before, but the message comprised $t = 16{,}382$ letters "A" plus the termination symbol.

As shown in Figure 2, the differences between the covert channel without encryption (denoted as *simple*) and the legitimate hash values are only visually recognizable if a suitable visualization method (in our case: differences modulo 8) is selected (in large hash values of e.g., 512 bit size, a (randomized) modification of the least significant bits would be invisible on charts that cover the whole range of hash values). The encrypted covert channel's values (denoted as *improved*) match those of the legitimate traffic.

However, both covert channels' hash values are barely distinguishable from legitimate values if the original traffic is not available. Several hash values of both channels are either close to (and a few matching) the legitimate values (*simple* channel) or partially close and mostly matching (*improved* channel) while following a pseudo-random distribution typical for hash values. In our tests, approx. 6.7% of the modulo results of the *improved* channel did not match those of the legitimate traffic while all other values matched exactly.

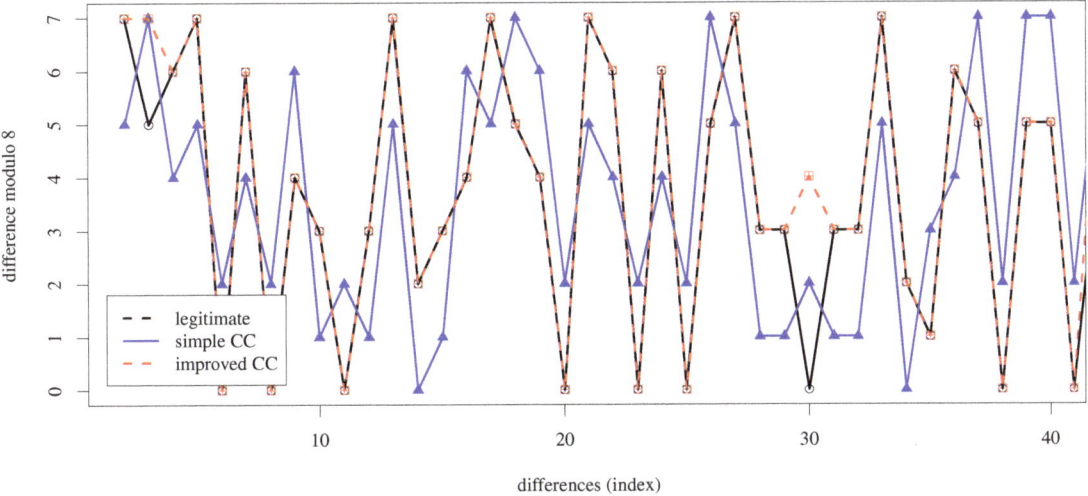

Figure 2. Differences between consecutive hash values for legitimate hash chains and covert channel with and without encryption, denoted as improved and simple, respectively.

6. Conclusions

Hash chains are an important element of today's inter-networked computing systems and are found, for example, in cryptocurrencies and authentication systems. For this reason, the exploitation of hash chains for covert channels is an attractive goal for attackers in several domains. We have presented the first covert channel in hash chains that is plausibly deniable and reversible. We have detailed how to create variants that differ in steganographic bandwidth and stealthiness. We have also presented non-trivial countermeasures against such a covert channel. Our experiments have shown that our channel might be detectable under realistic conditions only if no encryption is applied and authentication data are collected over a longer time-span. Thus, there are limitations both to the use of the covert channel—short-term only—and to the detection or limitation capabilities. The exact time spans will depend on the particular variant of the covert channel deployed, which in turn hangs on the width of the hash function used.

The covert channel has been presented in the context of network communication, yet it is not restricted to that. Instead of using network packets, the covert channel could also use a local system to break a security policy if A authenticates against B over an IPC path to which both CS and CR have access.

Future work will comprise further experiments, e.g., on other implementation variants, including the validation of countermeasures that can either prevent/limit or detect (e.g., with sophisticated machine learning methods) the proposed covert channels, and exploration of further application areas.

Author Contributions: The authors contributed equally to this work. All authors have read and agreed to the published version of the manuscript.

Funding: Jörg Keller's work is supported by the project *Secure Intelligent Methods for AdvancedReco Gnition of malware, stegomaLware & information hiding methods* (SIMARGL), https://simargl.eu), which has received funding from the European Union's Horizon 2020 research and innovation program under grant agreement No. 833042. Steffen Wendzel's work is partially supported by the project *Machine learning for Attack Detection using data of InduStriAl control systems* (MADISA), https://madisa.ztt.hs-worms.de funded by the European Union from the European Regional Development Fund (EFRE) and the State of Rhineland-Palatinate (MWWK ministry), Germany. Funding content: P1-SZ2-7 F&E: Wissens- u. Technologietransfer (WTT), Application No. 84003751.

Institutional Review Board Statement: Not applicable.

Informed Consent Statement: Not applicable.

Data Availability Statement: Data is contained within the article.

Conflicts of Interest: The authors declare no conflict of interest.

References

1. Lampson, B.W. A Note on the Confinement Problem. *Commun. ACM* **1973**, *16*, 613–615. [CrossRef]
2. Lamport, L. Password authentication with insecure communication. *Commun. ACM* **1981**, *24*, 770–772. [CrossRef]
3. Menezes, A.J.; van Oorschot, P.C.; Vanstone, S.A. *Handbook of Applied Cryptography*; CRC Press: Boca Raton, FL, USA, 1996.
4. Rivest, R. The MD5 Message-Digest Algorithm. In *Request for Comments (RFC) 1321*; Internet Engineering Task Force (IETF): Fremont, CA, USA, 1992.
5. National Institute of Standards and Technology (NIST). SHA-3 Standard: Permutation-Based Hash and Extendable-Output Functions. In *Federal Information Processing Standards Publication (FIPS PUB) 202*; NIST: Gaithersburg, MD, USA, 2015.
6. Bertoni, G.; Daemen, J.; Peeters, M.; Assche, G.V. The KECCAK reference, Version 3.0. *NIST SHA3 Submiss. Doc.* **2011**.
7. Haller, N. The S/KEY One-Time Password System. RFC 1760; RFC, Ed.; 1995. Available online: https://tools.ietf.org/html/rfc1760 (accessed on 13 January 2021).
8. Perrig, A.; Canetti, R.; Tygar, J.D.; Song, D. The TESLA Broadcast Authentication Protocol. *CryptoBytes* **2002**, *5*, 2–13.
9. Wendzel, S.; Zander, S.; Fechner, B.; Herdin, C. Pattern-Based Survey and Categorization of Network Covert Channel Techniques. *Comput. Surv.* **2015**, *47*. [CrossRef]
10. Chang, C.-C.; Lin, C.-Y. Reversible steganographic method using SMVQ approach based on declustering. *Inf. Sci.* **2007**, *177*, 1796–1805.
11. Mazurczyk, W.; Szary, P.; Wendzel, S.; Caviglione, L. Towards reversible storage network covert channels. In Proceedings of the 14th International Conference on Availability, Reliability and Security, Canterbury, UK, 26 August 2019; pp. 1–8.
12. Bindschaedler, V.; Shokri, R.; Gunter, C.A. Plausible deniability for privacy-preserving data synthesis. *arXiv* **2017**, arXiv:1708.07975.
13. Carrara, B.; Adams, C. Out-of-band covert channels—A survey. *ACM Comput. Surv. (CSUR)* **2016**, *49*, 1–36. [CrossRef]
14. Hanspach, M.; Goetz, M. On covert acoustical mesh networks in air. *arXiv* **2014**, arXiv:1406.1213.
15. Cronin, P.; Gouert, C.; Mouris, D.; Tsoutsos, N.G.; Yang, C. Covert Data Exfiltration Using Light and Power Channels. In Proceedings of the 2019 IEEE 37th International Conference on Computer Design (ICCD), Abu Dhabi, UAE, 17–20 November 2019; pp. 301–304.
16. Matyunin, N.; Szefer, J.; Biedermann, S.; Katzenbeisser, S. Covert channels using mobile device's magnetic field sensors. In Proceedings of the 2016 21st Asia and South Pacific Design Automation Conference (ASP-DAC), Macau, China, 25–28 January 2016; pp. 525–532.
17. Mazurczyk, W.; Wendzel, S.; Zander, S.; Houmansadr, A.; Szczypiorski, K. *Information Hiding in Communication Networks*; IEEE Series on Information and Communication Networks Security; Wiley: Hoboken, NJ, USA, 2016.
18. Zander, S.; Armitage, G.; Branch, P. A survey of covert channels and countermeasures in computer network protocols. *Comm. Surv. Tut.* **2007**, *9*, 44–57. [CrossRef]
19. Cabuk, S. Network Covert Channels: Design, Analysis, Detection, and Elimination. Ph.D. Thesis, Purdue University, West Lafayette, Indiana, 2006.
20. Xing, J.; Morrison, A.; Chen, A. NetWarden: Mitigating network covert channels without performance loss. In Proceedings of the 11th USENIX Workshop on Hot Topics in Cloud Computing (HotCloud 19), Renton, WA, USA, July 2019.

21. Saenger, J.; Mazurczyk, W.; Keller, J.; Caviglione, L. VoIP network covert channels to enhance privacy and information sharing. *Future Gener. Comput. Syst.* **2020**, *111*, 96–106. [CrossRef]
22. Zander, S.; Armitage, G.; Branch, P. Covert channels in the IP time to live field. In Proceedings of the Australian Telecommunication Networks and Application Conference (ATNAC), Melbourne, Australia, 4–6 December 2006.
23. Zhang, X.; Guo, L.; Xue, Y.; Zhang, Q. A two-way VoLTE covert channel with feedback adaptive to mobile network environment. *IEEE Access* **2019**, *7*, 122214–122223. [CrossRef]
24. Mazurczyk, W.; Caviglione, L. Steganography in modern smartphones and mitigation techniques. *IEEE Commun. Surv. Tutor.* **2014**, *17*, 334–357. [CrossRef]
25. Urbanski, M.; Mazurczyk, W.; Lalande, J.F.; Caviglione, L. Detecting local covert channels using process activity correlation on android smartphones. *Int. J. Comput. Syst. Sci. Eng.* **2017**, *32*, 71–80.
26. Wang, Z.; Lee, R.B. Covert and side channels due to processor architecture. In Proceedings of the 2006 22nd Annual Computer Security Applications Conference (ACSAC'06), Miami Beach, FL, USA, 11–15 December 2006; pp. 473–482.
27. Chen, C.Y.; Mohan, S.; Pellizzoni, R.; Bobba, R.B.; Kiyavash, N. A Novel Side-Channel in Real-Time Schedulers. In Proceedings of the 2019 IEEE Real-Time and Embedded Technology and Applications Symposium (RTAS), Montreal, QC, Canada, 16–18 April 2019; pp. 90–102.
28. Mileva, A.; Velinov, A.; Stojanov, D. New Covert Channels in Internet of Things. In Proceedings of the Twelfth International Conference on Emerging Security Information, Systems and Technologies (SECURWARE), Venice, Italy, 16–20 September 2018; pp. 30–36.
29. Wendzel, S.; Mazurczyk, W.; Haas, G. Steganography for cyber-physical systems. *J. Cyber Secur. Mobil.* **2017**, *6*, 105–126. [CrossRef]
30. Hildebrandt, M.; Lamshöft, K.; Dittmann, J.; Neubert, T.; Vielhauer, C. Information Hiding in Industrial Control Systems: An OPC UA based Supply Chain Attack and its Detection. In Proceedings of the 2020 ACM Workshop on Information Hiding and Multimedia Security, Denver, CO, USA, 22 June 2020; pp. 115–120.
31. Calhoun, T.E., Jr.; Cao, X.; Li, Y.; Beyah, R. An 802.11 MAC layer covert channel. *Wirel. Commun. Mob. Comput.* **2012**, *12*, 393–405. [CrossRef]
32. Anderson, R.; Needham, R.; Shamir, A. The steganographic file system. In *International Workshop on Information Hiding*; Springer: Berlin/Heidelberg, Germany, 1998; pp. 73–82.
33. Craver, S.; Li, E.; Yu, J. Protocols for data hiding in pseudo-random state. In *Media Forensics and Security*; International Society for Optics and Photonics: Bellingham, WA, USA, 2009; Volume 7254.
34. Rutkowska, J. Passive Covert Channels Implementation in Linux Kernel. In Proceedings of the 21st Chaos Communications Congress, Berlin, Germany, 27–29 December 2004.
35. Murdoch, S.J.; Lewis, S. Embedding covert channels into TCP/IP. In *International Workshop on Information Hiding*; Springer: Berlin/Heidelberg, Germany, 2005; pp. 247–261.
36. Abad, C. *IP Checksum Covert Channels and Selected Hash Collision*; Technical Report; Univ. of California: Los Angeles, CA, USA, 2001.
37. Chang, C.C.; Lin, C.Y. Reversible steganography for VQ-compressed images using side matching and relocation. *IEEE Trans. Inf. Forensics Secur.* **2006**, *1*, 493–501. [CrossRef]
38. Dittmann, J.; Hesse, D.; Hillert, R. Steganography and steganalysis in voice-over IP scenarios: Operational aspects and first experiences with a new steganalysis tool set. In *Security, Steganography, and Watermarking of Multimedia Contents VII*; International Society for Optics and Photonics: Bellingham, WA, USA, 2005; Volume 5681, pp. 607–618.
39. Graham, R.L.; Knuth, D.E.; Patashnik, O. *Concrete Mathematics*, 2nd ed.; Addison-Wesley: Reading, MA, USA, 1994.
40. Ugus, O.; Westhoff, D.; Bohli, J. A ROM-friendly secure code update mechanism for WSNs using a stateful-verifier tau-time signature scheme. In Proceedings of the Second ACM Conference on Wireless Network Security, WISEC 2009, Zurich, Switzerland, 16–19 March 2009; Basin, D.A., Capkun, S., Lee, W., Eds.; pp. 29–40. [CrossRef]
41. Lewand, R. *Cryptological Mathematics*; Mathematical Association of America: Washington, DC, USA, 2000.
42. Caviglione, L.; Gaggero, M.; Lalande, J.F.; Mazurczyk, W.; Urbański, M. Seeing the unseen: Revealing mobile malware hidden communications via energy consumption and artificial intelligence. *IEEE Trans. Inf. Forensics Secur. (TIFS)* **2015**, *11*, 799–810. [CrossRef]
43. Marsaglia, G. *The Marsaglia Random Number CDROM including the Diehard Battery of Tests of Randomness*; Technical Report; Florida State University: Tallahassee, FL, USA, 1995.
44. Rukhin, A.; Soto, J.; Nechvatal, J.; Smid, M.; Barker, E.; Leigh, S.; Levenson, M.; Vangel, M.; Banks, D.; Heckert, A.; et al. *A Statistical Test Suite for Random and Pseudorandom Number Generators for Cryptographic Applications*; Special Publication 800-22 Revision 1a; National Institute of Standards and Technology: Gaithersburg, MD, USA, 2010.

Article

An Adaptive Reversible Data Hiding Scheme Using AMBTC and Quantization Level Difference

Yan-Hong Chen [1], Chin-Chen Chang [2,3], Chia-Chen Lin [4,*] and Zhi-Ming Wang [2]

[1] School of Information, Zhejiang University of Finance & Economics, Hangzhou 310018, China; cyhong@zufe.edu.cn
[2] Department of Computer Science and Information Engineering, Feng Chia University, Taichung 407032, Taiwan; ccc@o365.fcu.edu.tw (C.-C.C.); zm.wang@fuho.com.tw (Z.-M.W.)
[3] School of Computer Science and Technology, Hangzhou Dianzi University, Hangzhou 310018, China
[4] Department of Computer Science and Information Engineering, National Chin-Yi University of Technology, Taichung 41170, Taiwan
* Correspondence: ally.cclin@ncut.edu.tw

Abstract: Hiding a message in compression codes can reduce transmission costs and simultaneously make the transmission more secure. This paper presents an adaptive reversible data hiding scheme that is able to provide large embedding capacity while improving the quantity of modified images. The proposed scheme employs the quantization level difference (QLD) and interpolation technique to adaptively embed the secret information into pixels of each absolute moment block truncation coding (AMBTC)-compressed block, except for the positions of two replaced quantization levels. The values of QLD tend to be much larger in complex areas than in smooth areas. In other words, our proposed method can obtain good performance for embedding capacity and still meets the requirement for better modified image quality when the image is complex. The performance of the proposed approach was compared to previous image hiding methods. The experimental results show that our approach outperforms referenced approaches.

Keywords: quantization level difference; AMBTC; reversible data hiding; high capacity

1. Introduction

With the rapid development of internet communication and computer technology, a large number of information is transmitted over the internet. When digital data are transmitted through the internet, some sensitive data may become vulnerable to the malicious users. Therefore, to ensure the security of the transmitted data, data owners either encrypt the transmitted data via traditional cryptographic algorithms or transfer data into an imperceptible way by using data hiding techniques [1]. In the last decade, multimedia-based transmission has become popular; as such, data hiding techniques are a secure and efficient method for such applications. Data hiding is a way to embed secret data into a digital cover media by modifying the original content, such that other users in a public network will not be aware of the existence of the embedded data. If malicious users have not noticed the transmitted data concealing confidential data, the safety of hidden data is guaranteed. Generally, a data hiding scheme can be divided into three categories, i.e., spatial domain, frequency domain, and compressed domain. The spatial domain method imparts some meaningful changes in the image pixels in order to embed information. The frequency domain method and compressed domain method embed the secret data into transformed coefficients and the compressed codes of digital images, respectively [2].

In order to transmit multimedia data efficiently on the internet, many researchers have proposed various compression methods to reduce the size of multimedia files, such as vector quantization (VQ) [3–5], discrete wavelet transform (DWT) [6–8], and discrete cosine transform (DCT) [9–11]. Qin et al. [3] proposed a data hiding scheme based on VQ compressed images and an index mapping mechanism. Ahmed et al. [6] proposed a data hiding method based on DWT. Their method hides a secret image inside a cover image by using two secret keys. Chang [11] et al. proposed a scheme to hide the secret information in the DCT coefficient domain. In this scheme, the image is divided into 8 × 8 blocks, where if two successive coefficients of the medium-frequency components are zero, the information is hidden in each block.

Block truncation coding (BTC) [12] is another efficient lossy block-based image compression technique. In recent years, many researchers have studied data hiding based on BTC and made improvements, such as absolute block truncation coding (AMBTC) [13], ordered dither block truncation coding (ODBTC) [14], error Diffusion Block truncation coding (EDBTC) [15], etc. BTC is characterized by low complexity and low memory, and thus it has become an ideal data hiding domain. Wu and Sun [16] presented a data hiding method in which each secret bit is embedded into the bitmap of the BTC compression codes. Kim [17] proposed a data hiding method for halftone compressed images based on ODBTC and exploiting modification direction (EMD). Guo et al. [18] introduced a data hiding scheme based on error-diffused BTC to embed an extremely large amount of watermarks without obviously damaging image quality. These methods are irreversible, and the host image is permanently altered and it cannot be recovered accurately after data extraction. However, in some applications such as medical image sharing, military image processing, remote sensing and multimedia archive management, the recovery of a host image is essential [19]. To address this problem, a reversible data hiding scheme [20] were proposed that can extract the hidden data and produce a lossless recovery of the cover image. As Zhao et al. mentioned [1], the key property of reversible data hiding is not only the secret data but also the host image can be accurately recovered in the recorder.

In 2008, Chang et al. [21] presented a reversible data hiding method aimed at BTC-compressed color images. In 2011, Li et al. [22] introduced a reversible image hiding based on the BTC-compressed approach. In this scheme, the histogram shifting and bitmap flipping technique were used to hide secret bits. In 2013, Sun et al. [23] introduced another reversible data hiding method for BTC-compressed using the joint neighbor coding technique. In 2015, Lin et al. [24] presented a reversible data hiding scheme for AMBTC-compressed images by combining secret bits with bitmap bits one by one.

In this paper, we propose an adaptive reversible data hiding scheme that is based on an AMBTC compression domain and quantization level difference. In this scheme, the cover image is compressed into corresponding quantizers and a bitmap image by absolute moment block truncation coding (AMBTC). Subsequently, a certain amount of the data bits will be embedded into this pixel according to the value of QLD. The rest of this paper consists of four sections: AMBTC's and Lin et al.'s methods are introduced in Section 2; the proposed algorithm is illustrated in Section 3; detailed experimental description and comparative analysis are provided in Section 4; and finally, the conclusions are offered in Section 5.

2. Related Work

2.1. Absolute Moment Block Truncation Coding (AMBTC)

As a variant of BTC, AMBTC was introduced by Lema and Mitchell [13] in 1984. During the encoding procedure, the algorithm divides the original image into a set of non-overlapped blocks with a size of $k \times k$. Assume that x_{ij} is the pixel value in location (i, j) of the block, the mean value u and its standard deviation α are computed by Equations (1) and (2), respectively.

$$u = \frac{1}{k \times k} \sum_{i=1}^{k} \sum_{j=1}^{k} x_{ij}, \tag{1}$$

$$\alpha = \sqrt{\frac{\sum_{j=1}^{k \times k} \left| x_{ij}^2 - u^2 \right|}{k \times k}}. \tag{2}$$

Then, each block is converted to two quantizers and a bitmap image bm. The two quantizers hm and lm for the block are computed by:

$$lm = u - \alpha\sqrt{\frac{q}{k \times k - q}}, \quad (3)$$

$$hm = u + \alpha\sqrt{\frac{k \times k - q}{q}}, \quad (4)$$

where q is the number of pixels that are greater than or equal to the mean value u. The bitmap $bm = \{m_{ij} | m_{ij} \in \{0,1\}, 1 \leq i, j \leq k\}$ is created as follows:

$$m_{ij} = \begin{cases} 1, & \text{if } x_{ij} \geq u \\ 0, & \text{if } x_{ij} < u. \end{cases} \quad (5)$$

Figure 1 shows an example to describe the procedures for the AMBTC scheme. Figure 1a shows the original image block of 4×4 pixels. Then, the block mean u and standard deviation α are computed, respectively, by using Equations (1) and (2). In this example, $u = 110$ and $\alpha = 10$. The bitmap generated by AMBTC is shown in Figure 1b. Finally, the quantization levels, namely lm and hm, are calculated by using Equations (3) and (4), respectively. Figure 1c shows the reconstructed image block.

108	97	112	98
123	115	125	103
125	115	108	87
110	130	115	86

(a) Original image block

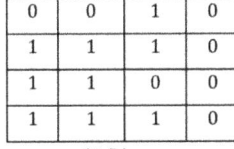

(b) Bitmap

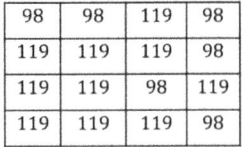

(c) Reconstructed image block

Figure 1. Example of absolute block truncation coding (AMBTC) encoding procedures.

2.2. AMBTC Scheme of Lin et al.'s Method

In 2015, Lin et al. presented a reversible data hiding scheme for AMBTC-compressed images by considering the mean value and the standard deviation to achieve a high payload and high-quality modified images. Following are details about the major steps of the embedding processing.

Step 1: Define three parameters, i.e., the bitmap bm, mean pixel value u and standard deviation α using Equations (1), (2) and (5), respectively.

Step 2: Define four different scenarios for each pixel of a given $k \times k$ block. As shown in Table 1, if the secret bit is "1", and the bit in bitmap is "0", then the corresponding scenario is "10" by combining secret bits with bits of the bitmap.

Table 1. Four scenarios for each pixel of a given block.

Scenario	Case00	Case01	Case10	Case11
secret bit	0	0	1	1
Bit in bitmap	0	1	0	1

Step 3: Determine the cover image block is embeddable or non-embeddable. If there are only one or two different scenarios, this cover block is a non-embeddable block. If the types of scenarios are equal to three or four, the cover is an embeddable block.

Step 4: Determine the hiding strategy. The detailed Algorithm 1 for hiding strategies is shown below.

Algorithm 1. Hiding strategy of Lin's method.

Input: current scenarios
Output: corresponding pixel value
cpv   *corresponding pixel value*
Switch(current scenarios){
        case00 : $cpv = u - \alpha$; *break*;
        case01 : $cpv = u + \alpha$; *break*;
        case10 : $cpv = u - \alpha - 1$; *break*;
        case11 : $cpv = u - \alpha + 1$; *break*;
}
return *cpv*;

Figure 2 shows an example of the strategy. Figure 2a shows the secret bits and the corresponding bitmap. Figure 2b shows a combination. There are four types of in this example. Figure 2c shows the result according to Algorithm 1.

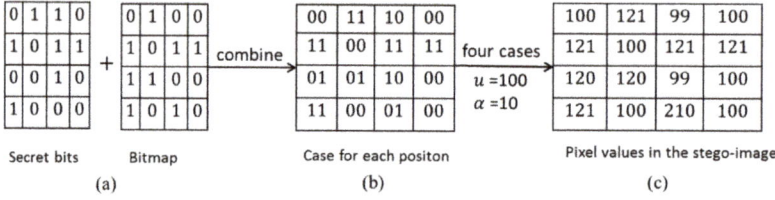

Figure 2. Example of Lin et al.'s hiding strategy.

3. The Proposed Scheme

This section may be divided by subheadings. It should provide a concise and precise description of the experimental results, their interpretation as well as the experimental conclusions that can be drawn. This section describes the details of our method. Our proposal utilizes an adaptive interpolation technique and AMBTC compression technique, to improve embedding capacity and image quality. As we utilize the difference of two quantization levels to adaptively embed the secret data into the cover image, our method can obtain a high embedding capacity. Moreover, our method still meets good image quality as we exploit the middle value of two quantization levels and the values of two thresholds to limit the shifting of values. The flowcharts of embedding and extraction phases for our proposed scheme are shown in Figures 3–6, respectively.

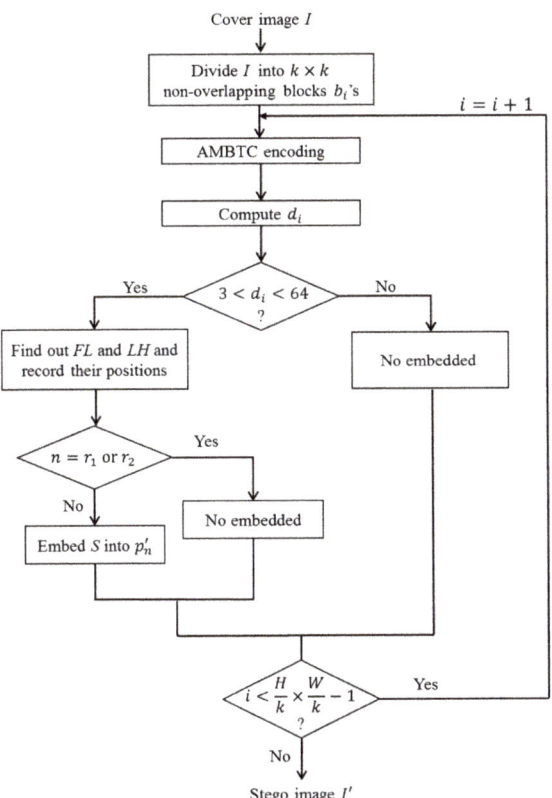

Figure 3. Flowchart of embedding phase.

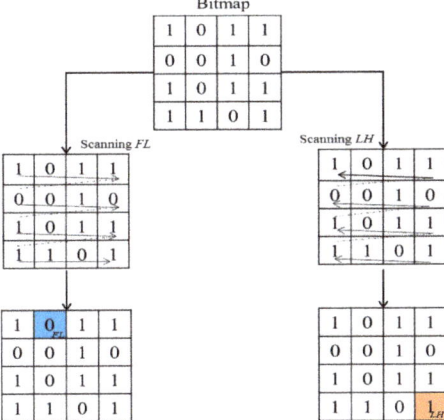

Figure 4. The example of FL and LH scanning.

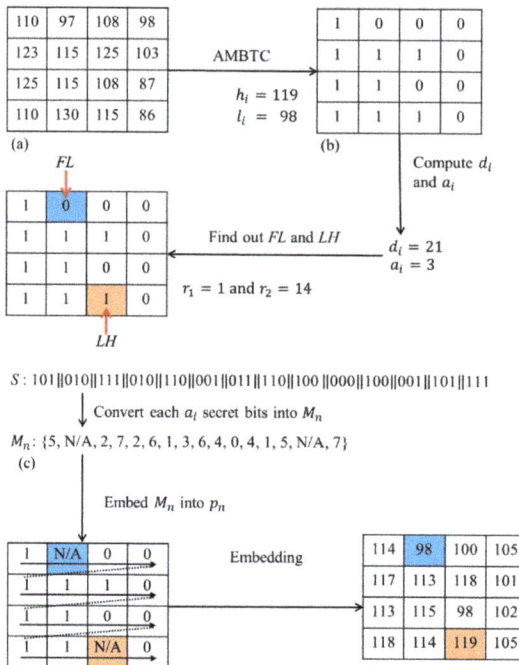

Figure 5. (**a**) Block b_i sized 4×4, (**b**) The bit map of block b_i, (**c**) Secret data S and (**d**) The modified block b'_i sized 4×4.

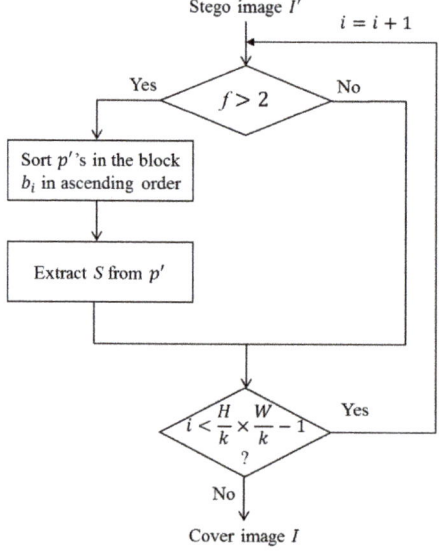

Figure 6. The flowchart of extraction and recovery phases.

3.1. Embedding Phase

The process of embedding phase is shown in Figure 3. Let I be an input cover image sized $H \times W$. Each block b_i is sized $k \times k$, where $i = 0, 1, \ldots, \frac{H}{k} \times \frac{W}{k} - 1$. Secret data S is a bit stream in binary form, and M_n is the decimal value of secret bits.

Input: Cover image I and secret data S.
Output: Modified image I'.
Step 1. Divide I into $k \times k$ non-overlapping blocks b_i's.
Step 2. Calculate the current processing block b_i using AMBTC algorithm.
Step 3. Compute d_i using Equation (6).

$$d_i = h_i - l_i, \tag{6}$$

where h_i and l_i are quantization levels of high value and low value, respectively.

Step 4. Determine the value of d_i. If $3 < d_i < 64$, go to Step 5. Otherwise, go to Step 7.

Here, if d_i is smaller than 3, the secret data cannot be extracted because of the middle value of two quantization levels could not be determined. For example, the values of h_i and l_i are 9 and 7, respectively. We cannot know whether the modified pixel value p'_n is $h_i - 1$ or $l_i + 1$ while p'_n is 8. Therefore, d_i must be greater than 3. And if d_i is greater than 63, it may cause a problem where the difference of the current processing block and its neighbor blocks are very large. As such, d_i should be smaller than 63.

Step 5. Find out the first $bp_n = 0$ (FL) and the last $bp_n = 1$ (LH) in the bitmap, where bp_n is the presented value in the bitmap and $n = 0, 1, \ldots, k \times k - 1$. FL and LH are the first value 0 and the last value 1 in the bitmap, respectively. The locations of FL and LH are r_1 and r_2, respectively, where r_1 and r_2 are $0, 1, \ldots$ or $k \times k - 1$. We show an example in Figure 4 to describe in detail the process of scanning FL and LH.

Step 6. Compute the value of a_i using Equation (7). Then, embed the M_n into each p_n using Equation (8),

$$a_i = \left\lfloor \log_2\left(\frac{d_i}{2}\right) \right\rfloor, \tag{7}$$

$$p'_n = \begin{cases} h_i, & \text{if } n = r_2 \\ l_i, & \text{if } n = r_1 \\ h_i - M_n, & \text{if } bp_n = 1 \text{ and } n \neq r_1 \text{ or } r_2 \\ l_i + M_n, & \text{if } bp_n = 0 \text{ and } n \neq r_1 \text{ or } r_2, \end{cases} \tag{8}$$

where M_n is the decimal value of the next a_i secret bits to be embedded, p_n is the pixel value in the block b_i and p'_n is the modified pixel value in the modified block.

Step 7. Modify the value of each p_n in block b_i using Equation (9) that no secret data are embedded.

$$p'_n = \begin{cases} h_i, & \text{if } bp_n = 1 \\ l_i, & \text{if } bp_n = 0. \end{cases} \tag{9}$$

Step 8. Repeat Step 2 to Step 7 until all blocks b_i's are processed.
Step 9. Obtain modified image I'.

We can get modified image I' when all steps are finished. We provide an example to further clarify our embedding process in Figure 5. In Figure 5, (a) shows an example of a 4×4 sized block b_i, (b) is the bitmap of block b_i, (c) presents secret data S and the decimal value M_n of each a_i secret bits and (d) shows the final result of modified image I'. In the first step, utilize the AMBTC algorithm to compute the block b_i and obtain two quantization levels l_i and h_i. As a_i is 3, S will be partitioned into multiple groups and each group contains three secret bits. Then, convert each group of a_i secret bits into decimal value M_n. The positions of r_1 and r_2 are utilized to substitute the values of l_i and h_i, respectively. Moreover, no secret bits are embedded in them. As such M_{r_1} and M_{r_2}, we use N/A to represent. In the next step, embed M_n into each p_n using Equation (8). And finally, S can be embedded into the block b_i and obtain the modified block b'_i.

3.2. Extraction and Recovery Phase

The processes for the extraction and recovery phases are shown in Figure 6. S will be extracted from modified image I'. When the block b_i belongs to a non-embedding case, there are only two values in it. Therefore, we do not need any extra information to record whether this block has secret data or not.

Input: Modified image I'.
Output: Secret data S and the cover image I.
Step 1. Divide I' into $k \times k$ non-overlapping blocks b_i'''s.
Step 2. Calculate the frequency f of the number of different pixels in the current processing block b_i'. The Algorithm 2 is described as follows.

Algorithm 2. Procedure for calculating the frequency.

Output: Frequency f
    for $i = 0$ to $k \times k - 1$. **do**
        if $p'_{i+1} \neq p'_{0,1,\ldots j}$. then
            $f = f + 1$;
        endif
        j++;
    end for

Step 3. Determine the value of f. If $f > 2$, go to step 4. Otherwise, go back to Step 2.

Step 4. Sort all p'_n's in the block b_i' in ascending order. The first and last values in the sorted sequence are l_i and h_i, respectively. And the positions of l_i and h_i are r_1 and r_2, respectively.

Step 5. Compute the values of d_i and a_i utilizing Equations (6) and (7), respectively. Extract the secret data from p'_n's using Equation (10).

$$M_n = \begin{cases} h_i - p'_n, & \text{if } p'_n > \frac{l_i + h_i}{2} \text{ and } n \neq r_1 \text{ or } r_2 \\ p'_n - l_i, & \text{if } p'_n < \frac{l_i + h_i}{2} \text{ and } n \neq r_1 \text{ or } r_2 \end{cases}. \quad (10)$$

Then, convert M_n into a_i secret bits and add in S.
Step 6. Recover block b_i' using Equation (11).

$$p_n = \begin{cases} h_i, & \text{if } p'_n > \frac{l_i + h_i}{2} \\ l_i, & \text{if } p'_n < \frac{l_i + h_i}{2} \end{cases}. \quad (11)$$

Step 7. Repeat Step 2 to Step 6 until all modified blocks b_i'''s are processed.
Step 8. Obtain the cover image I and secret data S.

After all steps are computed, we can extract S from modified block b_i' and recover each b_i' using min$\{p'_n\}$ and max$\{p'_n\}$ after sorting. We used l_i and h_i to replace the positions of FL and LH, respectively. This allows us to know l_i and h_i utilizing the ascending order of all p'_n's in modified block b_i' while extracting. This approach can avoid the problem when the value of M_n is 0. We also provide a detailed example of the extraction and recovery phases in Figure 7. In Figure 7, (a) presents the modified block b_i' that follows the previous example in Figure 5, (b) shows the results of extracted M_n and S in binary form and (c) is the resulting block b_i after recovery. Firstly, calculate the frequency f and determine whether the value of f is greater than 2. Then, all p'_n's in the modified block b_i' will be sorted in ascending order. The first and last values are l_i and h_i, respectively. According to the first and last values in a sorted sequence corresponding positions in modified block b_i', the positions of r_1 and r_2 are 1 and 14, respectively. Next step, M_n will be extracted from modified block b_i' using Equation (8). Each M_n will be converted into a_i secret bits and added in the S. In the last step, recover each p'_n using Equation (9). Finally, we can get block b_i and extract S from the modified block b_i'.

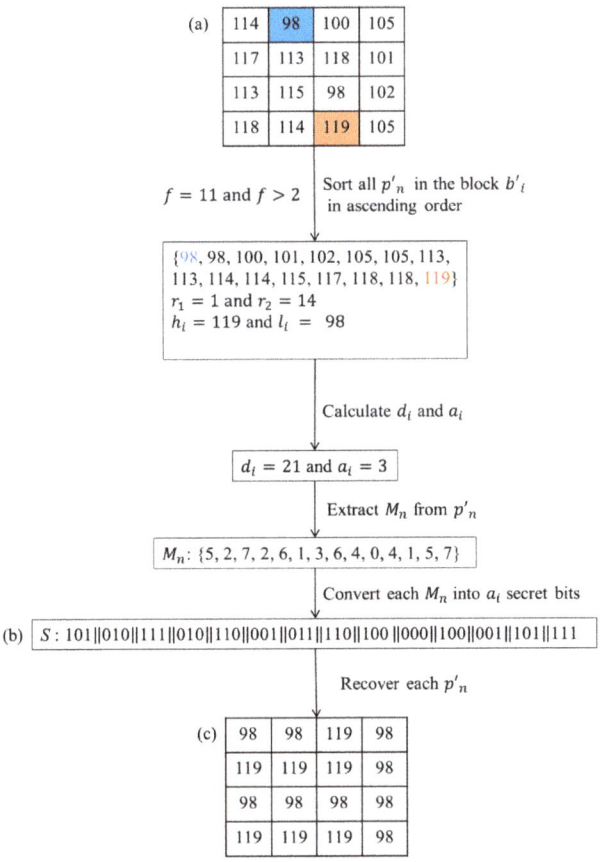

Figure 7. (**a**) The modified block b'_i sized 4×4, (**b**) Secret data S and (**c**) block b_i sized 4×4.

4. The Proposed Scheme

The section provides some experimental results to show the hiding capacity (bits) and image quality (dB) of our proposed scheme. In Figure 8, all of the experiments were performed with six commonly used grayscale test images: Lena, F-16, Sailboat, Girl, Toys, and Barbara. All are of the same size, 512×512. The size of each block b_i is 4×4. The embedded secret data are composed of a random bit-stream that was produced from a random number generator.

In these experiments, the visual quality of the modified images was evaluated by using peak signal-to-noise ratio (PSNR) as defined in Equation (12).

$$PSNR = 10 \times \log_{10}\left(\frac{255^2}{MSE}\right), \quad (12)$$

The definition of mean square error (MSE) is shown in Equation (13).

$$MSE = \frac{1}{H \times W} \sum_{i=0}^{\frac{H}{k} \times \frac{W}{k} - 1} \sum_{n=0}^{k \times k - 1} \left(p'^{i}_{n} - p^{i}_{n}\right)^2, \quad (13)$$

where p'^{i}_{n} and p^{i}_{n} are the stego pixels and original pixels in each modified block and original block, respectively.

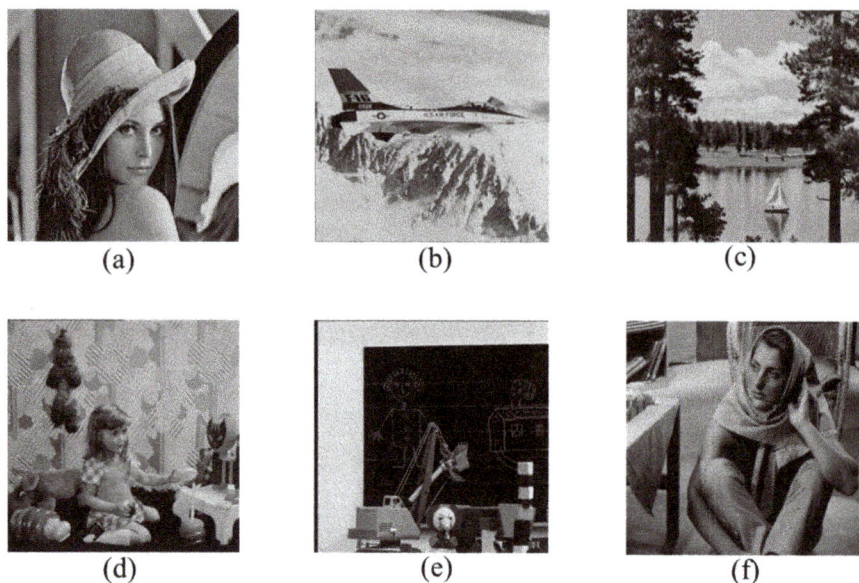

Figure 8. Test images (**a**) Lena; (**b**) F-16; (**c**) Sailboat; (**d**) Girl; (**e**) Toys; (**f**) Barbara.

To demonstrate the performance results for our proposed scheme, our method was compared with previous reversible data hiding methods in two aspects. In the first group, the proposed scheme was compared with other BTC-based schemes [21–24]. Figure 9a and Table 2 show the results of this comparison. Figure 9a shows, the good performance for embedding capacity that was achieved in our scheme. The proposed method can embed 56 bits in each 4 × 4 pixel block while the difference between two quantization levels is larger than 32. However, Lin et al.'s scheme can embed 16 bits in each 4 × 4 pixel block. And in the schemes of Chang et al.'s, Li et al.'s, and Sun et al.'s, each 4 × 4 pixel block can only be embedded 1, 2 and 4 bits, respectively. In our scheme, the capacity for, "Lena", "F-16", "Sailboat", "Girl", "Toys" and "Barbara", were 324,548 (bits); 267,386 (bits); 432,796 (bits); 388,780 (bits); 292,250 (bits) and 449,876 (bits), respectively.

Table 2. Comparative performance of PSNR (dB) for six test images between our method and other methods base on BTC.

Scheme	Lena	F-16	Sailboat	Girl	Toys	Barbara	Average
Our scheme	32.59	32.22	30.16	33.30	32.12	28.82	31.54
Lin et al.'s [24]	33.05	31.64	30.32	33.36	30.99	28.63	31.33
Li et al.'s [22]	32.34	31.93	30.41	33.44	31.15	28.82	31.34
Chang et al.'s [21]	Cannot be constructed by the modified code stream						
Sun et al.'s [23]	Cannot be constructed by the modified code stream						

In our scheme, the image obtained a higher embedding capacity even with complex images such as "Barbara" and "Sailboat", because our adaptive interpolation technique is related to the difference of two quantization levels. However, the capacity is relatively small in smooth images, such as "Lena", "F-16′ and "Toys". Table 2 shows a comparison of image quality. In Chang et al.'s and Sun et al.'s schemes, the cover image cannot be directly obtained from a stego compression code. Therefore, the two methods cannot be compared in terms of image quality of a modified image. From Table 2, the proposed scheme cannot achieve the best PSNR in every test image. In the "Lena", Lin et al.'s scheme achieves the best results, and Li et al.'s scheme provides the best results in the "Sailboat". But our method achieves a higher average. In brief, the first experiment shows that our scheme achieves the higher embedding capacity while maintaining relative good, modified image quality.

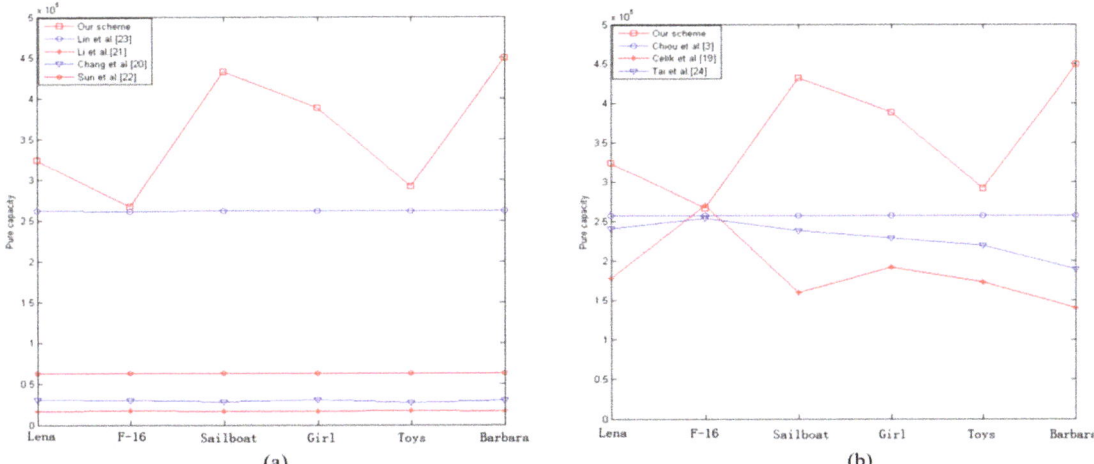

Figure 9. Comparative performance of pure hiding capacity for six test images between our method and other methods. (**a**) Comparisons with ours and other schemes based on BTC and (**b**) comparisons with ours and other schemes which are not based on BTC.

In the second group, we compared some reversible data methods that are not based on a BTC-compressed technique [4,20,25]. These three other techniques hide secret data in the spatial domain. As shown in Figure 9b and Table 3, our method obtains good performance in comparison with the other methods. In Chiou et al.'s scheme, secret data cannot be embedded into the blocks in the first row and first column. Tai et al.'s scheme and Celik et al.'s cannot embed secret data in some cases. In our method, although secret data cannot be embedded when the difference of two quantization levels is smaller than 4, our scheme still can obtain a better hiding capacity than other schemes when conditions were similar for PSNR. The experimental results show that, our proposed scheme was better than other reversible data hiding schemes.

Table 3. Comparative performance of PSNR (dB) for six test images between our method and other schemes.

Scheme	Lena	F-16	Sailboat	Girl	Toys	Barbara	Average
Our scheme	32.59	32.22	30.16	33.30	32.12	28.82	31.54
Chiou et al.'s [4]	31.05	30.23	28.43	31.11	28.73	25.53	29.18
Celik et al.'s [20]	32.54	31.33	30.41	32.76	31.15	29.82	31.34
Tai et al.'s [25]	31.61	29.84	27.25	31.43	34.84	28.42	30.57

5. Conclusions

This paper proposed an adaptive reversible image hiding method using AMBTC compression by considering the quantization level difference of each block. According to our adaptive embedding strategy, more bits are embedded into the image sub-block located in regions where the value of QLD is larger. However, in order to ensure the quality of the image, when the value of the QLD of a sub-block is greater than the threshold, this block will not embed information. Experimental results showed that the performance of the proposed scheme is better than the previous schemes in terms of payload and modified image quality.

Author Contributions: Conceptualization, Y.-H.C. and C.-C.C.; methodology, C.-C.L.; software, Z.-M.W.; validation, C.-C.L.; writing—original draft preparation, Y.-H.C. and Z.-M.W.; writing—review and editing, C.-C.L.; project administration, C.-C.C. All authors have read and agreed to the published version of the manuscript.

Funding: This research received no external funding.

Data Availability Statement: Data available in a publicly accessible repository.

Conflicts of Interest: The authors declare no conflict of interest.

References

1. Zhao, Z.; Luo, H.; Lu, Z.-M.; Pan, J.-S. Reversible data hiding based on multilevel histogram modification and sequential recovery. *AEU Int. J. Electron. Commun.* **2011**, *65*, 814–826. [CrossRef]
2. Chang, I.-C.; Hu, Y.-C.; Chen, W.-L.; Lo, C.-C. High capacity reversible data hiding scheme based on residual histogram shift-ing for block truncation coding. *Signal Process.* **2015**, *108*, 376–388. [CrossRef]
3. Cheng, P.-H.; Chang, K.-C.; Liu, C.-L. A reversible data hiding scheme for VQ indices using histogram shifting of prediction errors. *Multimed. Tools Appl.* **2015**, *76*, 6031–6050. [CrossRef]
4. Chiou, S.; Liao, I.; Hwang, M. A capacity-enhanced reversible data hiding scheme based on SMVQ. *Imaging Sci. J.* **2011**, *59*, 17–24. [CrossRef]
5. Nasrabadi, N.M.; King, R.A. Image coding using vector quantization: A review. *IEEE Trans. Commun.* **1988**, *36*, 957–971. [CrossRef]
6. Abdelwahab, A.A.; Hassaan, L.A. A Discrete Wavelet Transform Based Technique for Image Data Hiding. In Proceedings of the 2008 National Radio Science Conference, Institute of Electrical and Electronics Engineers (IEEE), Tanta, Egypt, 18–20 March 2008; pp. 1–9.
7. Al-Asmari, A.K.; Salama, A.; Iliyasu, A.M.; Al-Qodah, M.A. A DWT Ordering Scheme for Hiding Data in Images Using Pixel Value Difference. In Proceedings of the IEEE Eighth International Conference on Computational Intelligence and Security (CIS), Guangzhou, China, 17–18 November 2012; pp. 553–557.
8. Lai, B.-L.; Chang, L.-W. Adaptive data hiding for images based on harr discrete wavelet transform. In *Advances in Image and Video Technology*; Springer: Berlin/Heidelberg, Germany, 2006; pp. 1085–1093.
9. Lin, Y.-K. A data hiding scheme based upon DCT coefficient modification. *Comput. Stand. Interfaces* **2014**, *36*, 855–862. [CrossRef]
10. Alturki, F.T.; Almutairi, A.F.; Mersereauu, R.M. Analysis of blind data hiding using discrete cosine transform phase modula-tion. *Signal Process. Image Commun.* **2007**, *22*, 347–362. [CrossRef]
11. Chang, C.-C.; Lin, C.-C.; Tseng, C.-S.; Tai, W.-L. Reversible hiding in DCT-based compressed images. *Inf. Sci.* **2007**, *177*, 2768–2786. [CrossRef]
12. Delp, E.; Mitchell, O. Image Compression Using Block Truncation Coding. *IEEE Trans. Commun.* **1979**, *27*, 1335–1342. [CrossRef]
13. Lema, M.; Mitchell, O. Absolute Moment Block Truncation Coding and Its Application to Color Images. *IEEE Trans. Commun.* **1984**, *32*, 1148–1157. [CrossRef]
14. Guo, J.-M.; Wu, M.-F. Improved Block Truncation Coding Based on the Void-and-Cluster Dithering Approach. *IEEE Trans. Image Process.* **2009**, *18*, 211–213. [CrossRef] [PubMed]
15. Guo, J.-M. Improved block truncation coding using modified error diffusion. *Electron. Lett.* **2008**, *44*, 462. [CrossRef]
16. Wu, X.; Sun, W. Data Hiding in Block Truncation Coding. In Proceedings of the IEEE International Conference on Computational Intelligence and Security (CIS), New York, NY, USA, 11–14 December 2010; pp. 406–410.
17. Kim, C. Data hiding based on compressed dithering images. In *Advances in Intelligent Information and Database Systems*; Springer: Berlin/Heidelberg, Germany, 2010; pp. 89–98.
18. Guo, J.-M.; Liu, Y.-F. High Capacity Data Hiding for Error-Diffused Block Truncation Coding. *IEEE Trans. Image Process.* **2012**, *21*, 4808–4818. [CrossRef]
19. Peng, F.; Li, X.; Yang, B. Adaptive reversible data hiding scheme based on integer transform. *Signal Process.* **2012**, *92*, 54–62. [CrossRef]
20. Celik, M.; Sharma, G.; Tekalp, A.; Saber, E. Reversible Data Hiding. In Proceedings of the International Conference on Image Processing, Institute of Electrical and Electronics Engineers (IEEE), New York, NY, USA, 20 March 2006; Volume 2, p. II-157.
21. Chang, C.-C.; Lin, C.-Y.; Fan, Y.-H. Lossless data hiding for color images based on block truncation coding. *Pattern Recognit.* **2008**, *41*, 2347–2357. [CrossRef]
22. Li, C.-H.; Lu, Z.-M.; Su, Y.-X. Reversible Data Hiding for Btc-compressed Images Based on Bitplane Flipping and Histogram Shifting of Mean Tables. *Inf. Technol. J.* **2011**, *10*, 1421–1426. [CrossRef]

23. Sun, W.; Lu, Z.-M.; Wen, Y.-C.; Yu, F.-X.; Shen, R.-J. High performance reversible data hiding for block truncation coding com-pressed images. *Signal Image Video Process.* **2013**, *7*, 297–306. [CrossRef]
24. Lin, C.-C.; Liu, X.-L.; Tai, W.-L.; Yuan, S.-M. A novel reversible data hiding scheme based on AMBTC compression technique. *Multimed. Tools Appl.* **2013**, *74*, 3823–3842. [CrossRef]
25. Tai, W.-L.; Yeh, C.-M.; Chang, C.-C. Reversible Data Hiding Based on Histogram Modification of Pixel Differences. *IEEE Trans. Circuits Syst. Video Technol.* **2009**, *19*, 906–910. [CrossRef]

An Algorithm for the Detection of Hidden Propaganda in Mixed-Code Text over the Internet [†]

Andrea Tundis [1,*], Gaurav Mukherjee [2] and Max Mühlhäuser [1]

[1] Department of Computer Science, Technische Universität Darmstadt, 64289 Darmstadt, Germany; max@tk.tu-darmstadt.de
[2] Brox IT-Solutions GmbH, 70771 Stuttgart, Germany; gmukherjee@brox.de
[*] Correspondence: tundis@tk.tu-darmstadt.de; Tel.: +49-6151-16-23205
[†] This paper is an extended version of the paper published in the 15th International Conference on Availability, Reliability and Security (ARES 2020), Virtual Event, Dublin, Ireland, 25–28 August 2020; Article 76, pp. 1–7.

Abstract: Internet-based communication systems have become an increasing tool for spreading misinformation and propaganda. Even though there exist mechanisms that are able to track unwarranted information and messages, users made up different ways to avoid their scrutiny and detection. An example is represented by the mixed-code language, that is text written in an unconventional form by combining different languages, symbols, scripts and shapes. It aims to make more difficult the detection of specific content, due to its custom and ever changing appearance, by using special characters to substitute for alphabet letters. Indeed, such substitute combinations of symbols, which tries to resemble the shape of the intended alphabet's letter, makes it still intuitively readable to humans, however nonsensical to machines. In this context, the paper explores the possibility of identifying propaganda in such mixed-code texts over the Internet, centred on a machine learning based approach. In particular, an algorithm in combination with a deep learning models for character identification is proposed in order to detect and analyse whether an element contains propaganda related content. The overall approach is presented, the results gathered from its experimentation are discussed and the achieved performances are compared with the related works.

Keywords: propaganda detection; mixed-code identification; text analysis; machine learning; internet-based crimes; cyber terrorist networks; cyber-criminality

1. Introduction

Language is a medium of expression in human society. Communication is a form of social interaction that involves exchange or negotiation of information primarily through the use of the *language* [1]. As it is discussed in [2], languages are socio-cultural as well as individual products and, as such, they change over time, keeping up with the evolution of the social environment. IT has revolutionised the communication way [3] as evidenced by the amount of information generated and spread via social media, such as Facebook, Instagram, Twitter and YouTube. In particular, the growth of the Internet-based communication has become one of the basic necessities of the world. Thanks to such technology, many users attempt to use the Internet even for malicious purposes. The high number of users make it very easy for any kind of information to diffuse very quickly so as to influence the perception of the user itself [4]. This kind of information, mostly known as *viral messages*, is often not verified, from its authenticity point of view and it can result in outrage or hysteria. Furthermore, as discussed in [5], such methods can be used to shape public opinion, finances or even create panic in the society, that means it can be treated as an *infection of the mind*. Terrorist organisations, for example, use online networking to generate and promote propaganda based content to legitimise or instruct illegal activities to the public, as the huge amount of online registered users make the information spreading faster and easier [6–8]. That is why criminals exploit the Internet as an active means to perpetrate some crimes [9–12].

Especially, online social media is skillfully utilised by terrorists as a tool of persuasion and behaviour change (by including political opinion, marketing and sales, humanitarian and community acts) in order to cause significant damage as well as social unrest in sensitive places by using fake news and propaganda, which might result in individuals joining terrorist networks [13–16].

It is not trivial to monitor all ongoing activities even if such cyber communication takes place in the clear, without adopting any anonymous or encrypted communication techniques [17,18]. It is difficult to recognise it, especially if it is structured in such a fashion that avoids raising the necessary security flags while reaching the intended targets. The writing style, for example, is a strong way to spread propaganda while avoiding the authorities [19]. It can represent a big obstacle from a machine perspective, to automatically detect and correctly interpret a message written in clear as a plain text. There are a few ways to enable it, such as code-mixing and mixed-code text methods. *Code-mixing* is the term used when a person writes something using two different languages especially of two different scripts. For example, "Aap kaise ho?" is a text written for a Hindi person but using a Roman script. This is common parlance called a *Hinglish* text, and likewise: *Romanji* (Japanese in roman script), *Benglish* (Bengali in Roman script), *Roman Urdu* (Urdu in Roman script) and so on. Furthermore, when using code-mixing, the spelling of words tends to differ for different persons, while the variation of the phonetic usage of the Roman letters can result in varying interpretation adding to its complexity. The major challenge relies on properly monitoring these harmful messages circulating in the social network and removing or delegitimising them. This is a big concern in multilingual societies like in India where correctly identifying a potential threat is a huge hurdle. This creates a challenge for the machine to properly "understand" the semantics. In countries like India where multiple languages are used and social media is predominantly expressed in Roman script, a wide usage of mixed code to converse on a daily basis can be observed. However, this poses a problem to recognise the intended message in a mixed code environment. On the other hand, *mixed-code* text consists of using special characters to write words in such a way they would graphically resemble the intended words but from the machine point of view, it is considered a no-sense sequence of symbols. The question should be asked—What is the function of mixed-code text? The answer lies in the simplicity of the method. Mixed-code text only requires the user to use a bit of creativity and on the reader's part only the knowledge of the language as the reader in a flow would easily understand the intended text. However, a machine will take the text literally and would check for its content which in most cases would be dismissed as garbage. Consequently, there is a need for careful deliberation to re-evaluate text and to provide a method for improving its interpretation.

In this panorama, this article, which is an extended version of [20], focuses on the detection of hidden propaganda in mixed-code text, by proposing an algorithm for supporting the analysis of suspicious mixed-code text, based on the optical character recognition (OCR) analogy [21]. Specifically, a segregation approach is adopted to analyse the characters' combinations, which in turn are transformed into images. A character recognition model, based on machine learning techniques, is trained in order to recognise such modified letters of the alphabet. The process iterates through all possible combinations to find the intended word. A second model deals with the text classification, to determine whether a text contains hidden propaganda messages or not. Since such problem falls within the detection field, accuracy, precision, recall and f1-score have been employed as evaluation criteria for assessing the proposal's performances for the detection of hidden propaganda in mixed-code. From the conducted experiments, it results that each of those metrics reaches more than 91%, as a symptom of good performances, that are inline in comparison to the related works described in Section 2.

The rest of the paper is structured as follows: Section 2 provides an overview of the related works by distinguishing between mixed-code analysis and propaganda detection. An overview on optical character and image recognition, which represent the enabling technologies, have been introduced in Section 3. In Section 4, the most common identified mixed-code categories, the overall adopted analysis process along with the proposed algorithm are elaborated. Whereas its evaluation is presented and discussed in Section 5. Finally, the conclusion and future works are highlighted in Section 6.

2. Related Work

This section provides an overview on the related scientific contributions both in the field of (i) mixed-code analysis (see Table 1), which takes place when, in a conversation or communication, two distinct languages, syntax or written forms are employed [22]. It is generally used to overcome linguistic shortfalls, to help in understanding groups' dynamics and characteristics, as well as to grab various ethnic peculiarities which can define their group identities [23]; (ii) online propaganda detection, which is devoted to identify specific content that aims to incite the masses by influencing their mindset. An overview of the most popular related works is presented in Sections 2.1 and 2.2 respectively.

2.1. Mixed Code Analysis

A contribution centred on machine translation of the so called *Hinglish* text is proposed in [24], where Hinglish represents a communication way that uses a mix of Hindi and English terms within a conversation. The authors proposed a system centred on machine learning in order to translate Hinglish script. They discussed how the constraints of mixed code should be considered when defining a model in order to obtain an accurate interpretation of the mixed-code. They claimed that acceptable results were achieved in more than 90% of cases; however, any metrics and the quantitative results related to the evaluation approach have not been presented. Furthermore, the application context in which such experimentation was conducted has not been clearly specified.

In [25], the hate speech detection problem in code-mixed texts on social media has been faced, by exploiting a Hindi-English code-mixed dataset consisting of online posts on Twitter. Different types of textual-based features have been used to define a detection model: n-grams, word n-grams, punctuations, negation words and hate lexicon. The annotation consisted of two Factor-World Level and Hate/Normal speech, which were used to indicate which words of the text were English and which words were Hindi. N-gram was adopted to support the feature extraction (both at character and word level) in order to detect relevant words. Furthermore, punctuation and negative words were considered as a benchmark to determine potential hate speech or not. The experiment showed that the best result was achieved by combining all such features to train a SVM, thus achieving 71.7% accuracy.

In [26], an approach for language identification on social media has been elaborated. A dataset with Facebook posts and comments that contains code mixing between Bengali, English and Hindi has been built. The authors considered a text as mixed-code not only when the script was different but also either when the words of different languages were used randomly or sentences switch languages within a single text or paragraph. Different analysis techniques have been experimented, some based on a unsupervised dictionary approach and others on supervised word-level classification. However, no clear evaluation has been provided. Instead, the work proposed in [27] focused on the classification of offensive tweets written in Hinglish language. A Twitter dataset containing tweets in Hindi-English code switched language has been collected. The dataset has been organised into three main classes: nonoffensive, abusive and hate-speech. Convolutional Neural Networks (CNNs) combined with transfer learning have been used in the classification process by reaching 83.9% accuracy.

In [28], the identification of hate speech from code-mixed text on social media has been faced, by using a Hindi-English mixed code corpus as the initial baseline. A Long Short

Term Memory (LSTM) technique, based on subword level, has been mainly considered. The idea behind the subword level selection is to identify the root words and to match their variations. This is because in a mixed code setting the variation may differ for each writer. The hierarchical LSTM model as well as Random Forest (RF) and Support Vector Machine (SVM) have been experimented by using subwords phonetic. As Hindi is a phonetically accurate for writing, a phonetic input of the text has been also provided. The words were divided into consonant-vowel sequences and these sequences form the base of their attention model. This enabled the model to determine both the words that make up the vocabulary and to match the phonetic to such words as well. The results showed that the hierarchical LSTM reached the highest Recall and F1-score, whereas the SVM reached the highest accuracy, equal to 70.7%.

In [29], different analysis techniques for supporting sentiment analysis of textual information, after having normalised the influence of multiple languages in mixed-code script, have been experimented. In particular, several machine learning techniques, which are able to characterise the text by determining the polarity of a text have been used. The mixed code text used to train the model was initially identified to mark the words as Hindi or English. Such model used an Artificial Neural Network (ANN) to identify the affinity of the text and to mark it with values from "very positive" to "very negative" (−5 to +5) so as to provide a sentimental score. The results showed circa 80% accuracy. However, regarding the meaning of polarity, it is not clearly specified whether positivity means happiness or joy and negativity anger or sadness.

Another research contribution related to code-mixed text centred on sentiment analysis is described in [30]. It is based on the combination of two models: N-gram probabilistic model, which was called Multinomial Naive Bayes (MNB), and LSTM model centred on Tri-gram characters. In particular, the LSTM model has been used to cache deep sequential patterns contained in the text, whereas the low-level word combination of keywords has been faced with the MNB model, in order to compensate grammatical inconsistencies. The overall achieved accuracy was equal to 70.8%. Whereas in [31], the authors have extended the NLP techniques to detect humour in a Hindi-English mixed code environment. N-gram, Bag-of-Words (BoW), Common words and hash-tags have been used and experimented on a manually annotated dataset. SVM, Random Forest and Naïve Bayes have been experimented with a highest accuracy of 69.3%. In [32], instead, another NLP technique to normalise words in a code-mixed environment—as the spelling tends to vary for different persons—has been proposed. A Skip-gram model, which clusters the words of variation to deliver the base word as output in the normalised text, has been used. The results have shown an accuracy level of 71% and a F1-score equals to 66%.

Table 1. Mixed code related works.

Ref	Objective	Approach and Contribution	Evaluation	Dataset
[24]	Mixed-code translation	Unspecified	Accuracy: 90%	Custom
[25]	Dataset Hate speech in Mixed code	Textual-based features, SVM	Accuracy: 71.7%	Custom
[26]	Language detection	Data collection	Unspecified	Custom
[27]	Tweets classification	Data collection, CNN	Accuracy: 83.9%	Custom
[28]	Hate Speech identification	SVM, LSTM, RF	Accuracy: 70.7%	Custom
[29]	Sentiment analysis	ANN	Accuracy: 80%	Custom
[30]	Sentiment analysis	N-Gram, MNB, LSTM	Accuracy: 70.8%	Custom
[31]	Sentiment analysis	N-Gram, BoW, SVM, RF,NB	Accuracy: 69.3%	Custom
[32]	Text normalisation	Skip-gram model	Accuracy: 71% F1-Score: 66%	Custom

A clear aspect that emerged from the above identified related works is that such previous research studies have focused on mixed-code analysis by mainly dealing with the language translation. Such research direction differs from the purpose of this current work, as it focuses on the detection of hidden propaganda in mixed code as *leet text* [33], that is a particular form of expression, which is primarily used on the Internet. The distinguishing characteristic of such textual expression form lies in the combination of characters and symbols of the computer keyboard in order to graphically represent a text. This writing style makes the *leet text* a powerful way of communicating and spreading propaganda, as it allows for easy bypass of its automatic identification.

2.2. Online Propaganda Detection

Online propaganda is a modern way of conducting campaign centred on IT-based tool and in particular online social networking. Twitter represents one of the most used medium for propaganda and it is heavily utilised by extremist and terrorist groups to reach the mass. The recent interest in detecting online propaganda is documented by the different research efforts conducted in this field (see Table 2).

In [34], for example, the authors focused on the detection of extremist ISIS groups, by proposing a method to actively identify tweets containing propaganda related content. The method aimed to recognise not only patterns containing specific Hashtags but also user accounts by profiling them so as to enable their potential predictions. The method was centred on the Term Frequency (TF) of the suspected words in order to derive relevant information, whereas a Regression-based Neural Network (RBNN) has been used as classification algorithm, without quantifying the achievements.

Similarly, the detection of radical content was faced in [35], through the definition of a model. It was used to analyse the text produced by the users from the psychological perspective by considering specific behavioural patterns. In particular, the authors utilised TF-IDF to identify suspicious terms related to radical behaviour, which were used to train a Random Forest (RF), a Support Vector Machine (SVM) and a K-Nearest Neighbor (KNN) classifier by obtaining 94% accuracy, as the highest result.

A deep learning model for supporting the identification of Sunni extremist propaganda via text analysis is presented in [36]. Here, word2vec and doc2vec techniques have been adopted to detect specific relationships among extremist-related terms which in turn were used to identify and classify new text as propaganda or not. Among the conducted tests, Artificial Neural Networks (ANNs) showed the best classification results by providing accuracy and precision of about 90%.

In [37], the authors focused on the creation of a free available dataset as a benchmark to support the propaganda detection research activities, that has been used in different research competitions related to propaganda detection. It contains sentences that are annotated from experts as propaganda and not. In addition, the paper presents preliminary classification results by achieving about 63% of accuracy by using the Neural Network classification. Using the same database, in [38] the authors exploited the BERT classification to identify single nonpropaganda rows by employing ELMo, BERT and RoBERTa approach, by achieving 79% recall, 66% precision and 60% f1-score.

Whereas in [39], the authors focused on the assessment of radical and extremist online propaganda, by proposing a pyramidal conceptual model that enables to distinguish propaganda related content at different level of radicalisation. The model is centred on three sociological human aspects which characterise traits of radicals and terrorists. A preliminary experimentation was carried out in order to illustrate how to allocate propaganda items to the pyramid model.

Table 2. Mixed code related works.

Ref	Technique	Contribution	Evaluation	Dataset
[34]	RBNN, TF	Hashtag-centred detection of ISIS groups	Unspecified	EMNLP19
[35]	TF-IDF, SVM, KNN	Text-based detection of Radical users	Accuracy: 94%	Acquired
[36]	Word2vec, doc2vec, ANN	Text analysis of Sunni extremist content	Accuracy: 90%	Acquired
[37]	Neural Network	Data collection and text analysis	Accuracy: 63%	Custom
[38]	ELMo, BERT, and RoBERTa	Text analysis propaganda detection	Precision: 66%	EMNLP19
[39]	K-Means	Classification of Pro-ISIS users	Unspecified	Acquired

From the above reviewed papers, it resulted that online propaganda detection is an active research field towards analysis of extremist related content. However, it emerged that all previous research effort are limited on the analysis of natural language of a plain-text. Our scope is instead to deal with a form of expression which is not directly attributable to plain-text but which is made up to "hide" the real message, by composing different symbols to graphically resemble the standard alphabet.

3. Background

For the sake of completeness and to make the paper's content self-contained, an overview on basic concepts regarding character recognition and writing ways is given in Sections 3.1 and 3.2 respectively.

3.1. Optical Character Recognition

The objective of character recognition is to enable a machine to recognise characters by using optical devices, such as a camera. The machine should be able to capture the image of the character and associate it with its corresponding symbolic identity [40]. Optical Character Recognition (OCR) technique can be found as early as 1900 where the scientist Tyurin successfully implemented the idea and with the invention of modern computers, the research into this field has increased a lot. The OCR was initially developed to assist the visually challenged individuals to read the text, and then it was adopted into other application context such as banking, health and security in combination to Machine Learning (ML). A common OCR application is handwriting recognition, centred on smart devices that are capable of transforming handwritten text into its digital counterpart [41]. OCR is utilised to recognise languages of different origins not only in Roman script [42] but also in the case of degraded language documents. Another use of OCR to recognise handwriting is presented in [43], where the authors used the n-gram model, which produces groups of words that overlay on each other. The authors extended such model and utilised the likelihood score, from a statistical machine translation system, as main feature, so as to be able to capture the image of the words and to translate each image into other languages.

A further application of OCR is provided in [44], which describes a method to recognise Bangla handwritten numerical characters using local binary pattern. Whereas in [45], the authors used OCR technique to detect printed English and Fraktur text using Long Short Term Memory (LSTM). The authors described that the handwritten content may vary in the position and baseline of the text, as a consequence a text line normalisation approach has been used to uniformly position the text. Such normalisation approach was based on an dictionary, containing data generated on the basis of the connected component shapes and associated baseline. For recognition and classification, the authors implemented 1-D Bidirectional Long Short Term Memory model, in order to establish the ground-truth alignment by using a forward-backward algorithm, which also provides a decoding mechanism to map the frame network upon a sequence of symbols.

Further applications of OCR, for supporting the recognition of handwritten digits, are presented in literature. For example in [46], the use of Random Forest, Decision Tree and Hoeffding Tree as classifiers have been proposed to build a tool that can easily recognise the digits. For this, they utilised the handwritten digit dataset of MNIST5, that is preprocessed before being used, in order to extract potential characterising features. In such work, a comparative study among the different classifiers has been conducted by concluding that the Hoeffding tree was the most performing one by reaching 73% accuracy. Another approach to support character recognition was based on the use of the Tesseract OCR open source engine to train a Tamil OCR model [47]. In particular, a segmentation approach was adopted by using a box file system. Each character was numbered, so that the number of boxes was equal to the number of training characters. Starting from such boxed character a classifier has been trained by using various images with different font size type. The evaluation of the proposed OCR system was performed using 20 scanned images from 20 ancient Tamil books and over 14,000 characters, by obtaining 81% accuracy.

A method for the recognition of Roman Script and English language was proposed in [21], based on Artificial Neural Network (ANN) and Nearest Neighbour (NN) to detect and interpret scanned English documents in three different font types. Using such method, the authors achieved 98% accuracy, by experimenting it on a dataset consisting of English alphabets in different fonts created by themselves, which is not available. As a consequence, the database could have been biased. Unfortunately, this is not verifiable, as no information is available neither regarding such dataset nor on the adopted evaluation approach.

3.2. The Art of Writing

When we talk about *Word Art*, we typically refer to the graphic structural aspect with which words are written, commonly known as calligraphy. It is often considered to be the craft of writing text in an appealing form, and it is regularly used in font design, typography, logo and graphic design. Word Art can be depicted as a text modifier which includes visual enhancements to text like shadows, outlines, colors, skew and 3-D effects to make it more attractive to the user. *Text fonts* are also an integral part of the modern writing. Since there are multiple fonts to choose, a user can use a font to describe the purpose of the text and to emphasised the mood of the article. For example, a user might choose the calligraphy font for invitations and calibri font for formal documents or even create custom fonts to describe a unique style of presenting a textual content.

In [48], a distinction between the term of *Computer Art* and *Digital Art* is discussed. *Digital art*, which is considered more general, represents the use of the computers capacity to convert different media types (such as Music, Pictures, Movies, Story and Text) into a digital form and to process them for multiple purposes. For example, a digitally encoded video of an event can be integrated using music of another origin while displaying text of another. The integration is possible into one, as all of them are fundamentally a series of binary code. In contrast to this, *Computer Art* is the art created by exploiting any external methods, by only using the available tools. The initial stages were just art with characters available with the standard keyboard to create the images. These types of images are called ASCII art, which rely only on the use of standard characters to make images, due to the lack of other graphical resources and professional tools. The use of ASCII art is still prominent today in chats and forums like Reddit, Stackoverflow as well as by players in a multiplayer game communities. In addition, the symbols used to create the full picture are typically linked to the meaning and the context of the pictures itself.

As argued in [49], *ASCII art* is a more complex art form than the intended originally ones. It requires precision to provide the proper alignment of the text to avoid any misinterpretation, which in turn would give inconsistent result for recognition techniques like optical character recognition (OCR). Furthermore, with the help of the computers today, it is easier to provide text in multiple forms and fonts, as the operating systems offer built-in writing systems, that support a multitude of fonts, design styles as well as design tools for creating the so popularly called "Word Art".

Another form of writing text that combines "Text Art" and "Font" is called *Leet Text*, typically of websites, which uses characters found on the keyboard to type out text, by playing with the similarities of the characters to be represented. Since the language used on the Internet is predominantly English and the keyboard of most users have Roman characters on it, it is generally used for Roman scripts. Other languages are also possible but the scope may be limited. The term "leet" comes from the word "Elite" and it would be used online as a symbol of proficiency in certain fields and especially in Gaming. The representation of the word "leet" itself in leet text is represented as "l337". Leet is considered similar to ASCII or Word art and it is also synonymous of emotions. Leet code is based on conventions but no standard rules are defined.

Since leet speak is dependent on a language base for communication, it does adhere to its grammatical constraints. However, leet speak has some of its own unique sets of texts which are generally known to its users. It uses misspellings and abbreviations to convey a word or message and it uses numbers as valid letters to write a word. Furthermore, it has an extensive use of special characters to depict certain characters. Leet speak is also used to provide censorship to certain text which can be provocative or hate inducing. These texts require precision and practise to be understood and interpreted. More insights about the complexities of leet speak have been provided in [33]. For example, it is mentioned that there are many varieties of leet speak and that many others can be developed on the basis of the specific context.

4. Propaganda Detection in Mixed-Code Text

In this section, the proposed method for supporting the detection of online propaganda hidden in mixed-code text is elaborated. In particular in Section 4.1, first different mixed-code types are presented, and then the adopted research process is briefly introduced. In Section 4.2, the proposed normalisation algorithm for transforming mixed-code into standard text is elaborated, whereas the approach for the analysis and classification of propaganda-related content is described in Section 4.3.

4.1. Writing Styles and Mixed-Code Categorisation

The way of expressing thoughts in written form can take place differently. Indeed, not only a text is a composition of symbols and characters that are used to build a word in order to convey a message, but it can also be used to depict some phonetic structures or art forms. The basic way of using writing is called *Text on Document (ToD)*, which is characterised by the use of standard alphabetic characters, that is, the symbols belong to a specific language, whose structure is governed by a set of grammar rules, semantics and vocabulary. *ToD* is supposed to contain an explicit message easy to read and to understand. *Text in Visual Media (TiVM)*, instead, represents the use of the text, in graphical representations, to improve the visual information by imitating sounds or emotions. It might not necessarily follow grammar rules or having any semantic identity. Whereas, a *Text as Art Form (TaAF)* aims to emphasise the artistry of the writer, by using forms or symbols that are not part of the alphabet, in order to represent a code or a coded message in clear.

Mixed-code text belongs to *TaAF*, and according to the conduced research, we classified it into three main types (i.e., *Single row—multiple language*, *Single row—single language*, and *Multiple rows*) by considering two main parameters, as depicted in Figure 1: (i) the *language*, that is, whether the mixed-code text contains multilanguage factors or writing styles linked to one or more languages and (ii) the *graphical writing style*, that is, whether a standard row-based writing style is followed or multiple rows are used in order to graphically represent the alphabetic characters.

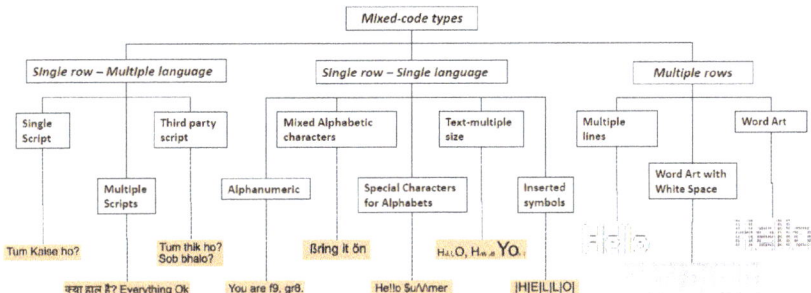

Figure 1. Mixed-code categories.

Moreover, for each of them further subcategories have been identified, which are described in the following:

- *Single Script*: the text is written in a particular script, but the basic language might be different. For example, when Hindi is written in Roman script, that means that the script used for Hindi is Devnagri but the usage of Roman script is adopted to write Hindi.
- *Multiple Scripts*: the words retain their original forms and scripts but different languages are adopted. The grammar is difficult to grasp; however, the greater number of words used with a particular language generally dominates the grammar rules.
- *Third party script*: the text is based on two different languages, but the script utilises a third party script whose grammar fluctuates between the two used languages.
- *Alphanumeric*: the mixed code language utilises alphabets and numbers to develop the scripts. It is important that the phonetics of the numbers are in accordance with the reference language.
- *Different Alphabetic/Language characters*: the text uses the intended script of the language, but there is also sporadic use of symbols from different languages. The symbols are not part of the language characters but do resemble some of the characters to provide the suitable replacement.
- *Special Characters for Alphabets*: the text uses the intended script of the language but it also utilises the special characters in the system to create the alphabet required to sell out the word. The use of special characters may depend on the characters it is required to replace. The characters can be depicted using a single special characters or multiple special characters. This also depends on the code that is being used, i.e., if there is a predetermined set of rules for such replacement, then the special character selection depends on that.
- *Multiple size*: the text is written over different height and width. The text may have some characters that vary in size, so as to make the text inconsistent with the standard practise of writing This is generally done to add more effect to the text.
- *Inserted symbols*: in this writing form the text is written normally, but it contains symbols inserted among the basic characters to produce a special effect or to decorate a word.
- *Multiple lines*: this is the way of using special characters to build a word or a letter that spans over multiple lines of the text. In this case, different symbols are used individually over multiple lines in such a way that they give the visual effect that a text is represented.
- *Word Art*: this is a variant of the previous one, by using letters or special characters not only to provide a textual information but rather to see the picture formed by carefully aligning texts over multiple lines. This type of arrangement is also called ASCII art.
- *Word Art with white space*: the text is written over a large area is such a way that the white area, left intentionally empty, gives the appearance of a text. It means that the text or characters are used to enclose the white space in such a manner to represent the word.

Due to the high diversity of such subcategories, their analysis requires in turn an individual and specific study. That is why the rest of this research work focused on one of them and in particular on the *Text as Art Form* called "Special Characters for Alphabets", which has not been investigated yet.

Figure 2 depicts the adopted analysis process. In particular, given a textual Input, a first check verifies whether the text, which is from now on referred to as *TaAF*, contains special characters. If so, the mixed-code text *Normalization Algorithm* is applied, so as to transform the *TaAF* into a standard computer readable text. At this point, the transformed text can be further analysed. In particular, the normalised *TaAF* is given in input to the "Propaganda detection classifier", trained on a specific dataset, which is able to discriminate whether it is Propaganda or Nonpropaganda related. If the textual Input is not a *TaAF*, the propaganda detection step can be directly applied. The next sections elaborate the proposed "Normalization Algorithm" as well as the training of the "Propaganda detection classifier".

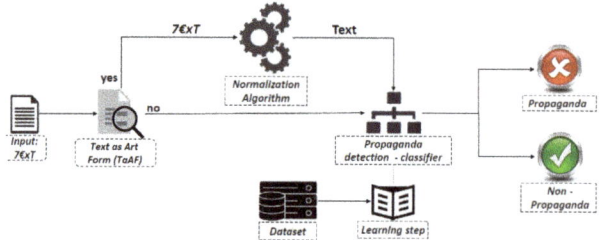

Figure 2. Research approach: data management, phases and work-products.

4.2. A Mixed Code Text Normalisation Algorithm

This section presents the proposed algorithm to normalise mixed-code text related to "Special Characters for Alphabets", whose pseudocode is reported in Algorithm 1. It consists of four main steps so labelled: (i) *Text Segregation*, which splits words by generating different subset of symbols, (ii) *Character Transformation*, that aims to derive, from each subset of symbols, letters of the alphabet, (iii) *Word Selection*, which deals with the generation and selection of existing words according to a dictionary on the basis of the derived letters, (iv) *Sentence Reconstruction*, which aims to replace the initially mixed-code text with the selected words in order to obtain a meaningful standard textual sentence.

A more detailed description of each step is exemplified through a simple reference example. In particular, given the sentence S in input, as it is represented through the equation (1), which contains a mixed-code text called from now on Art Form Word—*AFW* (e.g., "F{}{}T"), each step of the proposed normalisation algorithm is elaborated in the following.

$$S = My \; F\{\}\{\}T \; is \; cold \qquad (1)$$

Text Segregation step: this step has a syntactic function, and it works on the single words. It aims to create groups of symbols starting form the *AFW* in consideration. In particular, after splitting the sentence into subwords and identify those containing nonalphabetic characters, for each *AFW* the algorithm reworks its sequence of characters by grouping them differently, and generating several combinations, as it is shown in Table 3. In this approach a recursive operation is used to make combinations. It iterates through all the characters to make all the possible combinations. The process keeps one character constant and makes combinations with the rest of the remaining characters. Then it takes the first and second characters together and then makes combinations with the rest of the remaining characters. This operation is carried out exhaustively. In is assumed that, the order of the symbols through which the mixed-code text is built, and as a consequence the order of the combinations, reflects the order of the letters in the standard word. It means that the word has been written in the order it is meant to be read and it is not an anagram.

Algorithm 1: Preudocode for text normalisation

Data: String $S=\{W_1, W_2, ..., W_{k-1}, W_k\}$;
Placeholder=$\{P_1, P_2, ..., P_{k-1}, P_k\}$;
CandidateWords cw[];
Integer i=1; j=1; z=1;
Word w; CharactersGroup cg; String S_{Norm};
SegregationMatrix SM [K][N][M];
TransformedCharacter TC [M];

Text Segregation step: while $i<=$ S.size() do
    // - as long as there are words
    w=S.getWord(i); //take the i-th word
    if w.isNotMixedCode() **then**
        //if the i-th word is a regular word
        S_{Norm}.append$_i$(w); //it does not have to be normalised
    else
        S_{Norm}.append$_i$(P_i); // create a place holder in the i-th position
        $SM_{k=i}$.segregate(w); // segregate the i-th word
    end
    i++;
end

Character Transformation step: while $j<=$ SM.GroupSize() do
    // for each segregated word
    cg=SM.getGroup(j); // select the j-th group of characters
    if cg.isAnAlphabeticCharacter() **then**
        //if it is one of the standard alphabetic letters
        TC[j]=cg; //apply the rule-1 by considering it as it is
    else
        TC[j]=convertIntoSingleCharacter(cg); //apply the rule-2 by using OCR to transform the j-th cg group of symbols into one alphabetic character.
    end
    j++;
end

k=1;
Word Selection step: while $k<=$S.size() do
    z=1; while $z<=$SM(k).CombinationNumber() do
        //as long as there is a combination for each word
        c_z=SM(k).getCombination(z);
        c_z.replaceGroupsWithTheTransformedCharacter(SM,TC);
        if c_z.string().isAnExistingEnglishWord() **then**
            //if the generated word is not part of the English vocabulary, it is not considered
            SM(k).removeCombination(c_z)
        else
            // otherwise it become a candidate placeholder replacement
            cw.addCandidateWord(k,c_z)
        end
        z++;
    end
    k++;
end

k=1; **Sentence Reconstruction step:** while $k<=$S.size() do
    S_{Norm}.replacePlaceholder(k,cw(k).candidateWord());
    k++;
end

Result: S_{Norm};

Table 3. An example of segregation with Art Form Word (AFW) = "F{}{}T".

Combination	Group 1	Group 2	Group 3	Group 4	Group 5	Group 6	Group 7	...	Group M
1			F	{}	{}	T			
2			F	{}			{}T		
3		F{						}{}	T
...									
N	F{}{}								T

Character Transformation step: in this step, for each combination generated in the previous step the following transformation rules have been defined:

- *rule-1*: if a set of grouped characters coincides exactly with one standard alphabetic character (e.g., a, b, c, ..., Z), then it is considered like it is. For example, in all generated combinations when F and T are not grouped with any other symbol, they are interpreted as F and T.
- *rule-2*: if a set of characters consists of one not standard alphabetic character, including numbers (such as !, ?, @, 0, 1, 2 and so on), or it consists of a combination of one or more characters (e.g., F{, {}, {}T, }{, and so on) then an "optical character recognition—(OCR)" technique is applied. The idea is to emulate the human behaviour, from an optical point of view, so as to automatically recognise individual characters and letters. In particular, first each group of characters/symbols is transformed into images. Then machine learning techniques are exploited to recognise and associate each group of characters/symbols to a standard letter of the alphabet by trying to identify a match within the letters of the standard (English) alphabet. As it is shown in Figure 3, for each group of symbols different letters of the alphabet can be generated; however, the one with the highest similarity score is then chosen.

A classifier for character recognition has been trained by using the dataset provided in [50], which consists of a collection of character images of the alphabet belonging to the 26 English characters both handwritten and typed through a computer. Furthermore, other additional characters of other languages (such as ü, Ü, ä, Ä, ö, Ö, ß, Ø, ø and so on) have been further created in order to extend and enrich the initial dataset.

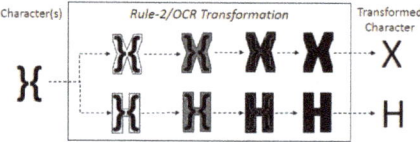

Figure 3. An example of a recognition rule.

To create such images, the use of python and the drawing library of Pillow [51] was used for creating the images. It aimed to incorporate certain non-English characters belonging to other languages. The images are made by using a dimension of 200 × 200 px for the width and height. They were generated in a gray scale, because for the character identification purpose RGB, the colour does not provide any additional information. The best performance for the character recognition have been achieved by using a Convolutional Neural Network (CNN). A training and testing set with a ratio of 80:20 and number of epochs equal to 15, were used to configure the CNN. Its performance, in terms of Evaluation Metrics, Confusion Matrix as well as training vs. testing loss, is depicted in Figure 4.

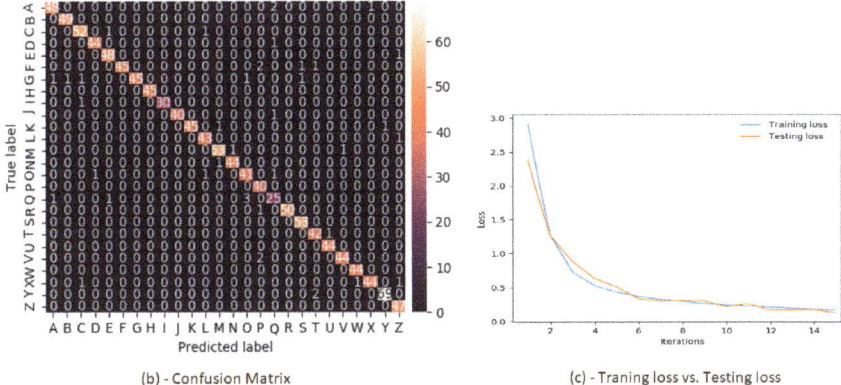

(a) - Evaluation Metrics

(b) - Confusion Matrix

(c) - Traning loss vs. Testing loss

Figure 4. Performances in the recognition of single characters.

Table 4 shows an example of character transformation by applying the above mentioned rules. For example, only the letters of the groups 3, 6 and M have been used as they are, whereas the rest of the groups generated from the segregation process have been first transformed into images and then mapped with single letters.

Table 4. An example of Character Transformation.

Group	Character(s)	Recognition Rule	Transformed Character
1	F{}{}	Rule-2/OCR	X
2	F{	Rule-2/OCR	A
3	F	Rule-1	F
4	{}	Rule-2/OCR	O
5	{}	Rule-2/OCR	O
6	T	Rule-1	T
7	{}T	Rule-2/OCR	E
...	}{}	Rule-2/OCR	L
M	T	Rule-1	T

Word Selection step: this part of the algorithm aims to derive candidate words that can replace the related *AFW*. First, for each *Combination* generated during the *Text Segregation step*, each group of symbols is replaced with its related *Transformed Character* obtained within the *Character Transformation step*. As it is shown in Table 5, a set of words which are syntactically written only with letters of the alphabet are built.

Table 5. An example on derived words.

Combination	Group	Transformed Character	Derived Word
1	F, {}, {}, T	F, O, O, T	FOOT
2	F, {}, {}T	F, O, E	FOE
3	F{, }{}, T	A, L, T	ALT
...	...	...	...
N	F{}{}, T	X, T	XT

The existence of such derived words is then checked against an English dictionary. Through this step, only the words that are part of the standard English language are selected and, as a consequence, used for further analysis. Figure 5 shows graphically an example of word selection, on the basis of their existence in the English dictionary.

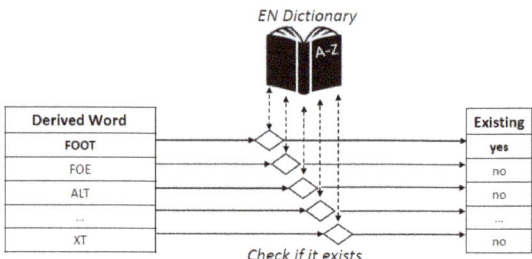

Figure 5. Selection of the derived words based on a dictionary.

Sentence Reconstruction step: this is the last part of the algorithm which is centred on two main input parameters: (i) all existing words that have been generated and selected, that means those that are part of the English dictionary and (ii) the initial sentence S containing a *placeholder* for each identified *AFW*. In particular, from the previous steps for each *AFW* a set of potential words have been derived and selected. As it is represented in Figure 6, at this point, the algorithm provides in output different versions of the normalised sentence $S_{Normalized} = \{S_1, S_2, ..., S_m\}$, this means, all sentences which are possible to reconstruct by replacing the *placeholders* with the generated words in all possible combinations.

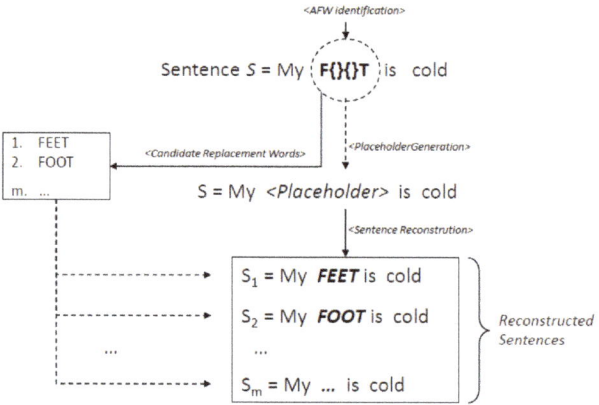

Figure 6. An example of the sentence reconstruction step.

In case of multiple sentences, all of them are evaluated. In particular, in the presence of an odd number of sentences, the final evaluation is based on the obtained majority value; in case of an even number of sentences, if the majority criterion is not applicable, then the evaluation is delegated to the human by requiring a manual intervention.

4.3. Dealing with the Propaganda Detection

In the previous section, the identification and transformation of a particular type of mixed-code text, based on "Special character for alphabets", has been faced by proposing an algorithm which is able to derive potential sentences in natural language. This section, instead, focuses on the description of the propaganda detection approach of Figure 2, which aims to automatically analyse the reconstructed sentences $S_{Normalized}=\{S_1, S_2, ..., S_m\}$, in order to discriminate whether they are related to propaganda or not and which one.

4.3.1. Machine Learning Approach

Among the available analysis techniques, machine learning (ML) is one of the most popular ones. It is adopted in different research fields by facing with (i) computational finance for the evaluation of credit risk and algorithmic trading; (ii) image processing and artificial vision for facial recognition, motion detection and object identification; (iii) computational biology for the diagnosis of tumors, pharmaceutical research and DNA sequencing; (iv) energy production for price and load forecasts; (v) automotive, aerospace and manufacturing sectors, for predictive maintenance; (vi) natural language processing for speech recognition applications and so on.

Furthermore, from the literature review, which is described in the related work section, it emerged that four main ML techniques represent the most popular algorithms in the automatic detection field, that is: (i) *Multinomial Naïve Bayes (MNB)*: which is a variant of Naive Bayes classifiers which uses a multinomial distribution for each of the features, (ii) *Support Vector Machine (SVM)*: that is a linear model for classification and regression problems which is used to solve linear and nonlinear problems, (iii) *Logistic Regression (LR)*: which is a linear predictive analysis algorithm based on the concept of probability to face with classification problems (iv) *Convolutional Neural Network (CNN)*: that is a type of artificial neural network, which is used in image recognition and processing, centred on deep learning to perform both generative and descriptive tasks.

As a consequence, given a sentence S, to be able to assess whether it is Propaganda or Nonpropaganda related, four different classifiers have been trained and evaluated (one for each of the above mentioned ML techniques respectively) regarding propaganda detection. The best one has been then selected.

4.3.2. Dataset Description and Evaluation Metrics

The four classifiers have been trained using an available and free downloadable dataset [52], which represents a research results achieved by a collaboration among the MIT Computer Science and Artificial Intelligence Laboratory of Cambridge (USA), the Qatar Computing Research Institute (Qatar) and University of Bologna (Italy). The dataset details are fully reported in [37]. It contains a collection of 15,847 textual items labelled with "0" and "1" to indicate Propaganda and Nonpropaganda. In particular, 4270 items are Propaganda related, and 11,577 are Nonpropaganda related. As the dataset was unbalanced, in order to reduce the bias of the classifier, two sampling techniques have been applied and evaluated for dealing with it: undersampling and oversampling approach. In particular, by applying the under sampling approach, we used the same number of textual items both for Propaganda and Nonpropaganda for a total of 8540, whereas by applying the oversampling technique we used all the 11,577 Nonpropaganda related items and we increased the number of Propaganda related item to 9440. In both cases, the generated datasets have been divided into two subsets: 80% of the items have been used to train the four models, whereas 20% of the items have been used to test the classifiers. To allow the comparison with previous research contributions, the trained classifiers have been evaluated through Accuracy, Precision, Recall and F1-Score, which are the most popular metrics used in ML.

4.3.3. Classifier Assessment

Different experiments have been conducted to determine the best classifier among the selected ones. More specifically, in order to reduce possible bias, that could have been arised from several factors, during the training and classification phase, MNB, SVM and LR classifiers have been assessed by using different vectorization approaches. In particular, Count Vectorizer, Term frequency–inverse document frequency, Term Frequency inverse document frequency with word n-gram, Term frequency inverse document frequency with character n-gram, were used. The overall performance reached from all classifiers, including the CNN, are reported in Table 6.

In particular, it resulted that the Convolutional Neural Network performed better than the other classifiers. By using an undersampled dataset, it reached the following results: 73% accuracy, 74% precision, 73% recall and 73% F1-Score. Whereas, as it is reported in Table 6, by oversampling the same dataset, better performances have been reached after retraining and reassessing the CNN-based classifier. In particular, it showed the following performances: 94% accuracy, 92% precision, 92% recall and 91% F1-Score, which have shown not only better performance than the other ones tested within this research work, but it is also inline in comparison to the performances of the other related works, that are reported in Table 2.

Table 6. Comparison of the performance achieved from each classifier with oversampling.

Trained Classifier	Accuracy	Precision	Recall	F1-Score
Multinomial Naive Bayes count_vectorizer	0.74	0	0.74	0.74
Multinomial Naive Bayes tfidf_vectorizer_word	0.71	0.70	0.70	0.70
Multinomial Naive Bayes tfidf_vectorizer_word_ngram	0.68	0.68	0.66	0.65
Multinomial Naive Bayes tfidf_vectorizer_ngram_chars	0.68	0.68	0.67	0.68
Support Vector Machine count_vectorizer	0.80	0.80	0.80	0.80
Support Vector Machine tfidf_vectorizer_word	0.82	0.82	0.82	0.82
Support Vector Machine tfidf_vectorizer_word_ngram	0.72	0.72	0.70	0.71
Support Vector Machine tfidf_vectorizer_ngram_chars	0.82	0.82	0.82	0.82
Logistic Regression count_vectorizer	0.79	0.78	0.79	0.78
Logistic Regression tfidf_vectorizer_word	0.73	0.72	0.72	0.72
Logistic Regression tfidf_vectorizer_word_ngram	0.68	0.68	0.66	0.66
Logistic Regression tfidf_vectorizer_ngram_chars	0.71	0.71	0.71	0.71
Convolutional Neural Network	0.94	0.92	0.92	0.91

5. Evaluation and Results Discussion

In the previous section, the proposed algorithm for supporting the analysis of mixed-code text has been described, as well as the approach for assessing and selecting the most promising machine learning classifier for the propaganda detection step has been contextually presented.

This section, instead, aims to discuss and show how the evaluation of the overall workflow has been conducted by explaining the encountered problem, by clarifying how the experiment has been setup, as well as by discussing the achieved results.

One of the problems encountered during the evaluation part concerned the lack of available dataset containing word art mixed code text and, especially, related to propaganda. To deal with it, the dataset described in Section 4.3 [37] has been taken in consideration as a starting point. In particular, a subset, called *SS*, of its instances has been selected by creating a smaller balanced dataset, that means by taking 50% of sentences labelled as propaganda and 50% of them labelled as nonpropaganda related.

After that, an online tool, called Universal Leet [53] has been used. Given in input to such tool a word W, it is able to automatically generate a possible related *Art Form Word* (W_{AFW}). As a consequence, the experiment dataset has been built by replacing in each sentence of the called SS subset, at least one word or even the full text with its related art form word, automatically generated from the above mentioned tool, so as to obtain a *Art Form Word* dataset (SS_{AFW}) with labels. In particular, at first we used alternatively three standard available modalities: *basic, advanced*, and *ultimate* leet to obtain the first version, and then in order to make such versions nonstandard but more human-like in terms of their variety, we have further updated part of them manually, so as to make them more difficult and less machine-related. All this encoding step has been done manually, because based on our knowledge we have not found any APIs, which allowed us to automate this process. An excerpt is shown in Table 7.

Table 7. An excerpt of the propaganda related dataset.

Id	Original Sentence $W \in SS$	Label	Sentence with $W_{AFW} \in SS_{AFW}$
01	Build the Wall	Propaganda	ßU!LD T│=│E \/\/ALL
02	Purge every homosexual	Propaganda	Pu│2ge every │=│omosexual
03	Abolish Wage System	Propaganda	Äbolish \/\/age $ystem
04	Whites should rule	Propaganda	Whit €s should │2ule
05	Right around 3 billion miles	Nonpropaganda	│2!g│-│t around 3 │3illion miles
06	America First	Propaganda	AmericÄ │=!rst
07	Here is the dirty secret	Propaganda	Here is the │)irtŸ $e(ret
...	...	...	...

Instead, the WordNet package [54] has been used as reference English dictionary, in order to implement the *Word Selection step* of the proposed normalisation algorithm, described in Section 4.2. It is centred on the Python's Natural Language Toolkit (NLTK) module and it consists of a database where the collected nouns, adjectives, adverbs and verbs are grouped into a set of cognitive synonyms, which are called synsets. As it has been already mentioned, on the basis on the results gathered from the classifier assessment described in Section 4, a CNN has been chosen for supporting the propaganda detection part of the process, as the trained classifier performed the best in comparison to the others. The configuration parameters, that have been used to setup the CNN classifier, are reported in Table 8.

Table 8. Configuration parameters of the CNN classification model.

Layer	Convolution
01	Conv2d(1, 100, kernel_size=(3, 300), stride=(1, 1))
02	Conv2d(1, 100, kernel_size=(4, 300), stride=(1, 1))
03	Conv2d(1, 100, kernel_size=(5, 300), stride=(1, 1))
04 (Fully Connected)	(fc1):Linear(in_features=300,out_features=2, bias=True

An example of the results, gathered by experimenting the method presented in Section 4, are reported in Table 9.

As it is possible to see in Table 9, for each sentence of Table 7, at least one reconstructed sentence is obtained. Indeed, according to the *Word Selection step* of the method, different "normal" words, and as a consequence multiple reconstructed sentences, can be generated from one single Art Form Word. Consequently, different evaluations are possible as for the sentence with Id = "1" or like the sentence with Id = "6" which is also reconstructed in different way but with the same result evaluation. Whereas, the sentence with Id = "7" is not properly reconstructed and then misclassified. To overcome the classification problem in case of discordant multiple classifications, the human intervention is required, in order to select one of the possible available alternatives.

Table 9. Reconstructed sentences and related classification results.

Id	Reconstructed Sentence(s)	Predicted Label(s)	Results
01	Build the Wall/Bag the wall	Propaganda/Nonpropaganda	True/False
02	Purge every homosexual	Propaganda	True
03	Abolish Wage System	Propaganda	True
04	Whites should rule	Propaganda	True
05	Right around 3 billion miles	Nonpropaganda	True
06	America First/America Fist	Propaganda/Propaganda	True/True
07	Here is the dirty met	Propaganda	False
...	...	...	...

Figure 7 summarises, instead, the confusion matrix at the end of the overall evaluation process based on the selected Convolutional Neural Network (CNN), which shows that only 9% of the instances are wrong classified and in particular only 5% of those related to propaganda are missclassified as nonpropaganda related.

True label	Propaganda	46%	5%
	Non-Propaganda	4%	45%
		Propaganda	Non-Propaganda
		Predicted label	

Figure 7. Confusion matrix of propaganda detection in hidden mixed-code text.

Whereas, Figure 8 shows the classification performances, in terms of accuracy, precision, recall and f1-score, by comparing the detection of propaganda in a standard text (i.e., with mixed code and as a consequence without applying the normalisation algorithm) with the detection of propaganda hidden mixed-code text. In particular, not only the diagram shows very similar performances, meaning that in presence of mixed-code, the normalisation algorithm is able to reconstruct and analyse appropriately the sentences; but it also highlights that the proposed approach is in average inline with the performances of the related works presented in Section 2, in terms of propaganda detection, by ranging from 90% to 92% in terms of accuracy, precision, recall and f1-score. Moreover, the correctness of the heuristic to normalise a text can be expressed as the number of correctly reconstructed sentences on the basis of the total original ones. Intuitively, a correct classification of a sentence/text is directly related to its correct normalisation process. This means that the classification values presented in Figure 8 represent, as a consequence, the lower bound of the heuristic to be able to correctly retrieve the original text starting from its TaAF representation.

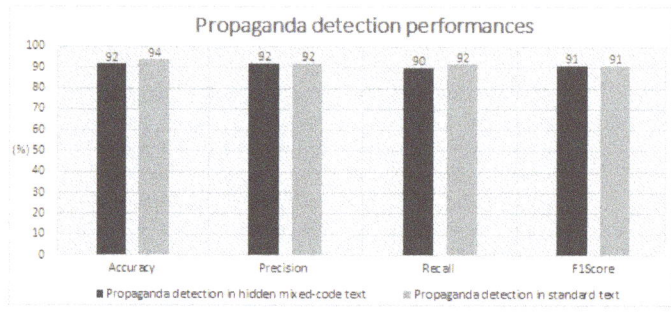

Figure 8. Results evaluation using CNN.

It is worth noting that the current results are improved, in comparison to those presented in the previous version of this work [20]. This result is not due to a new version of the presented heuristics, as its logic has not been changed, but it derived from a better training of the CNN algorithm, which makes less misclassification, by positively impacting on the overall process.

6. Conclusions

The paper dealt with the identification of mixed-code text for the detection of hidden propaganda. First a possible categorisation of different types of existing mixed-code on the basis of two parameters, related to the *language* and the *graphical writing style* has been provided. The study has been focused on the analysis of one type of *Text as Art Form* written on a single row (called "Special Characters for Alphabets"), by adopting a methodological approach centred on two main aspects: (i) mixed code text analysis and (ii) hidden propaganda detection. In particular, regarding the mixed code text analysis, a four-step algorithm (called *Text Segregation*, *Character Transformation*, *Word Selection* and *Sentence Reconstruction*) that supports both the identification of mixed code in text along with its normalisation into natural language has been proposed.

Whereas, regarding the hidden propaganda detection, a Convolutional Neural Network classifier has been chosen among other ML algorithms, as it provided the best performance in the detection of propaganda. The overall performance of the method has been experimented on a public available dataset containing a collection of 15,847 textual propaganda and nonpropaganda related items. The results showed good performances, by achieving 92% Accuracy and Precision, whereas 91% F1-Score and 90% Recall, which are on average better in comparison to the related work.

The impact of this solution lies in the ability to automate and consequently speed up the identification of sources and individuals, who use mixed-code to dissemination propaganda content, linked to extremist behaviour, so as to support the Law Enforcement Agencies (LEAs) and Police Forces (PFs) the fight against this phenomenon. Future works will focus on: (i) improving the performance of the current algorithm by defining a more efficient heuristic related to the Text Segregation step, in term of computational time. The current version generates all possible combination of symbols that works fine as long as the input is "reasonably contained". A smarter way to segregate the text needs be investigated to make it work also in larger context; (i) extending and experimenting the proposed method for supporting the detection of hidden propaganda by considering other types of mixed-code.

Author Contributions: Software, G.M.; Supervision, M.M.; Research, Writing—original draft, A.T. The authors contributed equally in all parts of the article in terms of literature review, adopted methodology, feature identification, model definition, experimentation and results analysis. All authors have read and agreed to the published version of the manuscript.

Funding: This work was partially performed in the context of the CHAMPIONs research project, which receives funding from the European Union's Internal Security Fund—Police, grant agreement no. 823705.

Informed Consent Statement: Informed consent was obtained from all subjects involved in the study.

Data Availability Statement: Not applicable.

Acknowledgments: The authors want to thanks José L. Diego, Project Manager at Valencia Local Police (Spain), for supporting this research activity.

Conflicts of Interest: The authors declare no conflicts of interest.

Abbreviations

The following abbreviations are used in this manuscript:

AFW	Art Form Word
ML	Machine Learning
OCR	Optical Character Recognition
NLP	Natural Language Processing
CNN	Convolutional Neural Network
ANN	Artificial Neural Network
LR	Logistic Regression
SVM	Support Vector Machine
MNB	Multinomial Naive Bayes
RF	Random Forest
LSTM	Long Short Term Memory
BoW	Bag of Word
TF	Term Frequency
TF-IDF	Term Frequency-Inverse Document Frequency
ToD	Text on Document
TiVM	Text in Visual Media
TaAF	Text as Art Form
NLTK	Natural Language Toolkit
LEAs	Law Enforcement Agencies
PFs	Police Forces

References

1. Richards, J.C.; Schmidt, R.W. *Language and Communication*; Routledge: London, UK, 2014.
2. Slobin, D.I. The many ways to search for a frog. *Relat. Events Narrat.* **2004**, *2*, 219–257.
3. Corea, S. Cultivating technological innovation for development. *Electron. J. Inf. Syst. Dev. Cities* **2000**, *2*, 1–15. [CrossRef]
4. Metropolitan Police 1. Available online: https://www.met.police.uk/advice/advice-and-information/t/ter-rorism-in-the-uk/signs-of-possible-terrorist-activity/ (accessed on 29 December 2020).
5. Nekovee, M.; Moreno, Y.; Bianconi, G.; Marsili, M. Theory of rumour spreading in complex social networks. *Phys. Stat. Mech. Appl.* **2007**, *374*, 457–470. [CrossRef]
6. Metropolitan Police 2. Available online: https://www.met.police.uk/advice/advice-and-information/t/terrorism-in-the-uk/ (accessed on 29 December 2020).
7. Bates, R.A. Dancing with wolves: Today's lone wolf terrorists. *J. Public Prof. Sociol.* **2012**, *4*, 1.
8. Tundis, A.; Huber, F.; Jäger, B.; Daubert, J.; Vasilomanolakis, E.; Mühlhäuser, M. Challenges and available solutions against organized cyber-crime and terrorist networks. In *WIT Transactions on the Built Environment*; WIT Press: Southampton, UK, 2018; Volume 174, pp. 429–441.
9. Jirovský, V.; Pastorek, A.; Mühlhäuser, M.; Tundis, A. Cybercrime and organized crime. In Proceedings of the 13th International Conference on Availability, Reliability and Security, ARES 2018, Hamburg, Germany, 25–28 August 2018.
10. Tundis, A.; Jain, A.; Bhatia, G.; Muhlhauser, M. Similarity Analysis of Criminals on Social Networks: An Example on Twitter. In Proceedings of the 28th International Conference on Computer Communication and Networks (ICCCN), Valencia, Spain, 29 July–1 August 2019; pp. 1–9.
11. Falcone, A.; Garro, A.; Tundis, A. Modeling and Simulation for the performance evaluation of the on-board communication system of a metro train. In Proceedings of the 13th International Conference on Modeling and Applied Simulation (MAS '14), Bordeaux, France, 10–12 September 2014; pp. 20–29.
12. Tundis, A.; Mazurczyk, W.; Mühlhäuser, M. A review of network vulnerabilities scanning tools: Types, capabilities and functioning. In Proceedings of the 13th International Conference on Availability, Reliability and Security (ARES 2018), Hamburg, Germany, 27–30 August 2018.
13. Chatfield, A.T.; Reddick, C.G.; Brajawidagda, U. Tweeting propaganda, radicalization and recruitment: Islamic state supporters multisided twitter networks. In Proceedings of the 16th Annual International Conference on Digital Government Research, Phoenix, AZ, USA, 27–30 May 2015; pp. 239–249.
14. Berzinji, A.; Abdullah, F.S.; Kakei, A.H. Analysis of Terrorist Groups on Facebook. In Proceedings of the European Intelligence and Security Informatics Conference, Uppsala, Sweden, 12–14 August 2013; p. 221.
15. Tundis, A.; Bhatia, G.; Jain, A.; Mühlhäuser, M. Supporting the Identification and the Assessment of Suspicious Users on Twitter Social Media. In Proceedings of the IEEE 17th International Symposium on Network Computing and Applications (NCA), Cambridge, MA, USA, 1–3 November 2018; pp. 1–10.
16. Tundis, A.; Mühlhäuser, M. A multi-language approach towards the identification of suspicious users on social networks. In Proceedings the International Carnahan Conference on Security Technology (ICCST), Madrid, Spain, 23–26 October 2017; pp. 1–6.

17. Tundis, A.; Böck, L.; Stanilescu, V.; Mühlhäuser, M. Limits in the data for detecting criminals on social media. In Proceedings of the 14th International Conference on Availability, Reliability and Security (ARES '19), Kent, Canterbury, UK, 26–29 August 2019; pp. 1–8.
18. Tundis, A.; Böck, L.; Stanilescu, V.; Mühlhäuser, M. Experiencing the detection of radicalized criminals on facebook social network and data-related issues. *J. Cyber Secur. Mob.* **2020**, *9*, 203–236. [CrossRef]
19. Cox, I.; Miller, M.; Bloom, J.; Fridrich, J.; Kalker, T. *Digital Watermarking and Steganography*; Morgan Kaufmann: Burlington, MA, USA, 2007.
20. Tundis, A.; Mukherjee, G.; Mühlhäuser, M. Mixed-code text analysis for the detection of online hidden propaganda. In Proceedings of the 15th International Conference on Availability, Reliability and Security (ARES 2020), Dublin, Ireland, 25–28 August 2020.
21. Mehta, H.; Singla, S.; Mahajan, A. Optical character recognition (ocr) system for roman script english language using artificial neural network (ann) classifier. In Proceedings of the the International Conference on Research Advances in Integrated Navigation Systems (RAINS), Bangalore, India, 6–7 May 2016; pp 1-5.
22. Auer, P. *Bilingual Conversation*; John Benjamins Publishing: Amsterdam, The Netherlands, 1984.
23. Auer, P. *Code-Switching in Conversation: Language, Interaction and Identity*; Routledge: London, UK, 2013.
24. Mahesh, R.; Sinha, K.; Thakur, A. Machine translation of bi-lingual hindi-english (hinglish) text. In Proceedings of the 10th Machine Translation Summit (MT Summit X), Phuket, Thailand, 12–16 September 2005; pp. 149–156.
25. Bohra, A.; Vijay, D.; Singh, V.; Akhtar, S.S.; Shrivastava, M. A dataset of hindi-english code-mixed social media text for hate speech detection. In Proceedings of the Second Workshop on Computational Modeling of People's Opinions, Personality, and Emotions in Social Media, New Orleans, LA, USA, 6 June 2018.
26. Barman, U.; Das, A.; Wagner, J.; Foster, J. Code mixing: A challenge for language identification in the language of social media. In Proceedings of the First Workshop on Computational Approaches to Code Switching, Doha, Qatar, 25 October 2014; pp. 13–23.
27. Mathur, P.; Shah, R.; Sawhney, R.; Mahata, D. Detecting offensive tweets in hindi-english code-switched language. In Proceedings of the Sixth International Workshop on Natural Language Processing for Social Media, Melbourne, Australia, 20 July 2018; pp. 18–26.
28. Santosh, T.Y.S.S.; Aravind, K.V.S. Hate speech detection in hindi-english code-mixed social media text. In Proceedings of the ACM India Joint International Conference on Data Science and Management of Data, CoDS-COMAD '19, Kolkata, India, 3–5 January 2019; pp. 310–313.
29. Sharma, S.; Srinivas, P.; Balabantaray, R.C. Sentiment analysis of code-mix script. In Proceedings of the 2015 International Conference on Computing and Network Communications (CoCoNet), Trivandrum, India, 16–19 December 2015; pp. 530-534.
30. Jhanwar, M.G.; Das, A. An ensemble model for sentiment analysis of hindienglish code-mixed data. *arXiv* **2018**, arXiv:1806.04450.
31. Khandelwal, A.; Swami, S.; Akhtar, S.S.; Shrivastava, M. Humor detection in english-hindi code-mixed social media content: Corpus and baseline system. *arXiv* **2018**, arXiv:1806.05513.
32. Singh, R.; Choudhary, N.; Shrivastava, M. Automatic normalization of word variations in code-mixed social media text. *arXiv* **2018**, arXiv:1804.00804.
33. Ferrante, T.; Ferrante, C.M. *E-Leetspeak: All New! The Most Challenging Puzzles Since Sudoku!* Author House: Bloomington, IN, USA, , 2008; p. 136, ISBN-10: 1438923554.
34. Zhou, Y. Pro-ISIS fanboys network analysis and attack detection through twitter data. In Proceedings of the 2017 IEEE 2nd International Conference on Big Data Analysis (ICBDA), Beijing, China, 10–12 March 2017; pp. 386–390.
35. Nouh, M.; Nurse, R.C.J.; Goldsmith, M. Understanding the radical mind: Identifying signals to detect extremist content on twitter. In Proceedings of the 2019 IEEE International Conference on Intelligence and Security Informatics (ISI), Shenzhen, China, 1–3 July 2019; pp.1–7.
36. Johnston, A.H.; Weiss, G.M. Identifying sunni extremist propaganda with deep learning. In Proceedings of the 2017 IEEE Symposium Series on Computational Intelligence (SSCI), Honolulu, HI, USA, 27 November–1 December 2017; pp. 1–6.
37. Martino, G.D.S.; Yu, S.; Barrón-Cedeño, A.; Petrov, R.; Nakov, P. Fine-grained analysis of propaganda in news articles. In Proceedings of the 2019 Conference on Empirical Methods in Natural Language Processing and 9th International Joint Conference on Natural Language Processing, Hong Kong, China, 3–7 November 2019.
38. Aggarwal, K.; Sadana, A. NSIT@NLP4IF-2019: Propaganda detection from news articles using transfer learning. In Proceedings of the Second Workshop on Natural Language Processing for Internet Freedom, Censorship, Disinformation, and Propaganda, Hong Kong, China, 4 November 2019; pp. 143–147.
39. Tundis, A; Shams A.A; Mühlhäuser, M. Concepts of a Pyramidal Model for Assessing Terrorist Propaganda. In Proceedings of the IEEE International Symposium on Network Computing and Applications (NCA), Cambridge, MA, USA, 24–27 November 2020; pp. 1–4.
40. Govindan, V.K.; Shivaprasad, A.P. Character recognition—A review. *Pattern Recognit.* **1990**, *23*, 671–683. [CrossRef]
41. Vamvakas, G.; Gatos, B.; Perantonis, S.J. Handwritten character recognition through two-stage foreground sub-sampling. *Pattern Recognit.* **2010**, *43*, 2807–2816. [CrossRef]
42. Dutta, S.; Sankaran, N.; Sankar, K.P.; Jawahar, C.V. Robust recognition of degraded documents using character n-grams. In Proceedings of the IEEE 10th IAPR International Workshop on Document Analysis Systems, Washington, DC, USA, 27–29 March 2012; pp. 130–134.

43. Devlin, J.; Kamali, M.; Subramanian, K.; Prasad, R.; Natarajan, P. Statistical machine translation as a language model for handwriting recognition. In Proceedings of the IEEE International Conference on Frontiers in Handwriting Recognition, Bari, Italy, 18–20 September 2012; pp. 291–296.
44. Hassan, T.; Khan, H.A. Handwritten bangla numeral recognition using local binary pattern. In Proceedings of the IEEE International Conference on Electrical Engineering and Information Communication Technology (ICEEICT), Savar, Bangladesh, 21–23 May 2015; pp. 1–4.
45. Breuel, T.M.; Ul-Hasan, A.; Al-Azawi, M.A.; Shafait, F. Highperformance ocr for printed english and fraktur using lstm networks. In Proceedings of the 12th IEEE International Conference on Document Analysis and Recognition, Washington, DC, USA, 25–28 August 2013; pp. 683–687.
46. Lavanya, K.; Bajaj, S.; Tank, P.; Jain, S. Handwritten digit recognition using hoeffding tree, decision tree and random forests - A comparative approach. In Proceedings of the 2017 International Conference on Computational Intelligence in Data Science (ICCIDS), Chennai, India, 2–3 June 2017; pp. 1–6.
47. Liyanage, C.; Nadungodage, T.; Weerasinghe, R. Developing a commercial grade tamil ocr for recognizing font and size independent text. In Proceedings of the 15th IEEE International Conference on Advances in ICT for Emerging Regions (ICTer), Colombo, Sri Lanka, 24–26 August 2015; pp. 130–134.
48. Lopes, D. *A Philosophy of Computer Art*; Routledge: London, UK, 2009.
49. Xu, X.; Zhang, L.; Wong, T. Structure-based ascii art. *ACM Trans. Graph.* **2010**, *29*, 1–9.
50. De Campos, T.E. The Chars74k Dataset: Character Recognition in Natural Images. Available online: http://www.ee.surrey.ac.uk/CVSSP/demos/chars74k/ (accessed on 29 December 2020).
51. Pillow. Available online: https://pillow.readthedocs.io/en/stable/ (accessed on 29 December 2020).
52. Shared Task on Fine-Grained Propaganda Detection NLP4IF, 2019. Available online: https://propaganda.qcri.org/nlp4if-shared-task/data/ (accessed on 29 December 2020).
53. Universal Leet Converter. Available online: http://www.robertecker.com/hp/research/leet-converter.php?lang=en (accessed on 29 December 2020).
54. WordNet Interface—NLTK Corpus Reader. Available online: https://www.nltk.org/howto/wordnet.html (accessed on 29 December 2020).

MDPI
St. Alban-Anlage 66
4052 Basel
Switzerland
Tel. +41 61 683 77 34
Fax +41 61 302 89 18
www.mdpi.com

Applied Sciences Editorial Office
E-mail: applsci@mdpi.com
www.mdpi.com/journal/applsci

www.ingramcontent.com/pod-product-compliance
Lightning Source LLC
LaVergne TN
LVHW070420100526
838202LV00014B/1494